THE ROMANCE OF
WISCONSIN PLACE NAMES

The Romance of Wisconsin Place Names

Second Edition

Robert E. Gard

WISCONSIN HISTORICAL SOCIETY PRESS

Published by the Wisconsin Historical Society Press
Publishers since 1855

© 2015 by the Robert E. Gard Wisconsin Idea Foundation
The Romance of Wisconsin Place Names was first published in 1968 by Wisconsin House.

For permission to reuse material from *The Romance of Wisconsin Place Names, Second Edition* (ISBN 978–0-87020–707–5 and eISBN 978–0-87020–708–2), please access www.copyright.com or contact the Copyright Clearance Center, Inc. (CCC), 222 Rosewood Drive, Danvers, MA 01923, 978–750–8400. CCC is a not-for-profit organization that provides licenses and registration for a variety of users.

wisconsinhistory.org

Photographs identified with WHi or WHS are from the Society's collections; address requests to reproduce these photos to the Visual Materials Archivist at the Wisconsin Historical Society, 816 State Street, Madison, WI 53706.

Printed in the United States of America

Designed by Ryan Scheife / Mayfly Design

19 18 17 16 15   1 2 3 4 5

Library of Congress Catalog Card Number: 68-29817

∞ The paper used in this publication meets the minimum requirements of the American National Standard for Information Sciences—Permanence of Paper for Printed Library Materials, ANSI Z39.48–1992.

For Helen Smith, tireless place name collector

A small cheese factory near Blue Mounds, ca. 1964

CONTENTS

Editor's Note ix

Foreword, by Jerry Apps xi

Introduction 1

A 5

B 17

C 49

D 75

E 93

F 106

G 123

H 138

I 159

J 163

K 169

L 178

M 197

N 227

O 241

P 253

Q 272

R 275

S 289

T 319

U 329

V 333

W 339

Y 365

Z 367

Image Credits 368

A grist mill near Nelsonville, in Portage County, ca. 1950

EDITOR'S NOTE

Fifty years ago, educator and writer Robert E. Gard traveled across Wisconsin in search of stories about the origins of our state's unique place names. Importantly, Gard shared the results of his research without casting judgment on the stories themselves. Today, some language contained in these stories may sound offensive to some readers, and slight editorial changes have been made to remove language considered insensitive by today's standards. We believe Gard's book provides an important snapshot of how Wisconsin residents of a bygone era came to understand these monikers, many of which exist today as mere memory.

A winding farm road near Gilmanton in Buffalo County, ca. 1963.

FOREWORD

By Jerry Apps

I first met Bob Gard in 1960, when I was a University of Wisconsin Extension Agent working in Brown County. Bob worked for the Extension office in Madison, and I asked if he could come up to De Pere and help me with a drama workshop for 4-H members. I knew next to nothing about plays, but I knew that a goodly number of 4-H people enjoyed putting them on and wanted some help in doing it.

Bob was a tall, lanky, slow-talking farm boy from Kansas, but he had become well known for helping local communities organize drama workshops and writing groups. I watched him that day working with young people and adults—impressing upon them the importance of really knowing the place where they lived and celebrating it on the stage.

When Bob teamed up with my friend L. G. Sorden to create the first edition of this book, I knew they would make a good pair. L. G. was a longtime Extension agent and administrator. He was short and rotund and had a considerable interest in Wisconsin history. L. G. knew the state and scores of people from whom he could gather information. Bob Gard knew how to write, and he had a great interest in history and the importance of place in people's lives. With L. G.'s help, Bob set out to gather the background for Wisconsin's place names. He looked to answer how a given place got its name, but he went further in many instances, ferreting out other stories associated with the names.

It was a difficult task. To accomplish it, Gard wrote, "Literally hundreds of workers assisted." He enlisted the county Extension offices—one in every county in the state—asking county agents to appoint "compilers" of place information. In several instances the county agents did the work themselves. Anyone with knowledge about a place was asked to send in information.

It was a tremendous task of organization as names, origins, and stories connected with the names rolled in. The first edition of *The Romance of Wisconsin Place Names* was published by October House in 1968. A revised copy with additional names was published by the *Milwaukee Sentinel*. The *Milwaukee Sentinel* printed many of the place name stories in a feature titled "Places," which appeared in the "Good Morning" section of the paper.

One of the challenges Bob encountered was in answering the question, "Is this information accurate?" This is a challenge every historian faces, and ultimately the historian does the best job possible.

It's a challenge I've run into myself. When I wrote the history of my hometown, Waushara County's Wild Rose, in the 1973 book *Village of Roses,* I sought out the history of the name and came up with three different stories. One version, told to me by an old-timer with a hint of a smile on his face, was that "the village was named after this young woman—Rose was her name. She had quite the reputation." The second version, mentioned by several people, was that the town was named after the wild roses that grew nearby. But the most accurate version, I believe, was based on the origin of the first settlers, who had come from a village called Rose in New York's Wayne County in 1850.

Wisconsin's place names give us a rich window into the state's history, beginning with its Native American roots. Many places in Wisconsin have Native American names, and even the name of the state itself comes from a Native American term. In addition we have Manitowish, Milwaukee, Oshkosh, Poygan, Poysippi, Waupaca, Waupun, Wausau, Waushara, Wautoma, and Wauwatosa, to name just a few.

French traders arrived in the late 1660s and would roam Wisconsin's wilds for many years. So French place names appeared. We have Butte des Morts, Chequamegon Bay, Couderay, Eau Claire, Eau Galle, Embarrass, Fond du Lac, La Crosse, Lac Court Oreilles, Prairie du Chien, and Prairie du Sac. But, as with so many place names, several different stories exist as to why a particular name was chosen. For example, Bob Gard quoted an old Clintonville newspaper account, reporting one resident's claim for how Embarrass got its name: "We came to this shallow, easily forded stream at mid-day . . . we decided to call it Embarrass because we could see its bottom."

The root of Eleva, in Trempealeau County, is not without controversy. Some people say it was named after a French village. But personally, I like the second account, which claims that when a grain elevator was built next to the railroad tracks, only the first five letters of "elevator" were painted on before winter set in and the workers left. Newcomers assumed Eleva was the name of the town, and because it was so simple, it soon was adopted. Wisconsin people have been known to do things like this. It's one of the reasons the state and its place names are so interesting, as each one has a story attached to it.

Wisconsin has many place names with origins in New England, New York, and Pennsylvania, as many early Wisconsin settlers came from these eastern states. Thus we have Batavia, Ostego, Rochester, and Salem, all named for New York places; as well as Sandusky for Sandusky, Ohio; Rutland, for Rutland, Vermont; and Vermont, after the state of Vermont.

Later, when many settlers arrived from Europe, they often named towns in Wisconsin after places in Europe. By 1900, more than forty ethnic groups had settled in the state. Thus we have Berlin, named for Berlin, Germany; Ostburg, for Ostburg, Holland; Slovan for Slovan, Czechoslovakia; Sussex, for Sussex, England; Valders, for Valders, Norway; Wales, for the country of Wales; and many more.

Other Wisconsin places are named for geographic and natural features, such as Beaver Dam, Clearwater Lake, Fairwater, Fox Lake, Green Bay, Green Lake, and Little Chute. And of course, we have places named for people famous and not so famous—places such as Jackson, Jefferson, Madison, Washburn, and Washington. Cornell, in northern Wisconsin, is named for Ezra Cornell, who was once president of Cornell University in New York State. In 1862, with the passage of the federal Morrill Act, sometimes known as the land-grant act, states were allotted tracts of federally owned land that could be sold for proceeds that could be used to create land-grant colleges. Cornell's land grant was in northern Wisconsin, and thus it can be said that Wisconsin helped to build Cornell University.

From Aaron, in Burnett County, to Zenda, in Walworth County, *The Romance of Wisconsin Place Names* will keep you up at night, learning about Wisconsin's history via its place names, sometimes chuckling and other times laughing right out loud as these fascinating little place name stories unfold.

In some ways *The Romance of Wisconsin Place Names* is a reference book, a place where you can go to learn a little more about your hometown. But in many ways it is much more than that, for it includes the stories of places throughout the state, submitted by the people who knew them. It is a book where story, people, and place all come together. First compiled and written in the mid-1960s, this book is a reflection of those times. As I often tell my writing students, to know where we are going, it is important to know where we've been—thus the importance of the book for today's readers. Beyond all of that, the book is vintage Bob Gard, who contributed much to our understanding of Wisconsin's people and its places.

Robert E. Gard

INTRODUCTION

By Robert E. Gard, 1968

The names of places lie upon the land and tell us where we are or where we have been or where we want to go. And so much more.

The names of places tell of those who came before us, of the ancestry of our ancestors, sometimes of their hopes and dreams, sometimes of what they saw when they came or what they hoped their children would see.

The names of Wisconsin register the peculiarities of her history. The first Europeans here were French—Nicolet, Marquette, Joliet, and later the French trappers and backwoodsmen—and Wisconsin is rich in names of French origin.

The first wave of settlement in Wisconsin came about two centuries after settlement of the eastern seaboard. These immigrants in the first part of the nineteenth century, coming largely from southern New England and the Middle Atlantic states, brought names from their former homes, names already old in New York State, Pennsylvania, Ohio, and Connecticut. By 1848, New York had contributed 120,000 settlers to Wisconsin, New England 54,000, Pennsylvania 21,000—to say nothing of those who came from Virginia, Missouri, Kentucky, Maryland, and Delaware.

By the middle of the nineteenth century, new Americans from northern Europe—Germany, Holland, Scandinavia—were leaving their mark upon the land, and naming places after towns and villages they had left behind them.

And always the Indians were there, and had named the land before the settlers came. Driven out of the East, tribes found refuge in the wilderness that was then Wisconsin—and drove other tribes still farther west. Names from a dozen different tribes, some of them passing through French orthography to reach their present form, still cover the land. And since the settlers were not skilled etymologists, the meanings of these Indian names are often difficult to come by. Many other names are translations of the Indian names—to the best of the settlers' limited linguistic ability.

In the second half of the nineteenth century came the lumbermen—and the railroads. Every lumber camp had to have a name (many of them now vanished), and every railroad siding and station (many now abandoned as the rail lines vanish).

It has been a pleasant task for us to compile this book of Wisconsin place names. They reflect so much of the state's tradition, settlement, and flavor. All around, on every side, the appeal of Wisconsin echoes and reechoes in its names: girls' names, early settler names, classic names, presidents' names, Bible names, names that were supposed to be something else, forgotten names, nostalgic names supplied by homesick immigrants, geographic names, names from wars, from other cities and places, from feats of strength, from heroes, from friendships, lovers, dreams; from railroads, poetry, and humor.

The place names of hamlets, crossroads, villages, townships, cities, counties, lakes, streams—all are monuments to someone's imagination, courage, strength, willpower, kindness, or devotion.

Wisconsin names are uniquely of the state and reflect its character.

Wisconsin, we believe, has a different look, a feel, a character that always makes one know that he is coming home almost the moment he crosses the Mississippi on the west, or crosses the Illinois line on the south. There is a special feel, a homeness that is Wisconsin. Mainly, perhaps, it is the look of the land, as though a kindly Providence created a special setting for a special people. For the descent of the glaciers from Labrador and Hudson Bay modified the land, leveled off the hills in places, filled depressions. And occasionally erosion left a landmark, or a whole series of strange stone formations, and when a settler saw these things he said, Castle Rock, or Tower Rock, or Elephant Mound, or Steamboat Rock, or Ferry Bluff.

Settlers followed the land, and the formation of the land. They settled on the kind of land where they thought they would find happiness and prosperity. In the hills, the hill people of Norway, Switzerland, Wales, Germany, and other far countries tended to settle, and they called the places New Glarus, Caledonia, Wales, Berlin, Vienna, New Holstein. Sometimes the settlers chose land for its flatness and fertility, and they sprinkled the crossroads and the meeting places with poetic names, or names of joy, or personalities, or hope: Black Earth, Belle Plaine, Cornucopia, Spring Valley, Star Prairie, Mount Hope.

We see all the periods of the state's history and settlement in the names. It was Marquette who first wrote the name of the great river of the state, calling it Meskousing, from which eventually came Wisconsin. René Menard left St. Esprit and La Pointe. The Voyageurs gave us Eau Pleine, Eau Claire, Eau Galle, De Pere, La Baie Verte, Lac Vieux, Desert, Butte des Morts.

We believe that place names are cherished today more than ever. As evidence, note the recent story of Winneconne, meaning "the place of skulls." (An Indian battle once took place around there.)

The Winneconne folks are very proud of their name and their town. Some time ago, Winneconne, by some unthinkable chance, was left off of the Wisconsin road maps. The Winneconne Chamber of Commerce, under the dynamic leadership of its president, Mrs. Vera Kitchen, immediately organized the community for action. For, if the village no longer existed, "fishermen could not know where to fish, industry would not know where to locate, employees could not know where to work."

Even poems were written about the situation:

Wisconsin must have had a mental lapse,
To take Winneconne off the highway maps.

A contest was started on "how to put Winneconne back on the map, with the winner to receive a wonderful all-expense weekend in Winneconne."

Governor Knowles tried to smooth the ruffled feathers of the irate citizens. He told them the name would certainly be on next year's maps. The Winneconne folks immediately made Knowles the chairman of the nationwide contest.

The winners of the contest were two Wisconsin girls residing in Washington, D.C., who suggested that Winneconne "secede and declare war."

Secession days were observed by officials with an appropriate program in the forgotten city on July 22 and 23, 1967, with the Winneconne navy, air force, and army standing by.

A "Declaration of Independence" was issued by the village president, James Coughlin. A sovereign state was declared, and a toll bridge over Wolf River was established to collect revenues for the new state. Later in the day the toll bridge was freed. Adequate funds had been easily collected to operate the new state . . . about seven dollars.

At 4 p.m. of the first day of independence, a phone call was received from Governor Knowles suggesting a negotiated return to Wisconsin. The next day, at noon, the negotiations were concluded, and Winneconne rejoined the State of Wisconsin in a flag-raising ceremony.

Many names are now forgotten. Dane County is dotted here and there with plats of imaginary cities whose locations are lost and whose very names have passed out of memory.

Superior City, Van Buren, Dunkirk Falls, Clinton, City of the Second Lake, City of the Four Lakes, Middletown, Troy, and Beaumont—all were deprived of their hope of greatness.

Superior City, on paper, contained nearly five hundred blocks. It had a wonderful location, lying as it did on the east bank of the Wisconsin River, among the bluffs, valleys, gullies, rattlesnakes, and ravines of four sections in the north part of Dane County. Provisions were made for the State Capitol, which, of course, was to be located in the middle of this great metropolis. Capitol Square was bounded by Broadway, State, Wells, and Taylor Streets. Another public square was reserved for a park. A lot of Easterners invested and lost their stake. In Superior City many lots were actually owned by renowned figures such as Daniel Webster and Henry Clay.

But present or forgotten, the place names of Wisconsin are always with us. They are in our present and their roots are in our past.

Antigo, ca. 1925

⇥ A ⇤

Aaron *Burnett County*
Aaron Cornelison was an early settler in Rusk township. The first postmaster, Lucy Cornelison, named the town.

Abbotsford *Clark County*
Named for Edwin H. Abbot, the financial genius of the old Wisconsin Central Railway.

Abbott *Sheboygan County*
Now called Sherman. The Abbotts were a prominent family in the community. Because of their Southern sympathies during the Civil War, they were forced to leave the community and the town's name was changed to Sherman—after General William T., of course.

A. B. C. Ridge *Crawford County*
Located in the Township of Utica, this ridge was named for three farmers that settled here: Andrew Mikkelson, Ben Rand, and Chris Anderson.

Ablemans *Sauk County*
First called Ableman's Mills from a flour mill owned by Colonel S.V.R. Ableman, who settled here in 1851. The town has also been called Rock Springs and Excelsior.

Ackley *Langlade County*
After the first settler in the area—a Frenchman with an Indian wife.

Acorn *Dane County*
This corner area was named for an early post office that operated from September 17, 1888, to July 13, 1898. The post office was named by Mrs. Kate Goddard, the postmistress, though her reason for choosing "Acorn" is unknown.

Adams *Adams County*
For either John Quincy Adams, the sixth president, or John Adams, the second president. The town was first called South Friendship. The citizens didn't like that name, so they appealed to the Chicago and North Western Railway, and the railway company finally decided on Adams because it was short.

Adams Valley *La Crosse County*
Named for V. M. and H. D. Adams, who came here in 1853.

Adamsville *Iowa County*
Named for John Adams, who, with David Hollister, erected a large gristmill here in 1854.

Adelaide Park   *Fond du Lac County*

W. W. Collins donated this land in the northwest part of the city of Fond du Lac to the city in 1935. The park was named for his granddaughter, Adelaide Boyd.

Adell   *Sheboygan County*

The original landowner, Christian Gersmehl, purchased land here in 1855. He platted out a settlement around the depot and called it Sherman's Station. It was later named Adell after an old post office that was active for a period.

Aetna   *Lafayette County*

The tale of this forgotten place in the New Diggings Township is that there was a limekiln on the spot that resembled the spouting of Mt. Aetna in Sicily.

Afton   *Rock County*

First incorporated as Middledale on July 7, 1854. The Postmaster General requested a change of name, because too many other towns and villages were called Middledale. A meeting, called in May 1855, was opened with prayer and the song "Flow Gently Sweet Afton." Everybody cried, "Let's call the village Afton."

Agenda   *Ashland County*

The result of a meeting on the formation of the township, at which items for discussion were titled "agenda."

Agnew   *Ashland County*

A civil engineer named Agnew worked for the Wisconsin Central Railroad when the line was built.

Ahnapee   *Kewaunee County*

The river and township were formerly spelled Ahneepee, a Potawatomi name meaning "where's the river," or "wolf river."

Ainsworth   *Langlade County*

Uncle Tom Ainsworth, born in Dorchester, England, 1839, owned the first store.

Akan   *Richland County*

This township was named for Robert Akan, who helped build the early road from Richmond to Rockbridge.

Alaska   *Kewaunee County*

The post office was established the same year the United States acquired Alaska from Russia.

Alaska Station   *Waukesha County*

From the many icehouses in the area, from which ice was shipped to Milwaukee breweries and to the resort hotels that once flourished in the vicinity.

Albany *Green County*

Some of the first settlers of the village and township came from Albany, New York.

Albertville *Chippewa County*

Albert Halvorsen was a barber from Eau Claire; he started the general store but never ran it himself.

Albion *Dane County*

Isaac Brown suggested the name. There was some opposition to it. Some of the settlers wanted to call it Salem, but the English settlers favored the old Roman name of their native isle.

Albion *Trempealeau County*

Again, the ancient name for England.

Alder *Ashland County*

Named for the black alder trees that abound in the locality.

Alderly *Dodge County*

The first three settlers were from Alderly, Scotland.

Algoma *Kewaunee County*

The first settlers arrived here on June 27, 1851. Abraham Hall, a New Yorker, erected a sawmill and a store here in 1852. The place was incorporated as Wolf River in 1856, but the name was changed to Ahnapee in 1858. The post office was established in 1859, and by 1873 there was a newspaper, the Ahnapee Record. Ahnapee became a city in February 1879. In 1899 it was renamed Algoma, an Indian word meaning "park of flowers," or "snowshoe."

Allen *Eau Claire County*

Charles Allen was an early settler and owner of the land on which the village was built in the early 1870s.

Allens Grove *Walworth County*

Founded by four brothers, Pliny, Sidney, Phillip, and Harvey Allen.

Allenville *Winnebago County*

Timothy Allen owned the land on which the railroad station was built.

Allequash *Vilas County*

An Indian term meaning "many fish."

Allis *Milwaukee County*

After E. B. Allis, the founder.

Allis Heights   *Dane County*

Named for Frank W. Allis, the owner of the land from the 1890s. This subdivision, in the town of Blooming Grove, was platted in 1927.

Allouez   *Brown County*

Named for Father Claude Allouez, a French missionary in the mid-1600s.

Allouez Bay   *Douglas County*

Also named for Father Allouez.

Allouez Park   *Oconto County*

Father Allouez is considered the first European to visit this area. He founded St. Frances Xavier mission here in 1665.

Alma   *Buffalo County*

Named by W. H. Gates after a Russian stream made famous during the Crimean War.

Almena   *Barron County*

Albert and Wilhelmena Koehler ran a store here, and in 1887 an application was made for a post office. The name was coined from Albert and Wilhelmena. The original name was Lightning City, from Lightning Creek, which ran through it. The post office department didn't like Lightning City.

Almond   *Portage County*

Founded in 1849 by settlers from Almond in New York State.

Alpha   *Burnett County*

The first postmaster was a butter maker named Mr. Guy E. Moves, who submitted the name Smaland Prairie, because so many of the first settlers were from the Smaland region of Sweden. But the post office department said the name was too long. The would-be postmaster found a shorter name by glancing at his cream separator, an Alpha Number One De Laval.

Alstead   *Burnett County*

Named for an early Norwegian settler, James Alstead, the site is now a forest, conservation, and wildlife area.

Altdorf   *Wood County*

Most of the Swiss families of the neighborhood came from Altdorf, Canton Uri, Switzerland.

Alto   *Fond du Lac County*

The village is near the spot where Chief Black Hawk once had a camp. The name was given to the place by Silas Miller, the third settler, who was the lay preacher of the Methodist Church—perhaps named for a singer in his choir.

Altoona
Eau Claire County

Altoona was platted in 1881 and was originally called East Eau Claire. It was incorporated as the city of Altoona in 1887. A division point on the old Chicago, St. Paul, Minneapolis, and Omaha Railroad, it is said to have been named by a man named Mr. Beal, who came from Altoona, Pennsylvania.

Alverno
Manitowoc County

Named for Mt. Alverno in Italy, where the Franciscan order was founded.

Amberg
Marinette County

W. A. Amberg was owner of the granite works here.

Amery
Polk County

In honor of William Amery, who was born in England in 1831. He came to this country in 1861, locating first in Stillwater, Minnesota, and later moving to St. Croix Falls, Wisconsin. Although he never lived in Amery, the town was named in his honor in 1887, the year of his death.

Amherst
Portage County

Judge Gilbert Park, who had been a logger in Canada, and Adam Uline, who was born and spent his boyhood days in Amherst, Nova Scotia, proposed this name for the township in honor of the hero General Jeffery Amherst. In 1900 a square mile of land was incorporated as a village with the same name.

Amherst Junction
Portage County

When the Green Bay and Lake Pepin Railway was constructed from Green Bay to Winona in 1872, it crossed the Wisconsin Central's rails at what had been mapped as Groversberg, named for an early settler. But the small settlement, located two miles northwest of Amherst at the intersection, was commonly called The Junction and later became Amherst Junction.

Amnicon
Douglas County

The name of two townships, a lake, a river, and a falls. Amnicon is a corruption of an Ojibwe word meaning "spawning ground," from the whitefish that enter the Amnicon River to spawn.

Amsterdam
Sheboygan County

Although few traces of the town remain today, it once was a thriving settlement on the lake shore in the town of Holland. Amsterdam was the only fishing village in the county. Henry Walvoord is said to have given the place its name after the city in the Netherlands.

Amy
Dunn County

Located about four miles southeast of Elk Mound and close to the Eau Claire County line, Amy is the site of a post office, a school, and a store. It was named after Amy Kellogg Morse, a prominent temperance worker.

Anah *Washburn County*

Walter Crocker, postmaster at Spooner, established a star route to a farm home and named the office Anah, after his sister.

Anacker *Columbia County*

This was once a station on the Soo Line from Portage to Stevens Point. The Anacker family still lives in large numbers around Portage.

Anderson Creek *Fond du Lac County*

This creek runs across land in Friendship Township that was once owned by W. Anderson.

Andersons *Burnett County*

Canute Anderson was the first settler here in 1851. He was twice a member of the Wisconsin Assembly, and he conducted the first post office unofficially in his own home. He was instrumental in organizing the Burnett County government.

Andrews Corners *Dane County*

Near the town of York, named for Justus Andrews of New York, and his descendants. The land has been in the family since before 1873.

Angelo *Monroe County*

Angelo was the first settler here.

Aniwa *Shawano County*

A corruption of an Ojibwe word meaning "superiority"; it is also a word meaning "those."

Anston *Brown County*

Named for a family of the vicinity.

Anthony *Eau Claire County*

Anton Brager was a worker in the general store. The place became Anthony in his honor.

Antigo *Langlade County*

From an Ojibwe Indian name meaning "balsam evergreen river" or "the place where evergreens can always be found." The name was first used by settlers around 1876.

Antioch *Richland County*

The community and the school both took their names from the church. The original Antioch was the place where worshippers were first called Christians.

Apostle Islands *Lake Superior*

These beautiful islands were named in part by the early Jesuits under the impression that there were twelve. Actually there are twenty-two: Basswood, Bear, Cat, Devils, Eagle, Gull, Hermit, Ironwood, Long, Madeline, Manitou, Michigan, North Twin, Oak, Otter, Outer, Raspberry, Rocky, Sand, South Twin, Stockton (Presque), and York. Some names have been changed since early days.

Apple Ridge   *Richland County*
A place in Ithaca Township, there were orchards here long before 1900.

Appleton   *Outagamie County*
In 1634 Nicolet paddled up the Fox River from Green Bay and claimed the territory in the name of France. In 1855, following the establishment of Lawrence College in 1847, the city of Appleton came into being, named after Samuel Appleton of Boston, father-in-law of Amos A. Lawrence. Mr. Appleton, although a man of eighty-six at the time, took great interest in the village bearing his name and bequeathed ten thousand dollars to Lawrence College to found a library. There were originally three villages where the city now stands: Lawesburgh to the east, Grand Chute to the west, and Appleton in the middle.

Appleton Junction   *Outagamie County*
From the city of Appleton.

Arbor Vitae   *Vilas County*
Named for the arbor vitae trees that grew so abundantly on the shore of what is now known as Big Arbor Vitae Lake. The name dates from around 1895.

Arbutus School   *Wood County*
Arbutus flowers once grew in abundance near this school in Port Edwards and still can be found here.

Arcadia   *Trempealeau County*
Suggested by Noah Comstock, from real or fancied resemblance of the valley to the state of Arcadia in ancient Greece. The name was actually given to the township by Mrs. David Bishop.

Argonne   *Forest County*
When the Soo Line Railroad was built in 1888, the site of the present town of Argonne was platted by Abraham Van Zile, and named after himself. The Van Zile post office was established on November 18, 1889, with Gale E. Bailey as postmaster. On May 20, 1892, the name was changed to North Crandon. On May 11, 1929, the name was changed to Argonne to honor those who had served in the armed forces during World War I.

Argyle   *Lafayette County*
In 1844 a committee applied to Washington for a post office, giving the name Hazel Green. The department informed them that a town by that name was already listed in Wisconsin. Then Allen Wright, a native of Scotland and one of the leading men in the settlement, suggested the name Argyle, in honor of the Duke of Argyle, whom he greatly admired. Wright had been a tenant of the duke.

Arimond's Picnic Ground   *Fond du Lac County*
This subdivision is laid out on Long Lake in Osceola. Jacob Arimond was a merchant in Dundee who owned this land. After his death in 1906 his widow had the land platted under this name.

Aristocracy Hills   *Wood County*

Once a part of early Grand Rapids, it was also called Quality Row. The more well-to-do residents lived on this rise behind the east bank of the Wisconsin River. It is now 3rd Street South in Wisconsin Rapids.

Arkansaw   *Pepin County*

In 1852, Willard F. Holbrook took a day off from work at the sawmill to go trout fishing with a friend from the East. Walking over the present Gap Hill, they came to a small stream, which Mr. Holbrook named Arkansaw because of a certain resemblance to the Arkansaw Creek. Holbrook later built a log cabin and established a furniture factory here. Local Indians said the plentiful trout in the Arkansaw River kept the water pure, and would not fish the stream for that reason.

Arlington   *Columbia County*

The source of the name is unknown. The place was settled in 1838 by a man named Clark M. Young. In 1844 he was joined by others, and in 1871 Mrs. Sarah Pierce and David Sullen platted a section of land upon which the village was started.

Arlington Heights   *Dane County*

The name was chosen for its suggestion of elegance or distinction. This subdivision was platted within the city of Madison in 1927.

Armstrong   *Fond du Lac County*

Asher Armstrong settled in the township in 1851. He was the first postmaster of Armstrong Corners Post Office when it was formed in 1862.

Armstrong Creek   *Forest County*

The depot, established in 1887, was named after a settler.

Arnold   *Chippewa County*

The village was originally called Still Hawn, for the firm of Sillman and Hawn, who operated a sawmill here. When the railroad came through, N. H. Deuel built a store and post office close to the railroad and named the village and post office for his oldest son, Arnold.

Arpin   *Wood County*

John D. and Antoine Arpin located the village about a mile east of the present site. They made a pond as a reservoir for logs and built their sawmill on the east side of it. In the meantime, Martin Pfyle had laid out another town called Martinsville about a mile south of Arpin, and just east of the railroad tracks, where he put up a store and cheese factory. A saloon was built in Martinsville and more people moved in. For a while it looked as though Martinsville would be the permanent site of the village. Meanwhile, another town was platted west of the railroad, and a store, saloon, and blacksmith shop were built. This third site was near the depot, and eventually the other settlements were abandoned.

Arthur   *Chippewa County*
For President Chester A. Arthur.

Ash Creek   *Richland County*
The heavy growth of ash timber in this area of Orion Township suggested the name.

Ashford   *Fond du Lac County*
Originally organized as the town of Chili. An act of the state legislature on January 26, 1854, changed the name to Ashford, suggested by the ash trees growing nearby.

Ashippun   *Dodge County*
In the early days, the district was known as Ashippun. It was plentifully supplied with ash trees, both white and black, as well as dense thickets of prickly ash. Scotch settlers wanted to call the place Ashburn. But the English settlers wanted to retain something of the time of the Indians. The name Ashippun was suggested by Mr. Samuel Marshall, the first town board chairman. Ashippun is an Indian name and may mean "decayed lungs," or it may have reference to the raccoon, since the Menominee word for raccoon is aspipun. The Ojibwe word for raccoon is aissibun. The prairie Potawatomi word for raccoon is ashippun. Ashippun is also, apparently, an Algonquin Indian name from Virginia.

Ashland   *Ashland County*
The Indian name for the place was Zham-a-wa-mik, from the Ojibwe term meaning "the long-stretched beaver." It was platted by the Milwaukee, Lakeshore, and Western Railroad in 1885 and was named Ashland by Martin Beaser, one of the original owners, in honor of the home of Henry Clay. Before this, the place was called Whittlesey, for Adolph Whittlesey, its first postmaster, then Bay City, and then Saint Mark for Saint Mark's in Venice.

Ash Ridge   *Richland County*
An area in Forest and Marshall townships, named for the ash trees on the ridge.

Ashton   *Dane County*
This corner area in the town of Springfield was named for the Ashton Post Office, which was probably named for Thomas Ashton, the president of the British Temperance Emigration Society.

Ashwaubenon   *Brown County*
The township and creek were named from the tract of land left by the great Menominee chief Ashwaubemie to his descendants, the families of Franks and La Rose. According to legend, this is where Waubenuquq, the beautiful Morning Star, was brought when Ashwaubemie carried her away from her people to make her his wife.

Askeaton   *Brown County*
The village may have been named after an Indian resident who had a painful mouth, since the Indian meaning of the name is "raw mouth."

Aspen *Burnett County*

This abandoned settlement was probably named for aspen trees, which were plentiful there.

Athelstane *Marinette County*

Athelstane is from the Scottish Athelstane, or Athel's stone.

Attica *Green County*

This village was first called Winneshiek, then Milford, but soon changed back to Winneshiek. The post office was called Attica, since there was at that time another office in the state named Winneshiek. The name Attica was suggested by Jeptha Davis, formerly from Attica, New York.

Aubrey *Richland County*

Aubrey was named for Auburn Cass, an early settler. Because there already was an Auburn in Wisconsin, Aubrey was substituted. This name was given to the little post office that was located here, in Ithaca Township, from 1899 to 1902.

Auburn *Fond du Lac County*

Glacial moraines in the township have created many recreational areas for vacationers. This name was chosen by two Adams brothers originally from Auburn, New York, which was named for Goldsmith's Deserted Village—"Auburn, the loveliest village on the plain."

Atwater *Dodge County*

A settlement called Mill Creek was changed in 1856 to Atwater by a Mr. Hillyer, who came from Atwater, Ohio.

Auburndale *Wood County*

The name was probably brought by English settlers. Or it may have been given this name because some of the daughters of an influential family, the W. D. Connors, had auburn hair.

Augusta *Eau Claire County*

Formerly known as Ridge Creek. The name was changed by Charles Buckman in honor of the capital of Maine, from which he came. A second explanation has it that some citizens proposed to name the place after the prettiest girl in town. They held an election, and Augusta Rickard, a visitor from Oak Grove, Wisconsin, was the winner.

Avalanche *Vernon County*

Named for the formation immediately east of the village, resembling a gigantic landslide.

Avoca *Iowa County*

The name may come from a poem by Tom Moore that mentions the sweet vale of Avoca. There is also the story that in 1857, a homesick Irishman said, "Sure and 'tis like the beautiful vale of Avoca in old Ireland."

Aztalan *Jefferson County*

The remains of the ancient city of Aztalan, considered one of the wonders of the Western world, were discovered in 1836 by N. F. Hyer. The name was chosen by Mr. Hyer because, according to Alexander Van Humbolt, the Aztecs of Mexico had a tradition that their ancestors came from a country to the north called Aztaland. The thought that these Wisconsin mounds might be the remains of the city of the ancestors of the Aztecs suggested the name. It is made up of two words, atl, "water," and an, "near." The Crawfish River is right at hand, and the Rock River is not far away.

Bayfield County's Robinson Lake, ca. 1935

⇥ B ⇤

Babb Hollow   *Richland County*
This location in Marshall was named for the Babb family, who came to the county very early.

Babb Ridge   *Richland County*
George H. Babb became prominent in the affairs of the town of Sylvan after he arrived in 1856. By the turn of the century, E. C., J. D., and John H. Babb, descendants of George, had land on this ridge in Sylvan Township.

Babb's Crossing   *Sauk County*
This is a bridge that crosses the Baraboo River in Reedsburg. It is named for John Babb's grandfather, one of the earliest settlers in the region.

Babb's Prairie   *Sauk County*
This level tract near Reedsburg is named for James W. Babb and his son, John, who settled in 1845.

Babcock   *Wood County*
According to old-timers, the town was built by a lumber baron named Babcock who had a sawmill in Nekoosa.

Back Bay   *Dane County*
Named for its position behind West Bay and Monona Bay, this subdivision has been absorbed into the city of Madison since its platting in 1902.

Bacon Creek   *Crawford County*
Early settlers named it for Sylvester Bacon. Bacon Creek runs from Highway 171 to the junction of the Kickapoo River.

Badaxe   *Vernon County*
Named for the river in the vicinity. In 1868 its name was changed to Genoa.

Bad River   *Ashland County*
Local Indians called this "Swamp River" because it flows through swampy land before emptying into Lake Superior. Settlers mistook the Ojibwe word maski, meaning "swamp," for matchi, meaning "bad," and therefore referred to it as Bad River.

Badger Mill Creek   *Dane County*
The Badger Mill, the first gristmill in the county, was built here in 1844. The creek rises in sec. 13, Verona, and flows southwest to join the Sugar River in sec. 28.

Badger Village   *Sauk County*
Built during World War II to house workers for the Badger Ordnance Works. After the war the village housed University of Wisconsin students who bused to the university.

Badger Valley   *Sauk County*
A vale nine miles east of Spring Green, named for the badgers that once were plentiful here.

Bagley   *Grant County*
Mary Bagley owned the land on which this village was built. In 1884, the Chicago, Burlington, and Quincy Railroad depot was erected. The St. Paul Land Company bought land from Mrs. Bagley and platted and named the village. William Thiessa bought the first lot and built a hotel, hauling the lumber over the river on the ice from Clayton, Iowa. On January 1, 1885, the building was open for business. This hotel has since been enlarged and is now known as the Burlington Hotel.

Baileys Harbor   *Door County*
Baileys Harbor is the first place on the Door County Peninsula to be settled as a village. One day in 1848, Captain Bailey was returning from Buffalo. As he headed his vessel down the lake toward Milwaukee, a storm came up and, since the boat was in danger of sinking, Captain Bailey had to look for a harbor. Suddenly, to the west, he saw a large, safe-looking inlet that was deep enough for the ship and well situated to act as a harbor. He stayed several days and explored the area, finding large stands of timber and a ledge of building stone. On returning to Milwaukee, Bailey told his owners of the stone and wood. The owners acquired the land around the harbor, and lumber and stone were brought by the ships to Milwaukee.

Bain Junction   *Kenosha County*
A name found on railroad timetables, but never a settlement. Taken from the Bain Wagon Company of Kenosha.

Baker Creek   *Crawford County*
In Clayton Township, named for the Baker family.

Bakerville   *Wood County*
In 1886 Bakerville contained a hotel, a gristmill, a sawmill, a general store, a blacksmith shop, and a wagon maker, but by 1923 only a cheese factory remained. The settlement, part of Lincoln Township, was at the common corners of secs. 23, 24, 25, and 26. It was named for James H. Baker, who owned land in the area.

Bakke Hill   *Dane County*
In Pleasant Springs, named for P. O. Bakke and his descendants, who owned the land from before 1890 until after 1911.

Bald Hill   *Dane County*
Part of Verona and Fitchburg, this large, wooded hill has a bare spot on its north side.

Baldwin   *St. Croix County*

The West Wisconsin Railway Company built a line from Tomah to Hudson, completing it on June 19, 1871. Baldwin was then called Clarkesville, after the General Freight Agent. But D. H. Baldwin was president of the company, and he and Jacob Humbird deserve the credit for this important line into St. Croix County.

Baldwin Pond   *Dane County*

Anson and Julius Baldwin settled adjoining land in Rutland.

Balmoral   *Richland County*

Part of Eagle Township, it was first known as Rodolf's Mill. Later it was known as Lawson, for William H. Lawson. The name Balmoral may have been assigned by the government in 1889, when the post office was established here. There does not appear to be any connection to Balmoral Castle in the Scottish highlands.

Balsam Lake   *Polk County*

The village and lake were named by the Ojibwe Indians.

Bancroft   *Portage County*

Named after the Reverend Warren G. Bancroft, a pioneer Methodist pastor who came here after the Civil War. Warren G. Harding, president of the United States, was named for Warren G. Bancroft. The village grew chiefly because of the railroad. A post office was established on May 17, 1876.

Bangor   *La Crosse County*

John Wheldon named the village after his birthplace in Wales. Wheldon came to the area in 1853 from New York State, after reading an article in an Eastern newspaper in which the author called the locality "a Garden of Eden." Mr. Wheldon constructed the first log cabin in Bangor, located on Indian camping grounds.

Banker Park   *Richland County*

Once snake-infested and weedy, the area was turned into a picnic place by Lee Banker and others.

Baraboo   *Sauk County*

As far as is known, this name is unique in America. Two Baribeau brothers had a mill at the mouth of the Baraboo River where it flows into the Wisconsin River south of Portage. The brothers had a serious disagreement and dissolved the partnership. The remaining brother then changed his name to Baraboo. Eventually both brothers left the region and moved to Canada. Histories of Baraboo written in the latter part of the nineteenth century tell of a Frenchman named Baribeau who traveled by boat or canoe along the rivers of Wisconsin. He had a trading post at the mouth of the Baraboo River, where he exchanged goods with the Indians. One historian calls this trader Jean. Another calls him Pierre, and a third mentions his name as Jacques. Since there was more than one Baribeau brother in the area, the histories may refer to three different men.

Barber's Bay *Dane County*

George Barber bought some land here in the town of Dunn in the 1890s. The bay is on the west side of Lake Kegonsa between Colladay's Point and Lund's Point.

Barker's Corners *Walworth County*

Named for early settlers. Later the area was called Millard.

Barneveld *Iowa County*

The surveyor for the railroad, a native of Holland, suggested the name. He had been a great admirer of Dutch leader Jonna Barneveld.

Barnum *Crawford County*

Part of Haney Township, Barnum was the name of a family of early settlers.

Barre *La Crosse County*

Probably named for Barre, Vermont. Some of the area's early settlers came from there.

Barron *Barron County*

In 1869 the name of the county was changed from Dallas to Barron in honor of Henry D. Barron of St. Croix Falls. Born in New York State, Barron moved to Wisconsin in 1851 and was for a time editor and postmaster in Waukesha. In 1857, he entered law practice at Pepin, where in 1860 he was appointed judge of the eighth circuit. In the following year Barron moved to St. Croix Falls. He was several times a member of the assembly and a state senator. In 1876 he was appointed judge of the eleventh circuit, a position he held until his death.

The village of Barron was named for him after it became the county seat. The location had previously been known as Quaderer's Camp. Knapp Stout Lumber Co. owned the land upon which Rice Lake had been founded and was naturally anxious to have Rice Lake made the county seat. A few independent thinkers in the county had other plans.

John Quaderer, who was originally a Knapp Stout foreman and was still contracting for them, was one of the leaders against company domination of county affairs. Another was Woodbury S. Grover, who had a farm in Dallas township. In the election of 1874, it was voted to move the county seat to Barron, and Grover was elected county clerk. He put the records in the seat of a chair hewn out of a log and, driving a team of horses with their feet covered so as not to make any noise, took the records to Barron and deposited them with John Quaderer. The chair is still kept in Barron.

Bartel *Ozaukee County*

A former station of the Chicago and North Western Railway, named after a local family.

Barton *Washington County*

The original name was Salisbury's Mills. When the Yankee population was replaced by incoming Germans, it was called Salzburg. For a while the village was also called Newark, but in 1853 its present name, Barton, after the founder, Barton Salisbury, was fixed. The township received its name from the village.

Bascom Hill   *Dane County*
On the University of Wisconsin campus, it is crowned by Bascom Hall, which was named
for John Bascom, an early president of the University of Wisconsin. It is also called College Hill or University Hill.

Bashaw   *Washburn County*
Bashaw may be part of the name of the great Ojibwe Indian chief Wabashaw, also spelled
Wabasha. It may also be named after a logging camp boss named B. A. Shaw.

Bashford Hill   *Richland County*
Before the establishment of the Bashford Post Office in 1895, this hill in Dayton Township was known as Sparling Hill, for the A. Sparling family. Some believe that it was
named for Coles Bashford, who was the governor of Wisconsin from March 1856 until
January 1858.

Baskerville Harbor   *Dane County*
Named for E. J. Baskerville, it adjoins Baskerville Park in Middleton and forms the
entrance of Pheasant Branch Creek into Lake Mendota.

Bass Bay   *Waukesha County*
Named after the Bass family living on the north side of Big Muskego Lake.

Bass Lake   *Dane County*
In early days this lake in Rutland contained many black bass.

Bassett   *Kenosha County*
Henry Bassett came to Randall Township in 1842 and purchased 120 acres of land. Soon
his son, Reuben Bassett, joined him. The village was named when Mr. Bassett gave the
land for the railroad.

Basswood   *Ashland County*
Thought to be a translation of the Ojibwe word for the island, Wigobiminiss.

Basswood   *Richland County*
The first post office, established in August 1869, was named "Lucas" for James Lucas,
a prominent farmer. About two months later, though, the name was changed to "Bass
Wood." In 1892 the spelling was changed to "Basswood," part of Eagle Township. The
basswood trees growing in the area were used to build the first schoolhouse.

Batavia   *Sheboygan County*
Probably named for Batavia, New York.

Bateman   *Chippewa County*
M. P. Bateman, an immigrant from Ireland, came to Chippewa County in 1854 by way
of Sun Prairie. An enterprising farmer, he operated a sawmill and dam at the mouth of

Paint Creek. At one time he used a muzzle-loading shotgun to defend the dam against men trying to run logs through it without paying the toll he demanded.

Bauer Valley   *Richland County*
Named for Nicholas Bauer, who settled in Westford in 1865.

Bay Beach   *Brown County*
Originally named Bay View Beach by a former ship captain named Cusick, who owned and developed the land.

Bay City   *Ashland County*
One of the early names for what is now the city of Ashland.

Bay City   *Pierce County*
After Saratoga was abandoned, Mr. Charles R. Tyler secured the town site by paying $1,700 in back taxes. He renamed it Bay City.

Bay de Noquette   *Brown County*
Bay de Noquette is possibly named for an Algonquin tribe located by the earliest French writers around Noquet Bay at the mouth of Green Bay. Noquet is believed to mean "bear foot" in Ojibwe. According to Nicolet, the Noquets were, at the time of his visit in 1634, on the shores of Lake Superior.

Bayfield   *Bayfield County*
La Pointe was the original name for the entire locality around Chequamegon Bay. A Jesuit mission, established by Father Allouez in 1665, was known as La Pointe du Saint Esprit. In the eighteenth century a French post was established here, which was called La Pointe. The name La Pointe was officially, in the nineteenth century, limited to the trading post on Madeline Island. About 1857, the town of Bayfield was promoted by Henry M. Rice of St. Paul, who named it for Admiral Henry W. Bayfield of the Royal Navy, surveyor of Lake Superior for the English government from 1823 to 1825.

Bay Settlement   *Brown County*
Located on the site of a Menominee village.

Bayside   *Milwaukee County*
The village was incorporated on February 13, 1953. It is part of the town of Milwaukee. The area is composed of several subdivisions adjacent to Lake Michigan, and the name is geographically descriptive.

Bay View   *Milwaukee County*
Named for its location on the Bay of Milwaukee and because of the fine view of the lake that can be had from here.

Baywood   *Dane County*

Woods along a small bay on the east shore of Lake Mendota mark the location of this subdivision. It has been absorbed into Maple Bluff since its platting in 1922.

Bean School   *Wood County*

A. B. Bean, B. F. Bean, and W. H. Bean owned land in the vicinity, so it is probable that this school in Hansen was named for this family or one of its members.

Bear Cave   *Richland County*

Also called Bear Den or Popp's Cave, this cave in Sylvan Township was once used by bears as their lair. There are three rooms of fairly large dimensions here, and settlers used to visit often.

Bear Creek   *Outagamie County*

Started as a lumber camp in 1850. A lumberman, Welcome Hyde, cut the first road into the area. There was no village in the whole township until the railroad was built in 1880. About this time F. M. Hyde built a store in what became Bear Creek Station. In 1885, the land west of the station was platted for Welcome Hyde and was named Bear Creek after the nearby stream. After a disastrous fire in 1902, in which three-fourths of the town was wiped out, the people rebuilt and called the town Welcome, after Mr. Hyde. The name was later changed back to Bear Creek.

Bear Creek   *Sauk County*

Indians named the creek for the bears they found here.

Bear Creek   *Crawford County*

A man named Bennett shot a bear in the area, and it has been called Bear Creek ever since. The creek runs through Clayton Township.

Bear Creek   *Richland County*

Several stories exist about its naming, all involving the killing of a bear. The creek runs through Buena Vista and Ithaca Townships.

Bear Lake   *Sheboygan County*

Named by a government surveyor, Nehemiah King. In 1835 he entered in his notebook, "We could not learn the Indian name of this lake with any certainty. From the circumstances of their having recently killed bears near it, we gave it the name of Bear Lake."

Bear Trap   *Ashland County*

An early settler caught a black bear in a trap here some time before the town was located.

Bear Valley   *Richland County*

Peter Haskin platted a little town at this site in Ithaca Township in 1855. When a post office was moved into the area, it was called Bear Valley, "Bear" from the Bear Creek and "Valley" from the nineteen-mile valley running down to Lone Rock.

Beaty Hill   *Dane County*

George Beaty of Pennsylvania settled here in 1854.

Beaver   *Marinette County*

The name of the township comes from a nearby brook.

Beaver   *Polk County*

This township was established November 11, 1885, and named for its many beaver dams.

Beaver Brook   *Washburn County*

Named for a stream in the vicinity, which in early days even as now was favorable for beavers. From the small lakes in its course, it appears the beavers built many dams there.

Beaver Creek   *Trempealeau County*

Tradition says two French trappers wintered here above Galesville and caught a large number of beavers. William B. Bunnell and James Reed also caught beavers here and gave the creek its name.

Beaver Dam   *Dodge County*

James B. Brower is said to have named it for the many beavers who built dams on the several little streams emptying into the river. The town was established by Thomas Mackie and his son-in-law, who came from Fox Lake.

Beaver Lake   *Waukesha County*

Named for the industrious native animal.

Bechaud Beach   *Fond du Lac County*

Located on Lake Winnebago, it was platted from land owned by the Bechaud Brewing Company. The company produced Bechaud Beer and, later, Empire Beer. They suspended operations in 1937.

Beckey's Spring   *Eau Claire County*

This wayside was named for an early settler who owned the land. It was a popular stopping place in the 1870s for loggers traveling to Eau Claire from Read's Landing near Wabasha, Minnesota, which was then a booming logging town with scores of hotels.

Beebe Branch   *Richland County*

Named for William Beebe, who came to Richland County before the Civil War and served in Company 1 of the Nineteenth Regiment.

Beechwood   *Sheboygan County*

Named for the large growth of beech trees in the vicinity.

Beetown *Grant County*

In the early part of 1827, Cyrus Alexander found a nugget of lead weighing 425 pounds in the cavity made by the overturning of a large bee tree. The discovery was called the Bee Lead, and thus originated the name of the town.

Beldenville *Pierce County*

The village of Beldenville sprang up around O. Belden's Mill.

Belgium *Ozaukee County*

Belgium was started by the Northwestern Railway Company, which built a station here in 1864 on land donated by Mrs. Nick Streff. The name sent to Washington for approval was Luxembourg by the people who originally came from the European country. When the papers were returned they bore the name Belgium, and the name Luxembourg was given to a town in northern Wisconsin in the Sturgeon Bay area. This was a mistake made by a secretary in Washington, D.C. Both towns kept the names assigned to them by the government.

Bell Center *Crawford County*

Dennis Bell was a prominent citizen of the area. Bell Center is centrally located within the township.

Bell Center Ridge *Crawford County*

First called Whiteaker Ridge after the Whiteaker family, it was later renamed Bell Center Ridge for the village of Bell Center. The ridge, in Clayton Township, runs east of Bell Center to Highway 61.

Bell School *Wood County*

In Saratoga, it was named by the children of the school in honor of Alexander Graham Bell.

Belle Fountain *Columbia County*

The town, which no longer exists, was first founded in the days of John Jacob Astor and named for a spring or creek nearby. The famous Wisconsin Indian interpreter Pierre Pacquette, who lived at Portage, also had a farm at Belle Fountain.

Belle Isle *Dane County*

Part of Blooming Grove. The name comes from the French, meaning "beautiful island," and it is also reminiscent of another location of the same name. On Winnequah Point, jutting into Lake Monona, the outer part of this point has been cut by artificial canals to form two islands.

Belle Plaine *Shawano County*

Means "beautiful plain" in French and describes the area.

Belle's Corners *Walworth County*

Probably took its name from the first postmaster, William Belle.

Belleville *Dane and Green Counties*

Founded by John Frederick, born in 1799 in Belleville, Canada. He came to Wisconsin in 1842 and camped that summer on the banks of the lakes where Madison now stands. He was in search of suitable water power for a gristmill and finally chose this site on the Sugar River. He built the first house in the area in 1845, a sawmill in 1847, and the gristmill in 1849.

Bellevue *Brown County*

When the township was organized, the people were having trouble finding a name. They finally turned to John Penn Arndt, a local pioneer, and he came up with Belleview, probably because of the good view from a nearby ledge. The spelling was changed later.

Bellinger *Taylor County*

Named for one of the early pioneers, John Bellinger.

Belmont *Lafayette County*

The first capital of Wisconsin. On October 25, 1836, the first meeting of the territorial legislature was held here. On December 8, 1836, the Supreme Court met at Belmont, but on December 23, 1836, Madison was chosen as the permanent capital. At the first session of the legislature, forty-two laws were passed. Several institutions of learning were incorporated, but because no money was appropriated for them, the projects failed— among them the establishment of Wisconsin University at Belmont. The name is derived from three mounds within the village limits, which the early French travelers called Belle Monte, meaning "beautiful mountain."

Beloit *Rock County*

Its names prior to 1837 were Turtle Creek and New Albany. Beloit's first settlers came from Colebrook, New Hampshire, where the New England Emigrating Company provided the means for a group to make the adventurous journey to the new Midwest settlement. A Major Johnston wanted a name as nearly like Detroit as he could induce his companions to accept. He suggested Beloit.

Bena *Bayfield County*

The name is a corruption of the Ojibwe word bine, meaning "partridge."

Bench *Crawford County*

Located in Wauzeka village, it was first known as the Reichmann Bench, after the Reichmann family.

Bender Hollow *Richland County*

In Forest Township. Daniel and Abraham Bender came from Indiana in April 1854 and were followed in the fall of that year by Peter Bender and twenty-six other relatives.

Benet Lake *Kenosha County*

The Benedictine Fathers, who owned the south half of the lake and some five hundred acres of land surrounding it, established a monastery and seminary here in 1945. The lake, which consists of about one hundred acres of water, has had many names. At one time it was called Cooper Lake, and later Shangri-La. The Benet Lake post office was established near the monastery, and the lake took on the name. Some of the property owners on the north end of the lake objected to the change and carried it to the court in Kenosha. The case was not contested, and in the end the judge decided that the lake should have two legal names—Shangri-La for the north half, and Benet Lake for the south half. The word benet is an old English form of the word "benedict," one of the famous saints of England being St. Benet Biscop.

Ben Hansen Park   *Wood County*
Benjamin Hansen was instrumental in the movement to clear the riverbanks in the city, previously used as dumping grounds, and to make them into parks. The park is located on the west bank of the Wisconsin River in Wisconsin Rapids.

Bennett   *Douglas County*
Named after Richard Bennett, who settled in 1884.

Benoit   *Bayfield County*
The first name was Thirty Miles Siding, which had something to do with the logging industry and the railroads. The next name was Peckville, then Peck, then Benoitville, and finally Benoit, after a French settler.

Benson   *Burnett County*
A branch of the railroad was built in 1884, connecting Grantsburg with the St. Paul and Duluth Railroad at Rush City. A station on that branch line at the store of Sven Johann Bengston (also written Benson) was named for the storekeeper. In 1885, the storekeeper applied for a post office, giving the name Benson, but there was already a Benson in Wisconsin, so the name was changed to Randall. The post office was discontinued in 1929 but the name remained for the community, which has now completely disappeared.

Benton   *Lafayette County*
The name Benton was chosen by the Murphys, early settlers and friends of Senator Thomas Benton of Missouri, a popular figure among the early miners of the area. The name was first used in the 1840s when Dennis Murphy became the first postmaster. Prior to that time the place was known as Swindler's Ridge.

Berdo   *Burnett County*
The postal archives record a post office established in 1860 by Canute Anderson, who named the place Berdo. The archives also show that the name was changed to Anderson in 1863. No one in the area seems to have heard of Berdo, leading to the conclusion that the settlers always called it Anderson. Berdo or Bardo is the name of a place in Norway from which many of the early settlers came.

Berg Hill   *Dane County*
John I. Berg was a Norwegian settler here in 1846.

Berlin *Green Lake County*

The post office was established in 1848. Hiram Conant was appointed postmaster, and the post office department asked him to select some name not already used in Wisconsin. Mr. Conant selected Berlin in honor of the famous European capital. Previously, the place had been called Strong's Landing, and later Strongville. At the spring election of 1851, it was decided that this place should bear the name of the post office. The change is said to have been made with appropriate ceremony. One account relates that a large hoop was placed around the shoulders of Mr. Strong and that he, with such music as was procurable, headed a procession that paraded the streets and listened to a dedication speech. During World War I, many cities changed their German names, but the Berlin Guard unit took the slogan "From Berlin, Wisconsin to Berlin, Germany." The name was usually pronounced Berlin before the war, and Berlin afterward.

Bermanville *Dane County*

This small group of houses in Fitchburg was named for Frank and Gene Berman, owners of the land.

Berry *Dane County*

Probably named for Berry Haney, the second settler of adjoining Cross Plains and a tavern keeper, postmaster, and ferry operator.

Berryville *Kenosha County*

Around this place are many large farms growing strawberries, raspberries, gooseberries, and blackberries.

Bethesda *Waukesha County*

The neighborhood surrounding the little Bethesda Church in the Welsh settlement in Genesee.

Beyenbruch *Manitowoc County*

Named for an early settler.

Bibon *Bayfield County*

Believed to be an Ojibwe word for "winter."

Big Bend *Waukesha County*

Named by Indians for the big bend in the Fox River, which flows on the west side of the village. The first settlers came in 1836 from Andover, Vermont.

Big Bull Rapids *Marathon County*

From downriver these rapids sound like the bellowing of a bull.

Big Ditch *Dane County*

Descriptive of a drainage ditch that connects Dunlap Creek with the Wisconsin River, in Mazomanie.

B

The Big Divide   *Richland County*
This watershed between the Baraboo River and the Pine River in Westford Township extends about seven miles in a zigzag line until it reaches the county line.

Big Eau Pleine River   *Marathon County*
Called "Soft Maple River" by the Indians, Eau Pleine is French for "full water."

Big Falls   *Waupaca County*
Big Falls was founded by a man named Whitcomb as a lumbering town in 1882. Since he had already founded a village named Whitcomb about forty miles north of Big Falls (long since disappeared), he named it Big Falls after the falls of the Little Wolf River, which runs through the town.

Big Foot Prairie   *Walworth County*
Named for Chief Big Foot of the Potawatomi.

Big Hill   *Rock County*
Located on the west bank of the Rock River, it was named by the Ho-Chunk after a hill in the vicinity.

Big Hollow   *Sauk County*
Big Hollow is a canyon or valley three miles long and three miles wide in the town of Spring Green. There are several hollows located along the bluffs here.

Big Patch   *Grant County*
At one time known as Kaysville, Big Patch was named by Welsh miners for a large area of sheet lead ore found in the vicinity. In their homeland, the Welsh often spoke of a patch of brush or a patch of timber, and so it came naturally to speak of a big patch of lead ore.

Big and Little Quinnesee Falls   *Marinette County*
Derived from an Indian word meaning "smoke" and refers to the spray that is constantly seen ascending from the bottom of the torrent high into the air on the Menominee River.

The Big Stone   *Dane County*
A large piece of gray stone lies in a meadow near Perry. A cheese factory took its name from this isolated stone.

Big Suamico   *Brown County*
The Big Suamico River comes from a French Indian name possibly meaning "big sand," "yellow beaver," or "yellow residence place."

Bill Cross Rapids   *Lincoln County*
Named for William (Bill Cross) Harrison, who lived opposite the Bill Cross Rapids on the Wisconsin River. He was one-fourth Sioux Indian and an ordained priest who had been sent to the area as a missionary. He later renounced the priesthood and married an Indian woman.

Billings Park   *Douglas County*

Frederick K. Billings, president of the Northern Pacific Railroad, was greatly interested in Superior. His family donated this beautiful site on the St. Louis River.

Birch   *Ashland County*

So named for the many white birch trees.

Birch Creek   *Chippewa County*

Also named for the predominance of birch trees.

Birch Island   *Burnett County*

Received its name from the lake on which it is located. Birch Island Lake peninsula running into the lake is covered with birches and looks like an island from a distance.

Birchwood   *Washburn County*

In 1903, soon after Wilbur Loomis set up a store and post office in Birchwood, he traveled to Shell Lake to petition the town board to set off some land for a new township to be named Loomis. By 1912 a group of citizens became peeved with Mr. Loomis and did not want to live in a township bearing his name, so they circulated a petition to change the name to Birchwood, the same as the village.

The village received its name from George M. Huss, who was the president of the Soo Line Railroad and bought up village plats along the right of way from Ridgeland to Reserve. White birch showed up so strongly along the lake shores that he named this village Birchwood. He had the village surveyed and lots and streets located in preparation for a land sale in the fall of 1901. He was a progressive man and possibly named all the villages on the line in 1901. The railroad crews tied up at Birchwood one winter and in the spring started to build out to the east and north. By the time they reached Reserve, they decided they had had enough grief and went no farther. The line was abandoned in 1936.

Birdds Valley   *Richland County*

Named for James Birdd, who settled in the Yuba area about 1866. In Czechoslovakia he was Wencil Ptak, ptak meaning "bird" in Bohemian.

Birnamwood   *Shawano County*

In 1881 the North Shore Railroad reached what is now the southern limits of Birnamwood. One of the railroad officials, accompanied by his son, a college student, rode to the end of the line in a caboose. There were large piles of burning wood and brush along the right of way, and the official's son left the caboose to explore.

The young man, a student of Shakespeare, quoted, "Macbeth shall never vanquished be, until Great Birnam wood to high Dunsinane hill shall come against him."

What a great name for a town, he thought. He convinced his father, and the name Birnamwood was marked on the map. The name was officially adopted in 1884 when the first permanent sawmills were built. Logs had been sawed before that by a small mill that was destroyed by a boiler explosion in 1883. The village was incorporated in 1895.

Biron   *Wood County*

Named after Francis Biron, who was born in 1816 in Canada on the bank of the St. Francis River. He left home at the age of sixteen with a cousin, Pierre Biron, and a friend. They came by boat around the lakes to Green Bay. In 1848, Francis Biron purchased a mill, and later a second, larger one. Here he prospered until his death in 1877.

Bischoff Island   *Grant County*

This is a government island, directly north of Sinipee. Mr. Casper Bischoff settled this island and named it for his father, an immigrant from Germany who was killed in the Civil War.

Bishigokwe-Sibiwishen Creek   *Ashland County*

A small creek in the Ashland area. Some people believed Bishigokwe means "a woman who has been abandoned by her husband." In the old days a French trader lived at the mouth of this creek. He suddenly disappeared, perhaps murdered. His wife continued to reside for many years in their old home—hence the name.

Bishop Ridge   *Crawford County*

In Freeman Township, it was named for early settlers by the name of Bishop.

Bitsedalen   *Dane County*

Said to have been named for an English-speaking family that settled in what became a solidly Norwegian community, it is Norwegian for "Bates Valley."

Bittersweet Island   *Dane County*

Near Mazomanie, bittersweet vines grow on this island in the Wisconsin River east of the lower part of Railroad Bridge Island.

Blackbird Point   *Fond du Lac County*

Located on the west shore of Lake Winnebago, it is named for a local family.

Black Brook   *Polk County*

This township was named for a creek of the same name. It was organized August 5, 1867, and the first town meeting was held in April 1868. A chairman, two supervisors, a clerk, a treasurer, and three justices of the peace were appointed.

Black Creek   *Outagamie County*

There is a black creek at the edge of the village. One of the first settlers laid claim to the land and staked out the village that he called Middleburg, but the name was not generally accepted.

Black Earth   *Dane County*

The name was taken from the creek that passes through the village. In August 1848, the legislature gave the township the name of Farmersville, incorporating the present town of Berry; but by an act of February 1, 1851, the name was changed back to Black Earth. The name was changed to Ray by an act approved in 1858. When the village was incorporated in that year, however, George High, as first president, officially named it Black Earth.

Black Hawk   Richland County
Black Hawk, leader of the Sauk Indians, possibly buried a cannon here during his 1832 retreat because it was too heavy to drag through the wilderness.

Black Hawk   Sauk County
This is a discontinued post office named for the Indian chief made famous by the Black Hawk War. After the battle of Wisconsin Heights near Sauk City, the Indians fled through the wilderness near here.

Blackhawk Cliff   Crawford County
Legend has it that Chief Black Hawk and his horse jumped off this cliff while being pursued by cavalry. The horse was injured, but Black Hawk was later found hiding in the Black Hawk Tree. The Blackhawk Cliff is located east of Prairie du Chien.

Black River   Jackson and Trempealeau Counties
Named by the Ho-Chunk and the Ojibwe. The water in the river appears to be very nearly black.

Black River   Sheboygan County
Named by the Potawatomi, because of the color of the water.

Black River Falls   Jackson County
The first settlers arrived at this place in the spring of 1819 and established a camp at the falls. Since that time, there has always been a settlement here. Many old-timers still call the city The Falls.

Black Wolf   Winnebago County
Named after an old Indian chief of the Ho-Chunk tribe.

The Black Woods   Dane County
The woods were thick and dark in settlement days, but now they are much reduced.

Blackwell and Blackwell Junction   Forest County
Both places were named for John Blackwell, owner of a nearby sawmill.

Blaine   Burnett County
This township, established in 1902, was probably named for John G. Blaine, the Progressive Republican at the 1902 convention.

Blair   Trempealeau County
Originally platted as Porterville and named after early settlers, the Porter family. But after the railroad was built in 1873, and the village had begun to develop, it was called Blair, for

John Insley Blair, of Blairstown, New Jersey, a stockholder in the Green Bay and Western Railway Company.

Blakely Hollow *Richland County*

Joseph and Martha Blakely made the trip from Galena by oxcart or on foot and settled here in Forest Township at the head of Goose Creek.

Blake's Prairie *Grant County*

Named for an early settler, Page Blake.

Blanchardville *Lafayette County*

Lead ore and the close proximity of waterways brought the first settlers into the area. Nearly all the early immigrants were miners, but by the late 1840s the rich agricultural resources of the region had become known.

Samuel Horner built a dam and a gristmill on the Pecatonica River here in 1848. The next year, Cyrus Newkirk, a Virginian, bought it and ran it for almost five years, then sold it to George White. Alvin Blanchard purchased it on May 26, 1855. In 1857, Blanchard and Cyrus Newkirk signed as owners of the village of Blanchardville and offered land for sale to the public. In 1858, Blanchard became the first postmaster of his town.

The whole community had been called Zarahamia by the Latter Day Saints of the area, but Blanchard's name supplanted all others and has continued.

Blenker *Wood County*

This was mainly logging territory until about 1884, when the railroad came. Mr. John Blenker moved in from a neighboring village, started a store, and became the first postmaster.

Blanding *Burnett County*

A post office from 1886 to 1901. It was named for William Blanding, a logger, who lived in St. Croix Falls.

Blodgett *Waukesha County*

For C. A. Blodgett, an early settler. This settlement is also called Goerke's Corner, after Fred Goerke's Saloon and Inn.

Bloody Run Creek *Wood County*

In times of high water, the ferrous material lying on the bottom of the creek bed is stirred up and gives the creek a reddish color. The creek runs through Grand Rapids Township.

Bloom *Richland County*

Isaac McMahn moved here from Ohio and brought with him some apple seeds, from which have grown the many trees bearing delicious fruit and the beautiful blossoms from which the township takes its name.

Bloom City *Richland County*

Bloom City was named for its location in the township of Bloom. Israel Cooper was responsible for the name.

Bloomer   *Chippewa County*

Sylvester Van Loon and his companion, William Priddy, natives of New York, left their homesteads in Sauk County in July 1855 and came north. They intended to acquire homesteads on land available beyond the sawmill town of Chippewa Falls.

They had heard something of Bloomer Prairie, so-called after an ambitious merchant from the Mississippi town of Galena, Illinois. In the summer of 1848 he had sought to build a dam and sawmill at Eagle Rapids, a point on the Chippewa River where the Wissota dam was built three-quarters of a century later.

Bloomer's men scouted for hay on the prairie north and west and secured an ample supply despite an extremely dry season. However, he gave up the sawmill project in early fall, sold his supplies and equipment to H. S. Allen of Chippewa Falls, and returned to Galena. But the prairie where his crew of men had procured hay was henceforth called Bloomer's Prairie, and finally simply Bloomer.

Bloomer Prairie   *Chippewa County*

Arriving at the falls, having walked the entire distance, the two men, Van Loon and Priddy, inquired further about Bloomer Prairie. Both acquired homesteads through which flowed beautiful Duncan Creek, embracing a portion of the future city of Bloomer. As settlers moved in they decided to call the village Vanville, in honor of Mr. Van Loon. This name eventually died out. When the railroad went through, officials designated the station Bloomer, after Bloomer Prairie. The name was officially changed in 1877.

Bloomer Millpond   *Chippewa County*

The pond backed up by the dam, made for the mill on Duncan Creek in the city of Bloomer.

Bloomingdale   *Vernon County*

In spring the valley and hillsides were literally covered with wildflowers and the blossoms of wild plum trees. The early Norwegian settlers referred to the area as "Blome Dalen." Blome is the Norwegian word for "flower," and dalen, pronounced "dah-len," means "valley." Eventually it came to be called Bloomingdale.

Blooming Grove   *Dane County*

Reverend John G. Miller, superintendent of schools, is credited with naming the township. He traveled much, and as he frequently said, he had never seen a section of the country in which there were such fine groves and so many wildflowers. He said the locality was literally a blooming grove. The name stuck.

Blooming Prairie   *Walworth County*

So named for the carpet of blooming flowers in the area.

Bloomington   *Grant County*

The village was first called Tafton, for a Mr. Taft who had built the first mill in 1841. By 1867 the villagers were on the outs with Mr. Taft some financial trouble. About the same time, the Spencer Blacksmith Shop got the patent on a new device for sowing oats. This was a vigorous spur to agriculture, and local people expressed their elation in the name

Blooming Town, soon converted to Bloomington. In 1867, by an act of the legislature, the name Bloomington was applied to both the township and the village.

Bloomville   Lincoln County

Named for the Bloom family, who were early settlers in the area, this tiny village was established by 1891.

Blue Bill Point   Dane County

As early as 1865, hunters were calling this point on the right bank of the Yahara River in Westport by this name, due to the fact the blue-bill ducks were plentiful here.

Blue Mounds   Dane County

The village was named by early French missionaries for three high mounds nearby and the bluish hue of the earth on their banks, caused by the presence of copper.

Blue River   Grant County

When the railroad first came through in 1856, the village was called Minnehaha, but soon afterward the name was changed to Blue River. The river was named for a Mr. Blue, who owned a farm through which the river ran, just east of the present village.

Blueberry   Douglas County

The Ojibwe Indians found this a place where blueberries grew in abundance.

Bluff   Sauk County

This discontinued post office on the east Sauk road in the town of Sumpter was near a large bluff.

Bluff Siding   Buffalo County

Named for the precipitous rocky bluffs at this point.

Blum's Creek   Dane County

Named for John Blum, who acquired the land in the 1890s. Formerly called Inama's Creek, only the lower part of the creek is known as Blum's Creek; the upper part is called Madison Creek. The creek runs through Roxbury and Mazomanie.

Boardman   St. Croix County

Originally called Lone Tree, it was renamed for Francis R. Boardman, who arrived in 1856 and became the first postmaster and merchant. It is located on Ten Mile Creek, a branch of the Willow River, which flows about a mile to the west. The creek and river became a center for sawmills and gristmills. The first settlement was made in 1853 by C. A. Boardman and S. L. Beebe. These two names are still prominent in the area.

Boat Yard Hollow   Grant County

Boat Yard Hollow is located halfway between East Dubuque, Illinois, and Eagle Point bridge. Flatboats were built on this site about 1848, and a ferryboat across the Mississippi River was established at Boat Yard Hollow in that year.

Boaz   *Richland County*

This little village in the western part of the town of Dayton contains a store or two, a church, the Boaz Mill, mechanical shops, and a few residences. The population has remained stationary for many years since Richland Center, with its better market facilities, has cut off the trade. The village was platted in the winter of 1857–58; the first store was opened in 1857. The Boaz sawmill, named after the biblical character, was an important establishment in the town.

Bogus Bluff   *Richland County*

Numerous legends tell of a band of counterfeiters who operated on the hill south of Lone Rock as early as 1842. Many have searched for the treasure that was thought to be buried in the tunnels here. The bluff is in Buena Vista Township.

Bois Brule River   *Douglas County*

The name is French, meaning "burned wood," and was given to the river by French voyageurs.

Bolt   *Kewaunee County*

Named for Mr. Bolt, the owner and operator of the first general store in the area.

Bolton   *Vilas County*

Its first settlers came from Bolton in Massachusetts.

Boltonville   *Washington County*

Named in honor of Harlow Bolton, who started it in 1854.

Boma Ridge   *Crawford County*

In Utica Township. Named for a man called Boma from La Crosse, who used to go coon hunting here.

Bomkamp Hollow   *Richland County*

In Orion Township. The land purchased by Hubert Bomkamp in 1896 was still in the family in 1971.

Bonduel   *Shawano County*

Named after the Reverend F. Bonduel, a Green Bay priest, who founded the Catholic mission at Keshena in 1853. The legend is that on his journey through Bonduel, he held services for the Indians in a birch-bark chapel erected near Gumaer's Point.

Bone Lake   *Polk County*

The Sioux had battles with the Ojibwe here, and a legend says that bones were found in the area of the lake.

Booger Gut   *Crawford County*

In Utica Township. Thought to have been named by local sophisticates, it is located in the Blackhawk-Kickapoo Watershed area.

Boom Bay   *Winnebago County*

This bay on the north shore of Lake Poygan in Winnebago County connects with the Wolf River by a canal that was used to float logs from the river into the bay. When the logs reached the bay, they were sorted and rafted, later to be towed to Oshkosh and beyond. The canal shortened the distance to Oshkosh by seven miles. The operational center at Boom Bay was called the Boom House.

Borea   *Douglas County*

A station on the Soo Line and Great Northern Railroad. Boreas, in ancient mythology, was the god of the north or the north wind. The name was chosen because the community is so far north.

Borghilda Spring   *Dane County*

In Deerfield. Discovered in 1844 by Borghilda Groven, a settler from Norway, on land on which she and her husband had squatted. The spring feeds Koshkonong Creek.

Borth   *Waushara County*

A bustling trading and social center near Lake Poygan in Waushara County, Borth is a sort of halfway station between Oshkosh and Berlin. Named for August Borth, the first postmaster, it was also an important church center in the early years. The place lost its importance after the automobile came into general use.

Bosak's Creek   *Polk County*

Named for the Bosak family, who were pioneers in Polk County, this stream empties into Somers Lake.

Boscobel   *Grant County*

There are three possible sources for the name of Boscobel. Some say the name is a Castilian vulgarism for "beautiful wood." Others say it was named for the friendly little English wood that sheltered Charles Stuart after the luckless battle of Worcester. A third group says that an early settler had two cows, one Boss, one Bell. When he called them to come home at night, he would sing out: "Co Boss, co Bell!"

Bosstown   *Richland County*

Part of Sylvan Township. William Henry Dosch, familiarly known as "Boss" Dosch, owned a store built on the site of the old Bailey and Hull sawmill. As a child he was sick for some time and became accustomed to the attention he received so that he later "bossed" the family. Later in his life the family called him Uncle Boss.

Boulder Junction   *Vilas County*

Once a junction of railroad lines. There are many large boulders nearby.

Bouska Hollow   *Crawford County*

Part of Bridgeport Township. It is named for the Bouska family.

Bowen's Mill   *Richland County*

Part of Richland Township. William J. Bowen bought the sawmill owned by James M. Cass in 1854. In 1867 a flour mill was erected. Four generations of Bowens have been associated with the mill.

Bowler   *Shawano County*

An attorney for the Chicago and North Western Railway Company named Bowler was instrumental in the purchase of the right-of-way for the company.

Boyceville   *Dunn County*

The Boyce family operated a mill at the west end of the village.

Boyd   *Chippewa County*

The surveyor for the railroad that came through in 1893 was named Boyd.

Boydtown   *Crawford County*

Robert Boyd made the first settlement in the township of Marietta in 1844.

Boyle Hill   *Crawford County*

This hill in Clayton Township was named after the Boyle family.

Boyleston   *Douglas County*

A station on the Great Northern Line to St. Paul. The man who named this was from Massachusetts. Instead of selecting a name with local significance, he repeated names of Bay state towns. Boyleston was one.

Brackett   *Eau Claire County*

Settled in 1854 and named for an Eau Claire postmaster.

Bracy   *Burnett County*

This post office was in existence from 1884 to 1908 and was named for the first postmaster, Burtred G. Bracy.

Bradley's   *Walworth County*

Now called Elkhorn, this settlement was originally named after a tavern keeper of the early 1850s.

Bragg School   *Fond du Lac County*

Located in the city of Fond du Lac, it was named for Edward Stuyvesant Bragg. In 1850 he moved from New York to Fond du Lac, where he was one of the youngest members of the legal profession.

At the outbreak of the Civil War he volunteered for service and recruited a company of "Bragg's Rifles." He took part in many campaigns and was promoted to brigadier general at the head of Wisconsin's Iron Brigade. Following the Civil War, he served in Congress and later in the diplomatic service in Cuba, Mexico, and Hong Kong.

In 1884 Bragg seconded the nomination of Grover Cleveland for the presidency. His statement, "They love him most for the enemies he has made," was adapted and used as the campaign slogan.

Branch   Manitowoc County

The first settler located at the mouth of the Branch River was E. Lenaville, who set up a sawmill about 1838. The community was first known as Lenaville. Later it was known as Zalesburg, from the name of an early settler from Germany. The village was named Branch when the post office was established in 1857. W. R. Williams was the first postmaster.

Brandon   Fond du Lac County

The village was built up after 1856 when the railroad went through. In the early days it was known as Bungtown. It was named Brandon by William Lockin, an early settler, after a town in Vermont.

Branstad   Burnett County

For Ole C. Branstad, one of the early settlers and donor of the land on which the creamery was built in 1896. A hamlet and farmstead on a fjord near Oslo, Norway, named Branstad, was his original home. The hamlet in Norway was burned to the ground in olden times and the name in Norwegian means "burned village."

Brant   Calumet County

Once called Branch Creek, but so many places were named Branch that the citizens decided to change the name to Brant.

Brantwood   Price County

A logger named Brant had a landing here and it was often referred to as Brant's Landing. The present name was chosen for the site of a new mill, about 1894.

Brass Ball Corners   Kenosha County

Named from a tavern built by Seth Huntoon in the mid-1850s. The original brass ball that was the tavern sign has long disappeared, but for many years a mine buoy that had washed up on a Florida beach hung above the highway to carry on the brass-ball tradition. Highways 50 and 83 in Salem Township.

Brauns   Taylor County

Named after a real estate and timber dealer named George Braun.

Breakneck Hill   Fond du Lac County

A steep and dangerous drive up the ledge of some of the limestone crevices near Oakfield.

Break Neck Hill   Dane County

J. B. Runey, the first settler of Oregon, had a fatal accident when his wagon overturned here in Fitchburg.

Breakneck Ledge and Breakneck Road   *Fond du Lac County*

Located in Oakfield Township, they are named for a steep slope down the ledge, which is particularly precarious in winter.

Brear-Beaux or Grandfather Bull Falls   *Wisconsin River*

These are the largest falls on the Wisconsin River and were called "Long Falls" by the Indians. These falls have never been successfully crossed by European settlers, but one instance is known where Indians have passed them safely. In 1849, as the story goes, the falls were navigated in a birch-bark canoe by two Indians named Black Nail and Crow after they had made appropriate prayers and an offering to the gods—two yards of scarlet broadcloth and a brass kettle.

Breed   *Oconto County*

Named by George M. Breed, who was the first postmaster of the village.

Brehm   *Taylor County*

Named for a storekeeper in the area.

Brewery Creek   *Dane County*

This small creek flowed past a brewery before entering Black Earth Creek. It rises in the southeast of Berry and flows into the village of Cross Plains.

Briar Hill   *Dane County*

The slopes on which this subdivision of Madison is located were overgrown with berry bushes.

Bridge Creek   *Eau Claire County*

This township is named for the creek that passes through it. It became a township with representation on the county board in 1857 and originally included most of the east half of Eau Claire County.

Bridgeport   *Crawford County*

The first half of the name of this township derives from the fact that a bridge here connects Crawford and Grant Counties. The second half of the name came from the old ferry crossing to the "ports" of each county.

Briggsville   *Marquette County*

In the fall of 1850, Alexander Ellis Briggs of Vermont arrived here with a group of homesteaders. Mr. Briggs became a partner of Amplius Chamberlain, and the two men negotiated for the right to build a dam across Neenah Creek to provide waterpower for a sawmill. The first lumber manufactured was some heavy oak planks and joists used in the building of the first jail at Portage. The dam, begun in the fall of 1850, made a lake to the west about three miles in length. It was named Lake Mason for the carpenter who built the mill.

Brigham Park *Dane County*

Given to Dane County by the Brigham family, it is dedicated to the memory of Charles Ilsley Brigham and Col. Ebenezer Brigham. Ebenezer was a prospector, an innkeeper, and a colonel in the Black Hawk War.

Brighton *Kenosha County*

Named for "the old home of pioneers."

Brill *Barton County*

Named after Judge Brill of St. Paul, Minnesota, an attorney for the railroad company. At the time the officials made their first trip over this line, Judge Brill was with them. When they came to this first station out of Rice Lake, they asked Judge Brill if he would like it named after him. It was a stopping place along the river for the Knapp Stout Lumber Company.

Brillion *Calumet County*

The original name of the township and city was to have been Brandon. But the 1856 session of the county board found that the adjoining county of Fond du Lac had a town named Brandon. T. N. West, as postmaster, sent in the name Pilleola, a combination of letters from the names of two of his daughters. But the department turned down the proposed name and called the office Brillion.

Bristol *Kenosha County*

The name was suggested by David Wilder, an early settler who came from Bristol, New York.

British Hollow *Grant County*

The men in the area always spent the evenings together at the general store or tavern. The question of a new name for the place arose. One man was mistakenly under the impression that the French still claimed the land. He said, "While the French still claim this place, it won't be long before the British have it, and as we are mostly English here, let's call it British Hollow."

Brittingham Bay *Dane County*

Named for the adjoining Brittingham Park, which was named for its donor, Thomas E. Brittingham. The small bay is in the west end of Lake Monona in Madison.

Brodhead *Green County*

Edward H. Brodhead, of Milwaukee, was connected with the Chicago, Milwaukee, and St. Paul Railway. Concerned for the development of the new village, he offered to present a bell for the first church erected, providing the village was named for him. The Methodist church, organized on June 13, 1856, won the bell. It was a Meneeley bell, weighing 795 pounds, and it cost $400. One Sunday morning about 1880, the bell cracked and had to be sent to Milwaukee to be recast. With this exception it has hung continuously in the belfry and still rings the call to worship each Sunday.

Brodtville   *Grant County*

Named for Josh Brodt. A post office was established in 1864 and closed in 1883.

Brookfield   *Waukesha County*

Brookfield must have received its name from the many brooks and wide fields in the area. It was incorporated in 1954 with an area of seventeen square miles.

Brooklyn   *Green County*

Brooklyn station and township were named by John E. Glunt, the engineer in charge of locating the railroad, after the borough in New York City.

Brooklyn   *Sauk County*

Brooklyn, Wisconsin, was named for Brooklyn, New York, which was named for Breuckelen, Holland. Named by R. G. Camp, it is one of the original towns in the northeast portion of the county. The name means "broken up land" or "marshy land."

Brooks   *Adams County*

The village was platted as Brookings in 1911. The Chicago and North Western Railway did not approve of the name, because there was already a Brookings on their line in the Dakotas. After much deliberation, it was finally decided to call the village Brooks. There is a very nice brook or trout stream just to the east of town.

Brooks Cove   *Walworth County*

This cove, a part of Beulah Lake, is named after David Brooks, a local landowner.

Brookside   *Oconto County*

Named for its location—beside a brook.

Broughton Park   *Sheboygan County*

Named for Charles E. Broughton, who bought eighty acres of Sheboygan marsh and gave it to the county for a park.

Brown County

Named for Major General Jacob Brown of the United States Army. General Brown, who lived from 1775 to 1828, was born in Pennsylvania and was a successful leader in the War of 1812. At its close he retained command of the Northern Division, and in 1821 was made General in Chief of the Army.

Brown Deer   *Milwaukee County*

Before it was called Brown Deer, this settlement was called White Deer. The name White Deer was given to it by Dr. E. B. Walcott, the Brazelton brothers, and Anson W. Buttles when they spied an albino or white deer while hunting in the vicinity. But brown deer were more common in the area, and the conformists had their way!

Brown Hollow   *Crawford County*

It was named for the Brown family.

Brown Hollow
Richland County

According to legend, this hollow in Richland Township was named for a man named Brown, who was a rebellious, copperheaded Democrat. He was said to be so obnoxious that the home guard went to his home, pulled him out of bed, and gave him an impromptu bath in the creek.

Browning
Taylor County

Named for an early settler.

Brownlee
Washburn County

Passing tracks were provided every six miles along the Soo Railway in Washburn County. Brownlee was the site of one of these, named for one of the railroad's contractors.

Brownsville
Dodge County

Alfred D. Brown, who came from England to the United States in 1846, brought with him to Lomira Township, in 1850, the first stock of goods. He also brought the second threshing machine into the township from Milwaukee, which he used with horses bought in Chicago. He settled eighty acres of land. The railroad station and village were named in his honor in April 1878.

Browntown
Green County

This village was for many years known variously as Brown, Irion, or Wood's Mill. When the village was laid out, it was named in honor of William G. Brown, who was one of the mill's builders. Mr. Brown was born in Missouri, though he was reared in New Orleans. His early life was passed on the Mississippi River, first as cabin boy on river steamers and afterward as second mate. Later in life he learned the business of a millwright and built the mill at Browntown. He went to California for a short time in 1849, after which time he was known as William "Grizzly" Brown.

Bruce
Rusk County

After a son of the famous Weyerhaeuser lumber family.

Bruemmer Park
Kewaunee County

Named for O. H. Bruemmer, who contributed to its establishment. Mr. Bruemmer was a one-time mayor of Kewaunee, district attorney, and chairman of the county board.

Brule River
Douglas County

Official maps give the name Bois Brule to the beautiful river, generally called the Brule River. The French explorers in the early 1600s probably named it. The name means "burned wood." Another account explains that the river was named for French explorer Etienne Brule, who came to Canada with Champlain in 1608. Brule was thought to be the first European to see Lake Huron, and probably the first to set eyes on the Brule River.

Brule–St. Croix Waterway
St. Croix County

The St. Croix River and the Brule River formed a waterway connecting Lake Superior with the Mississippi River.

Brunet Falls *Chippewa County*

Brunet Falls was platted in 1902 and is now a part of Cornell. It was named for Jean Brunet, who had a trading post and portage depot here.

Brush Creek *Richland County*

Samuel Swinehart named this creek in Richland Township in the 1840s when he noticed the unusual amount of brush growing in the streambed.

Brushville *Waushara County*

The name was chosen not for the woody foliage in the area, but for the Brush family. Eliphalet Brush was its second postmaster. The post office was discontinued February 15, 1906, and Brushville is presently a "ghost" village in the northeastern part of the county.

Bryant *Langlade County*

Named for S. M. Bryant from Milwaukee, the owner of most of the farmland and timber in the vicinity.

Bryngelson's Hill *Dane County*

This small hill on the edge of Lake Waubesa was once owned by Sever Bryngelson, a Norwegian settler.

Bryn Mawr Church *Dane County*

This Presbyterian church was named for Bryn Mawr, Pennsylvania, which gave it some financial support. It was built in 1896 in Cottage Grove.

Buckbee *Waupaca County*

Named for Colonel J. E. Buckbee of the Sixth Michigan Regiment of the US Volunteers.

Buck Creek *Crawford County*

A large number of deer were seen in the area at the time this creek in Freeman Township was named.

Buck Creek *Richland County*

The story is told of an old drunken man who mounted his horse with a flourish and proclaimed, "I am the greatest buck from Buck Creek." A more plausible account of the naming of this creek in Richland Township tells of the sighting of a deer of unusual size grazing along the stream.

Buckhorn Corners *Dodge County*

In the early days of Dodge County, a military road and four territorial roads converged at a point in the town of Trenton. In 1844 Captain Hugh McCallum built a large hall and opened a tavern at this site. It was called Buckhorn Corners because a large five-point buck had been shot in the vicinity, and a large pair of buck horns had been placed over the tavern entrance.

Bucknerville   *Waukesha County*

This former settlement was named for the Buckner family, early settlers.

Buena Park   *Racine County*

Buena is Spanish for "beautiful," and Buena Park is a beautiful area along the west bank of the Fox River in the township of Waterford. It was recorded as a subdivision in 1926 by the Class family, and it grew into a well-known summer area during the years before World War II. Since the early 1950s, the area has changed to one of permanent homes. A log cabin, which was the home for three different families until about 1906, still stands on the Class farm.

Buena Vista   *Grant County*

This place near Potosi is Spanish for "beautiful view." A group of early settlers named it.

Buena Vista   *Richland County*

Named at the suggestion of Mrs. J. W. Briggs. The name Buena had been suggested by a returning soldier from the Mexican War. Mrs. Briggs suggested the name would be incomplete simply as Buena and thought that Vista should be added.

Buena Vista   *Waukesha County*

A summer resort at the west end of Pewaukee Lake.

Buffalo   *Buffalo County*

The name Buffalo attached to county, river, and township reflects buffalo in the vicinity long ago. Father Louis Hennepin, in his account of his voyage of 1680 up the Mississippi, calls it the River of Wild Bulls.

Bufton Hollow   *Richland County*

Located in Forest Township, this land was owned by Evan Bufton in the 1890s.

Bugitsquian   *Sheboygan County*

This historic Indian village is located in the Sheboygan Marsh region of the town of Rhine. Bugitsquian was inhabited chiefly by the Ojibwe, and only during the summer months, but a handful of Menominee and one Potawatomi chief also lived here. In 1856, this village consisted of fifty or sixty wigwams and a population of about 250 people. Most of the remaining Indians left this region in 1869 or 1870. The name is believed to mean "great swamp" or "river flat marsh."

Bull's-Eye Bluff   *Wood County*

Pilots of lumber rafts coming down the Wisconsin River judged their position in the river by a knoll on the top of this bluff as they navigated the bend in the river between Edwards Island and the riverbank. The bluff is on the east bank of the river in Wisconsin Rapids.

Buncombe   *Lafayette County*

For "Buncombe" Gillett, the owner of an adjoining farm, who was a prominent politician when the railroad station and town was established.

Bunker Hill *Richland County*

It is the highest point in the county, and its physical features are thought to resemble the hill near Boston where the Americans fought the British in 1775. A fight at a dance hall in the Westford Town Hall gave the community its name, though. According to legend, a fight there grew so furious that one of the fiddlers jumped out of the window and was found in Irontown with the sill still around his neck and the bow in his hand.

Burke *Dane County*

Early settlers named this area for Edmund Burke, one of Ireland's most illustrious men.

Burkhardt *St. Croix County*

The settlement of Burkhardt, township of St. Joseph, was named by Guy W. Dailey (1827–1899) when he was a member of the Wisconsin Legislature in about 1880. The name is in honor of Christian Burkhardt (1834–1931), owner and operator of the mills here. The settlement had been known as Bouchea.

Burlington *Racine County*

Named for Burlington, Vermont, by E. D. Putnam, who said that his native Vermont had one city celebrated above all others for its location and scenery. He proposed the name of that town for his new home in Wisconsin.

Burma Road *Richland County*

This little road in the Horse Creek area of Richland Township was named for the Burma Road in Indochina.

Burnett County

Named for Thomas P. Burnett, an early Wisconsin legislator. Although born in Virginia, Burnett emigrated to Kentucky as a child and was there educated, practicing law in Paris, Kentucky. In 1829 he was appointed Indian Agent at Prairie du Chien and made his home there until 1837, when he moved to Cassville. He returned to the practice of law and was influential in Wisconsin territorial legislation. He was, at the time of his death in 1846, a member of the Wisconsin Constitutional Convention.

Burnett *Dodge County*

The township and village were named after Ellsworth Burnett, who was killed in 1835 by an Indian while accompanying James Clyman on a search for land from Milwaukee to the Rock River region. According to the popular story, the men bought a canoe from an Indian woman on their trip down the Rock River. When the woman's husband returned home and found his canoe gone, he went to look for the men who bought it. He got close to Burnett, who was in camp, and shot him. Then he waited for Clyman, who was gathering wood, to come back to camp. Clyman discovered what had happened and turned to run but was wounded by a bullet. He finally arrived at Milwaukee.

Burnham and Scott Hill *Richland County*

In about 1900, John T. Scott owned a farm at the foot of this hill in Richland Township, and O. J. Burnham had a farm and orchard at the top.

Burnside   *Outagamie County*

Named for General A. E. Burnside of Rhode Island, an officer in the Civil War.

Burnside   *Trempealeau County*

Named for General Ambrose E. Burnside, Commander of the Army of the Potomac in the Civil War.

Burnt Ground Camp Site   *Wood County*

In early Wood County days, this spot in Rudolph was a rendezvous for Indians engaged in fur trading because it was the only cleared space along the Wisconsin River for miles.

Burton   *Grant County*

The old mill constructed by Daniel R. Burt on Grant River was the nucleus about which a post office, store, and blacksmith shop were built.

Burton Ridge   *Crawford County*

The Burton family lent their name to this ridge in Haney Township. It is also known as Vinegar Ridge.

Burton Brook   *Calumet County*

An early English family named Brook lived in the area.

Bush Creek   *Crawford County*

In Wauzeka Township, it was named after an early pioneer family.

Butte des Morts   *Winnebago County*

The name means "hill of the dead." It was so named because of the large number of Indian burials there. Many of the burials are reburials of skeletons brought from a distance. Another story recounts that a great Indian battle took place here between the Fox and the French, Menominee, Potawatomi, and Kickapoo.

Butternut   *Ashland County*

On the east side of a lake in the area was a grove of butternut trees, twenty-four to thirty inches in diameter, having a crown spread of sixty to seventy feet.

Byrd's Creek   *Richland County*

D. H. Byrd came to the county in 1847 and built his cabin along the creek in Richwood Township.

Byron   *Fond du Lac County*

First settled in 1889, and probably named after the poet.

Cameron, ca. 1907

⇥ C ⇤

Cable   *Bayfield County*
In 1878 this was the end of the line on the Chicago, St. Paul, Minneapolis & Omaha Railway. Named after the first locomotive engineer who pulled a train into this stop.

Cable   *Grant County*
R. Cable owned the first hotel in this community.

Cadott   *Chippewa County*
Jean Baptiste Cadotte (or Cadeau) was the son of a famous French Canadian fur trader who settled on Madeline Island, where he married a Ojibwe woman and established a fur trading post. Young Cadotte established a trading post at a falls on the Yellow River about three-fourths of a mile downstream from the present village. For many years, it was known as Cadotte Falls. It is not known when the final letter was lost, but when the village was first settled by Robert Marriner in 1865, it was called Cadott and was platted under that name ten years later. Young Jean's brother, Michel, was educated in Montreal, Canada, and married Equaysayway, the daughter of White Crane, the village chief on the island. Michel Cadotte built the settlement at La Pointe.

Cahoon Mine   *Sauk County*
An iron mine that opened in 1911 about two miles south of Baraboo was named in honor of former assemblyman Wilber Cahoon.

Cainville   *Rock County*
Mr. Seth Caines gave the land for the depot.

Caldwell Prairie   *Racine County*
Old maps of Racine County show a post office by this name in the northwest corner. Joseph and Tyler Caldwell had settled here in the spring of 1836. Caldwell Prairie was never platted as a town. It was located in Section 5, Township 4, Range 19.

Caledonia   *Columbia County*
Named by Scottish settlers after the Latin name for Scotland. It was probably named by the McDonald brothers, who settled there in 1836.

Caledonia   *Racine County*
Named by Scottish settlers. This area also had Welsh, Irish, Bohemian, and German settlements.

Caledonia   *Trempealeau County*
Named by Alexander and Donald McGilvray and other Scottish settlers.

Calhoun   *Waukesha County*

George E. Calhoun owned the farm on which the railroad station was built.

Calumet   *Fond du Lac County*

The word is the Norman-French form of chalumet, a tube or reed, which was applied by French Canadians to the Indian "pipe of peace." Calumet was a former Menominee village on the east shore of Lake Winnebago. It had 150 inhabitants in 1817. Various tribes held peace councils there.

Calumet County   *Calumet County*

Calumet County was, at various times, the home of six Indian Nations—Menominee, Ojibwe, Sac, Fox, Potawatomi, and Ho-Chunk. Once a Ho-Chunk chief told a commander at Fort Howard in Green Bay, "If you come in peace, you bring too many soldiers; if you come for war, you bring not enough!"

The name is incorporated in a county insignia with the motto, "We extend the calumet." The insignia is appropriately made up of two crossed Indian peace pipes surrounded by a chain of Indian beads.

Calumet County Park   *Calumet County*

The hill in the park is known as Riley's Hill, according to Margaret Schomish Niles, who lived with her parents at the brickyard operated by Cook and Brown Company in the park area. Riley lost his life falling off a load of hay being brought into the brickyard. The park was named by the Calumet County Board of Supervisors in 1939.

Calvary   *Fond du Lac County*

Named by F. M. Barrett, a railroad contractor from the Calvary Convent, located near the station.

Calydon   *Sauk County*

When the United States geological surveyors were at Durwards Glenn at the time of the making of a contour map of this region, they asked B. I. Durward, the poet-painter who resided there, for the name of the stream flowing through the glen. He replied, "The Calydon." It comes from "Caledonia," and is the poetical expression of the word.

Cambria   *Columbia County*

In 1844 John Langdon and four sons started a sawmill on Duck Creek using a hand-operated pit saw. One man stood in a pit and the other on a frame holding the tree trunk lengthwise over it. Soon they built a dam over the creek for power, and the place was called Langdon's Saw Mill. When a flour mill was added, the Langdons called the place Florence. The Langdons had no money left to buy machinery for their flour mill, so they borrowed from James Bell. When they failed to meet payments Bell took possession and changed the name to Bellville. Bell sold the property in 1851 to two men of Welsh descent and left the town. By this time the Welsh people were coming in to settle and they gave the town the old Roman name for Wales. The Welsh call their country Cymru.

Cambridge
Dane County

According to Robe Dow Jr., grandson of Judge Dow, a pioneer of this area, the name Cambridge was affixed to the community in 1847 by Alvin B. Carpenter, who, with the Keyes brothers, obtained title to the land and platted the village. "I have been told by one of Mr. Carpenter's contemporaries," Dow said, "that this selection of the name was influenced by a romance of his boyhood days. A sweetheart of his youth lived in Cambridge, New York."

Cameron
Barron County

Mr. Stanley, the surveyor who platted the original village and the township of Stanley, named this village after his friend, State Senator Cameron of La Crosse. The village had its beginning in 1879, when a few people settled along the foot of a bluff about one and a half miles south of the present site.

To their disappointment, the Omaha Railway tracks were laid north of Old Cameron. Then the Soo Line Railway built its east-west line to cross the Omaha Railway tracks, and the people decided to move their town north to the railway junction. Stores and houses were loaded on sleds in the winter and wheels in the summer and taken across the fields on both sides of the tracks to the present location, which had been called Cameron Junction by the railroad company.

Campbell
La Crosse County

Named for Lt. Governor E. D. Campbell, who was elected in 1857.

Campbell Hill
Dane County

Named for Edward, Hugh, and John Campbell of Virginia, who built a stone house here that became a stopping place for travelers.

Campbellsport
Fond du Lac County

Pioneers settled in this area near the east branch of the Milwaukee River in 1843 and named their settlement Crouchville in honor of Ludlow (or Ludin) Crouch, one of their leaders. Mr. Crouch was originally a New York pedagogue who selected this spot because it had potential waterpower. A few years later a group of emigrants from Kassel, Germany, settled here. In 1856 the name was changed by Emil Brayman to New Cassel in honor of Hesse-Cassel, his birthplace in his homeland.

Shortly after the Civil War there were rumors that a railroad would be built through the area. But the Air Line Railway rerouted its line, passing one mile west of New Cassel. Officials desired to establish a station on H. B. Martin's farm. Mr. Martin would sell no fractional part of his farm but offered the whole of it for $10,000. Stuart Campbell purchased the farm and gave the railroad company three acres. The company later bought three more and platted a village. Jacob Haessly named the place Campbellsport in August 1873, on the day the deed for Martin's farm was signed.

For many years the two villages went their separate ways with two post offices. Finally, in 1902, they decided to unite under the name of Campbellsport.

Camp Creek   *Richland County*

Cyrus, William, and Hartwell Turner, T. L. Jackson, and John Fuller and their families camped at the mouth of this creek in Forest Township before crossing the Kickapoo River in the fall of 1854. Indians also used it as a camping ground.

Camp Dewey   *Dane County*

Admiral George Dewey, who had just won the battle of Manila, was honored by having his name given to this camp in Dunn on Lake Kegonsa.

Camp Douglas   *Juneau County*

On the morning of September 20, 1864, the work train of the Milwaukee Railroad let off three passengers to set up a camp that would supply cut wood for the locomotives. They were two middle-aged men and a young girl—Amp Chamberlin of Kilbourn, James Douglas, and his daughter, Ann Eliza Douglas. Six weeks later Mr. Douglas had a crew of men to board. Mr. Chamberlin acted as clerk and paymaster.

One mile west of this camp was another operated by a Mr. Temple. To distinguish this camp from his own, Mr. Douglas put a sign by the railroad track that read Camp Douglas, and Mr. Temple also erected a sign, Camp Temple.

Mr. Douglas moved his camp to the railroad track and remained there four years, sawing the wood with power from a horse treadmill. In the meantime a telegraph office was built and the section men built shacks nearby.

The Omaha Railroad came through this section by 1870. It crossed the Milwaukee Railroad one-half mile east of the wooding camp, and the telegraph office was moved from the wooding camp to the crossing. A depot was built, and the junction became known as Camp Douglas. The wooding camp then became Old Camp.

Camp Gallistela   *Dane County*

This "tent colony" summer camp of the University of Wisconsin on the shore of Lake Mendota was named for Mr. and Mrs. A. F. Gallistel, who were instrumental in its founding and operation. Dean Scott Goodnight suggested the name, and it was chosen by a vote of the students at the camp in 1925.

Camp Hamilton   *Fond du Lac County*

Soldiers were trained for service in the Civil War at this site in the city of Fond du Lac. Col. Charles S. Hamilton, later a general, commanded the troops stationed here.

Camp Lake   *Kenosha County*

An old Indian campsite with a view of three lakes, a rolling timbered hillside, and a pleasant glade.

Camp Randall   *Dane County*

Named after Alexander W. Randall, governor during the American Civil War, it was turned over to the state in 1861 for use as a military training rendezvous. The state's largest staging point, a hospital, and a stockade for Confederate prisoners of war were located here. It presently belongs to the University of Wisconsin and is the site of Camp Randall Stadium.

Candy Corners   *Eau Claire County*
A small community no longer in existence, named for a store in the township of Brunswick. The storekeeper doled out candy to the children when their parents paid bills.

Canute Brook   *Burnett County*
Canute Brook and Hagen Creek are tributaries of the Trade River flowing through what is now the town of Anderson. They were named for Canute Anderson and Charles Hagen, who owned large haying meadows and sold hay to loggers.

Capital City View   *Dane County*
So named because this subdivision of Blooming Grove had a view of Madison, the state capital.

Caraboo Spring   *Fond du Lac County*
Twenty-five feet across, it is the source of the Grand River. It may have been named for the caribou that were once found in Wisconsin.

Carcajou Place or Carcajou Point   *Jefferson County*
Carcajou is believed to be the Algonquin word for "wolverine." It is a common Indian term used from the northern Cree to Alaska.

Carlton   *Kewaunee County*
James Carlton was one of the earliest settlers.

Carramana   *Rock County*
Platted in 1836. The name means "Walking Turtle," after an old Ho-Chunk chief.

Carr Creek and Carr Valley   *Sauk County*
Both "stream and vale" are named for David Carr.

Carroll College   *Waukesha County*
Named for Charles Carroll, a signer of the Declaration of Independence.

Carrollville   *Milwaukee County*
Named by Patrick Carroll. The name of the post office is Otjen, after Theobald Otjen, a member of Congress from Wisconsin.

Carson   *Iron County*
John B. Carson, a prominent railroad man of Ohio, Illinois, and Indiana, and an enthusiastic fisherman, penetrated the country around Carson long before any settlers lived there and before the railroad came.

Carters Siding   *Forest County*
John Carter built the first house.

Carver's Cave   *Buffalo County*

About thirteen miles below the Falls of St. Anthony is a remarkable cave known to some Indians as Wakon-teebe Cave. Jonathan Carver renamed it.

Cascade   *Sheboygan County*

In about 1848, James Preston, his wife, and Huntingdon Lyman settled this land. It was a good place to develop waterpower, using the rapids in the north fork of the Milwaukee River. A village was settled, most of the people coming from Buffalo, New York. The place was so wicked it's believed they called it Nineveh after the wicked city of the Bible. Years afterward, Henry Chambers and John Preston met in the town of Nineveh (Nineva) and renamed it Cascade, after Cascade Falls in Colorado.

Casco   *Kewaunee County*

The first settler, in 1855, was Edward Decker, a lumberman from Casco, Maine. After the lumber was gone he became a banker.

Cashton   *Monroe County*

This village is located at a bend where an old Indian trail turned west. This was a trading post and station for stagecoaches following the trail from the south toward Sparta and points north. Cashton was first known as Mt. Pisgah. In 1857 a post office was established called Hazen's Corner. The Viroqua branch of the Milwaukee Railroad was built through the village in 1879 by William Henry Harrison Cash, who had acquired title to a large portion of the village property. He also built the railroad station and christened the village.

Cassell and Cassell Prairie   *Sauk County*

Tract of land in the town of Troy named for Dr. J. N. Cassell. The post office has been discontinued.

Cassville   *Grant County*

Between 1816 and 1820 a man named Shaw stopped here while on a trip down the Mississippi River. In 1824 Thomas Hymer found a deserted cabin here. The settlement began in 1827 and was named in honor of Lewis Cass, governor of Michigan Territory, which included the present state of Wisconsin.

Castle Place   *Dane County*

Benjamin Walker built a castlelike house near here in 1863. This subdivision within the city of Madison was platted in 1903.

Castle Rock   *Grant County*

The township was originally called Blue River. The name was changed to Castle Rock after a peculiarly shaped rock nearby.

Caswell Springs   *Crawford County*

Located west of Gays Mills in Utica Township, it was named for the Caswell family.

Cataract   *Monroe County*

Perhaps from the little falls in the creek that runs along the north edge of the settlement. The township is called Little Falls.

Catawba   *Price County*

A story goes that some railroad surveyors who passed through here got a little drunk on Catawba grape wine. But the name is probably derived from the Choctaw word katapa, which may mean "divided, departed, a division."

Cat Island   *Apostle Islands*

The Indian name was Kagagiwanjikag Miniss, meaning "island of hemlock trees." It was known locally as Hemlock and also as Shoe. The outline of the island is not unlike that of a cat, and one early observer likened it to a shoe. The official name became Cat Island, but it is sometimes garbled into Caterhemlock, combining it with the earlier Indian label.

Cato   *Manitowoc County*

In 1848 the US government sold this parcel of land to Jonas C. Burns. Later it became the property of John E. Harris, who is credited with being the promoter of the town. It was called Harris and Harrisville until he left the area. The settlement was then a part of Rockland Township.

In 1845 it became a separate township named Nettle Hill, presumably from an overgrowth of nettles in the old cemetery at the top of the hill. In 1858, when the Manitowoc-to-Menasha railroad was built through the township, Alder Hickok, the first town chairman, changed the name to Cato because he had come from Cato in Jefferson County, New York.

Cave of the Mounds   *Dane County*

This sizable cave, discovered in 1939, was named for the nearby Blue Mounds.

Cave Rock   *Richland County*

In Buena Vista Township. An unauthenticated tale tells of a Canadian who in 1792 disappeared along with his gold-laden boat when lightning loosened a rock ledge south of Lone Rock bridge.

Cavour   *Forest County*

In 1887 the Soo Line was built from Minneapolis to Michigan. This village was named after a railroad timekeeper called Count Cavour.

Cayuga   *Ashland County*

Cornell University, which held large tracts of land in the vicinity, named this for Cayuga Lake in New York, the location of the university. Cayuga, New York, was named after a tribe of Indians in the Iroquoian Confederation who formerly occupied the shores of Cayuga Lake. Cayuga means "the place where locusts were taken out."

Cazenovia   *Richland County*

In 1848 Allan Perkins found that this site in Westport Township much resembled that of his former home in Cazenovia, New York. "Cazenovia" is the Latinized form of Cazenove, the name of Theopilus Cazenove, who was an agent for the Holland Land Company.

Cecil   *Shawano County*

In 1883 the Milwaukee, Lake Shore, and Western Railway (later Northwestern) extended its line from Clintonville to Oconto. When the railroad was finished in 1884 the new settlement at the head of Shawano Lake was named after a railroad man, Cecil Leavitt.

Cedar   *Iron County*

From the cedar or arbor vitae trees in the area.

Cedarburg   *Ozaukee County*

The name means "village in the cedars." There is also a story that the name came from the castlelike house of Dr. Fred Leaning, which sat on a hill surrounded by cedars.

Cedar Falls   *Dunn County*

Situated a few miles up the Red Cedar River from Menomonie, the presence of falls at this point led to the construction of a waterpower dam and to the name of the village. A large sawmill provided the economic base for a once thriving community of 250.

Cedar Grove   *Sheboygan County*

During the early fall of 1847 a small group of settlers from Gelderland and Zeeland in the Netherlands, under the leadership of Reverend Pieter Zoone, arrived at what is now Cedar Grove. The site had been purchased from the government in 1846 by G. H. TeKolste. This territory had been known by the Indians as Salina.

The ship Phoenix, carrying 127 Dutch settlers, burned within sight of Sheboygan with only forty-six survivors, of whom twenty-five were Dutch, and some of these people settled here in Cedar Grove. At the south end of the village stood the log house of Sweezy Burr, which became the post office in 1849. Backwoodsmen, pioneers, and Indians gathered at Sweezy Burr's for provisions and mail.

The Reverend Pieter Zoone lived at the north end of the town but was forced to obtain his mail at the south end. One day as he was standing in front of the post office with a group of people, he looked out at the large tract of cedar trees—about forty acres—and proclaimed that the settlement be named Cedar Grove. A nearby settlement called Amsterdam was moved to Cedar Grove after the coming of the railroad by 1871.

Cedar Point   *Walworth County*

Settlement on the east shore of Williams Bay. The Indian name was Ke-she-ge-ki-ah-ke-tah-ke-wum, meaning "cedar hill" or "cedar ridge."

Center Bluff   *Dane County*

This strikingly isolated bluff in the town of Dane has its position between branches of Spring Creek and the ranges of bluffs to the north and south.

Center Creek *Richland County*

Earlier called Camp Creek because of the camping ground on the creek, it later became known as Center Creek because of its proximity to Richland Center.

Centerville *Grant and Iowa Counties*

Located directly on the line between Iowa and Grant Counties.

Centerville *Manitowoc County*

It is midway between Manitowoc and Sheboygan.

Centerville *Trempealeau County*

Named from geographical location of Trempealeau Prairie. Originally called Martin's Corners after an early settler.

Centuria *Polk County*

About 1900 Cyrus Campbell of Minneapolis purchased land here. He got the Soo Line to build a railroad into the area. Settlers coming there soon began to feel the need of a town—Frederic and St. Croix Falls were too far to visit often for needed supplies. The result was Centuria, founded at the turn of the century.

Ceresco *Fond du Lac County*

Named for Ceres, the Roman goddess of agriculture, it was the home of the Wisconsin Phalanx, an experiment in communal living directed by the French social philosopher Charles Fourier. The communal longhouse is one of the last vestiges of the settlement.

Chaffey *Douglas County*

The Chaffey family established a colony in 1890.

Chambers Island *Door County*

This second-largest island in Green Bay received its name in 1816. The territory that became Wisconsin had been ceded to the United States in the treaty of 1783, but England did not relinquish her hold until July 1815. In August 1816, Colonel John Miller with five hundred men were sent to take possession of this distant western region. This party named many of the localities along the way. Chambers Island was named after Colonel Talbot Chambers, who commanded the expedition.

Champion *Brown County*

After an English explorer.

Champion Valley *Richland County*

In the 1880s many Champion grain binders and mowers were in use in the valley near Henrietta.

Chapel Hills *Walworth County*

A small church is located on a nearby hill.

Chapultepec   *Trempealeau County*

From Mount Chapultepec, Mexico. Charles J. Cleveland, whose father was a veteran of
the Battle of Chapultepec, was an early settler of Big Tamarac. The hill nearby seemed to
resemble the Mexican mountain described by his father.

Charlesburg   *Calumet County*

In 1863 Carl Franzen donated the statue of St. Charles to the local parish in honor of his
first name, which is Charles in English. Land for the site of the church was furnished by
Jacob Berg. The settlers named the town for these two benefactors.

Charlestown   *Calumet County*

Probably named after the Charlestown Indians, who came here at the same time as the
Brothertown and the Stockbridge. Some believe the name to be connected with the St.
Charles Catholic Church at Charlesburg since the two churches were sister missions. It
appears, however, that the Indian derivation is more accurate.

Charlotte   *Grant County*

The origin of the name is uncertain, but the first child born to European settlers in Wisconsin, at Fort Crawford, was named Charlotte Wisconsin Clark by parents, who were
traveling to Fort Snelling, Minnesota.

Charme Hollow   *Crawford County*

The name is of French derivation, but the exact source is not known. There were a large
number of families named Du Charme that lived nearby, but it is not certain that this
name was applied to this hollow in Eastman Township.

Chaseburg   *Vernon County*

Named for P. E. Chase, who came here from the East about 1854 and established a gristmill near the present schoolhouse site.

Chegwin School   *Fond du Lac County*

Rose Chegwin was a grade school teacher who taught in the city of Fond du Lac from
1890 until her retirement in 1938.

Chelsea   *Taylor County*

Named by President Colby of the Wisconsin Central Railway after a town near Boston,
Massachusetts. The name is English, and the village was given an invitation to attend the
festivities of the coronation of Queen Elizabeth II on June 22, 1953. The invitation was
issued to all the places named Chelsea throughout the world.

Chenequa
Chenequa Lakes
Chenequa Lake   *Bayfield County*
Chenequa Springs   *Waukesha County*

Dr. Increase A. Lapham, in his book Wisconsin, published by P. C. Hall at Milwaukee in 1844, says, "The Indian name is Chenequa or Pine, given in consequence of a few pine trees having been found on a small neck of land or island in this lake."

Rev. E. P. Wheeler, an authority on Wisconsin Indian names, thinks Chenequa may have been derived from the Potawatomi word Gih-chi-nah-quak, or "big tree grove."

John Blackhawk, an authority on the language and customs of his tribe, thinks the name might have been derived from the Ho-Chunk word *chenukra*, or "village."

A map of Wisconsin Territory 1839, prepared by Capt. Thomas T. Cram, government topographical engineer, calls it Gay Lake, probably derived from the Potawatomi word que (quay) meaning "woman"—the Ojibwe word is ikwe or akwe. Huron H. Smith, the ethnobotanist, states that Chenequa means "Indian woman" or "Indian maiden," and that the word is Ojibwe rather than Potawatomi. Chene is an abbreviation of inishinabe, meaning "Indian."

Chequamegon Bay
Chequamegon Point
Chequamegon National Forest   *Ashland County*

This name appears to be a corruption of the French spelling of the Indian word shau-gau-wau-me-kong, meaning "a long narrow strip of land running into a body of water"—such as a lake or bay—or, more literally, "hardly any water rising toward beach." There were many pronunciations and spellings. Schoolcraft defines Chequamegon as "low land." In Bishop Baraga's dictionary Jabonique is called a needle, and this low sandy point resembles a needle. Writer Edward Jaken says the point was probably first named Jawaumika, meaning "large extended breakers."

There is also the legend of the beaver who made the bay and island, which may have caused writers to imagine that the word Amik, "beaver," was part of this name. The legend says that Menobosho was hunting for the great beaver in Lake Superior, which was then a beaver pond. The beaver took refuge in Ashland Bay. Menobosho built a dam from the south shore of the lake to Madeline Island. As he threw fistfuls of mud from the bay into the lake, they formed the Apostle Islands. The dam was too soft, and the beaver escaped into Lake Superior. One Indian interpretation of the word says it means "at the soft beaver dam."

Cherokee   *Marathon County*

Named for the Cherokee Indians. The word has several meanings, one of which is "cave people."

Cherry Valley   *Richland County*

In Bloom Township. The name is reminiscent of Cherry Valley, New York. Joseph Cherry, a native of England and a farmer of some means, was listed on the 1850 census, but whether he ever was in Bloom is not known.

Chester   *Dodge County*

Named after Chester in Hampden County, Massachusetts, which was named after Chester, England.

Chetek   *Barron County*

In 1836 Joe Trepannier operated a trading post on what is now known as Red Club House Point. Records show that in 1852, when government surveyors arrived, they found Louis Montra buying furs from the Indians. The Ojibwe word for Chetek is Jede-sagaigan, Jede meaning "swan" or "pelican," and sagaigan meaning "an inland lake." Surrounding the lake are various Indian burial grounds. The first dam was built in early 1860 by Knapp Stout & Company, logging pioneers, and many of their employees are thought to have married Indian women.

Chetek was incorporated as a city in 1891, the smallest settlement in the United States to have the status of a city, and the first and only one to pass directly from township to a full-fledged city. Its population at that time was 531.

Chicken Hill   *Dane County*

Everybody on this hill in Dunkirk seemed to be raising chickens.

Chicken Ridge   *Richland County*

In Dayton Township. A 1934 newspaper reported that the 120 Plymouth Rock capons of Ernest Barnes "were a sight to behold."

Childs Station   *Rock County*

Situated on the farm of John Child.

Childstown   *Crawford County*

In Scott Township, also called Plug Town, it was named after a man by the name of Childs.

Chili   *Clark County*

In about 1880 the Chigaco and North Western Railway built through this area to take care of the sawmills. There was a sawmill about a mile east of where the railroad put in a siding called Cedarhurst. Another sawmill was built at the present site of Chili and grew to be a large operation. One cold day during the winter of 1881 the railroad officials came for the purpose of selecting a name. It was so cold they did not want to get out of the train, so one of them said, "Let's call this stop Chili because it is really chilly here."

Chilton   *Calumet County*

In 1835 Moses and Catherine Stanton settled on the banks of the Manitowoc River, where they built a mill. They named their settlement Stantonville. John Marygold came in 1858 and platted the village. He decided to call it Chillington after his native home in England. Patrick Conahue was sent to the county seat at Stockbridge to register the name. Along the way, probably at Portland or Branch Creek, Patrick stopped to imbibe strong liquor and became somewhat hazy.

When he got to Stockbridge the registrar interpreted his message as Chilton. This name, however, is not a coined term. Mary Chilton was the first Pilgrim to step on Plymouth Rock. For a number of years Chilton Canning Company called a brand of peas Mary Chilton. She was pictured on the label. The depot area was originally called Chilton Center.

Another story, by J. H. Hamilton, says that in 1852 or 1853 the question of a name for the city was submitted to a vote of the residents. His father, W. H. Hamilton, had a friend and neighbor whose old home in England was called Chillington, and he was anxious to have that name for the new town. The evening before the election this gentleman called at the Hamilton home and asked the eldest girl, Gratia, then twelve, to write the ballots for him. In error she wrote Chilton, and that name won.

Chimney Rock *Richland County*
This rock formation in the Town of Ithaca resembles a chimney.

Chimney Rock *Trempealeau County*
From the towering, ragged rock, the highest point in the vicinity. It was originally called Devil's Chimney and was a landmark to travelers.

Chippanazie *Washburn County*
When lumbermen set out to fell a tree, they would saw through the proper distance, and then chop a notch on the side to which the tree was to tall. This was called to "chip-in-a-zee."

It is also said that the name was first applied to the creek and is the Indian term for "crooked water."

Chippewa *Ashland County*
Chippewa is considered a popular adaption of the Indian word Ojibwe, a tribe of the Algonquian Nation. The word means "to roast till puckered up" and refers to the puckered seam on their moccasins, or the puckering of the skins in the toe of their moccasins.

Chippewa City *Chippewa County*
The first settlement was a sawmill in 1851. The town thrived until the money panic of 1875, when it was abandoned and most of the residents moved to Durand. In 1938 Procter LaDuc of Canada bought the land and opened a fishing resort. Chiefs of the Ojibwe tribe were said to have met in council at this site.

Chippewa County
Named for the Chippewa River. Several bands of the Ojibwe tribe settled on its headwaters, to which they had fought their way from Lake Superior against the Dakota or Sioux.

Chippewa Falls *Chippewa County*
This settlement received its name in 1836 from a pioneer, Jean Brunet, because of the large falls on the Chippewa River at this site. At one time it had the largest sawmill under one roof in the world.

Chittamo *Washburn County*

The Ojibwe Indian word for "squirrel." It was also the name of an Indian subchief who lived there for many years.

Chitwood Hollow *Richland County*

John Chitwood came to Richwood in the 1850s and he died here in 1905.

Chiwaukee Prairie *Kenosha County*

Chiwaukee Prairie is the largest unbroken prairie in Wisconsin. The two-hundred-acre prairie is so named because it is located between Chicago and Milwaukee. More than three hundred species of plants grow on the sandy ridges and swales of what was once the shoreline of glacial Lake Chicago, the predecessor of Lake Michigan.

Christiana *Dane County*

Named by Mr. Grunnel Olson Vindg in honor of the Norwegian city in his native land. It should have been spelled Christiania.

Christiana *Vernon County*

From the city in Norway.

Christ Ridge *Crawford County*

In Marietta Township, it was named after the Christ family, as were Christ Hill and Christ School.

Cisco River *Winnebago County*

Cisco is an Indian word believed to mean "trout of an oily nature."

Citron Creek *Crawford County*

Pioneer families along this creek in Seneca Township used to grow a melon used for pickling, called the "citron."

Clam Falls *Burnett County*

Formerly Ga-Essikag-Kakabikang, which is Ojibwe for "there are clams" (ga-essikag) and "a waterfall" (kakabikang).

Clam Falls *Polk County*

This settlement was named for the nearby falls on the Clam River. The Indians called the river Kiesca-Seba, meaning "clam shell river."

Clam Lake *Ashland County*

This lake, and Lower Clam Lake and Little Clam Lake, were named by the early loggers for the abundance of clams. In the early days muskrats covered the shorelines with clamshells.

Clarence *Green County*

B. J. Tenney built a small store here and the town was known as Tenneyville. In honor of Squire Derrick, the name was changed to Clarence, the name of the town in which he had resided in New York.

Clark County

The place was named, according to the record in the Wisconsin Historical Collection by Dr. Lyman C. Draper, in honor of General George Rogers Clark, the conqueror of the Northwest during the American Revolution. Dr. Draper was an acknowledged authority on the life of General Clark and was also secretary of the Wisconsin Historical Society in 1853 when Clark County was named. There is also a story that the county was named after A. W. Clark, an early settler.

Clark Mills *Manitowoc County*

A Mr. Clark had a sawmill and a gristmill on the river.

Clarno *Green County*

The first man who came to Green County was Andrew Clarno, who selected a parcel of land for his farm in 1829.

Clayton *Crawford County*

This township was named after a person named Clayton, who came from Ohio or some other state in the East.

Clayton *Polk County*

Clayton Rogers was a boss in the mill at the settlement and a captain in the army. Vernon Tanner homesteaded this site about 1872.

Claywood *Oconto County*

A settlement was given this name because of the clay soil in a large woods.

Clear Creek *Crawford County*

Located in Marietta Township. Clear water makes a clear creek. It was the site of Indian engagements in early times.

Clear Creek *Eau Claire County*

The township became separated from Otter Creek in 1882 and was named for the creek that crosses it.

Clear Lake *Polk County*

The name of this village was to have been Clark's Lake after one of the oldest families, but it was found that there already was a Clark's Lake in Wisconsin at that time. The lake was then named Clear Lake, and the village was given the same name.

Clearwater Lake *Oneida County*

The post office in this small community was established about 1905, and the name was chosen because of a large clear lake in the area.

Cleghorn *Eau Claire County*

There was a station on the Foster Railroad here from 1913 until the railroad was discontinued. Settlers came in numbers during the 1850s, and it became a center for good farming. Named after Lewis Cleghorn, one of the early settlers.

Cleveland *Chippewa County*

A settlement was established here in 1850 called Birch because of the many birch trees. The township separated from Eagle Point, and on March 28, 1885, it was named Cleveland in honor of the new president of the United States.

Cleveland *Manitowoc County*

Known as Centerville Station when the depot was established in 1873. The new railroad had bypassed the lake port, Centerville, one mile to the east. In 1885, when a post office was established, it was renamed in honor of President Cleveland.

Cliff House *Sauk County*

Abandoned hotel and discontinued post office on the north shore of Devils Lake. It was originally called Minnequkan, after a lake by that name in North Dakota. W. H. Marsh, the builder of the hotel, renamed it because it was located under the high cliff.

Clifton *Grant County*

Bosman Clifton, a pioneer settler, owned land in an area known as Martinville. When his daughter died at the age of seven, Clifton offered to donate one and a half acres for a church, and a town grew up around it with his name.

Clinton *Rock County*

This post office was named on August 12, 1843, presumably after Governor De Witt Clinton of New York. Numerous cities in the East were named in his honor, and the emigrants brought the name with them when they resettled in the West. Twenty-seven active US post offices are named Clinton.

Clinton Junction *Rock County*

The original location of this town was called New York by J. M. Bartlett, who laid it out. The name was changed in 1855 by the Iowa Land Company, which bought the town site and nearby land, to Ogden for W. B. Ogden, president of the Chicago and North Western Railway. Several of the early settlers had come from Clinton, New York, and they were influential in getting the legislature to name the town Clinton Junction.

Clinton Square *Sauk County*

This park in Lyons was named for Governor De Witt Clinton of New York. Governor Clinton was one of the projectors of the Erie Canal. W. H. Canfield was a surveyor on the new waterway, and afterward, in 1846, when he was deputy district surveyor for Sauk

County in the territory of Wisconsin, he made a plat of Lyons and named the public square or central park for the Empire State executive.

Clintonville *Waupaca County*

The very first settlers in this little community called it Pigeon. Norman Clinton and his family were on their way to a logging camp on the Embarrass River in February of 1855 when their ox became sick and they were forced to stop at Pigeon. They built a rude hut, and after a few days they decided this was a good place to live. The Clintons became the first permanent settlers, although others had come and gone before. The village was incorporated in 1879.

Cloverland *Vilas County*

Early settlers found clover growing in the open spaces here and hoped it would become a good farming area.

Club Harbor *Fond du Lac County*

This three-story hotel is located in the village of Pipe. It was built by Henry Fuhrman as a stagecoach inn. Part of the basement was built of black walnut, and square nails were used throughout. A spring still flows under the northeast corner of the basement.

Clyman *Dodge County*

In 1837, so the story goes, two frontiersmen, a Mr. Burnett and a Colonel Clyman, left Milwaukee on a hunting and trapping expedition in the area that later became Dodge County. They walked to the east fork of the Rock River, where the village of Theresa now stands, and procured a canoe to travel downstream to the Ox Bow. Here they stopped to make camp and were attacked by Indians. Burnett was killed.

Clyman, slightly wounded, took flight and was pursued by one of the Indians. After running several miles through the woods, Clyman came to a fallen tree. He leaped over it, then dropped down behind it. The Indian jumped over the tree and ran on. Clyman remained quiet until about midnight and then resumed his flight. After several days of wandering he found his way back to Milwaukee. The two Indians later told this story of the murder and chase to Solomon Juneau, fully corroborating the account by Colonel Clyman, who later returned to his campsite area to settle.

There was an old territorial road going north from Watertown, and other settlers also came to establish farms. The township was named Clyman, and a village on the Chicago and Northwestern Railway was incorporated in 1924. Clyman Junction became another settlement one mile to the north, where the Chicago and Northwestern Railway was crossed by the Milwaukee, Sparta, and Northwestern. Colonel Clyman was said to have greatly resembled General George Washington in personal appearance.

Cobb *Iowa County*

Originally called Cross Plains because the old territorial road crossed the level plains or prairies here. Captain Amasa Cobb renamed it when he became a congressman and was influential in getting a post office established and a railroad built through the area. He had been a captain in the Black Hawk War, and his unit had camped near this site.

Cobban *Chippewa County*

Joseph Cobban, a farmer and industrialist, owned land here. He was born in Inverness, East Canada, in 1838, and came to Chippewa Falls in May 1867.

Cobblers Knob *Crawford County*

Located in Wauzeka Township, there is no obvious meaning to the name.

Cochrane *Buffalo County*

After one of the officers of the railroad company that built the first line through the area.

Colburn *Chippewa County*

Established in 1886 and named after the man who built the dam and operated the mill.

Colby *Clark and Marathon Counties*

Gardner Colby of Boston, Massachusetts, of the Colby-Philips Construction Company, built the railroad for the Wisconsin Central Company. His son, Charles L. Colby, became president of the company.

Cold Spring Farm *Fond du Lac County*

Not only is there a cold spring on the farm, but Isaac Tallmadge, the original owner, came from Cold Spring, New York. Located in Empire Township, it has been known by this name for over one hundred years.

Coleman *Marinette County*

A Mr. Coleman owned much of the land in the area.

Coleman Hollow *Crawford County*

Located in Utica Township, it is named for the Coleman family.

Colfax *Dunn County*

At first Colfax was called Begga Town because "rutabeggas" were raised by so many of the farmers. Later, in about 1868, the name was changed in honor of Senator Schuyler Colfax, who served as vice president under Ulysses S. Grant.

Colgate *Washington County*

Probably after James B. Colgate of the famous Colgate family.

Collins *Manitowoc County*

In the year 1895–96 the Wisconsin Central Railroad built a branch line from Hilbert to Manitowoc. Most depots along the line were named after a prominent family in the community. This settlement was to be named Valleskey, but Mr. Gustave Valleskey refused the use of his name. The railroad superintendent rode the first train to travel this branch on July 4, 1896, and named the station after himself.

Coloma   *Waushara County*

Charles White, who returned from the goldfields of California in 1852, named this township after Coloma in California, where gold was discovered. Coloma Corners grew up near the west side of the township. When the railroad came through it missed Coloma Corners by two miles, so a little village called Coloma Station began, which later became known as Coloma.

Colonel Heg Memorial Park   *Racine County*

Colonel Hans C. Heg was an outstanding Civil War hero and was killed in action during the war. At the time he was Wisconsin's top-ranking officer. The park brochure states: "Heg Park is a memorial to Old Muskego, a Norwegian mother colony and a place of significant beginnings in the fields of religious, social, and cultural development. It was here that the first Norwegian Lutheran church in America was built, the first Norwegian newspaper was printed, and the first Temperance Society among Norwegians in America was organized. Here, in a churchyard on Norway Hill, rests the body of Colonel Hans C. Heg, who was killed in the Battle of Chickamuaga while in command of a Scandinavian regiment called the 15th Wisconsin."

Columbia County

In 1846, when the territorial legislature set off their county from the rest of Portage County, it narrowly escaped being named York, as petitions for that name had more signatures than the one for Columbia. But James T. Lewis, with characteristic pertinacity, induced the legislature to strike out York and substitute Columbia. Apparently this name came from the Columbia River in Oregon. The name also honors Christopher Columbus.

Columbia Park   *Wood County*

This park in Marshfield was known until 1915 as "the city park" or "the north side park." In August of 1915 the Marshfield Civic Pride and Park Committee suggested that the park be designated by "a name that all know of . . ."

Columbus   *Columbia County*

One of the first settlers to come here was Major Dickason, who built a little log cabin on the banks of the Crawfish River near where the depot now stands. He brought with him sixty or seventy head of cattle, upward of twenty horses, and four or five wagons. He believed that the open spots in the woods and the little prairie areas alone would be ample space for all the demands of agriculture, and that the wooded ground would never be cleared but would always remain hunting grounds. Shortly after he arrived he staked out twelve lots near his cabin for a village and called it Columbus.

Colwell   *Taylor County*

The Colwell brothers were farmers and sawmill operators in the eastern part of Taylor County.

Combined Locks   *Outagamie County*

Named for the canal locks in the Fox River at this point.

Commonwealth *Florence County*
The mine of the Commonwealth Iron Mining Company was located here.

Comstock *Barron County*
Named in honor of H. S. Comstock, who lived in Cumberland and became the county judge. He was a lawyer, a leader, and a promoter of the new territory.

Congress Hall *Sauk County*
Named by the Toping family about 1850 for the form of the first chamber at the entrance to the glen. It is situated between Delton and the Wisconsin River.

Conners Point *Douglas County*
Benjamin H. Connor preempted this site.

Connorsville *Dunn County*
Named after David Connors, an early pioneer, Connorsville is located in the northwestern part of the county. Nearby is a farming community of Slovak people, many of whom came here from the coalfields of Pennsylvania.

Conover *Vilas County*
Seth H. Conover of Plymouth built the first summer resort and hotel on Big Twin Lake in 1883.

Conrath *Rusk County*
Frank Conrath and his brother Charles logged this area and later settled here.

Cooks Valley *Chippewa County*
A township first settled by Jacob Cook and Zerah C. Willis in 1858.

Cooksville *Rock County*
In the town of Porter, it was laid out by John Cook in 1842. Daniel and John Cook and their families came here in 1840.

Cooley Creek *Crawford County*
In Freeman Township. It was named for Aaron Cooley.

Coomer *Burnett County*
This hamlet was named after William Coomer, a merchant at Taylor Falls. Nothing remains of the original settlement, but a church and a school still carry the name.

Coon Valley *Vernon County*
The first settler was Helge Gulbrandson, who came from Norway in 1849. For some years the valley was called Helgedalen, meaning "Helge valley." In 1865 a post office was established and called Coon Valley because so many raccoons were found in the region. Before the settlers came, steamboats on the Mississippi River had landings along the river where

they stopped for wood. One landing where Coon Creek emptied into the Mississippi was identified as Coon Slough.

Cooper Hill   *Richland County*
This hill in Richland Township was named for the Cooper family.

Cooperstown   *Manitowoc County*
Allen A. Cooper was an early settler and the first postmaster.

Copper Creek   *Sauk County*
Copper ore was found in this stream in Winfield. The "floating ore" came down from the north in glacial times.

Coral City   *Trempealeau County*
While digging for a dam on the north side of the creek, some funny-looking rock was found. Granville McFarland told the Wrights that it was coral. Mr. Wright soon caught on that he was being tricked but named the site Coral City anyway.

Core Hollow   *Richland County*
William, David, and George Washington Core were the first of the Core family to settle in the hollow in the Akan and Dayton Townships.

Corliss   *Racine County*
The settlement was formerly known as Western Union Junction. The village was surveyed by Samuel D. Austin on August 13, 1901, for the Brown Corliss Engine Company of Milwaukee. Three days later the plat was filed in the register of deeds under the name of Corliss.

Cormier   *Brown County*
George Cormier was highway commissioner for many years.

Cornell   *Chippewa County*
Formerly called Brunet's Falls after Jean Brunet, who operated a portage and trading post here. It was renamed after Ezra Cornell, who was president of Cornell University at the time of the Land Grant College Act, when the university and the Cornell family acquired large holdings of pinelands in Wisconsin.

Cornucopia   *Bayfield County*
Mr. F. J. Stevenson was so impressed by the abundance of fruits being grown here about 1900 that he chose the horn of plenty title.

Corwin   *Richland County*
In Westford Township, named for Oliver Corwin Sabin, for whom Sabin in Sylvan Township also was named. He became the first postmaster of Corwin in January 1895.

Cottage Grove *Dane County*

The first known settlement was in 1838, and in 1840 William C. Wells, Amos Harris, and Horatio Catlin bought land. Wells named the town for a beautiful grove of burr oaks that surrounded his first house. This house served as home, tavern, and post office for many years.

Cotton House *Brown County*

Built by John P. Arndt about 1840, it was originally the home of Arndt's daughter and her husband, Captain John Window Cotton, a retired army officer. The house is considered one of the finest examples of Jeffersonian architecture in the Middle West.

Couderay *Sawyer County*

The name is an adaption of a French phrase, court oreilles, meaning "short ears." Radisson and Groseillers, the first Europeans to visit this area in 1659, found Ottawa Indians, whom they called The Short Ears. The area was a favorite habitat of many tribes because of the abundant game and fish, wild berries, and wild rice. The Sioux Indians lived here before the Ottawa, and the Ojibwe lived here after 1745. It is said that Indians and early English and American explorers referred to the area as Ottawa Sagaigan, meaning "Ottawa Lake." Couderay was the first mill town on the upper Chippewa River.

Coulee Country *La Crosse County*

Rugged valleys in this area collect rivers that feed the Mississippi. The early French called such a valley a coulee. Coulee Country is known widely through the writings of Hamlin Garland (1860–1940), a Wisconsin author.

Coulter Hollow *Richland County*

William Coulter came to the town of Marshall in 1877 to settle.

Coumbe Island *Richland County*

Located in Richwood Township. John Coumbe was the first European settler in the area.

County Line *Racine County*

The boundary between Milwaukee and Racine counties runs through the railroad station grounds. The post office is Lamberton.

Crab Tree Corners *Grant County*

An abundance of crabapple trees grows in the vicinity.

Cranberry Center *Juneau County*

Called Mas-ki-gimi-nika-nang by the Ojibwe Indians, meaning "place where cranberries grow."

Cranberry Island *Dane County*

Cranberries grew here but not elsewhere in the neighborhood. It is also known as Timber Island.

Crandon
Forest County

First named Ayr for the city in Scotland. It was renamed in 1885 after Major Frank P. Crandon, an official of the Chicago and North Western Railway, which owned nearly half the lands in Forest County. Major Crandon was influential in getting the legislature to create Forest County from Langlade and Oconto Counties.

Samuel Shaw, editor of Forest Leaves, describes Major Crandon in the June 18, 1885, issue: "He is warmly interested in the development of the county and hopes to meet our people next month. They will find him to be a gentleman of keen perception, courteous manners, generous impulses, strong convictions, and great force of character. Three twos express his weight, and every ounce is warmed up by the blood of noble manhood."

Samuel Shaw had been superintendent of schools in Madison and was the first land agent for the Chicago and North Western Railway. He advertised lands for sale at fifty cents to three dollars per acre in his newspaper. Mrs. Samuel Shaw was the first postmaster at Crandon.

Crane City
Polk County

There once was a grove of about eighty acres of white pine near Palmer Lake where thousands of big cranes nested. They would bring fish for their young from trout streams and lakes farther away. About 1883 or 1884 "William McCarthy and Peter Hueber of Clear Lake cut all the grove and hauled the logs to Gregory and sawed them into lumber and shipped it west to the pineries."

Wortley Prentice tells of the Indian dances he witnessed at Crane City and of the great sorrow it caused them when the nesting trees were destroyed. He writes:

"Readers, you can't imagine what sad disappointment and sorrow the destroying of Crane City caused the Indians. For centuries it was one of their happy hunting grounds. Every Indian far and near knew the time by the moons when to come and enjoy their feast of the young crane, squab, young doves, or pigeons. The Indians would congregate for miles around to feast on these young cranes and would never kill the old ones unless by mistake. That meeting would be looked for each year, and every family that could get there would be dressed in their best clothing. They would always get there about two weeks before the young cranes could fly and kill the young squabs and dress and cook them in every way imaginable. Believe me they were very palatable especially when anyone was hungry. The flesh when cooked was as white and tender as any meat or fowl I ever saw. When the Indians met they would all be one big family and you could imagine it was a real love feast."

Cranetown
St. Croix County

All that is standing here now is the "old company store," probably the only remaining vestige of the sawmill days in the county. Named for the Crane family, who ran a sawmill on Beaver Creek in the 1890s, it was once a community of several hundred persons.

Crawford County

Named for Fort Crawford, built in 1816 by Major Willoughby Morgan of the United States Army. William H. Crawford was Secretary of the Treasury under President James Monroe.

Crescent Park *Dane County*

E. N. Edwards gave this park in Dunn its name in 1901. The shape of the Lake Waubesa shore along which it lies gave him the idea for the name.

The Crex Meadows Wildlife Area *Burnett County*

A State Conservation Area named after the Crex Carpet Company of New Brighton, Minnesota, which owned the area and harvested wire grass there for the manufacture of grass carpets from 1905 to 1915.

Crivitz *Marinette County*

Formerly called Ellis Junction after the Ellis family. Judge Bartels renamed it for his native place in Germany.

Cross Plains *Dane County*

Berry Haney, one of the early settlers in the area, became the first postmaster in March 1838 and named the town after his home in Tennessee.

Crossville *Calumet County*

A little settlement, now forgotten, at the northern tip of Lake Winnebago, where tolls were collected on the road that crossed from Winnebago to Calumet County.

Crow Hill *Richland County*

Located in Dayton Township. An old newspaper account states that Mrs. Flora Miller, a correspondent for the Richland Rustic, gave the hill its name because of the many crows that flocked here. A more plausible explanation is that the name came from the Crow or Groh family.

Crow Hollow *Crawford County*

Located in Haney Township. Henry Crow operated a sawmill here.

Crowley Ridge *Crawford County*

Northeast of the village of Eastman, it was named after the Crowley family.

Crusan Slough *Richland County*

This slough in Buena Vista was owned by G. Crusan. Later it came to be known as the Sand Prairie Slough.

Crystal Lake *Dane County*

Formerly spelled "Cristal" and also "Chrystal," this clear, shallow lake near Roxbury was first named on an 1859 map.

Cuba City *Grant County*

In 1848 this territory belonged to Mr. Nicholas, and at his death it was divided among his children. The small settlement, called Western, became the stopping place for teamsters driving from the mines of Mineral Point to Galena. There was a hotel with a root house and pasture for the horses that were exchanged here for fresh ones. Mr. Craiglaw built the first house, and the name of the settlement became Craiglaw for a time.

The Wisconsin State Journal of October 27, 1941, has this account of how the name was changed to Cuba City:

> *Legend has it that when William Stephens, Madison Y. Johnson, and Solomon Craiglaw platted the village some seventh years ago, there was some disagreement among the partners as to what the name of the fledgling should be. At a meeting of the three one day, Johnson asked if the others had thought of a name. Stephens answered, "We'll call it Stephensville."*
>
> *At this, Craiglaw shouted, "You be damned. We won't."*
>
> *Stephens, evidently not lacking a sense of humor, then said quickly, "That's it, we'll call it Yuba."*
>
> *And that was the name for a short time until it was discovered that there was another Yuba in the state. Then the initial Y was changed to C, and the village was Cuba. There are old plat books with a printed C pasted over the Y.*
>
> *The post office was officially Cuba, Wisconsin, until the 1920s. Then, during Assemblyman W. H. Goldthorpe's term as postmaster, he asked the Post Office Department to change the name to Cuba City, citing as his chief reason for the request that there were no less than five Cubas in the United States, which caused much confusion in handling the mail. He also pointed out that the railroad express office had always been Cuba City. Why that was, no one seems to know. As a result of Goldthorpe's petition, the post office department changed the name to Cuba City, Wisconsin.*

Cudahy
Milwaukee County

Named for Patrick Cudahy, who began in 1862 as a delivery boy for Heinecke's Grocery. Milwaukee was little more than a frontier town then, and Patrick was thirteen years old. Later he carried meat for the Roddis Packing Company and became superintendent of several packing houses, including the large Plankinton & Armour plant. In 1888 Mr. Plankinton retired, and Patrick, with his brother, John, purchased his interest and started the firm of Cudahy Brothers. Patrick built a new plant south of Milwaukee's city limits in 1893. New industries were attracted to the area, and the community grew and prospered. In 1906, Cudahy became a city, but old Chicago and North Western Railway records show that the railroad called the village Cudahy before it was officially named.

Cumberland
Barron County

Originally Cumberland encompassed four townships and was organized as Lakeland in 1876 with a post office by that name. During the winter of 1879, John A. Humbird, president of the Chicago and North Western Railway, asked that it be changed to honor his hometown of Cumberland, Maryland, and Judge Barron ordered the change. Cumberland is often called Island City because it is located on an irregularly shaped island at the southern end of Beaver Dam Lake.

Curtiss *Clark County*

In 1880 Charles Curtiss, a civil engineer, was sent to Clark County by the Wisconsin Central Railroad Company to survey for a branch off the Soo Line. He bought two hundred acres of land, cut off the best timber, and had it sawed in the mill owned by Mr. Bass. He stayed in the area for only two years. No one seemed to know where he went, but the railroad named the village after him. The first post office was named Quar, in 1881, but was changed to Curtiss in 1882.

Cushing *Polk County*

This settlement was named after Caleb Cushing when the post office was established in 1870. Cushing had purchased several thousand acres of agricultural college granted lands that were logged by the Cushing Lumber Company and resold by the Cushing Land Agency managed by Major J. Stannard Baker and resident agent Henry D. Barron. Caleb Cushing was born in Salisbury, Massachusetts, in 1800 and graduated from Harvard at the age of seventeen. He served in the Massachusetts legislature, and in Congress from 1834 to 1842. He negotiated the first treaty between the United States and Canada. He served as a colonel in the Mexican War, and was attorney general under President Franklin Pierce. He died at his home in Massachusetts on January 2, 1879.

The type of soil found here, a clay loam with some lime, believed to be windblown from the western states, is known as Cushing loam, and is so called wherever it is found in the United States.

→ D ←

Dacada *Ozaukee County*
An adaptation of the Indian word Dakota. There are mounds in the area that are thought to have been built by Dakota Indians. The first European settlers came from Luxembourg in 1846. They were considered a sturdy people and very religious.

Dacada *Sheboygan County*
Named after the Dakota Indians, who once lived in this area.

Dahl Place *Fond du Lac County*
On the east side of the city of Fond du Lac, it was given the middle name of Peter D. Humleker.

Dairy Belt School *Wood County*
In the town of Richfield, probably named to call attention to the fact that there were many dairy farms in the area.

Dakota *Waushara County*
Named for the Indians of the Dakotas, meaning "allies." It was also written Lakota, Lahtoka, and Nakota and was used as the common name of all confederated Sioux tribes.

Daleyville *Dane County*
Sometimes called Dahleville, it was named for Onon B. Daley (originally Dahle) and his descendants. In 1853 this native Norwegian opened the first store in town and made himself the unofficial postmaster for the neighborhood.

Dallas *Barron County*
Barron County was originally called Dallas County after George Dallas, vice president of the United States from 1845 to 1849. In 1869 the name was changed to Barron County. The village of Dallas took the name when it was incorporated on June 26, 1903.

Dalton *Green Lake County*
When the Chicago and North Western Railway established this station in 1911 they named it in honor of Mrs. John (Jeanette Blackwood) Dalton, who had sold them the town site. Mrs. Dalton left Scotland when she was fourteen years old and came to Wisconsin from New York State with her husband and baby daughter in 1851.

Dalton is located along the old Military Road established in 1828 to follow an Indian trail from Green Bay to Prairie du Chien via Portage. Mr. and Mrs. Dalton built a farm and raised fourteen children.

Mrs. Dalton had her first train ride in the railroad official's private coach when the first passenger train traveled the new line. She was asked what name she wanted to give the new station. She replied that Pleasant Valley was all right, as that was the name of the rural community and the local Congregational church. The officials told her it was a good suggestion, but it had already been named Dalton.

Dam Site   *Polk County*

Located at the site of the old Ridler's Mill, it was built up several decades ago on the Apple River where it is crossed by Highway 8.

Danbury   *Burnett County*

This town site was built in 1911 on the Soo Line Railroad and may have been named after Mr. Dan Springer, the contractor who did the grading for the railroad. It is also said that a man who worked on the railroad suggested the name of Blueberry. They discussed the subject with Mr. Ed L. Peet, a real estate dealer and the chief promoter for the new site. Mr. Peet discussed the matter with his friend John Daniel Glass, the principal landowner in those early days, and the name of Danbury was chosen. The old-timers say that Mr. Peet was the guiding star for this new "pet project" and was responsible for the beginning of several of its industries. He might have named it Nettland, after his wife, or Edsville after himself, or just Peet. But he envisioned a second Danbury, Connecticut, and thus chose the middle name of his friend.

Dane   *Dane County*

The county was named by James Duane Doty in honor of Nathan Dane, a judge and member of Congress from Massachusetts and framer of the Ordinance of 1787 establishing the Northwest Territory. Early settlers named the village after the county.

Daniels   *Burnett County*

Named for Daniel Johnson, an early settler and a prominent citizen. Set off as a new town about 1905–10.

Danville   *Dodge County*

Daniel Busset is said to have left Columbus, Wisconsin, to go down the Crawfish River to a mill site that looked good to him. He laid out a village there and called it Danville. When the railroad decided to swing north and miss Danville, his plans were ruined. Danville lost its post office, which took the name of Elba, but there were so many Elbas, they decided to name it Astico.

Darbellay   *Kewaunee County*

This discontinued post office in Red River Township was named after a Belgian who eventually moved to the city of Kewaunee and engaged in the farm implement business.

Darboy   *Calumet County*

When the first Catholic church was dedicated in this vicinity, it was named Guardian Angel. The community was later called Buchanan, probably in honor of the president. In 1877 a post office was named Darboy in memory of Georges Darboy, archbishop of Paris.

Darien *Walworth County*

John Bruce came from New York in 1837 and bought up most of the land that is now the township of Darien. He set aside a strip of land consisting of three acres to be known as The Commons as early New England towns had always done. This area is now known as Bruce Park or Darien Village Park. Mr. Bruce sold lots around The Commons and gradually it became known as Bruceville. In 1838 many settlers came from Darien, New York, and decided to change the name. By 1860 Darien was said to have been the largest shipping point for stock, grain, and pine lumber between Milwaukee and the Mississippi River.

Darling's Gap *Fond du Lac County*

The break in the ledge near the brickyard in Oakfield Township marks the site of Darling's Gap. Reverend Samuel Darling once owned this land.

Darlington *Lafayette County*

In the spring of 1850, J. M. Kee and J. B. Lynde, an agent for Joshua Darling of New York, purchased the land in this area.

Darnells Corners *Richland County*

Also called Dayton Corners, because of its location in Dayton Township, this name is for R. J. Darnell, who had a store and roadhouse on the Black River Road.

Dartford *Green Lake County*

Named by and for its founder, Anson Dart, who came here in 1845.

Darwin Station *Dane County*

Located in Burke. Origin unknown.

Davig Ridge *Crawford County*

Located in Utica Township. It was named for the Davig family.

Davis Ridge *Crawford County*

This ridge near Freeman Township was named for the Davis family. It is located on Highway 82 coming into DeSoto from Vernon County.

Dawn *Sauk County*

Dawn was given its name to symbolize the beginning of the married life of S. H. Kerfoot and his bride after they came from Virginia to Lake View, Chicago. It was the summer home of the Kerfoot family and is located on the Wisconsin River near Kilbourn.

Dayton *Green County*

Dr. Kirkpatrick and his family came from the vicinity of Dayton, Ohio, in 1852, and named the settlement after his native town.

Deaddog Hole *Dane County*

Known as such by local sportsmen, tradition has it that a dead dog was found in 1898 floating over this particularly deep spot on the Wisconsin River.

Dead Man's Curve *Grant County*

A bend in the road named by the railroad and others because of the many deaths that occurred there.

Dead Man's Spring *Sauk County*

James Babb named the spring in 1846 after a man died near it. The man who died here was a surveyor. His name has been forgotten.

Dean Park *Douglas County*

Denis and Peter Dean were among the first settlers in Superior in the 1850s. Peter bequeathed this land to the city for a park. Denis Dean was the first postmaster of Superior.

Deansville *Dane County*

Founded by Richard Dean in 1860 when the railroad went through.

Death Point *Crawford County*

A number of auto wrecks and a plane crash in the area gave this name to this location in Clayton Township.

Decatur *Green County*

A post office was established here in the winter of 1841–42 with John Moore as postmaster. He named it in honor of Commodore Decatur, and the township took that name also.

Deckers *Ozaukee County*

The Decker family owned property and were early settlers here.

Decorah Peak *Trempealeau County*

Named after One-Eyed Decorah, a Ho-Chunk chief who, according to tradition, took refuge in a cave near here after being wounded in an Ojibwe attack on his village.

Deerbrook *Langlade County*

Probably named for a tributary of the Eau Claire River where many deer were seen drinking. An earlier name on old maps is said to have been Dexter.

Deerfield *Dane County*

Alek Nelson was the original owner of most of the land here. He was instrumental in bringing the railroad and built some of the first business places. The people wanted to name the village Nelson, but he refused. There was quite a large lake nearby where many deer roamed, and it is believed the name was chosen because of them. Most of the people were of Norwegian descent.

Deer Park *Saint Croix County*

Otto Neitge, known as the Dutch Hunter, came in 1853 and built his cabin on a knoll. He was attracted by the abundance of game, especially deer. Just below his cabin was a pond or watering place, and in 1858 Otto built a nine-foot fence to enclose 160 acres around the pond by setting oak posts side by side in a three-foot trench. Along the outside of the fence were several places where deer could jump into the stockade but could not jump out. Old-timers say there were as many as four hundred deer in the enclosure at one time. There was enough water and pasture to allow the deer to live well. The Dutch Hunter marketed the venison in St. Paul and Ft. Snelling, Minnesota.

In 1874 the North Wisconsin Railroad built its line right through the deer park, and Otto Neitge abandoned his park.

DeForest

Dane County

Isaac DeForest was born in 1819 in Albany, New York, of Belgian parents. He came to the township of Windsor in 1854 and purchased land where the village of DeForest now stands. This land had been bought from the government by James Stephenson in 1845, at $1.25 an acre. Deforest paid $25 an acre, platted one-acre lots, and sold them for $100 each. He farmed about 2,200 acres. In 1860 he harvested 25,000 bushels of wheat with eight reaping machines and sixty men. After the Civil War the price of wheat declined from $2.00 per bushel to almost nothing. DeForest sold his land in 1868 and moved to Kansas. Mr. DeForest was the first postmaster at Token Creek in the township of Windsor in 1865.

De Haas Lake

Fond du Lac County

Dr. Carl De Haas made his home here after he immigrated to the United States in 1847. After he arrived in America he wrote letters to his homeland that were later published under the title Winke fur Auswanderer (Hints for Emigrants).

Dekorra

Columbia County

Named for the Ho-Chunk Dekorra family that claimed as their ancestor the French fur trader DeKauray.

Delafield

Waukesha County

The town was first known as Nehamabin or Nemahbin—probably an Indian name given to the lake before the town was established. Early settlers also called it Hayopolis, possibly because of the abundance of native grasses. Some think this term may have come from the Greek word heliopolis, meaning "city of the sun."

The name finally chosen honored Charles Delafield, who came from New York in 1843 to start a mulberry grove here. It was Nelson P. Hawks, proprietor of the Delafield House, once known as Hawks Inn, who proposed his friend's name for the new post office. Mr. Hawks was known as a great joker and storyteller and became the first postmaster. Mrs. Hawks made the tallow candles that were used by the first legislature in Madison. She dipped them in hot deer's tallow and coon's oil and suspended them across a pair of quilting frames to harden.

De-La-Mater Hollow

Crawford County

De-La-Mater is a family name. The hollow runs from 131 to High Ridge near Clayton Township.

Delavan   *Walworth County*

Henry and Samuel Phoenix, founders of Delavan, were in sympathy with the temperance movement of the 1830s, and when they platted the town, they insisted that there be total abstinence in the town. They named it after Edward Cornelius Delavan, a rich man of Albany, New York, and a prominent temperance leader in this country until 1870. To the best of anyone's knowledge, Mr. Delavan never visited the city.

Delavan Lake   *Walworth County*

The Ho-Chunk Indians are said to have called it Kay-chunk-er-rah, meaning "turtle." The Potawatomi Indians were still here when the first settlers came in 1836. They called it Wau-ba-shaw-bess, meaning "swan lake."

Delavan's Circus Colony   *Walworth County*

Edmund and Jeremiah Mabie stopped over in Delavan in 1847 to hunt prairie chicken near Delavan Lake. They liked the area so well that they established the winter quarters for their circus here. At the time, it was the largest and most profitable circus in existence. The idea for forming the P. T. Barnum Circus was developed here in 1871 by W. C. Coup, who was the first man to put a circus on rails and to use a second and third ring.

Dell Creek   *Sauk County*

Named after a stream that had a number of cliffs along its bank. The name appears as early as 1845 on government plats.

Dells   *Eau Claire County*

So named for the steep rocky banks along the creek here. The first mill was built in 1861 to grind wheat, buckwheat, and feed grains.

The Dells   *Wisconsin River—Adams, Columbia, Juneau, and Sauk Counties*

The French word is dalles, meaning "the narrows of a river" or "between the cliffs," and Dells is an adaptation. The Ho-Chunk name was Nee-hah-kecoo-na-herah, meaning "the place where the rocks strike together."

Dellwood   *Adams County*

In 1912 when the first railroad came through Adams County, this was named Arkdale Station, as there was another settlement known as Arkdale about five miles north. Later the name was changed to Holmsville after the Holm family, who were pioneers of the area. In 1925 the Badger State Development Company of Chicago bought a tract of land along the Wisconsin River south of the settlement and divided it into lots that were sold to a number of families and called the Dellwood Subdivision. About a year later Holmsville was officially changed to Dellwood.

Delta   *Bayfield County*

The township was named by the Duluth South Shore and Atlantic Railway, which went through here in 1890. It is a meeting place (or delta) of the south fork, west fork, and main fork of the White River, famous as a trout stream.

Delta   *Grant County*

A settlement formerly called Buhl and now named after the delta in the river.

Delton   *Sauk County*

Edward Norris, who platted the town, called it Norris. When the post office was established it was called Loretta, the first name of Mrs. Norris. Afterward the name was
changed to Delton, a contraction of Dell Town.

Denmark   *Brown County*

Many of the early settlers came from Denmark. In 1876, D. Benecke operated a cheese
factory that was known as New Denmark.

Denniston House   *Grant County*

Daniels, Denniston, and Company of New York offered to give this building to the state
without charge if Cassville was chosen as state capital. It wasn't. Nelson Dewey later
acquired the house as part of his vast properties, and he opened it as "Denniston House"
in 1854. It has been run as a hotel since that time.

Denoon Road   *Racine County*

This road on the north boundary of Norway Township and Denoon Lake in Waukesha
County is all that remains of one man's dream. James Denoon Reymert planned and plot-
ted a village, but it was never built. Reymert published the first Norwegian newspaper in
the United States, the Nordlyset.

Denzer   *Sauk County*

Discontinued post office in Honey Creek Township, named after William Denzer.

De Pere   *Brown County*

In 1634 Jean Nicolet, the first European known to set foot in Wisconsin, portaged around
the rapids in the Fox River just south of the present city of De Pere. In 1671 Father Claude
Allouez, Jesuit missionary, came at the invitation of the Potawatomi Indians and erected
the first chapel in Wisconsin at the foot of George Street. He named the site Rapides des
Pères—"Rapids of the Fathers." The chapel was destroyed during the Fox Wars and never
rebuilt, but a memorial tablet has been erected.

Father Marquette and Louis Joliet spent the winter of 1673 in De Pere. From 1685
to 1763 the St. Francis Xavier mission and trading post in the little settlement was the
headquarters of the Northwest Territory of New France. The village of De Pere, comprising the present first and second wards, was incorporated in 1857, and in 1870 West De
Pere was a separate village comprising the present third and fourth wards. The two were
consolidated in 1890.

DeQuases   *Taylor County*

Named for a family known as DeQuases or DeQuassie, who lived in the town of McKinley.

Deronda   *Polk County*

Abe and Charlie Sylvester had come from Green County to settle here about 1867. In 1886, when the railroad was built, a meeting was called to select a name in Sylvester's small crossroads store. Most of the voters wanted Sylvester, but there was already a post office by that name in Green County. Lucina Sylvester, a daughter of Abe, was reading the book Daniel Deronda by George Eliot. At her suggestion they called their post office Deronda.

Des Moines   *Burnett County*

This settlement was known as Sucker Lake until summer residents from Iowa had it changed.

DeSoto   *Crawford and Vernon Counties*

This site on the Mississippi was a French trading post for about twenty years. It was known as Winneshiek's Landing after a Ho-Chunk Indian chief who came regularly to trade his furs. The first settlers were several French families named Godfrey. The settlers did not like the Indian name. They selected Formora or Formosa, but it seemed too lackadaisical. Finally they chose DeSoto, after the Spaniard who had discovered the Mississippi River. The village was platted in 1854.

The Devil's Chimney   *Dane County*

This sandstone pillar near Primrose stands fifty feet high and is apart from the rocks about it. Other nearby formations have been identified as "the Devil's Washbasin" and "the Devil's Bootjack."

Devils Lake   *Sauk County*

One tribe of Indians is said to have called the lake Minnewaukan, or "evil spirit lake." The Ho-Chunk called it Ta-wak-cun-chuk-dah, or "sacred lake," because the water was to them the abode of water demons. Peter Folsom, an early explorer and surveyor, is said to have named the lake in 1842 because it was set in a deep hollow that resembled the crater of a volcano. The first station was called Kirkland, after Noble C. Kirk. When the Cliff House was established it had a post office known as Devils Lake, and the railroad called the Kirkland station Devils Lake. This became confusing to the Post Office Department and the railroad company. When the Cliff House was discontinued it was decided to change the name officially to Devils Lake.

Devil's Pond   *Fond du Lac County*

It was once thought to be a bottomless pond in which a farmer's wagon and team of horses disappeared.

Dewey   *Douglas County*

This railroad station and post office was named after Commodore George Dewey, hero of Manila Bay.

Dewey's Corners   *Trempealeau County*

The name applied to Old Arcadia, from the family of that name prominently identified with its early history.

Dexterville   *Wood County*

According to tradition, George Hiles named Dexterville after Dexter, his balky white mule. It is worth noting, however, that the Farmington, Michigan, birthplace of Hiles was only about thirty miles from Dexter, Michigan.

Diamond Bluff   *St. Croix County*

Named by a Vendean loyalist of the army of Jacques Cathelineau, who fled from France to Quebec in 1793. He proceeded westward and arrived on the Mississippi River near the present city of Diamond Bluff in 1800 and called it Monte Diamond. He lived there until 1824, and the neighborhood was known among the Indians for many years as "Old White Man's Prairie."

Diamond Hill   *Trempealeau County*

The name was inspired by a legend of unrequited love involving Lucy, the Irish schoolteacher at the Little Lone Star country school, and Sam Heggen.

Dickeyville   *Grant County*

The settlement, started about 1849, was named after Mr. Dickey, an early settler. It was called Dickeysville, and later Dickeyville.

Dieter Hollow   *Richland County*

Named for Christopher Dieter (Deilder) and his son Louis (Lewis), who came to America from Germany in 1846 and to the town of Akan in 1859.

Dillman   *Milwaukee County*

Named for a nearby farmer.

Dixon Ridge   *Crawford County*

Named for the Dixon family. It runs from Lynxville to Highway 27 south of Seneca.

Dobie   *Douglas County*

A post office and station on the South Shore Railroad that was named for David Dobie, a prominent lumberman.

Dodge   *Trempealeau County*

The township was named after William E. Dodge, a financier and philanthropist from New York. He was associated with the construction of the Green Bay and Western Railroad.

Dodge County

Named in honor of General Henry Dodge, governor of the Wisconsin Territory.

Dodgeville   *Iowa County*

On October 3, 1827, Henry Dodge, Jesse Shull (the founder of Shullsburg), John Ray, and James M. Strode arrived here. Mr. Dodge came with his wife and children and four slaves. He staked out an extensive mining claim that covered what is now the business section of Dodgeville. The next year, dissatisfied because of the way the government treated the miners, he moved to the grove that now bears his name. He purchased a thousand acres of land and built a large residence, a smelting furnace, and a stockade that was called Fort Union. The town was first called Minersville. Henry Dodge became the first governor of the Wisconsin Territory in 1836.

Dog Hollow   *Richland County*

This hollow, near Ithaca, is named for a valley in Big Willow that got its name from the menacing dogs in the valley in early sheep-raising days.

Dogtown   *Dane County*

A local dweller is said to have kept numerous dogs at this corner in Fitchburg that were an annoyance to passing travelers. The name may also suggest insignificance—as would the expression "one-horse town."

Donersville   *Burnett County*

The first post office in the Trade Lake area was located in the home of the postmaster, Samuel Doner, who lived between Little and Big Trade Lakes. Donersville was established in 1870, in the same year the name was changed to Trade Lake.

Dongola   *Burnett County*

This town and post office in the Sand Lake area was active between 1899 and 1912. The name chosen by the first postmaster, Hiram Ingalls, was Gondola, but his choice was misspelled Dongola, and the name remained. Another story states that the name was chosen after Dongola kid, a kind of leather that was popular at that time.

Dooney   *Trempealeau County*

This railroad stop was once known as Dooney's Siding after James B. Dooney, general agent of the Green Bay Railroad. It consisted of a wood yard, a stockyard, and a railroad platform and switch.

Door County

The Menominee name was Kenatao, meaning "cape." It is said that a party of Indians were crossing between Washington Island and the mainland when they were overcome by the swift current and drowned. The channel was then called Death's Door, and when the county was organized in 1851 it was called Door. The French voyageur term was La Porte des Morts, meaning "door of the dead."

Doran   *Burnett County*

The name is thought to be of Swedish origin, though "it smacks strongly of the Emerald Isle."

Dorn's Spring　　　　　　　　　　　　　　　　　　　　*Dane County*

This spring in Westport is named for P. J. Dorn and his descendants, who, since before 1873, have owned the land on which it rises.

Dorwin's Mill　　　　　　　　　　　　　　　　　　　　*Pepin County*

This scenic place is located about five miles east of Durand. The owner, a Mr. Dorwin, built a drainage tunnel through the sand rock because many farmers complained of their land being flooded.

Dotyville　　　　　　　　　　　　　　　　　　　　*Fond du Lac County*

Named for James Duane Doty, the territorial governor.

Douglas County

For Stephen A. Douglas, US Senator from Illinois and Democratic candidate for the presidency in 1860. He is said to have been interested in the original company to promote a city at the head of Lake Superior.

Douglass Corners　　　　　　　　　　　　　　　　　　　　*Walworth County*

Former name of the village of Walworth, named after Christopher Douglass.

Dousman　　　　　　　　　　　　　　　　　　　　*Waukesha County*

Talbot C. Dousman was born in Mackinaw, Michigan, in 1816 and moved to Milwaukee in 1836, where he boarded with Solomon Juneau while he built a warehouse and started his lumber business. Later he moved to Mukwonago township, where he erected a log cabin and farm buildings. When the Chicago and North Western Railway was built in 1881 there was much rivalry between Mr. Dousman and a Mr. Hardell as to where the station should be located. The railroad company compromised by putting the station between the two locations. The land was very marshy, and the station was referred to as Bull Frog Station. Later the name of Dousman was transferred from a post office across the town line. Talbot Dousman was a brother of Hercules Dousman of Prairie du Chien fame. One account says that the town was named after Colonel John Dousman, an early and influential citizen of Wisconsin.

Dover　　　　　　　　　　　　　　　　　　　　*Dane County*

West of Mazomanie near Highway 14 is the site of old Dover. In 1844 nearly seven hundred settlers were brought by the British Emigration and Temperance Society. When the railroad chose Mazomanie as its station, settlers moved their houses there. In 1850 Dover was booming.

Dover　　　　　　　　　　　　　　　　　　　　*Racine County*

Captain John T. Trowbridge was the first settler here in 1836 and the first postmaster of Dover. He originally named the town Brighton, after Brighton, England, his previous place of residence. When towns were reorganized in 1850 the name was changed to Dover, another English name, probably to avoid confusion with Brighton in Kenosha County.

Downing   *Dunn County*

James Downing bought a farm in the St. Paul area with his friend William James Doughty, who had been a cookee in a logging camp and also a cook on a passenger steamer from St. Louis to St. Paul. Both of the men married, and Downing entered the Civil War. When he returned the two friends worked for Knapp, Stout and Company in what is now Dunn County. In 1867 they bought eighty acres of railroad land for six dollars an acre and brought their families there to live. They logged the timber, floating the logs down Tiffany Creek and Hay River into Red Cedar River. When the Wisconsin Central Railway was built in 1884, the settlement became officially known as Downing.

Downsville   *Dunn County*

Located eight miles south of Menomonie on Highway 25, it was named after Captain Burrage E. Downs, who built a dam across the Red Cedar River at this point and operated a sawmill here. Downsville is in "Caddie Woodlawn" country and is close to some well-known sandstone quarries. The Dunn County Historical Society operates a lumber museum, "Empire in Pine," at Downsville.

Doylestown   *Columbia County*

The first settlers were Orin Kincaid and Daniel James in 1848. The next year Damon C. Starr and Eason Starr purchased land where the village now stands. The town was named Otsego because the settlers had come from Otsego, New York. Orin Kincaid was the first town chairman. In 1865 Lemuel H. Doyle purchased 120 acres from Damon Starr and 115 acres from Eason Starr. He platted a village and named it Doylestown, although there were only four families living there. For the next five years the town did not grow, so Mr. Doyle offered a free lot to anyone who would erect a building on it This brought on the Doylestown boom, during which some thirty homes were built in a single year. Lemuel H. Doyle was known as a man of fine character, great energy, and solid perseverance. During the 1880s he established newspapers in many different localities. The Badger Blade of Rio and the Wyocena Advocate survive him, but the Portage Advertiser, the Rio Reporter, and the New Era at Fall River were short-lived.

Drammen   *Eau Claire County*

Called Lent when settled in the 1870s. Early settlers who came from Drammen, Norway, changed the name when it became a town in 1877.

Drammen Valley   *Dane County*

Many of the early settlers came to Perry from Drammen, Norway.

Dresser   *Polk County*

When the Soo Line Railroad was built through this area in 1885, Samuel Dresser, a landowner, donated some land to the company. The railroad station was a junction point and was named Dresser Junction. In 1940 the village board shortened the name to Dresser.

Drummond   *Bayfield County*

Frank H. Drummond brought a crew of men here in 1882 to cut timber. The first lumber camp was built about where the railroad depot now stands. The story is that some member of the crew, probably a shanty boss, wrote the name Drummond on a piece of board in large letters and nailed it over a root house door.

Dry Hollow *Crawford County*

From Bell Center to Bell Center Ridge, it is a dry run.

Drywood *Chippewa County*

Two creeks, Big Drywood and Little Drywood, rise near here. An early farmer's map shows the land covered with windfalls, possibly timber destroyed by a tornado or high winds prior to 1866.

Du Bay Lake *Marathon County*

The lake was the site of a trading post operated by John B. Du Bay, the son of an Indian trader.

Du Bay Trading Post *Portage County*

Lake Du Bay, created in 1942, covers the original site of the trading post established in 1834 by John Baptiste Du Bay.

Du Charme Ridge *Crawford County*

Located near Eastman Township. Named for the numerous Du Charme families that lived in the area.

Duck Creek *Brown County*

Early trappers named the creek for the great number of ducks that nested on its banks every spring. Or they may have gotten the name from the Menominee, who called it Sesi-puke-tahe-kone, meaning "ducks landing from flight." The place is said to be famous in Menominee folklore.

Dudley *Lincoln County*

A lumber company operating here asked that the settlement be named after Henry Dudley, one of its employees.

Duffy Creek *Crawford County*

East of Seneca, it was named for the Duffy family.

Duha Ridge *Crawford County*

Near Eastman Township, it is named after the Duha family.

Dull Ridge *Crawford County*

Near Clayton Township, Dull Ridge was named after the Dull family.

Dunbar *Marinette County*

This township had a population of about two thousand when the logging camp and lumber mill were operating during the 1880s. The cook at the logging camp was named Dunbar. It is said that the trains dropped off supplies for all the various logging camps at this stop, where Mr. Dunbar took charge of them. When the train was coming near his camp, the crew would say, "What's for Dunbar today?"

Dundas   *Calumet County*

The railroad tracks were laid, and men were building the station when they noticed some bear tracks around the buildings. They decided to call it Bearfoot Station. Later it was changed to Montford, but there was another Montford in Wisconsin. So the name was changed again in memory of a railroad engineer on the Chicago and North Western Railway named John Dundas.

Dundee   *Fond du Lac County*

The settlement was platted in 1864 and named for the local post office. Local Scots suggested the name, which was after the city in Scotland.

Dundee Kame   *Fond du Lac County*

This cone-shaped mound of glacial debris is in the vicinity of the little village of Dundee.

Dunn   *Dane County*

Named by an error for Door, or possibly Dover, which were early names for this location. The name was so poorly written when it was submitted to the engrossing clerk of the assembly that he mistook it and recorded "Dunn."

Dunn County

In honor of Charles Dunn, first chief justice of the Wisconsin territory.

Dunnville   *Dunn County*

From the Wisconsin State Journal, January 6, 1963:

> *The west is not the only place where ghost towns dot the countryside. Wisconsin also has abandoned frontier towns.*

Dunnville, once the county seat of Dunn County and a prosperous lumbering center, now is a weed-covered patch of land. The encroaching forest almost hides the few crumbling ruins twelve miles out of Menomonie, on County Trunk H. It is still on the state highway maps, but there is no population figure for Dunnville.

Dunnville was founded in 1840 by a man known as Lamb, a veteran, probably of the War of 1812. He chose the site because of its location at the junction of the Red Cedar and Chippewa Rivers. Lamb built an inn for lumbermen who came down the Red Cedar River on log drives. Soon often, a lumber mill was built by the Knapp, Stout Company.

The community was named after Charles Dunn, then a state senator and formerly chief justice of the Wisconsin Territory. When Dunnville became the Dunn county seat in 1854, there were warehouses and log cabins, trading posts and a wooden courthouse.

The county seat gained an unsavory reputation because of the rough class of transient lumbermen, fur trappers, and hunters. Gamblers and gunmen also were among the town's residents. There was at least one murder in Lamb's Inn, after he sold it to his brother-in-law, Arthur McCann. A mill hand got into an argument in a card game and

McCann threw a heavy scale weight at him. The mill hand fatally wounded McCann, then escaped into the dense woods to freedom.

After the murder, life in the rowdy village went on as before, with dreams of future greatness. Then, in 1858, the courthouse burned to the ground. Dunnville was county seat of an area including the present Chippewa and Pepin Counties. When Dunn County was cut down to its present size, also in 1858, a more central location was desired. Without a vote, the seat was summarily moved to Menomonie.

Before that, there was chaos in Dunnville as the board of supervisors argued over building a new courthouse or moving the county seat. After the county board moved to Menomonie, Dunnville reverted back to its wilderness state.

A sign near seldom-used railroad tracks still proclaims Dunnville. The tracks appropriately lead into the backwaters of the Chippewa River.

Dunrovan
Dane County

The name is a pun on "done rovin,'" which the present owner says he is. It was formerly called Montjoy.

Durand
Pepin County

The first settlement was located at the mouth of Bear Creek, two miles north of the present city, and was called Chippewa. The snow was four feet deep in the winter of 1856–57, and in the spring the Chippewa was flooded so badly that the buildings and post office were moved to what is now Durand.

Miles Durand Prindle had journeyed up the Chippewa River in a keelboat and obtained government land on the site of the present city in the summer of 1856. He was not the first arrival—Alexander Babatz had been living in a claim shanty in the neighborhood for several years, and Charles Billings had a small cabin on the bank of the river that he used for shelter when he came upriver. Prindle and Billings platted a town and cut off timber so buildings could be erected. The town was named Durand when the plat was surveyed in 1856.

Durst Hollow
Richland County

The land, in Ithaca Township, was purchased by Gerhardt A. Durst in 1876 and has remained in the family for more than seventy-five years.

Durward's Glen
Sauk County

Bernard Isaac Durward of Scotland, an artist and a poet, found this secluded place in 1861. He bought forty acres and built a house, a studio, and a chapel of native stone. In his studio, built in 1887, are paintings by Bernard and his son Charles, as well as some of the family possessions.

Dutch Gap
Fond du Lac County

Dutch Gap is a watercourse in the city of Fond du Lac. In the city's early history Martin Road was plagued with flood problems each spring. This ditch was dug to alleviate the problem. Since the section of the city that benefited from the ditch was occupied by Germans, it came to be known as Dutch Gap.

Dutch Ridge   *Crawford County*

First known as German Ridge, the name was later changed to Deutsch Ridge, which later became Dutch Ridge.

Dutch Settlement   *Sheboygan County*

The origin of the early settlers is reflected in many of the names of places and families in this vicinity.

Duvall   *Kewaunee County*

An abandoned post office in the township of Red River named for Joseph Duvall, a merchant, banker, and elevator owner who had made a fortune in lumbering.

Dyckesville   *Brown County*

Named for Louis Van Dycke, who was an early settler and founded the village. He operated a general store for many years.

Dyckesville   *Kewaunee County*

Named for the Van Dycke family, who eventually moved to Green Bay and started a brewery. This appears to be the same family that stemmed from Louis Van Dycke.

Dye's Settlement   *Sheboygan County*

"Deacon" A. O. Dye and his family moved from the present site of Sheboygan to settle in the town of Lima in 1838. Other families bound to them by ties of kinship, common nationality, and similar social and religious views settled nearby, and the neighborhood became known as Dye's settlement. A post office, called Mentor, was established in 1849, but the place never attained the status of a village.

A postcard image of Ephraim, ca. 1907

⇥ E ⇤

Eagle   *Richland County*

Even before the eagle became the national bird, this was a popular place name in the county. Eagle Township was probably so named because eagles were fairly numerous in Wisconsin at the time.

Eagle   *Sauk County*

One of the original towns in the county, it was probably named for the national emblem.

Eagle   *Waukesha County*

A group of prospectors or surveyors who were crossing a section of prairie in 1836 saw a large bald eagle rise up. These men were Mr. Thomas Sugden, John Coats, and a Mr. Carton. They named the area Eagle Prairie, and when a settlement was started it was called Eagleville. Later it was called Pittman after the man who recorded the plat. When the railroad was built in 1850, the village was called Eagle Center.

Eagle Heights   *Dane County*

This section of land northwest of the university campus at Madison is the highest elevation on the south shore of Lake Mendota and a significant spot in Ho-Chunk history. The Indians called it Sho-he-taka, meaning "horse hill." They went there frequently to fast and gain inspiration from the horse spirit that was thought to live there.

Eagle Point   *Chippewa County*

The name of a weigh station on the railroad assumed by the township in 1855. There were many eagles around the area in early times.

Eagle Point   *Crawford County*

Early settlers saw eagles in the area when they arrived here. The point is located at the confluence of the Kickapoo River and Plum Creek.

Eagle River   *Vilas County*

The Indian word for the lake and river was mi-gis-iwis-ibi, meaning "eagle," because so many of these birds nested in the area. When the Milwaukee, Lakeshore, and Western Railway platted the village in 1885, it was given the name of the river.

Eagleton   *Chippewa County*

A settlement established in 1876 in the township of Eagle Point.

Earl   *Washburn County*

In 1880 when the Chicago, St. Paul, Minneapolis, and Omaha Railroad was extended to Ashland, one of the subcontractors was named Earle. He built a trestle across a creek and marsh at Veazie. When a passing track was put in, he placed a signboard near it bearing his name. Later a little depot was built and a village established. The name on the signboard was adopted for the post office, dropping the final "e."

East Ellsworth   *Pierce County*
Anthony Huddleson built the first log home here in 1855. He lived in the town all his life and died at the age of 101. The town was named in honor of Colonel E. E. Ellsworth of Civil War fame.

When the Omaha Railway built an extension from River Falls to the county seat at Ellsworth, it was located about a mile east of the courthouse because this area was in a valley, and there was no way of getting track up the West Ellsworth Hill. A depot was built in the woods, and then a grain elevator, a saloon, and other buildings were added. A separate post office of East Ellsworth was established, while the area around the courthouse became the town of Ellsworth.

Eastman   *Crawford County*
The original name was Batavia, but another village had adopted this title. It was changed by popular consent to Eastman, the name of several residents.

East Pepin   *Pepin County*
A post office and a few buildings in the township of Albany took this name because they were located in the far eastern part of the county.

East Troy   *Walworth County*
So named by the first settlers from Troy, New York. The first claim was on the banks of Honey Creek near the present site of the East Troy mill, where a Mr. Roberts pitched his tent. Asa Blood came to join him and to build the first house.

In 1836 this settlement was one township known as Troy, but seven years later it was separated into Troy and East Troy townships.

East Troy Railroad   *Walworth County*
Running between East Troy and Milwaukee from 1907 until 1939, the East Troy Railroad is the last vestige of Wisconsin's once broad network of electric interurban railways.

East Wisconsin City   *Rock County*
Dr. James Heath kept a country store and a tavern here, "with entertainment for man and beast." His home, store, tavern, and office, on the east bank of the Rock River and opposite Wisconsin City, made up the entire city.

Eaton   *Brown County*
Named for an early settler.

Eaton   *Manitowoc County*
Named after Chauncey Eaton, who came from Illinois in the year 1839 and engaged in the lumbering business. It is said that he never lived in this township, but lived across the line in the town of Liberty.

Eau Claire and Eau Claire County
Named after the river, which was called Wah-yaw-con-ut-ta-gua-yaw-Sebe by the Ojibwe Indians, meaning "the water of the river is clear." The Chippewa River was coffee-colored, and Indian and French voyagers traveling downriver noticed the water become clear when this new river joined it. French explorers of the seventeenth century translated the Indian term to Eau Claire.

The settlement was originally in Chippewa County, which was divided in 1855 into three counties. The southernmost was known as Clear Water. Eau Claire had never appeared in the official records until R. F. Wilson and W. H. Gleason platted the village, and for a while it was called both Clearwater and Eau Claire. In 1856, when a county was formed, both the town and county were established as Eau Claire. A large percentage of the population at that time were French people who had come from Canada.

Eau Galle *Dunn County*
Probably named by the French voyageurs, as the name is French, meaning "gravel bank."

Eau Pleine *Marathon and Portage Counties*
French word meaning "full of water" or "plenty of water."

Ebenezer *Dane County*
This subdivision in Blue Mounds was named for Ebenezer Brigham, thought to be the first settler of Dane County.

Eblesville *Fond du Lac County*
Named for Andrew Eble.

The Eddy *Wood County*
Formerly a part of the Wisconsin River within the Wisconsin Rapids city limits, at this point the river's current flowed in an opposite direction to the main current as the river swept past a bend. This was a local swimming place.

Eden *Fond du Lac County*
Adam Holiday founded this settlement in 1845. The story is that when the settlers gathered in a log cabin among the pines and debated about a name, Holiday declared, "Since it is recorded that Adam dwelt in the Garden of Eden, I know of no better name for our town." He then commented on its beauty, richness of soil, great fertility, and abundance of fruits given by the hand of God.

The settlers unanimously agreed but shortened the name to Eden. Or perhaps it was named after John Eden, an early settler.

Edgar *Marathon County*
William Edgar of New York City was employed by the Milwaukee, Lake Shore, and Western Railway. When the town was platted by the railroad company in 1891, Edgar's name was attached to the plat. Later he became interested in other lands and owned a sawmill near Wausau.

Edgerton   *Rock County*

When the railroad was built northeast of the village of Fulton, the station was called Fulton Station. Several stores and Finney's Hotel were built, and as the community grew, citizens resented the railroad's attempt to identify their settlement with Fulton. In 1859, an informal caucus was held, and C. H. Dickinson, who had come in 1854, headed a committee that met with Benjamin Edgerton, chief surveyor for the railroad company. Since Edgerton had been influential in determining the route of the railroad, he was asked if his name could be used. He replied, "Better wait until I am dead. I might do something in the meantime to discredit the name."

Edgewater   *Sawyer County*

This settlement on the north edge of Lake Chelsea was always known as Edgewater. In 1903, when the Wisconsin Central Railroad entered the area, it was officially named by George Huss.

Edmund   *Iowa County*

Edmund Baker gave land to the railroad company in 1865 to have the station named after him. In those days the railroad was a big asset to a community. A town grew up around the station, and at one time it had a grain elevator and stockyards. Big shipments of cattle and hogs from all the surrounding area were shipped from here.

Edson   *Chippewa County*

Edson Chub, the first settler, came in 1857 and erected a sawmill in 1860 on Hay Creek. Chub Road, which was built and maintained by him, was quite a showpiece in those days of rough trails. Present-day county highway MM follows this old road almost exactly. Edson Center, an adjoining settlement, was established in 1869 but was absorbed into the town of Boyd. It is said the residents of Edson did not raise the necessary $5,000 for constructing a railroad, but Boyd was able to do it.

Edwards   *Sheboygan County*

Edward Neuhaus was the first postmaster of this pioneer hamlet.

Egg Harbor   *Door County*

Potawatomi Indians called it Che-bah-ye-sho-da-ning, meaning "ghost door." In 1825 there was a sham battle between the crews of two boats who attacked each other with eggs—all in the spirit of fun. Another account states that Mr. Increase Claflin named most of the places on this peninsula. On entering the harbor he is said to have found a nest full of duck's eggs.

Eight Corners   *Wood County*

Located in Sigel Township. Once this was the only intersection along the Centralia-Vesper road where crossroads met to form at least eight corners; all others were "T" intersections that came to a dead end at the Centralia-Vesper road. From 1878 to the present, however, the intersection has had more than eight corners. This location was an early meeting place in the county.

Ekdall   *Burnett County*

A community with a church, school, and post office was located in the township of West Marshland, north of Grantsburg, from 1891 to 1917. It has since disappeared completely. A large group of Swedish people settled here and gave the post office the name that means "oak slope" or "oak dale." Olai Johanson wanted his post office called Meadow Hill, but more people favored Ekdall because there were so many oak trees in the area.

Another story says that Norwegian settlers claimed this location, and Even Ryen named it Ekdall after a gaard in Norway.

Ekleberry Corners   *Richland County*

Located in Bloom Township. In 1879 Willis Ekleberry came from Indiana with his wife in hopes of improving her health.

Eland Junction   *Shawano County*

Named by E. H. Rummely, an officer of the Milwaukee, Lake Shore, and Western Railway Company, which platted the village in 1888. The eland is a variety of antelope discovered by David Livingston in central Africa. Rummely may have chosen this name because of the herds of wild deer in the area.

Elba   *Dodge County*

The first settlers, who came in 1843, could not agree upon a name, so a meeting was held at the farm of Mr. Thompson, but no agreement could be reached. A Mr. Robinson was delegated to meet with the Secretary of State in Madison, and the two chose this name after Saint Ailbe, an Irish bishop, since most of the settlers were Irish.

Elba   *Oconto County*

Named after the island in the Mediterranean.

Elcho   *Langlade County*

B. F. Dorr, the pioneer surveyor in this area, selected this name after a place in Scotland that is pronounced the way this name is spelled.

Elder Bowman's Bluff   *Dane County*

Elder (the Rev. Joseph) Bowman and his family owned the land from before 1861 until after 1926.

Elderon   *Marathon County*

Calvin P. Day of Waupaca, a Civil War veteran; his wife, Martha Jane; and their five children homesteaded 160 acres here in 1878. They built a house of logs and lived a lonely life as there was no one except an occasional Indian for miles around.

It was a joyful time when a traveler would stay overnight to rest. During the summer of 1880, a man drove a rig into the yard and introduced himself as a traveling minister organizing Sunday schools. Would Mrs. Day like to have one here? Would she! Oh, yes!

He stayed and organized the Sunday school. He said it was so peaceful and quiet and spoke of the beautiful elderberry blossoms growing along the banks of the small stream and the edge of the marsh. When he was preparing to leave, Mrs. Day asked, "What shall we name our new Sunday school?"

The man thought for a while and said, "I don't know. Let me have a little while to think it over and I will write you."

Sometime later Mrs. Day received his letter with a little card inscribed, "The Elderon Sunday School." The letter said, "Remembering the beauty of those elders and the peace of your place, Elderon means peace to me. Let us name your Sunday School Elderon."

Eldorado   Fond du Lac County
The town was originally platted as Eldon by the Pioneer Town Site Company in 1888, but the Post Office Department in Washington objected to that name. Eldorado was chosen by John O. Henning because he had dug for gold in Eldorado County, California.

Electric Park   Chippewa County
A station on the Chippewa Valley Electric Railway between Chippewa Falls and Eau Claire, established in 1898 by Arthur Applegard, president of the railway, and Superintendent H. G. Sawrence. It is now known as Lake Hallie Amusement Center in the township of Lake Hallie and has picnic spots, boating, and merry-go-rounds.

Elephant Trunk Rock   Richland County
In Ithaca Township. Legend tells of a man on a coal-black horse, who, each time there was a death in the community, would tie the horse to this rock and wander about the hills and valleys bringing the death angel. In another tale, a man went to this rock to admire a horse tied to it. A man suddenly appeared above on the cliff; the horse turned, kicked, and struck the stranger dead. These legends explain why the rock was earlier called "the Devil's Hitching Post." This more realistic name is given because of the resemblance of the rock to an elephant's trunk. The rock has not only a trunk, but also features that can pass for a head, eyes, and folded-back ears.

Eleva   Trempealeau County
About one hundred Sioux and Ho-Chunk Indians migrated here in 1857 and stayed for a season or two. In 1863 the first rough shanty, sixteen by eighteen feet, was built by J. D. Cooker out of tamarack logs. The next settler was D. J. Odell, who came in 1869. In 1877 the village was platted, and other settlers came. At first it was called New Chicago and then Dog Town. R. P. Goddard of Mondovi is said to have chosen Eleva after a French village.

Another account states that a grain elevator was erected beside the railroad tracks, and only the first five letters of elevator were painted on it when the men left their scaffolds for the winter season. Newcomers assumed that the uncompleted word was the town's name and used it until it became familiar and was officially adopted.

Elk Creek   Richland County
During a fierce snowstorm a herd of elk gathered together at the head of this creek near Sylvan Township. They tramped down the snow for over a mile and stayed there for some time, protecting themselves from predators.

Elk Creek   *Trempealeau County*
Named in 1842 by William B. Bunnell and William Smothers while hunting here. The valley of Elk Creek is usually called Pleasant Valley.

Elk Grove   *Lafayette County*
A beautiful and valuable growth of heavy timber extends for miles through the center of this township. In early times it had game of all descriptions, and it is said that early settlers found elk horns here.

Elk Point   *Richland County*
A story is told about a dog that was chased by an elk and was forced to jump off a high rock on the top of this hill near Forest Township.

Elkhart Lake   *Sheboygan County*
The village started as a part of the German settlement of the town of Rhine on the edge of the lake called Elkhart by nearby Indians. Popular belief is that the shape of the lake resembles the heart of an elk, but actually it is very irregular, with many nooks and bays.

According to Potawatomi legend, a young Indian maiden was scorned by her lover, Wapita, who in turn loved another chief's daughter. In despair the girl told her troubles to an old Indian woman, who said to her, "Weep not! Wapita loves the other girl now because her eyes are softer and her hair more silky than yours. But drink the heart's blood of an elk and you shall be more beautiful. Then, however, you will cease to love Wapita!"

The Indian girl went to the shore of the lake just after a mighty storm had brought down tall trees and made the spirit of the waters angry. Although lightning flashed, the air and the waters were still. Just then an elk came bounding from the woods. She shot it with an arrow and took out the heart with her hunting knife. As she drank the blood, her eyes became as dark as the dead elk's and her hair soft and silky.

When she returned and saw Wapita, his heart was filled with love, but hers was hard and cold. In vain he strove for her favor, but she laughed at him. Then despair and grief filled Wapita, and in madness he threw himself into the lake, which became his grave.

Elkhorn   *Walworth County*
In July 1836, Colonel Samuel F. Phoenix was traveling along an army trail when he came upon a stretch of prairie and sat down under a burr oak tree to rest. He looked up into the branches and saw a large elk's horns that someone had hung there. He named the prairie Elkhorn, and the village also took the name.

Elkmound   *Dunn County*
The land here rises to a lofty bluff of 1,220 feet, a lookout for the Ojibwe Indians. Settlers came in the 1860s. Occasionally they saw an elk on the top of the bluff.

Ella   *Pepin County*
First called Shoo Fly by settlers who came by water. Rail travelers called it Maxville. Ed Roundy gave it the name Ella, after his first child.

Ella Wheeler Wilcox Creek *Dane County*

Flowing into the Yahara River, this creek passes near the childhood home of Ella Wheeler Wilcox in Vienna.

Ellefson Hill *Crawford County*

Located in Freeman Township, named after the Ellefson family.

Ellison Bay *Door County*

The Indians called it Joe-Sahbe Bay. Sahbe was a son of Neatoshing, also known as Mishicott. Government surveyors recorded Ellison Bay on their map in 1865, after John Ellison, who promoted the settlement. His name was Johan Berndt Eliasen, but it was changed in this country. It is said he did not know the place had been named after him until he saw one of the maps in 1867.

Ellisville *Kewaunee County*

Deacon Ellis was an early settler and a pioneer lumberman from Montpelier, Vermont.

Ellsworth *Pierce County*

Pierce County was first visited by Europeans between 1675 and 1679. In 1680 Father Louis Hennepin, a French Catholic missionary, hunted with a party of Sioux Indians here. The French set up forts and trading posts along Lake Pepin.

In 1855 Anthony Huddleston, the first settler, claimed a section of land. Other families soon followed. The town was known as Perry.

There was a rivalry between the towns of Prescott and River Falls over the county seat. In 1861 a small majority favored moving the county seat farther east. Lines were drawn from northwest to southeast and from northeast to southwest. Where these lines crossed happened to be in the western part of the little town of Perry, located on a high ridge in dense timber. A courthouse was built, and the name was changed to honor Colonel E. E. Ellsworth.

Elmer Ephraim Ellsworth (1837–61) was famous for his Zouave company of Chicago, which toured the North giving exhibition drills. He was a friend of Abraham Lincoln and accompanied him to Washington in 1861. When the Civil War began, Ellsworth recruited a regiment from the volunteer firemen in New York City, and dressed and trained them in the Zouave manner. At Alexandria, Virginia, in May 1861, he removed a Confederate flag from the Marshall House and was shot and killed by the proprietor. His death was the first officer casualty on the Virginia front.

Elm Grove *Waukesha County*

A station on the first railroad in Wisconsin, the Milwaukee and Mississippi, built in 1852. Named for its beautiful elm trees.

The old plank road to Watertown passed through here. In 1848 James D. Doty, former governor of the Territory, became president of the group that sponsored the construction of the road. Trenches were dug eight feet apart in which white oak boards one and a half inches thick, eight inches wide, and twelve feet long were laid as stringers. The planks were oak boards three inches thick and eight feet long laid crosswise and pounded down with a heavy maul until they rested on the stringers. Nails were not used, as they might work loose and injure the hooves of horses. Planks were occasionally washed out in low places by heavy rains.

Tollgates were erected every ten miles, and half-toll gates between. No toll was collected for going to church, or from any person going to a parade or a review.

Elmhurst   *Langlade County*

One account derives the name from Elmhurst, Du Page County, Illinois. Another says that it was named for the elms in the area.

Elmo   *Grant County*

In 1854 Emanuel Whitham built a large frame house at the junction of the Galena and Platteville and Mineral Point Roads and kept a tavern called the Junction House. In 1875 the railroad company built a depot called Junction, and the next year a post office was established. The name was changed by M. Y. Johnson, after the novel St. Elmo.

Elmore Village   *Fond du Lac County*

Ulrich Legler, who built a sawmill and a gristmill here in 1857, first called it Leglerville. Ashford Post Office was located here for a while, but it was later moved to another part of the township, so the local post office was renamed Elmore. Andrew Elmore, for whom it was named, was nicknamed "The Sage of Mukwonago." He served in the state legislature and held other public offices. Elmore was also the early home of Nicholas Senn, a surgeon of international renown.

Elmwood   *Pierce County*

Name suggested by the elm trees that grew here.

Elmwood Beach   *Calumet County*

Charles and Georgia Phillips chose the name because of the trees.

Elo   *Winnebago County*

Oshkosh arranged to have a branch built to Ripon in 1872 to connect with the Milwaukee and St. Paul Railroad. The distance is twenty miles. The little hamlet that grew up around the halfway station in the center of the township of Utica was called Utica Center. The people wanted a post office and appointed Richard Styles, a storekeeper, to correspond with officials in Washington, D.C. The request was granted provided Mr. Styles selected a short name that was different from any other in the state. In a hymn book he had brought from England he found a hymn by the name of Elo, which means "face of God."

But Elo never had a train station; the train merely slowed down, and the baggage man dropped and picked up the mail from a platform.

Elroy   *Juneau County*

The town platted adjacent to the gristmill was on the side of a hill and about two city blocks square. Except for a few buildings grouped around the mill there were only scattered farmhouses. James Madison Brintnall suggested the name LeRoy because he had lived in LeRoy, New York, as a boy. Some say he chose this name from a place in Scotland. Since Mr. Brintnall's family made up almost a fourth of the population in the community, the name was accepted. But the Post Office Department rejected it because there already was a LeRoy, Wisconsin. James Brintnall's daughter, Lydia, suggested they reverse the first two letters to change it to Elroy. In 1858 an Elroy Junction was established when the railroad was built.

Elton
Langlade County

Elton Larzelere was the son of Charles H. Larzelere, one of the first settlers to come into the Upper Wolf River Valley.

Embarrass
Waupaca County

A French word was first attached to the river. It means to impede, to obstruct, or to entangle. Many of the early lumberjacks were French Canadians. When they tried to send logs down the river they found it almost impassable because of the many snags and other debris. They called it Rivière Embarrase.

An account in an old Clintonville newspaper says, "We came to this shallow, easily forded stream at mid-day on the Embarrass River. We decided to call it Embarrass because we could see its bottom."

Emerald Grove
Rock County

Named after another location, "that gem of the prairie."

Emmet
Dodge County

The first settlement in Dodge County. Named after Robert Emmet.

Emmet
Marathon County

Said to have been named after the Irish martyr.

Empire
Fond du Lac County

In 1851 this township was set apart from Taycheedah and named by Alfred T. Germond in honor of New York, the Empire State, his early home. Other settlers also came from Dutchess County, New York, including Colonel Henry Conklin and US Senator N. P. Tallmadge.

Endeavor
Marquette County

Eli A. Child, a Congregational minister, and his wife, Emma L. Child, founded an academy at a place known as Merrill's Landing, in 1891. They named it Christian Endeavor Academy after the Christian Endeavor Society. Trustees of the academy purchased a farm of 250 acres, platted the village of Endeavor on part of it, and sold lots at twenty-five dollars each to run the school. A building of the academy still stands.

Engine Creek
Richland County

Located in Henrietta Township. This appears to be a corruption of Indian Creek, which appears on a number of both old and recent maps.

Engle   *Columbia County*
A community in the northeast corner of Randolph township was known as Inglehart after an early family of that name. When the Chicago and North Western Railway built a line through the area in the early 1900s, they chose a different location for the whistle-stop and named it Engle to distinguish it from the other settlement.

English Ridge   *Richland County*
Located near Marshall Township. In the early 1850s James Brighton, Richard and William Minett, and Joseph Moon came to this ridge from England.

English Settlement   *Racine County*
English Settlement is a rural community in western Racine County; it is not a governmental unit and has no formal boundary lines. Part of the settlement is in Rochester, but most of it is located in Dover. Emigrants from England settled here in 1842. A one-room schoolhouse was built in 1845, and a church was built in 1846. The English Settlement Church still serves the people of the community.

Ephraim   *Door County*
The first twenty-six settlers came by water from Tank Colony in Fort Howard of Green Bay to make a beachhead near the hills of northern Door County. They arrived in May 1853, under the leadership of Pastor Iverson of the Church of the Brotherhood or the Moravian Church. They chose the name Ephraim, meaning "doubly fruitful," from the Bible.

Erdman   *Sheboygan County*
William A. Erdman operated a tavern on the Sheboygan-Calumet Plank Road and became the first postmaster.

Erickson   *Pepin County*
A post office named after the first settlers.

Erin   *St. Croix and Washington Counties*
Many Irish settled here.

Estella   *Chippewa County*
First settled in 1873. Warren Flint, who housed the post office in his store from 1880 to 1895, named it after his wife.

Esther Beach   *Dane County*
Named for Esther, the daughter of Charles Askew, an owner of a summer resort on Lake Monona. Given some time between 1904 and 1911, the name is widely remembered but has been superseded by "Hollywood at the Beach."

Ettrick *Trempealeau County*

John Cance (or Chance) came from Glasgow, Scotland, in 1855 and became the first postmaster. He chose a name from Marmion by Sir Walter Scott. Ettrick Forest was a mountainous region of Scotland.

The first store was erected in 1870 by Iver Pederson—a three-story building with a saloon in the basement, general merchandise on the street level, and a church on the top floor. He also built a flour mill, organized the creamery and woolen mill, promoted the Ettrick State Bank, and donated the ground for the Living Hope Lutheran Church.

Eureka *Polk County*

Elias Hoover chose as a name the Greek word meaning "I have found it." The first town meeting here was held in 1874, and by 1877 the population was up to four hundred.

Eureka *Winnebago County*

Israel G. Trow purchased this site in 1846, but through an error in the Green Bay Land Office it was assigned to J. R. Hall. Mr. Hall encountered financial difficulties, and the land was sold to Walton C. Dickerson, a brother-in-law of Mr. Trow. Mr. Dickerson said it was just the site he had been looking for. There was a beautiful view of the river, spring water available, and hard dry ground for building sites. He named it Eureka from the Greek, meaning "I have found it."

Euren *Kewaunee County*

A trading center established by the Bottkoll Brothers, who operated a sawmill, elevator, general store, and cheese factory. They had come from Euren, in Bavaria, Germany.

Evansville *Rock County*

First called the Grove because of the beautiful trees on the west and north. After 1845 the name was changed to honor Doctor Calvin (or J. M.) Evans, a much-loved physician.

Evergreen *Washburn County*

Named for the abundant forests and pastures.

Evergreen Valley *Calumet County*

Early pioneers here were noted for their progressive and frugal way of life. They loved farming and the soil. Crops grew well for them, so the area came to be known as Evergreen Valley.

Ewers Hollow *Richland County*

John and William Ewers came from Ohio in 1855. In the 1970s the Ewers family operated a mill in this part of Marshall.

E-Woo-Sanau *Dane County*

A Ho-Chunk word for the spring at the base of Maple Bluff, Madison, meaning "he thirsts."

Excelsior *Richland County*

When the first building was erected in this area, one of the men who was a part owner instructed the workmen to paint "Excelsior" on it. Several years later at the dedication of the post office the speaker of the day said, "Excelsior means excellence."

Exeland *Sawyer County*

The Arpin Lumber Company owned timberland in Weirgor township and built a railroad from the logging town of Atlanta in Rusk County to their own logging operations. At the same time the Wisconsin Central Railroad was building its line from Chicago to Duluth. A race between the two companies developed to complete a line to the stands of white pine and hemlock that were so plentiful in the Weirgor area. The Arpin Company won. The crossing of the two tracks, or X, prompted the name for the village that sprang up here.

Exeter *Green County*

The first settlement in Green County established in 1827 was named after Exeter in England.

⇥ F ⇤

Fairchild   *Eau Claire County*

Established in 1850 as part of Bridge Creek Township, it became an early logging center. In 1870, when the West Wisconsin Railroad was built, the village was named by Garry Graves in honor of Lucius Fairchild, the tenth governor of the state, who held office from 1866 to 1872.

Fairfield   *Sauk County*

The town was first named Flora by Timothy Adams after an old sweetheart. The residents did not like the name, and a petition was circulated by John Crawford to change it. A number of towns and counties in New England were called Fairfield from the beauty of their fields.

Fairfield   *Walworth County*

It was first known as Maxsonville, after its first settlers, Joseph Maxson and his son Austin. Joseph operated the first post office and lived in a log house. Soon after the post office was established, for an unknown reason, the name of the settlement was changed to Fairfield. This little settlement is located at the intersection of County Trunk C and County Line Road.

Fair Play   *Grant County*

First settled in 1833 and known as Hard Town because of the rough miners who came here to prospect. In 1841 a rich lead mine was discovered by some honest landholders. Claim jumpers laid plans to take the claim over, but the lawful owners banded together to protect their find. Bloodshed seemed inevitable. Someone called for a parley, and one member of the party said, "Let us have Fair Play and render unto Caesar the things that are Caesar's." The result was a favorable decision for the rightful owners. The mine became known as Fair Play and the village adopted the same name.

Fairview   *Burnett County*

The name tells it all.

Fairview   *Crawford County*

Located in Utica Township. One can see for miles in every direction from this location.

Fairwater   *Fond du Lac County*

The village was located on a favorable spot on the Grand River where a flour mill was built by a Mr. Dakin and a Mr. Lathrop. For ten years it was the commercial center of a large tract of rapidly developing country, but in 1856 the railroad left it out in the cold. Apparently its good location on the river prompted the name.

Fairy Chasm *Milwaukee County*

The two daughters of Jacques Donges, Elsie and Irma, were called his fairies when they played in the chasms and ravines of this area, which had an unusual growth of wildflowers, plants, and ferns, making it a sort of fairyland.

Fairy Springs *Calumet County*

A stretch of beach along Lake Winnebago with numerous small springs. In 1928 Gust Dorn recorded the name.

Fall Creek *Eau Claire County*

First named Cousins after Mr. Henry Cousins. Changed to Fall Creek for the stream on which it was located. The small falls disappeared when the stream was dammed to make a fish pond.

Fall River *Columbia County*

Alfred A. Brayton moved to Wisconsin with his father's family in 1837 and settled in Aztalan. The following year he married, and in 1845 he brought his family to the upper Crawfish River. He named the settlement for the power site he was developing, and also because his father's family had come from Fall River, Massachusetts.

Falun *Burnett County*

Edward C. Johnson, the first postmaster, chose this name after the city of Falun in Sweden, from which a large group of the early settlers had come in the 1870s.

Famacheon Ridge *Crawford County*

Located in Eastman Township. The Famacheon family settled here.

Fancy Creek *Richland County*

This creek, which crosses near Rockbridge and Marshall, was thought to resemble Fancy Creek in Sangamon County, Illinois.

Farmersville *Dodge County*

A group of Bavarian families settled just north of Mayville in the 1840s. They were farmers and tradesmen. The crossroads here was named for the farmers.

Farmington *La Crosse County*

The township contains some of the finest farming lands in the county.

Farmington *Polk County*

The excellent farmlands in the area gave this township its name. A store and a hotel were operating here before the town was organized.

Farmington *Washington County*

The town was created by an act of the state legislature in 1847 and named Clarence in honor of the son of Jonathan Danforth. A year later the name was changed to Farmington.

Fayette *Lafayette County*

The name is a contraction of LaFayette.

Fellows *Rock County*

Named for a nearby landowner.

Fence *Florence County*

A few homesteaders started a logging community here using Armstrong Creek, seven miles away, as a post office and trading center. The settlement was called Big Popple, after the river that runs through it. Samuel K. Harrison, owner of a grocery store, started a petition for a separate post office, and it was granted in 1905. The post office department suggested three different names: Podunk, Big Popple, and Fence.

A meeting was called, and Mr. Olous Annunson suggested Fence because it was short and easy to remember. The name Fence originated from the early Indians' method of killing deer for their winter supply of meat and hides. Each fall a huge brush fence was built and a picket fence directly behind it. Deer were driven toward the fence. When they jumped over the brush they landed on the sharp pickets behind.

Fence Lake *Vilas County*

The Ojibwe first called the lake Mitchigan, meaning "a wooden fence to catch deer near its banks." The translation of this meaning was adopted by settlers.

Fennimore *Grant County*

During the Black Hawk War John Fennimore started a farm on a section of land adjoining the Old Military Road leading to Prairie du Chien. He chose the site because it had a large spring. During the war he disappeared and was never heard of again. Other farmers moving into the area decided to remember him by calling their settlement Fennimore Center. Center was dropped from the name in 1881.

Fenwood *Marathon County*

The Milwaukee, Lakeshore, and Western Railway platted the village in 1891. Thick trees and shrubbery grew in a nearby fen or marsh.

Ferguson Hollow *Crawford County*

Part of Utica Township. Several Ferguson families lived here.

Ferron Park *Burnett County*

F. Ferron owned a stock farm on McKenzie Lake.

Ferryville *Crawford County*

At first called Big Landing, or just Landing, by settlers who crossed the Mississippi by boat to Lansing, Iowa, which was a market center in the 1850s. Later a ferry service was established, and the town was platted as Ferryville.

Fiddler's Green *Richland County*

Part of Rockbridge Township. A number of legends offer explanations for the name. One tells of a group of young men who were on their way to Fancy Creek. They were fiddlers from Smith Hollow and they were going to play at a dance there. Night overtook them while traveling, and they lost their way in the darkness. Having nothing better to do, they sat around a campfire fiddling.

Another reports a fiddler being paid in ham rather than money. Wolves began to follow him on the way back from his engagement. He climbed a tree and fiddled until the hungry animals left.

Fifield *Price County*

The first settlement was known as Flambeau in Chippewa County. When Price County was established in 1879 the town was officially named in honor of Sam E. Fifield of Ashland, who had timber interests in the area. Mr. Fifield was a state assemblyman, a state senator, and later lieutenant governor. His Ashland residence, at the intersection of Ellis Avenue and US Highway 2 on the shore of Chequamegon Bay, still has the stepping stone at the curb inscribed with his name.

From the Milwaukee Journal, December 28, 1930:

Fifield needs a bard to sing the saga of the "fightin'est town" in the world in its heyday—to recite the feats of the Cochranes and the Kennedys, of Michigan Smith and Pat Kelly, and of the boss of them all, Leo Kaliski.

Fifield is a sleepy little village now. All summer long the tourists stream through, for it is at the crossroads of northern Wisconsin, the junction of Highways 70 and 13. Sportsmen know it as a headquarters for fishing and deer hunting, but to most of those who come and go it is just another little village.

The main street, so empty now, had 27 saloons in its four blocks back in the eighties. The woods for miles around were full of lumberjacks. Three or four big logging operations were in progress and Fifield was the center of action for 10,000 or 15,000 men. It never was a lumbering town of the type of Escanaba and Saginaw in Michigan or Hurley in Wisconsin, with a "Hell's Half Mile" of dives and harlots. Fifield was just rough and tough. The "jacks" were seldom "rolled" or knocked on the head. Knife and gun play was almost unknown, except when a gun sometimes flashed to make sure that no one interfered while two fighters rolled around in the muddy street, biting and gouging, to see which was the better man.

The fame of the bullies of Fifield spread the country over. The Cochranes probably were the most famous fighting family. George, Miles, Sam, and Tom No. 1 and Tom No. 2, brothers and cousins, came from the lumber camps of Maine. Pat Kelly also came from Maine and went back, but George Cochrane sent for him to return to Fifield.

In those days men fought for the love of battle. Most of the time ill feeling was wholly lacking. They fought to see which was the better man. A bully from some other town, itching to see if he could best the famous men of Fifield, would come to town, hunt up the man he wanted to fight, and line up at the bar beside him.

After buying the Fifield bully a drink the visitor usually would follow the standard formula:

"I hear you're a pretty good man."

"Yeah? What about it?"

"Well, I'd like to take you on."

Dan Menzie, now a guide at Fifield, recalls the old days vividly.

"They usually got action," he said, "and most of the time they got licked. We had some great fighters here in those days. Why, back in the eighties it used to keep us kids busy running up and down the street to see which was the best scrap. Sometimes there were a dozen fights going at once in the four blocks.

"I remember one time McDonald and Finney—they were ring fighters—were standing on the street when a teamster named Harvey came along. One of them called Harvey a big hayshaker and the other one made some wisecrack.

"'You fellows are going to run into a snag,' says Harvey.

"One word led to another and Harvey collared those two fellows and before he got through with them he dragged them over to the pump and doused their heads good.

"Michigan Smith heard about Harvey beating the two prizefighters and there was nothing to it but he had to find out if he could handle Harvey. Harvey was teaming out in the woods and Smith went out and got a job loading. Whenever he loaded for Harvey he would bungle the job and beef about everything Harvey did. It went on for a day or two and Harvey didn't take long to see what Smith was up to, so one trip he told a couple of fellows to watch. Then he got the team into bad position and cussed out Smith for the way he loaded.

"Smith got down and went for Harvey and the teamster gave him about the sweetest trimming he ever got."

One of the legends of Fifield is that Leo Kaliski went down to Milwaukee when John L. Sullivan was barnstorming. He lined up with some other huskies who had stripped to the waist for the champion's inspection, and Sullivan, after passing along the line, returned to the Fifield bully and said, "This is the best-looking man, I'll box with him."

"No," replied Kaliski, "I won't get in the ring with you, but if you'll come out back of the theater I'll fight you rough and tumble."

"I'll fight you in the ring," said Sullivan, "but not in the alley."

One of the memorable battles of Fifield was between Pat Kennedy, now a Park Falls rooming house keeper, and Charlie Wilson, when Wilson arrived from Park Falls to avenge his brother, who had been worsted by Kennedy. Another famous fight, between Michigan Smith and Pat Kelly, is recalled by F. G. Traenkle, one of the oldest men of Fifield.

"They went to it hammer and tongs!" he said. "It was a whale of a fight and they were both good men. Finally they lay in the street, too exhausted to fight any more. Kelly was chewing Smith's finger and Smith was chewing Kelly's ear and once in a while one of them would get up enough gumption to reach over and make a weak pass at the other one. Well, it was a standoff and the boys called it enough.

"Kelly was a State o' Mainer and while he and Smith were standing at the curb, washing up, 10 or 15 State o' Mainers—the Cochranes and the rest of them—gathered around and began to pick on Smith. It looked as if they were going to jump him.

"Leo Kaliski was crippled up with rheumatism then and walked with a cane, but he forgot his rheumatism and stood on the sidewalk over Michigan Smith, waving his cane to keep them back.

"'I can lick any State o' Mainer!' he roared. 'I'll take you one at a time! Leave him alone!' And when they didn't get back from Smith he rapped a couple of them over the head with his cane. He bent their knees for them, too."

The bartenders of Fifield were fighting men. Sometimes a visiting bully would challenge one of the bartenders and they'd put everybody out and lock the doors and go to it. Once in a while, when the visitor licked the bartender, he'd unlock the door and call in the crowd, "Come on fellows! Let's clean up." Then the victor and the crowd would get gloriously "lickered" on the beaten man's stock.

"The town never was the same after it burned in 1903," said Dan Menzie. "That was a big fire. Some kids were playing in an old icehouse. They started a fire under a chair and tried to see who could sit the longest. The sawdust in the icehouse caught fire and most of the town went up in smoke."

Fifield made a bid for a more important place in the world while it was a booming lumber town. Price County was organized in 1879. Its whole area previously was embraced in the town of Worcester, Chippewa County. The town election in 1878 determined which village would be the seat of the town government and, later, the county seat.

Phillips was an older village, but by 1878 Fifield had increased to almost the same voting strength and in the April election put a whole ticket into the field against the Phillips ticket. Everyone knew that the real issue was removal of the town government from Phillips to Fifield.

Fifield canvassed friendly territory thoroughly and lined up a heavy vote. The polls opened at Phillips at 9 a.m. and at 7 p.m. the train from the north arrived with 126 voters aboard from Fifield, North Fork, Butternut, and Wauboo, solidly arrayed to back Fifield's claims. W. F. Huiz, candidate for town chairman, was major domo of the party. He paid the fares and gave each man a ballot printed on red paper—the straight Fifield ticket. Most of the men were unable to read, so this method was taken to aid them in voting.

The editor of the Phillips Times was in the crowd which met the train. He saw the red ballots and learned what was up. He ran to his shop and dug up similar red paper, on which he printed the Phillips ticket. Then he had friends quietly distribute these ballots among the newcomers.

Huiz watched the ballots go into the box at the polls until he had seen enough red rickets go in to assure victory for Fifield. Then he and his friends went off to celebrate. When the ballots were counted, the red ones were in the majority, but enough of the Fifield faction had become confused and cast the wrong ballot to give Phillips's ticket a clear majority.

The heyday of the Fifield bullies had not arrived, but its reputation for fighting was growing. It was a wild day in Phillips, with street fights galore, and when the train started north with the defeated faction, trainmen and officers were powerless. Conductor Tom Mitchell didn't try to collect a single ticket. He locked the coach doors after all were aboard and let the battle rage. Even so, one man was thrown out of a window and had to hike the rest of the way to Fifield. When the *doors were unlocked and the wild crowd poured out at Fifield, Mitchell found every window broken and all the seats smashed.*

Finnegan
Brown County

William Finnegan lived in the Duck Creek area and operated a large brickyard.

Finney Patch
Grant County

A mining settlement near Galena named after a Mr. Finney, who owned a mine with a Mr. Williams as his partner.

Fish Creek
Ashland County

In the Ojibwe language it was Gigonsi-Sibiwishe, meaning "a little fish creek." Gigons is a small fish or minnow and sibiwishe is a small creek.

Fish Creek
Door County

Formerly the site of an old Menominee and Ojibwe village called Ma-go-she-kah-ning, meaning "trout fishing."

Asa Thorp, who is credited with promoting this settlement, first felt the call of the wild while tending a lock of the Erie Canal with his father in 1844. One day he stepped onto a passing scow and joined the caravan of fortune hunters bound for the West. At Buffalo he transferred to a lake steamer and traveled to the crude little town of unpainted shanties, mud, filth, and riots known as Milwaukee.

As a boy Asa had learned the trade of making butter firkins, tubs, and similar woodenware. From Milwaukee he walked into the wilderness along a pioneer road, paying his way by stopping at each new settler's cabin to make woodenware. The road dwindled into a path and then a blazed trail that ended in Dodge County, where he bought land.

One day he was sitting in front of a store repairing butter firkins when a tall stranger accosted him. "Say," he said, "you ought to quit that puttering with butter firkins and come with me to Rock Island and make fish barrels."

"Rock Island!" said Asa. "What county is that in?"

"Dunno," said the stranger. "We ain't got no county down there."

"What state or territory is it in?"

"Dunno that," replied the stranger, "and what's more, don't care. We have no state, county, or town organization. We pay no taxes, and have neither lawyers nor preachers. But we have fish, and we have money. It will keep you busy twenty-four hours a day to make fish barrels at your own price. If you want to make money, come along with me."

Asa went to Rock Island (next to Washington Island, now owned by the state) late in the fall of 1845, but most of the fishermen had left. He took passage on a lake steamer, where the captain told him of the difficulty of running the boats because of lack of wood for fuel. The entire Door County peninsula was one vast forest, but there was not a pier from Washington Harbor to Green Bay where they could take on a dry stick.

As they passed the place where smoke from Increase Claflin's newly built cabin could be seen rising above the treetops, the captain said, "Now there is just where a man could build a pier and earn lots of money by selling wood to the steamers."

Asa made a sketch of the shoreline, and when he reached Menasha, he compared his sketch with the government maps and recognized the harbor of Fish Creek that the captain had pointed out. He filed preemption claims on all land south and east for a considerable distance. In 1853 he built his pier and gave employment to many men cutting cordwood for the passing steamboats. Fish Creek became an important business center.

Fisherville   *Manitowoc County*
John Fisher built a cheese factory here.

Fish Hatchery Road   *Dane County*
In Fitchburg, the State Fish Hatchery is located along this road.

Fitchburg   *Dane County*
Named for the post office and the precinct, the post office name is said to have been suggested by Ebenezer Brigham of Blue Mounds. It is probably reminiscent of Fitchburg, Massachusetts, which was near his birthplace, Shrewsbury.

Fitzgerald Station   *Winnebago County*
The Fitzgerald family came from Ireland in 1830 and settled in New Brunswick. Later they moved to Presque Isle, Maine, and in 1848 they came to Oshkosh. In 1860 James Fitzgerald bought 125 acres from a Mr. Porter and cut off the oak timber and burned it to clear the land for farming. Morris and Daniel Fitzgerald bought adjoining land. The three brothers built large brick houses and were instrumental in having a station located when the railroad was built in 1871. The site has since been abandoned.

Five Corners   *Ozaukee County*
Highway 60 crosses Highway 143 at this intersection. The fifth corner is made by the Covered Bridge Road running northeast from an old tavern built by John Rinn. The settlement was formerly known as Kennedy's Corners after John Kennedy, who ran a saloon here.

Five Points   *Richland County*
Because there are five roads leading away from it, Five Points seemed an appropriate name.

Flintville   *Brown County*
Richard Flint was an early settler and the first supervisor in the township of Suamico.

Flora Fountain   *Grant County*
Mrs. William Beswick, the wife of the carpenter who built the sawmill, selected this name. Flora was for the myriads of wildflowers that grew on the surrounding bluffs, and Fountain for a spring on the bluff across the river. Early settlers conveyed this springwater across the river in troughs made of basswood bark, forming a fountain.

Florence   *Florence County*
Iron ore was first discovered on a high hill near here by Hiram Damon Fisher in 1873. He called his find Eagle Mine after the Spread Eagle (or Badwater) Lakes. Later Dr. Nelson Powell Hulst, an engineer for the Milwaukee Iron Company, joined Mr. Fisher to

resurvey the find and develop it, and he became the first superintendent of the Menominee Mining Company. At Mr. Fisher's suggestion the following letter was written to Dr. Hulst's wife:

> *Mrs. Hulst:*
>
> *The time is come when we must give a name to the new town in Wisconsin at the end of the railroad now building, and to the mine in the vicinity, now called Eagle, but which name we do not wish to keep as there is already an Eagle Post Office in Wisconsin. The company owns all the land around the lake where the town will be located. It will be a lively town.*
>
> *We shall put an anti-whiskey clause in all deeds and we expect it will be as much noted for its temperance and morality as for its-its-its-well, anything the future may develop.*
>
> *We all wish to call the new town and the mine Florence in honor of the first white woman who had courage enough to settle (for awhile) in that rugged country I mean the first white woman known to us.*
>
> *Will you permit your name to be so used?*

Mrs. Florence Terry Hulst gave her consent.

Fogo Hollow   *Richland County*
Near Rockbridge Township, John Fogo came from Scotland in 1820 and settled at Fancy Creek in 1853.

Fond du Lac   *Fond du Lac County*
Formerly a Menominee village named Wanikamiu, meaning "end of lake." Early French explorers settled at Green Bay and used the Indian way of traveling the Fox River–Lake Winnebago waterway as a route to trading centers. The terminal point was at the south end of Lake Winnebago. The French referred to it as Fond du Lac, meaning "end or foot of the lake," or "bottom of the lake," or, more figuratively, "that part of the lake which is farthest, most remote." A town in Minnesota at the head of Lake Superior was also called Fond du Lac.

Fontana   *Walworth County*
On September 25, 1839, a gathering was held in a small log house at the head of the lake. It consisted of the seven pioneer heads of the families in the neighborhood. Mathias Moore suggested the town be named Fontana. They thought it was a French word for "a place of many springs."

Footbridge   *Kewaunee County*
Before the advent of roads in this area, a huge tree was felled to drop across the Kewaunee River. The upper side of the trunk was adzed to a flat surface to create a footbridge. The first practical settlement of the county began here in 1836, and the first sawmills and gristmills were built here. Footbridge is presently the home of the county park.

Footville *Rock County*

In 1836 James T. Watson, a real estate agent from New York City, bought a large tract of land from the government and started a settlement. Because Mr. Watson was unmarried, the area was known as Bachelor's Grove.

Ezra A. Foot came to Bachelor's Grove in 1843, traveling from Milwaukee in an oxcart. He built a log house that became the first schoolhouse, and later a gravel building. The post office was established in 1845, and mail was delivered twice a week by the Janesville to Galena stage. Mr. Foot was named a delegate to the Constitutional Convention in 1847.

Forest *Fond du Lac County*

The first post office was called Oasis. It became known as Forest because of the valuable stands of hardwood.

Forest *Richland County*

Early settlers found this area to be heavily wooded and virtually a wilderness. The first post office in this township was established in 1855.

Forest County

Named for the dense forests that covered it.

Forest Junction *Calumet County*

Mrs. Charlotte Quentin had thirty acres of this settlement platted as the village of Forest. A short time later George Baldwin platted eighty acres on the opposite side of the street as Baldwin. Two railroads were built that crossed in the village, and the Post Office Department declared the official name Forest Junction in 1873.

The Forest of Fame *Dane County*

This park in Mount Vernon contains trees from several parts of the world honoring Washington, Theodore Roosevelt, Pershing, Lincoln, Robin Hood, William Tell, LaFollette, and others. The Honorable John S. Donald had the idea for the park, which was started in 1916.

Fort Atkinson *Jefferson County*

During the Indian uprising of 1832 the federal government sent troops to southern Wisconsin under the command of Brigadier General Henry Atkinson. He built a stockade that was known as Fort Coscong (one of the many ways of spelling the name, which was finally adopted as Koshkonong). About forty-five hundred regulars were stationed near the fort during the Black Hawk War. When settlers came in 1836 they changed the name to honor General Atkinson.

Fortney Road *Crawford County*

In Clayton Township, this back road from Johnstown to Soldiers Grove is named after a family.

Fort Winnebago   *Columbia County*

A township was given this name after the fort that was built here. Originally the township was called Port Hope after the name of a port on the Fox River that never was more than a hope. The fort was constructed in 1827 and was one of three major military posts. Fort Crawford at Prairie du Chien and Fort Howard at Green Bay were the other two.

Foster   *Eau Claire County*

Homesteaders in the 1850s called this settlement Emmett. The name was changed to honor George E. Foster, who built the railroad through the community and was known as one of Wisconsin's most eccentric men.

Foster   *Fond du Lac County*

A post office in Eden Township established by Egbert Foster. It was discontinued in 1880.

Foster's Ferry   *Rock County*

William B. Foster built a ferry in the southern part of Fulton township.

Fosterville   *Vilas County*

John M. Foster, president and general manager of the Vilas Lumber Company, located here. It is now an abandoned railroad town.

Fountain City   *Buffalo County*

The Sioux called it Wha-ma-dee. In 1839 Thomas A. Holmes, a pioneer of both Milwaukee and Janesville, was journeying with thirteen others to the mouth of the St. Croix River when they were forced to make a landing because of ice. The place was called Holmes' Landing. A settlement grew, and in 1855 the name was changed to Fountain City because of the numerous springs that emerge from the bluffs along the Mississippi River.

Fountain Prairie   *Columbia County*

Named for the numerous springs of fresh water.

Four Corners   *Burnett County*

In early days a rival hamlet grew up near Trade Lake at a crossroads where County Route Y makes a sharp turn. It became known as The Corners and later Four Corners. Charles F. (King Karl) Anderson, an early settler at the corners, was the postmaster of Trade Lake from 1870 to 1874, but he operated it in Four Corners.

The Four Lakes   *Dane County*

This is the collective name of lakes Kegonsa, Waubesa, Monona, and Mendota, and of the region about them. They form a chain connected by the Yahara River.

Four Mile House   *Fond du Lac County*

This tavern near the east branch of the Fond du Lac River received its name because it was four miles from the village of Fond du Lac. The Four Mile post office was located in this tavern until it was discontinued in 1900.

Four-X *Dane County*

Two roads cross in Westport, forming an "X" and four corners. A saloon here also had the same name, but whether the saloon or the crossroads had it first is uncertain.

Foxboro *Douglas County*

An exile from Massachusetts named this town and several others after towns in his home state.

Fox Hollow *Richland County*

Located near Dayton Township. A freed slave by the name of Fox came here after the Civil War and lived in a small house on land that the other pioneers called Fox's Hollow.

Fox Lake *Dodge County*

The Indian name for the lake was Hos-a-rac-ah-tah, meaning "fox," or perhaps "fish spear." It was corrupted into the word Waushara. Jacob Brower, the first settler, who arrived in 1838, was told the Indian word meant Fox Lake, so he platted his land under that name. The Hamilton Stevens family bought adjoining land and platted it as the Village of Waushara. There was some confusion until 1850, when the Stevens family moved away and Fox Lake became the name of the entire settlement.

Fox Point *Milwaukee County*

Originally there were two names for Fox Point. One was Dutch Settlement, because of the Hollanders who migrated here, many of whom were French Huguenots who had moved to Holland and wanted to be considered Dutch, although they had French names. Early surveyors called the point of land at Doctor's Park Fox's Point. It stuck.

Fox River *Kenosha County*

Named after the river, which had an Indian name that was translated as Fox River or Fire River.

Foxville *Dane County*

A small village founded by A. Fox.

Francis Creek *Manitowoc County*

Joseph Poquin operated a tavern on the Green Bay Road that he called French Creek after a nearby stream that was so named for the many French settlers there. The Post Office Department changed the name to Francis Creek because there was another French Creek in the state, but this post office was closed when rural free delivery was established out of Manitowoc. In 1917 businessmen petitioned for the post office to be reopened, and in granting the petition the US government changed the name to Axelyn because there was another Francis Creek in the state. Leo Meyer, a young teacher who was later drowned on a school picnic, circulated a petition to have the post office officially named Francis Creek, and the request was honored.

Frankfort *Pepin County*

A village started on Dead Lake Prairie, and records seem to indicate it was named for an Indian fort that was built there. Dead Lake and Silver Birch Lake used to be one body of water, but the river changed its course, bringing sand into the lake and eventually dividing the two lakes. For this reason the village never developed.

Franklin *Kewaunee County*

John Franks was one of the organizers of the town, and it was named Franksville in his honor. Soon after the name was shortened to Franklin.

Franklin *Manitowoc County*

Said to have been named after Benjamin Franklin.

Franklin *Vernon County*

This town was the last in the country to which the name Bad Ax was applied. It was changed from Bad Ax to Loch Haven by the board of supervisors. The following year, in 1858, it was given the name of Franklin.

Franksville *Racine County*

In 1791, when Jacques Vieau came from Milwaukee to open a trading post, it was known as Skunk Grove. The village got its present name in the mid 1870s. It was a switching point on the Chicago and North Western Railway, and trains laid over here. They say a certain brakeman known only as Frank used to leave the train to pay court to a certain girl in the town, and this became a standing joke on the line. The settlement was referred to as Frank's Villa and then Franksville.

Frederic *Polk County*

William J. Starr owned some twelve hundred acres of land, a part of the Caleb Gushing land grant. It was hardwood timber and had been passed over when the pine was harvested earlier but became salable when the Soo Line Railroad built tracks from Dresser to this area in 1901. The village started as a sawmill town, and Mr. Starr named it after his son, Frederic. From 1902 until 1906, this sawmill was the largest hardwood mill in the United States, but it was dismantled in 1906 and the land sold for farms.

Fredonia *Ozaukee County*

First known as Stoney Creek. When the Wisconsin Central Railroad was built, a man from Fredonia, New York, suggested the name.

Freedom *Outagamie County*

From the Waupun Herald, August 29, 1921:

> *Many years ago an old [African American man] by the name of Andrew Jackson was a familiar figure on the streets of Appleton. He was frequently seen on the steps of the Old First National Bank Building, playing southern melodies on his flute or selling peanuts and popcorn to the children.*

Old Andrew had lived in a small, rude hut on a little farm out in the township. He had built the hut after a torturous journey from the South where he had escaped from his slave master in 1850. When the township was organized the people voted to name it Jackson, and a delegation was sent to inform him of the honor.

The old man shook his head decisively. "No gentlemen," he said. "Don't call it Jackson, no sir! Call it Freedom, because here's where I got my freedom."

Freeman   *Crawford County*
Early settlers named this township for the free men of all nationalities.

Freistadt   *Ozaukee County*
On March 10, 1844, Pastor Leberecht Krause said to a meeting of his Trinity Evangelical Lutheran Church, "After living here without a name for five years, it is time we chose a name for our settlement." Then, after quoting from the Bible on how various places got their names, he suggested Freystatt, meaning Free Place. They had left Germany for religious freedom and had found it here. The spelling was changed to the High German form.

Freitag Memorial Park   *Calumet County*
A wooded area given to the community of Forest Junction by Edward Freitag.

Fremont   *Waupaca County*
Old-timers say the village was named after Colonel John Fremont, who explored California and fought in the Mexican War.

French Creek   *Trempealeau County*
The name points back to the days of Rocque, a trapper and trader who built a cabin near the present Galesville in 1820.

French Town Road   *Crawford County*
At one time there was a town in this area called French Town. The road runs north of Prairie du Chien.

Frenchville   *Trempealeau County*
Takes its name from its location on French Creek. According to tradition, Joseph Rocque, a French trapper and trader, built a cabin near here.

Freya   *Burnett County*
A hamlet seven miles northeast of Grantsburg named after the Scandinavian goddess of love.

Friendship   *Adams County*
The original settlers came from Friendship, a small town in Allegheny County, New York.

Friesland   *Columbia County*

A town grew up in 1845 at the crossroads in the center of Randolph Township called Randolph Center. In 1910 the Chicago and North Western Railway extended a branch to the town. The name had to be changed if a post office was to be established because of the closeness of another town named Randolph. By this time Dutch people had moved in and bought the farms. Mrs. Vander Werff proposed the name Friesland after the province in the Netherlands.

Frisby   *Wood County*

Located near the Wood County Asylum, this railroad station in Marshfield was named in honor of Dr. Almah Frisby, a member of the state Board of Control during the first decade of this century, and a frequent visitor to the asylum on her inspection tours.

Frog Creek   *Washburn County*

Named for the many frogs.

Frog Station   *Kewaunee County*

A crossroad settlement where the Kewaunee River creates a series of deep pools. The pools have an abundant population of frogs, and the noise of their combined chorus on a still summer night prompted the name.

Frye Hollow   *Richland County*

Located in Sylvan Township. George Frye came from Tennessee to Sylvan in 1865.

Fussville   *Waukesha County*

Named after the first settler.

An aerial view of Gays Mills, date unknown

⇥ G ⇤

Gagen   *Oneida County*

Daniel Gagen was a landowner and pioneer in the area. Another account derives the name from the Ojibwe word gagego, meaning "no."

Gagen's Hill   *Vilas County*

Home of the first settler, Daniel Gagen, on Eagle Waters.

Gale   *Trempealeau County*

A township named for Judge George Gale, jurist, educator, and author.

Galesville   *Trempealeau County*

Judge George Gale purchased two thousand acres of land, including the present site of the city, in 1853. He founded Gale College, an institution of the early days.

Galloway   *Marathon County*

A logging camp in the wilderness here was known as Hunter's Camp after a Mr. Hunter, who was in charge of the logging operations. He worked for the Moore and Galloway Lumber Company of Fond du Lac. The name was changed to honor Mr. C. A. Galloway, one of the owners of the lumber company, who also owned land in the immediate area.

Gander Ridge   *Crawford County*

Located in Clayton Township. The ridge is named for the Gander family.

Gardner   *Door County*

F. B. Gardner was one of the founders of the community.

Gardner's Prairie   *Walworth County*

The southeast corner of the town of Spring Prairie was named after Palmer Gardner in 1836.

Garfield   *Polk County*

It was named for President Garfield.

Garner Lake   *Richland County*

Edom Garner settled on a farm in Richwood in 1866. Charles Garner's home was near the lake.

Garrison   *Sauk County*

Abandoned village and post office at the Lower Narrows of the Baraboo River, named for Mr. and Mrs. Andrew Garrison, who lived there.

The Hatton Lumber Company Camp in Galloway

Garth
Oneida County

The Garth Lumber Company set up operations here in the early 1890s.

Gaslyn
Burnett County

The lake and the creek, and later the town, were named for a logger and timber cruiser, Dave Gaslyn. The post office operated from 1902 to 1919.

Gatliff
Racine County

People who visited the Racine County Insane Asylum were served by the small railroad station west of Racine at Gatliff. The asylum later became the Racine County Hospitals and then High Ridge Hospitals. Gatliff was supposedly named after a farmer who once owned land on the west side of Highway 31, north of the railroad tracks.

Gault Hollow
Richland County

Samuel D. Gault came to Richland County shortly after the Civil War. After a couple of years in the town of Richland, he settled in the town of Bloom, where this hollow is located.

Gaynor Park
Wood County

Named in honor of John A. Gaynor, a well-known judge in the city of Wisconsin Rapids, this area of grass and trees was evidently intended as a park, but the name is known by only a few elderly residents, and the area is nameless for most residents.

Gays Mills   *Crawford County*

James Gay came from Virginia in 1848 and found the Kickapoo River ideal for water-power. He built a sawmill first and then other mills to grind grain, and employed a number of people. Farmers from miles around brought their grain to Gay's mills. In 1890 when the railroad and a post office were established, Gays Mills became the name, without the apostrophe.

Genessee   *Waukesha County*

Once called Jenkinsville for Benjamin Jenkins, an early pioneer who built the first gristmill. Mr. Jenkins supposedly renamed it after his former home of Genesee in New York State. Genesee is said to mean "there it has high banks."

Genesee Depot   *Waukesha County*

In 1852 the Chicago, Milwaukee, and St. Paul Railroad wanted to buy a right-of-way through Genesee, but the residents thought it would jeopardize the stagecoach route, so they refused. Consequently the railroad made a turn instead of going straight. A depot was built at the turn, which was known as Genesee Depot.

Geneva   *Walworth County*

The surveyor, John Brink, named the lake and the town after Geneva, New York, because the lake reminded him of Seneca Lake adjoining that city.

Genoa   *Vernon County*

The settlement was laid out by Joseph Monti in 1854 and named Bad Ax after the river in the vicinity. In 1868 Italian settlers thought it resembled Genoa in Italy because of its hills and rivers.

Genoa Junction   *Walworth County*

The village was laid out about 1859 by James F. Dickerson and became a mill site named after Genoa, New York. When two railroad lines formed a junction here, the word Junction was added to avoid confusion with Genoa, Illinois.

Georgetown   *Grant County*

The town was originally named Smelser after J. M. Smelser, who came in 1833. George Wineman built a log and frame L-shaped house in 1848 as a residence and general store that became popular for miles around. When the post office was established in 1849 George Wineman was postmaster.

Georgetown   *Polk County*

This township was named for George P. Anderson, an early settler. He was a Civil War veteran and the first settler in 1873.

Germantown   *Richland County*

Located in Westford Township. This little settlement near Cazenovia came into being in 1869 at the time of the influx of immigrants into the northern part of the county.

Germantown   *Washington County*

From 1840 there was a constant flow of German settlers to this township, until they had purchased the lands of all the other settlers.

Gibbsville   *Sheboygan County*

A village founded by the three Gibbs brothers, James H., Benjamin L., and John D., in 1836. John D. Gibbs was the first postmaster in 1846. The post office was discontinued in 1907.

Gibraltar   *Grant County*

In 1828 Asa E. Hough built a furnace and a sawmill on the Platte River a few miles from Paris and named it Gibraltar (or Gibralter). This settlement was never recognized as a town.

Gibson   *Manitowoc County*

Named to honor Darious Peck, one of the early settlers, who came from Gibson, Pennsylvania.

Gibsons Corners   *Dodge County*

John Gibson settled here in 1844.

Giddings   *Sauk County*

Discontinued post office in the township of Excelsior named for Joshua Reed Giddings, an American statesman.

Giddings Mills   *Sheboygan County*

A settlement on the Onion River, about ten miles south of Sheboygan Falls, named after David Giddings. In 1854, it had a flour mill, two sawmills, a store, and several mechanics' shops.

Gifford   *Waukesha County*

Also called Gifford's Station and named after Gifford's Resort, which was famous in the 1870s and 1880s.

Gigito-Mikana   *Ashland County*

An old Indian trail. The Ojibwe held a celebrated council in the area.

Gile   *Iron County*

Gordon H. Gile of Oshkosh was one of the owners of the Northern Chief Iron Company here. Another account says that a timber cruiser and surveyor named Miles Giles had the settlement named after him in lieu of some wages owed to him.

Gilead   *Kenosha County*

Asabel W. Benham moved here in 1844 and claimed nearly all the land in the vicinity. He built a frame house, the first in the village, and christened it Gilead in honor of the place in Connecticut from which his parents came. The village is now Wilmot.

Gillett *Oconto County*

First called Gillett Center after Rodney Gillett, who, with his bride, Mary Roblee Gillett, settled there in 1858.

Gillingham *Richland County*

Harvey Gillingham, an Englishman, and his family of thirteen children came here in 1852 from Ohio. They traveled by way of the Ohio, Mississippi, and Wisconsin Rivers to Orion, and then by oxteam to the new settlement. The town was named when the first postmaster was appointed in 1881. There is a Gillingham in Kent, England.

Gills Landing *Waupaca County*

Named for John Gill.

Gills Rock *Door County*

The Potawatomi Indians called it Wah-ya-qua-kah-me-kong, meaning "head of the land," or "land's end." Elias Gill owned about one thousand acres of land in the vicinity.

Gilman *Pierce County*

B. F. Gilman was the first settler in the township.

Gilman *Taylor County*

Named after a son of a Mr. Moore of Stanley, a nearby town. Mr. Moore was supposed to have had an interest in the SM&P Railroad.

Gilmanton *Buffalo County*

Joel Mann, a relative of Horace Mann, the famous educator, built a mill here in 1859. It was the first business place in the town, then called Mann's Mill. Later it was called Loomis Settlement because so many members of the Loomis family lived here.

Samuel Gilman and his four sons had come from New England in 1855. A member of their family signed the Declaration of Independence. One of the four sons served in the Wisconsin Assembly.

Gilmore *Grant County*

Small settlement near Sinsinawa Mounds named after one of the early settlers, a Mr. Gilmore.

Girdler Hollow *Crawford County*

Located near Utica Township. This hollow was named for the Girdler family.

Glasgow *Trempealeau County*

A number of hardy Scotsmen made their new home here.

Gleason *Lincoln County*

Salem Gleason and his wife, Sarah Jane, journeyed to the northern Wisconsin wilderness in the fall of 1880 in a covered wagon. At Jenny (Merrill) they heard trappers, hunters, and other travelers tell of the fabulous beauty of the country farther north. At a bend in the road where the Prairie River meandered through tall pines, maples, oak, and birch, the fall colors were unbelievably beautiful, and the Gleasons decided to settle there.

Their log house became a stopping place for all travelers, including Indians. A settlement grew, and Mr. Bradley from Tomahawk built a branch railroad line to it, and then a bank. Many people thought the town should be named Bradley. An old Indian was heard to say, "Call it Salem—he is a good man." A meeting was called, and the people voted to name their town Gleason.

Glenbeaulah   *Sheboygan County*

The site was first named Clark's Mill for Hazel P. Clark, who set up a sawmill with William Pool in 1850. Mr. Clark owned a 320-acre farm, and no one thought of developing a village here. In 1856 Edward Appleton contracted to build a railroad and acquired a tract of land that was platted into lots. He coined the name of the village by combining the word glen, which describes its location, with Beulah, the name of his mother. Beulah is a scriptural name supposed to mean "beautiful land," or "land of flowers." The town is nestled in a glacial valley of the beautiful Kettle Moraine hills. Originally the name was spelled as two words, Glen Beulah.

Glendale   *Milwaukee County*

At one time this was part of the town of Milwaukee and was also known as the town of Lake. Glendale was voted by the townspeople as a more popular name.

Glendale   *Monroe County*

James R. Lyon, an early settler, is said to have fancied the name.

Glen Flora   *Rusk County*

When the Soo Line Railroad built its line to this site in 1885, loggers moved in. The railroad built side tracks, commonly known as spurs. The main spur was called Miller's Spur after one of the loggers, a Mr. Miller. In 1887, when the town needed a post office, Mr. Miller submitted the names of his two children, Glen and Flora.

Glen Haven   *Grant County*

The earliest name was Stump Town in 1836. A few years later it was renamed Ray's Landing, after Richard Ray and his brothers. In 1857 George Burroughs, who had come from Scotland, and five other men platted the town as a part of Cassville, but two years later it became a separate village. The villagers suggested it be named Burroughsville. Mr. Burroughs declined the honor but said he would choose a name. "Call it Glen Haven," he said, "after the glens of Scotland and the haven so like heaven nestled between the bluffs and wooded hills."

Glenmore   *Brown County*

Settled by Irish people and presumably named after a place in Ireland.

Glenville
This region southeast of nearby Baraboo was named by C. L. Pearson for the glen-like appearance of the locality. The area was once identified as the site of "the little red schoolhouse."

Glenwood
The Glenwood Manufacturing Company, originally the Webster-Glover Manufacturing Company, with headquarters at Hudson, settled the area in 1885.

Glidden
Originally called Chippewa Crossing. Glidden was the name of one of the incorporators of the Wisconsin Central Railroad, which pushed tracks to the community in the 1870s.

Gobin Hollow
Located near Scott Township. Just off Sleepy Hollow and Light Foot Hollow, it was named for the Gobin family.

Gobin Hollow
Located near Richwood Township. Named for the Gobin families, who lived west of Excelsior.

Goerke's Corners
Originally named Blodgett after C. A. Blodgett, an early settler. Frederick Goerke, blacksmith, wagon maker, and innkeeper, operated a saloon and inn at the corner where several roads crossed.

Goetz
The settlement was part of the town of Sigel until 1887. It became a separate township named after Henry Goetz, who came from Germany in 1860 and settled on a farm here.

Gogebic Iron Range
From the Ashland Press, February 9, 1884:

> *Several months ago we undertook to ascertain the true interpretation of the word Go-ge-bic, or A-go-ge-bic. We have consulted the best authorities both at home and abroad, and have had the opinions and assistance of those who not only speak and write the Chippewa language, but those who have made the Indian language of the different tribes a study. Among the latter we may mention the Reverend Fathers Jacker, Terhost and Chebul, who are perhaps as well versed in the Indian tongue as any persons living. We have encountered difficulties from the first, from the great variety of opinions of our own local Indians, and those who appeared quite conversant with the Chippewa language. No two of them could or did give it the same meaning, and so we have consulted those who are acquainted with other tribal tongues. We think we can now give our readers the true and literal meaning of the word Agogebic.*

Before doing so, however, we will give the interpretations that have been furnished us.

A friend, who would not like to have his ability to understand Chippewa questioned, claims it means "a thick snake." Perhaps this is suggested by the form of the lake, or by the fancied resemblance between Gen-e-big, a snake, with the second half of the word Agogebic. Nor would the Indian for "thick snake," kep-a-gag-gen-e-big, ever have been changed into Agogebic.

The Marquette Journal claims that it is a Chippewa word signifying "little fish"—or else Schoolcraft, who made Indian language a life study failed to interpret it properly.

Another claims it is not a correct Chippewa word, and in order to be a name or a compound word in the Chippewa language it would have to be mah-ko-ge-bing, or mah-ko-nee-bing. The former would be a name composed of "lake," "water" and "bears," and the latter a compound word meaning "bear in water."

Another claims it means a "lake lying still or hidden." As far as we can learn there is no ground for this interpretation.

Some . . . Indians claim it means "small bush having a red berry."

An esteemed correspondent writes, "The word agogebic is certainly a Chippewa word, but in my opinion it is a corruption and should be a-go-gi-bi. It is composed of two words, an adjective a-god-jin, meaning "hanging" and a substantive ni-bi, meaning "water." In this composition the a-go-gi-bi, means "hanging water," or "water that would not be there if it had a ready outlet."

Unfortunately for this interpretation, the lake has a ready outlet at its northern end in the east branch of the Ontonagon River.

Another esteemed correspondent writes that Lake Agogebic is named from a-go-gib, a certain aquatic plant said to be found on it. If this be so, the term probably consists of the formative element ag-wa-go, relating to mould or rust, and ib, relating to water, and the literal meaning of the word would be "something covering the surface of the water like mould or rust," or, shortly, "water mould." Unfortunately for this interpretation, we cannot find that water flannel, or any aquatic plants that throw off a rust or mould to cover the surface of, or make stagnant the water, exists at Lake Agogebic. On the contrary it has always been noted for its clear waters.

Bishop Baraga, in his dictionary of the Ojibwa or Chippewa language, has it a-ko-gib, the name of a lake in Upper Michigan, and a-ko-gi-bing, at in, from or to that lake. The most common pronunciation of the word with the Indians, is a-ko-ge-bing, and is mostly employed by them in the locative sense; when they use it they mean they have been at, come from, or are going to the Lake Agogebic.

As far as we can learn, Bishop Baraga never visited Lake Agogebic, nor is it probable that any of the missionaries or travelers either ancient or modern ever penetrated so far into the interior.

The last correspondent, who translated the word to mean something rusty or mouldy covering the surface of the water, seeing we are not satisfied with such a poetical translation, set to work further to confirm his opinion. He consulted the dictionary nearly related to the Ojibwa or Chippewa, which has preserved many of the older forms of the Algonquin tongue. In the dictionary of the Cree language by the Rev. Alb. Lacombe, on page 288, he found the very words he wanted. We give the English translation of ak-wa-ku-piy, a "green or dirty grass or herb that covers certain lakes in summer." Ak-wa-ku-pi-sa-ka-hi-gan, or "a green lake covered or overspread with green herbage."

The above Cree term rendered into Ojibwa, or Chippewa, according to the ordinary rules of translation, would be ag-wa-gi-bi, or a-go-gi-bi (wa and o being almost indiscriminately used). Hence a-go-gi-bi, sa-ga-i-gan, was the original name for Lake Agogebic. Sa-ga-i-gan means "inland lake." In course of time the word sa-ga-i-gen or "lake" was dropped, and the remaining a-go-gi-bi, or a-go-gib finally became our present Anglicized, a-go-gee-bic, ago-ge-bic, a-go-gi-bic or go-ge-bic.

We think the last translation settles the etymological puzzle of Agogebic beyond a doubt and believe the translation of Father Lacombe, from the Cree term meaning "green lake" to be the correct, poetical, appropriate and literal interpretation of Ago-ge-bic, or, as it is now written, Gogebic.

Goodman   *Marinette County*

The James B. Goodman family founded the town in 1908 when they bought a large tract of timber, built a sawmill and a number of houses, and rented the houses to their employees. Later they built a planing mill, dry kilns, a chemical plant, and a veneer mill. They owned the whole town until 1955, when they sold out to Calumet and Hecla Inc. and sold the houses to the employees.

Goodrich Ferry   *Rock County*

Located at the foot of Lake Koshkonong, it was operated by a man bearing that name.

Goose Creek   *Richland County*

Located in Forest Township. A number of stories give various origins for the name. Willard Manley of the Democrat selected this one for publication:

"Two pioneer women became involved in a bitter quarrel over a goose which both claimed. The strife waxed bitter until it came almost to hair pulling. The creek was not named for the goose but for the women who were so foolish as to fight over a bird."

Gordon   *Douglas County*

Antoine Guerdon or Gordon, as he was later called, landed his canoe in 1860 at the site where the Eau Claire River empties into the St. Croix. (The Ojibwe Indians called the place Amick, meaning "beaver.") Gordon had come from the La Pointe Trading Post on Lake Superior to renew relations with the Indians to extend the fur trade for the Northwest Company that had its post at Lac du Flambeau. He built a trading post that became popular with the Indians and later became a supply point and stopping place along the St. Paul to Bayfield mail route. In addition to being a popular trader, Mr. Gordon also became a spokesman and counselor to the Indians and set up a school and a church where they were welcomed with the settlers.

Gordon   *Sauk County*

A telegraph station between Reedsburg and La Valle on the Chicago and North Western Railway. It may have been named for William W. Gordon, president of a railroad in Georgia.

Gotham   *Richland County*

Originally Richland City. Because of confusion with Richland Center the name was changed, although a Mr. H. M. Bock used his influence to have it changed back to Richland City three times. W. A. McNurlin, a storeowner, is credited with suggesting the name after his friend, Captain M. W. Gotham, who was postmaster when the post office was moved from the riverfront nearer to the railroad.

Captain M. W. Gotham became a Great Lakes sailor at the age of eighteen and commanded steamers for more than thirty years. When he married Clara Campbell, a Richland County girl, he decided to live in Richland City because it reminded him of his former home on the St. Lawrence River. In the winter months he enjoyed matching tall tales with the river men who worked steamers and lumber rafts on the Wisconsin River. He was sixty-one when he and two of his sons perished with the Macy on Lake Erie.

In the winter of 1902 the steamer Sylvanus J. Macy, commanded by Captain Gotham, was towing the schooner Mabel Wilson, commanded by his brother, Captain J. E. Gotham. They were on Lake Erie bound for Kenosha with cargoes of hard coal, the last trip of the year. When a heavy storm struck, the men on the Macy heroically cut loose the towline before their own ship went down. The Wilson reached Detroit, and the crew told of seeing the lights on the drifting Macy disappear suddenly about three o'clock in the morning.

Gothic Mill Pond   *Fond du Lac County*

The Gothic Mill was erected on its shores in the city of Ripon in 1853. The mill was an imposing stone structure three stories high.

Governor's Island   *Dane County*

Governor Leonard J. Farwell formerly owned this and adjoining land. It was originally an island on the north side of Lake Mendota, but it became joined to the mainland in about the 1850s, forming a peninsula. The name is still used, however.

Grafton   *Ozaukee County*

From 1840 to 1846 the village was known as Hamburg, probably for Hamburg, Germany, the ancestral home of Jacob Eichler, an early settler. Phineas M. Johnson, Jacob Adreana, and William Bonniwell built the stone block that became the courthouse and renamed the settlement Grafton. No reason for choosing this name is recorded, but it may have been suggested by Irish settlers who were becoming more numerous. One of the main shopping streets in Dublin is Grafton Street. There is also a Grafton County in New Hampshire, a Grafton township in Worcester County, Massachusetts, and a Grafton in Taylor County, West Virginia. The name was changed to Manchester in 1857 and changed back to Grafton in 1862.

Grand Marsh
Adams County

There is a large marsh north of the town. Farmers for miles around referred to it as the Grand Marsh. The village was born in 1911 when the Chicago and North Western Railway built tracks through Adams County. It was almost burned down at one time but has been partially rebuilt.

Grand Rapids
Wood County

The Indian name was Ah-da-wa-gam, "on the other side," or "across a river or lake," or "two-sided rapids." There are falls or rapids in the Wisconsin River here. A village west of the town called Centralia was consolidated in 1899.

Grand River
Fond du Lac County

The name is a translation of the original Ojibwe name "Washtanong."

Gran Grae
Crawford County

Located in Wauzeka Township. Legend has it that early settlers were nearly wiped out by a hailstorm. One of the settlers made the remark, "What kind of grand place is this?" Ever since, it has been called Gran Grae.

Grant County

Named for the river, which was named after a Mr. Grant, a famous trapper and Indian trader. He lived in a cabin on the riverbank when Wisconsin was still a territory. His cooking utensil was a brass kettle that he wore under his cap on his head. One day he encountered a war party of Ho-Chunk. One Indian struck Grant on the head with his tomahawk, producing no other effect than a sharp ring from the kettle. The Indians recoiled in terror, exclaiming "Manitou!"

Granton
Clark County

Older people generally agree that the name was adapted from Grant Township, which is said to have been named after General Ulysses S. Grant.

Grantsburg
Burnett County

The Indian name was Kitchi-Maski-gimi-nika-ning, meaning "at the great cranberry place." The Honorable Canute Anderson came to the area in 1851 and established the first post office in his house. He later built a sawmill and laid out the village site, naming it after General Ulysses S. Grant, who was popular at the time because of his victory in the Battle of Vicksburg.

Grant's Corners
Fond du Lac County

Located in Springvale, the site was named for O. Grant, who owned a farm here.

Grant Springs
Crawford County

Once a valuable water source for travelers on the old road from Wauzeka to Steuben, it was named for the Grant family, who were early pioneers.

Granville   *Milwaukee County*

Named by C. T. Everts, an early settler from Granville, Washington County, New York. John Carteret, Earl of Granville, was a British statesman.

Grass Lake   *Dane County*

This shallow lake near Dunkirk has grass growing in it.

Gratiot   *Lafayette County*

Henry Gratiot, a friend of Colonel Hamilton, came because of the lead diggings in 1824 and started Gratiot's Grove, which was turned into a stockade during the Black Hawk War. He is said to have been instrumental in treaties with the Indians.

Gravel Store School   *Dane County*

There used to be a store here with gravel on the walls, the first store opened between Albion and Milwaukee.

Gravesville   *Calumet County*

Originally known as Lodi but was renamed by Leroy Graves, who built a sawmill in 1850 and established a number of other businesses.

Greasy Hollow   *Crawford County*

Located near Marietta Township. A road was built at the upper end of Clay Creek, and when it rained the road got very slippery.

The Great Divide   *Ashland County*

This watershed separates the two principal drainage areas of Wisconsin. Water falling on the north side eventually finds its way into the Atlantic Ocean. Water falling on the south side flows into the Mississippi and down to the Gulf of Mexico.

Green Bay   *Brown County*

The Menominee name was Putci-wikit or puji-kit, meaning "a bay in spite of itself," or "a bay in spite of everything." Fort Howard was built here and named for a US Army officer. Early French settlers called the bay La Baie Verte or Green Bay from the deep greenish hue of the water. The French are also said to have called it Baie de puants because Radisson and Groseilliers called the Ho-Chunk Indians puants, or "stinkards," and La grande baie, "the large bay"—later corrupted to Green Bay. Augustin de Langlade and his distinguished son, Charles, who are thought to be Wisconsin's first permanent European settlers, lived here. The first farm was cleared and planted here in 1745.

Greenbush   *Sheboygan County*

Sylvanus Wade, his wife, Betsy, and nine children came to this wilderness in a covered wagon in 1844. There was no road, only a crude trail marked by blazed trees, and often it was necessary to cut brush and trees to get the wagon through. The woods were inhabited by Indians and wolves. When they arrived and Betsy saw all the trees and bushes, she said, "We will have to call this place 'Greenbush' just like the town we came from in

Massachusetts." Sylvanus built a log cabin and then a blacksmith shop. By 1851 he had completed the famous Wade House, an inn where travelers could stop for food and shelter.

Green Cloud Hill   *Grant County*

A hill in Wyalusing State Park named after a Ho-Chunk chief.

Green County

Said to have been named in honor of General Nathanael Greene of the American Revolution.

Greendale   *Milwaukee County*

This was once an Indian village, and a burial ground was discovered north of the administration building. One of the first log cabins in Milwaukee County was built near here. The discovery of a man-built stone dam, some sixteen feet underground, during the construction of the sewer system in 1937 indicates a much earlier habitation of this region—possibly thousands of years prior to the Indian village. In 1936 the Resettlement Administration began the construction of three new communities, known as the Greenbelt Towns, one of which is Greendale. It was a government-owned housing community on 3,400 acres of government-owned land. The community was laid out with a greenbelt of parkland, garden areas, and farms encircling the urban development.

Greenfield   *Sauk County*

A town named by Nathan Dennison for Greenfield, Massachusetts, his former home. The eastern town was named for a river that intersects it and was originally called the Green River District.

Green Lake   *Green Lake County*

Anson Dart, the first settler, arrived in 1830 and started a community known as Green Lake Center. The land he acquired was near two small lakes called Twin Lakes. He built a mill, but by 1845 the water level had fallen so the mill could not operate. Mr. Dart moved his family across the lake to its outlet on the Puckyan River, where he built a dam, another mill, and a ford across the river. A village grew up known as Dartford, for Dart's ford. In 1871 the railroad was extended to Dartford but named its station Green Lake. Mail became confused with Green Lake Center so Dartford changed its name to Green Lake, and Green Lake Center became Center House.

Green Lake County

Named for the large lake that lies near its center. Ho-Chunk Indians called it Ti-cho-ra, Tira meaning "lake" and cho meaning "green," because of the distinctive emerald color of the water. The French translated it to Lac du Verde. Other Indian names associated with the lake are wi-la-hi-ta, meaning "sunset," Chi-po-lo-ke, meaning "wigwams at old campsites," wi-cha-wa, meaning "corn grows at local camps and villages," and cho-hoth-ni, meaning "green water."

Greenleaf   *Brown County*

The Milwaukee Railroad built a track through the community about 1870, and the name was chosen either for the contractor who did the grading or for the president of the railroad.

Greenstreet   *Manitowoc County*

A Bohemian community where a Mr. Zelenka had a store, a saloon, and the post office. Zelenka is Bohemian for Green.

Green Valley   *Shawano County*

William Donaldson, the first town chairman, named the township for the many evergreen trees, especially pine and hemlock.

Greenville   *Outagamie County*

In the spring of 1848, John Culbertson of Madison, Indiana, left his home with his four sons to settle in Wisconsin. They arrived in the month of April, when everything was green. They named the new place Greenville, which was extended to the township. The Chicago and North Western Railway established Greenville Station near the post office Becker named for Anton Becker. In 1895 the post office was moved to Greenville Station, and Becker post office was discontinued.

Greenwood   *Clark County*

In 1844 when the first settlers arrived here, one-fourth of Clark County was covered with white pine. It is estimated that as much as 800 million feet of timber was cut here and sent down the Black River by 1873. Two or three years later the pine was almost gone. The name of Greenwood was given by Miss Mary Honeywell, probably because it was in the midst of the pineries, and since there were many hardwood forests as well.

Gresham   *Shawano County*

August Schmidt bought two acres here on the banks of the Red River and erected a two-story building. His son Walter was the first child born to European settlers in the locality. His store was the only place available when the new post office was established in 1885, and Mr. Schmidt became the first postmaster. The name Gresham honors Postmaster General Gresham in President Chester A. Arthur's cabinet.

Griffin   *Burnett County*

A hamlet nine miles north of Grantsburg, named for Ira Griffin, one of the cranberry kings of the district.

Griffin Hollow   *Crawford County*

Located in Clayton Township. Named for a family who allowed people to water their horses on their land.

Grimms   *Manitowoc County*

The depot and post office were first known as Shaving Street. The road north from the village was very low and muddy. Cedar shingles were made in the village and their shavings hauled along this road to cover the low area. Later the name was changed to Grimms after Louis Grimm, on whose property the depot had been built.

Grinsell Creek *Richland County*

Edward Grinsell, a native of Ireland, owned land in the town of Henrietta.

Grubbville *Columbia County*

A former name of Beaver Dam. "Grubbing it" was a term used in the lumber business.

Gudex Cemetery *Fond du Lac County*

Located in Ashford, it contains the graves of the Gudex family.

Gull Lake *Washburn County*

Early settlers saw several seagulls fly over the lake and gave it this name.

Guthrie *Waukesha County*

Charlie Guthrie's general store and post office became the nucleus of this neighborhood that grew into a hamlet.

⇻H⇺

Hadleyville *Eau Claire County*
The Hadley family owned a hotel on the stage route through Pleasant Valley township. A settlement was established in 1870 with a store, school, and post office.

Hainesville *Door County*
Named in honor of its founder, Tallak Haines, who settled at Sawyer Harbor in 1864.

Hake Hollow *Richland County*
John Hake made the first settlement in the town of Willow in June 1852.

Hale *Trempealeau County*
The first settler was George Hale, who came from Glastonbury, Connecticut, in 1858.

Hales Corners *Milwaukee County*
William Hale built the first log cabin here in 1837. His grandfather was one of five brothers who came to New York before the Revolutionary War. He built the South Side Hotel in 1861, held several town offices, and was appointed postmaster by President James Polk.

Halfway Prairie Creek *Dane County*
The earliest name of this creek was "Halfway Creek," which gave its name to the prairie through which it flows. It marked the midpoint between Cross Plains and Sauk City for travelers. The creek's main source is Indian Lake, and it flows westward through Berry and Mazomanie to join Black Earth Creek.

Half Way Spot *Grant County*
A tavern located halfway between Arthur and Platteville on the Sherwin farm. It was probably called Sherwin Inn at the time, but old-timers refer to it as Half Way Spot.

Hall Bottom *Richland County*
Located in Akan Township. George Hall was given one hundred sixty acres of land in lieu of money for his services in the Mexican War. After two years he sold his right to the land.

Hallie *Chippewa County*
Hallie Sherman (Mrs. A. S. Miller) was the daughter of Captain Sherman, a Civil War veteran who owned the area and operated lumber mills known as Blue Mills. The logs were stored in a natural lake of a particularly lovely blue color.

Halls Branch *Crawford County*
Located in Haney Township. It was named after an early Hall family.

Halunkenburg
Dane County

The German meaning is "Lout's Town." It is a nickname for Springfield Corners and its neighborhood, in which lived a group of rough and spendthrift farmers who did a lot of fighting and drinking, both in their community and in nearby villages. After a time, it was said of any disorderly person, "He must be from Halunkenburg."

Halverson Ridge
Crawford County

Located in Clayton Township. Sometimes referred to as Rosemeyer Ridge, it was named after the Halverson family.

Hamburg
Marathon County

Emigrants from Pomerania, Germany, settled this area.

Hamilton
La Crosse County

The town was formed from the union of Neshonoc and Barre. The new name was suggested by John M. Coburn, who came to Wisconsin with Dr. Ranney and had spent one year in Hamilton College, Clinton, New York. It is also suggested that Colonel William S. Hamilton, son of Alexander Hamilton, had claims in the lead-mining area. His diggings were said to have been called Fort Hamilton.

Hamilton
Ozaukee County

The earliest settlement was known as the New Dublin District. The majority of the settlers had come from Ireland. Valentine Hand built a hotel that became a rendezvous for old-timers where they cracked jokes and sampled the owner's bourbon. At one of these get-togethers it was suggested the name be changed to Hamilton District. At first there was opposition, but the name was changed in 1847 to honor Captain William Hamilton, brother of Alexander Hamilton. Captain Hamilton was detailed to deliver cattle from Chicago to the military at Fort Howard. The New Dublin District was a stopover or campsite and probably a watering station for these early cattle drives.

Hamilton Quarries
Fond du Lac County

These quarries in Byron were purchased by Irenus K. Hamilton in 1894. He had been involved in lumbering operations before the purchase.

Hamline
Burnett County

Named for Leonidas Lent Hamline, bishop of the M. E. Church.

Hammel
Taylor County

Named after an early settler who was a horse dealer.

Hammond
St. Croix County

In 1855, a firm of Boston speculators transferred the rights and titles to this region to Mann, Hammond & Co. R. B. Hammond of Waukesha and J. R. Ismond built the first sawmill. Nine Indians came to investigate the newcomers on their first morning, and Mr. Hammond bought venison from them, establishing a friendship. In March of 1856 a company of six families, twenty-three people, set out from Racine in four covered wagons and a democrat wagon drawn by horses for the women. They arrived on July 2. On July 4 all settlers in the community, about sixty people, turned out for a rousing celebration. Speeches were made and Old Glory floated for the first time on the village site. Mr. Hammond was present, a dedication was performed, and the name of Hammond was formally given to the community.

Hampden
Columbia County

One of the early settlers was an admirer of John Hampden, the English patriot.

Hancock
Waushara County

When the township was settled in 1854 it was named Sylvester, because the pioneers found a man named Sylvester cutting marsh hay at the west end of Pine Lake. The reason for changing the name to Hancock is not given, except that the post office of Hancock had been established.

Haney
Crawford County

The first settler was John Haney, who came in 1844.

Haney Ridge
Crawford County

Located in Haney Township. John Haney was the first settler in the area in 1844. He was buried in the Haney Valley Cemetery near the spot where he first settled.

Haney Valley
Crawford County

Located in Haney Township, it is named after the township.

Hanover
Rock County

The first settlers were driven out by Indians in 1769. Early the following spring they returned. Several massacres followed, but by 1771, peace and security were established. The original name was Bass Creek. It was changed by John Higgins, owner of the town site, to honor his German neighbors, some of whom had come from Hanover Township in the northeastern part of Pennsylvania, Luzerne County. Many of these settlers had originally come from Hanover, Germany.

Hansell
Richland County

Joe Hansell came from Bohemia and settled in Henrietta in the latter part of the nineteenth century.

Hansen
Wood County

Named after M. R. Hansen, who settled here in 1883.

Happy Corners
Grant County

Families used to gather for evenings of dancing and visiting. After one particularly enjoyable evening Miss Barbara Richards suggested the name.

Happy Hollow   *Richland County*

Located in Willow Township. First it was known as Cress Hollow, for a man called Cress who lived here. The name was changed after Mr. Wristley, the owner of the sawmill, heard the farmers whistling and singing at their work. He remarked, "This is the happiest valley I ever saw."

Harris   *Marquette County*

Named in honor of James Harris, an early settler.

Harrisburg   *Sauk County*

Discontinued post office in the town of Troy named after John W. Harris. It was originally spelled Harrisburgh.

Harrison   *Calumet County*

In 1852 the town of Lima was created from the town of Stockbridge. Later the town was bonded to build plank roads, and when it became difficult to meet the payments voters decided to change the name, thinking they could thus avoid their obligations. They selected the name in honor of William Henry Harrison, ninth president of the United States and the first to die in office. He had been an Indian fighter, and his campaign of "Tippecanoe and Tyler Too" won votes for his coonskin cap, log cabin, and hard cider. He gave his inaugural address for three hours in the rain, then danced and celebrated at his inaugural ball The next day he had pneumonia, and he died a month later.

Harrison   *Lincoln County*

The town was originally called Mitchell after an old settler. The name was changed to honor President Benjamin Harrison.

Harris Ridge   *Crawford County*

Named after William Harris in 1856, it is located in Marietta Township.

Harshaw   *Oneida County*

A foreman of one of the sawmills on Bear Creek was named Harshaw. A relative with this same name was killed at the mill soon after it started. The foreman thought some memorial should be erected, so he put up a post near the place of the accident with Harshaw printed on it. When the Chicago, Milwaukee, and St. Paul Railroad was built through the site in 1887, the railroad company accepted the name for their station.

Hartford   *Washington County*

The minute book of the first town meeting records the name of Wright in April 1843. It is said that people objected to this name because Mr. Wright was still living in the community. They wanted the name of Benton but were informed by the territorial legislature that there already was a Benton in Wisconsin. The next selection was Hartford, which was granted by the Legislature in 1847. A number of explanations for Hartford are offered: Pike Lake, about a mile to the east, is a perfect heart shape, and on the north end is a ford or dam, which suggests Hartford. A number of settlers came from Connecticut, and the name may have been adopted from Hartford, Connecticut. The Indian name for the area is said to have been Nokam, meaning "heart," because one part is heart shaped.

Hartland   *Waukesha County*
The first settler in 1838 was Steve Warren, and the settlement was named Warren. In 1842 a Mr. Christ Hershey bought Warren's property, and the community was called Hersheyville. One account states that it was called Hershey's Mills. The Indian name is said to be Sha-ba-qua-nake, meaning "a growing group"—of trees, people, or anything that grows. Hartland is said to mean literally "heart land," but no explanation for this name is given. It was incorporated as Hartland in 1892.

Hartman   *Columbia County*
Named for a postmaster, Joseph Hartman.

Hatch   *Chippewa County*
The railroad built a spur line to load logs and pulpwood that was being cut here. Presumably the logger was a man named Hatch. It was also known as Hatch's Spur.

Hat Island   *Door County*
Named by Mr. Increase Claflin, who thought it resembled the shape of a hat.

Hatley   *Marathon County*
Matthew LeBarian chose this name from Hatley, Quebec, Canada, from whence he had come.

Haugen   *Baron County*
Senator Haugen gave the community his name.

Haven   *Sheboygan County*
Formerly a rail stop known as Seven Mile Creek. No reason for the name of Haven is given.

Hawkins   *Rusk County*
The first name of this community was Main Creek. One account states that Mr. Hawkins was one of the first lumbermen in the area, another that he was an official of the Soo Line Railroad.

Hawkins Creek   *Richland County*
Located in Rockbridge and Westford. In early days a man named Hawkins trapped along the creek, but some say the creek was named for Captain Hawkins. In the early 1850s he lived in the first shack in the valley. He built a dam across the stream and spent several months rafting logs down to Sextonville and Richland City.

Hawthorne   *Douglas County*
One account states that there were thickets of hawthorne or a hawthorne grove that grew like an island in the dense forest. Another account states that the name was suggested by the wife of David Evan Roberts, a probate judge of Douglas County, who wished to

commemorate the famous author Nathaniel Hawthorne. A logger named Hawthorne is said to have cut enough logs to fill a pond here in 1882, before the railroad was built.

Hay Creek   *Eau Claire County*
The first settlers in 1875 selected this name because of the lush growth of wild hay along the stream.

Hayton   *Calumet County*
The community was first known as Wallerville, in honor of Parley Waller, one of the original settlers and businessmen. The name was later changed to School Section because of some state school property arrangement. Still later it was Dicksville—Dick was a common Calumet County name, and there was a Dicksville Institute in New York State. The community was also known at one time as Charles town, probably because the Charlestown Indians had migrated there.

In 1873 the name was officially changed by the post office department to Hayton, possibly from the abundance of hay in the area, the "-ton" being added to give it an English flavor. Some reports say that hay was flooded out of the marshes and dumped on the banks of the river, and people came to call the village Haytown. It is also reported that an early postmaster was named Hayton.

Hayward   *Sawyer County*
The Ojibwe name was Ba-ke-abash-kang, meaning "a swamp that is a branch of a larger swamp." Anthony Judson Hayward, a lumberman, located a site for a sawmill on the Namekagen River, and a town grew up around it.

Hazel Green   *Grant County*
The first miners came in 1825, and a fight between James Hardy and Moses Meeker for the possession of a mine gave the site the name Hardy's Scrape, since Hardy was the winner. This degenerated into Hard Scrabble, which was the official name until 1838 when the post office was established, and it was thought the village should have a name more appropriate to its beautiful location. Captain Charles McCoy of the Black Hawk War suggested Hazel Green. Some people claimed he came from Hazel Green in Kentucky. It was also said that the town site was originally covered with hazel bushes.

Hazelhurst   *Oneida County*
Cyrus Yawkey built the sawmill and the town in 1887 and was the big logger in the area until 1911. Mrs. Yawkey is said to have selected the name. A hurst is an old Saxon term for a thicket. Mrs. Yawkey was impressed by the many clumps of hazel brush on the village site.

Hazelton   *Grant County*
Formerly called Ora Oak, it was renamed after Congressman Hazelton. The post office was established in 1880 and closed in 1897.

Hazen Corners   *Crawford County*
Aaron Hazen was an early settler in this area in the township of Eastman.

Heafford Junction *Lincoln County*

The Soo Line Railroad was built through the area in 1885. Later tracks were laid for the Marinette, Tomahawk & Western Railroad, from near Heafford to Tomahawk. It was to join the Grand Trunk Railway, but the man financing it died, and the project was never completed. The Chicago, Milwaukee, and St. Paul Railroad was built in 1890. The first depot agent was a Mr. Heafford, and the settlement was named Heafford Junction.

Heart Prairie *Walworth County*

Named by James Hodlen in 1837 because of its shape.

Hegg *Trempealeau County*

Colonel Hegg was the commander of the Fifteenth Wisconsin Norwegian Regiment in the Civil War.

Helenville *Jefferson County*

The first post office was established in Mr. Ortgies Bullwinkle's store and called Bullwinkle. Mr. Bullwinkle had the name changed for his wife, Helen.

Hell Hollow *Richland County*

Located in Ithaca Township. A man purportedly of rather irascible character lived in the hollow. When he moved to Sauk County, another Hell Hollow appeared. Some say the name came from the rough and slippery road that wound through the hollow.

Hematite *Florence County*

Named for the hematite iron that was plentiful in the area.

Hemlock Island *Portage County*

The Ojibwe Indians called this island in the Wisconsin River Kaga-giwan-jikag, meaning "place where there are hemlock trees."

Henpeck *Richland County*

Located in Buena Vista Township. A story tells of a hen that built her nest under the steps of the schoolhouse. When the chicks hatched, the children attempted to handle them and were pecked.

Henrietta *Richland County*

This township was named for the second daughter of James Laws of the Laws Ferry era. She was a popular teacher and later was the wife of Reverend L. Leonard in Richland Center.

Herbster *Bayfield County*

Billy Herbster worked for the Cranberry Lumber Company as the camp cook. He was one of the few men in camp who could read, and letters were addressed to lumberjacks there in his care. Before 1895, it was known as Cranberry River.

Herman
Sheboygan County

The town was originally called Howard after one of the earliest businessmen, H. B. How-ard, proprietor of Howard's Hotel. He also established a trading center now known as Howard's Grove. The name was changed by German settlers to honor the great national Teutonic hero Hermann, who conquered the invading Roman army under Varus at the Battle of Teutoburg Forest in 9 AD.

Herpel Hill
Crawford County

Located in the township of Haney, it was named for the Herpel family.

Hersey
St Croix County

The village was once a busy sawmill town, named for Samuel E. Hersey in 1856. Hersey was a partner in a large sawmilling operation in Stillwater, Minnesota.

Hertel
Burnett County

Otto Hertel was a storekeeper who became the first postmaster.

Hessian Hollow
Dane County

Located near Blue Mounds. This is an alternative name for German Valley used occasion-ally by the Native Americans, not in its specific sense, but with Colonial overtones that suggest suspicion of foreigners.

Hewitt
Wood County

When the Wisconsin Central Railroad Company extended its roadbed from Stevens Point northwestward toward Abbottsford, the stopping places were known by numbers. The place that is now Hewitt was Number 28, indicating that it was twenty-seven miles from Stevens Point. The next name was Kreuser, because a man by that name was the first to sign the petition applying for a post office. Mr. Hewitt was a lumberman from Menasha who had a side track built near Number 28, known as Hewitt Side Track. When a depot was built in 1882, the words "side track" were dropped.

High Bridge
Ashland County

The Ojibwe name was Jomia-sibing, meaning "at silver creek" or river. There is a deep-cut ravine along Silver Creek here. The Wisconsin Central Railroad built a bridge some ninety feet high to cross the creek, and the village became known as High Bridge.

High Cliff
Calumet County

A high cliff along Lake Winnebago became popular for the making of bricks and the quar-rying of limestone. Henry Raymond, the first postmaster, called it Clifton. Some people referred to the settlement as Lower Cliff because it was at the bottom of the escarpment. About 1885 a tavern and dance hall were built on the top of the cliff and became known as High Cliff. The post office also took this name because there was another Clifton in the state.

Highland
Douglas County

A town built on the high land of the Brule River.

Highland   *Iowa County*

Elihu B. Goodsell built the first log cabin here in 1840. When a village was partly laid out he named it Franklin in honor of his broker, and also in honor of a favorite son of Mrs. William Suddeth. Mr. Goodsell and John Barnard, the second settler, registered the complete village plat in 1846 as Highland.

High Ridge   *Crawford County*

Located in Clayton Township. Also known as Orchard Heights, it was given its name because of its height.

Hika   *Manitowoc County*

When early settlers established a village called Centerville they ran into trouble with postal authorities. "There is already one Centerville in Wisconsin, and one is enough," the Postmaster General said. They promptly tagged the village Hika, although no one knows why.

Hilbert   *Calumet County*

The railroad station was once known as Hilbert Junction, although nobody knows why, and the post office shortened it to Hilbert.

Hilburn   *Walworth County*

A family of that name lived in the area.

Hiles   *Forest County*

Franklin P. Hiles of Milwaukee purchased large blocks of timberlands in the vicinity of Pine Lake at the head of the Wolf River. He built a lumber camp and a sawmill for the Forster-Whitman Lumber Company.

Hilgen Spring Park   *Ozaukee County*

Frederick Hilgen built a fine resort and park in 1852. It had two good hotels, a bandstand, a spring, a bathhouse, a fountain, flower beds, and gravel walks on about seventy acres of land. It was visited by people from St. Louis, Chicago, and New Orleans.

Hillcrest   *Douglas County*

A station on the Soo Line Railroad located at the top of the hill going up from Lake Superior.

Hillington   *Dane County*

Because this subdivision in Madison was suggestive of England, the name was chosen with others (Rugby Row, Eton Ridge, etc.) from a Baedeker guide book.

Hillpoint   *Sauk County*

William Burmester built a new store and wanted a name for the area. On a Sunday afternoon in 1907, he and Mike Drea, Henry Kohlmeyer, Henry Schluter, Dick St. John, Frank Krueger, and Sam Roberts selected this name.

Hillsboro *Vernon County*

Vilentia Hill made the first claim and broke the first land in 1850. Later he was joined by his brothers, William and Alonzo. The first spelling of the name was Hillsborough.

Hillsdale *Barron County*

In 1872 the Mooneys came to this community and started a sawmill. A post office was established, named Mooney's Mill, and mail came on a stage that ran between Barron and Menomonie. By 1895 the timber supply was exhausted, and the mill closed. Miss Jeannette Smith, the postmistress, suggested the name be changed to Hillsdale, probably because the land has hills and a dale.

Himley Lane *Crawford County*

Running from Trout Creek to Sugar Grove, this road in Clayton Township was named for the Himley family.

Hines *Douglas County*

Edward Hines was a lumberman from Chicago.

Hingham *Sheboygan County*

People who settled here came from the New England states and chose this name after Hingham, Massachusetts.

Hipke *Taylor County*

A man by this name was connected with the Northwestern Lumber Company of Stanley, and at one time the company had land and timber holdings in this area.

Hixton *Jackson County*

In 1818 the region now known as Hixton Township was a part of Crawford County. In 1851 it was set off as a part of La Crosse County, and in 1853 Jackson County was established, but actual boundaries were not laid out until 1883.

The greater part of Jackson County was first called Albion. In 1844 Hixton was a part of the town of Alma, and in 1860 it was platted as the town of Williamsport, probably because many of the settlers had come from Williamsport, Pennsylvania. In 1865 the name was changed to Hixton, with the town of Curran included, and in 1880 Curran became a separate township.

John L. Hicks and three other men were walking through the area on their way to Minnesota to take up land. They camped overnight on the spot where the first building was later erected. The next morning Hicks looked around and liked the area with the river nearby so much that he decided to stay. He built the first log house and became the first chairman of the Town of Alma. Hixton is a shorter way of spelling Hick's Town.

Hoard *Sheboygan County*

A post office probably named after William D. Hoard, governor of Wisconsin from 1889 to 1891.

Hobart
Brown County

Bishop Hobart was the Episcopal bishop of New York who had jurisdiction over this area in the early days.

Hobart Park
Calumet County

Harrison Hobart, an early resident, donated this picturesque area to Chilton. He left Chilton as captain of Company K, Wisconsin Volunteer Infantry, in April 1861, at the start of the Civil War, and was imprisoned in the notorious Libby Prison, from which he made a daring escape.

Hobart's Mill
Sheboygan County

This was the location of a steam sawmill in the town of Holland. The Hobarts—Frank, Edward, Hiram, and Aaron—were an early family of millers. A post office was established here in 1868 and was discontinued in 1876.

Hobbs Woods
Fond du Lac County

This well-known wooded area in Byron was on a farm once owned by John Hobbs. In 1973 the Environmental Quality Council of Fond du Lac County acquired it because it was a virtually untouched habitat for many species of flowers, trees, and shrubs.

Hoboken Beach
Dane County

This location on Lake Monona is identified on a 1900 map as "Hoboken Club." This had been a "tough neighborhood," and the folk-etymological explanation for the name indicates that it refers to the "hobos" who frequented the beach.

Ho-Bo-Sa-Che-Nug-Ra
Rock County

The Indian name for the Ho-Chunk village on the east bank of Rock River, about two miles north of Beloit. It was known as the village of Standing Post.

Hodunk
Walworth County

An old settler living in the town of LaFayette beside a steep hill could be heard to say, "Hodunk, hodunk" to his span of mules as he traveled down the hill.

Hog Island
Wood County

Located near Remington. Hogs were placed on this low-lying island to forage for food.

Hogs Back
Crawford County

An unusual land formation gives this location its name. It is located in the Township of Haney.

Hogsback Mill
Pepin County

Mr. Place, a hunter, is said to have remarked on one of his many hunting trips that took him over a hill, "It was like going over a hog's back."

Hogskin Hollow
Richland Center

Located in Eagle Township. It is said that the skins of stolen hogs were found hung on a tree in the thief's yard.

Hoke Hollow
Richland County

In the early 1850s John and Jemina Hoke and their eleven-year-old son, George, came to the town of Ithaca. George lived here until he enlisted during the Civil War. After the war, he returned and stayed here until 1868, when he moved to Sextonville.

Holcombe
Chippewa County

The early settlement was known as Little Falls because of the falls on the Chippewa River here. Holcombe was the name of the surveyor at the time of the land grant change. In 1960 the name was legally changed to Lake Holcombe because of the numerous residents on the lake formed by the power dam on the river, but the "Lake" portion has not been commonly used.

Holland
Brown County

Dutch emigrants settled here in 1848.

Holland
Sheboygan County

The town was first settled in 1841 and was organized in 1849. The settlers were principally Hollanders, hence the name.

Hollandale
Iowa County

In 1887 Bjorn Holland built a small shack and put in a stock of goods to supply the construction crew working on the Illinois Central Railroad. A small farming community grew, first called Bennville and later Hollandale, both after Mr. Holland.

Hollidays
Fond du Lac County

Benjamin Holliday owned the land through which the railroad was built.

Holmen
La Crosse County

Norwegians settled this area, calling their town Frederickstown, and later Cricken. In 1851 a Mr. Holmen was one of a group that surveyed the territory, and later he became a state senator in Indiana. It is said that C. A. Sjolander, the first postmaster, asked that the town be named in honor of Senator Holmen. Another account states that the name was chosen because of the location of the town, holm being the Norwegian word for a projection of low, level rich land extending into the water. Holmen is also said to be a berg in Norway.

Holway
Taylor County

Nymphus B. Holway was a lumberman from La Crosse who had considerable land holdings in Taylor County. He may also have been an early settler.

Holycross   *Ozaukee County*

This locale is believed to have been chosen by a Holy Cross Catholic father to establish a Wisconsin branch of their Boston, Massachusetts, seminary. A small church and school were built, but the funds to develop it did not materialize; the winters were too severe, and the project was abandoned. The parish was organized on September 14, 1845, the day of the Feast of the Holy Cross. The church here claims to possess relics of the original Holy Cross of Christ from Mt. Calvary. The settlement grew as a Luxemburg farming community.

Holy Hill   *Washington County*

From The History of Washington County, 1885:

Many years ago a farmer whose home was among the hills, was returning from the neighboring village of Hartford, late at night. The full moon had just risen, and as he approached St. Mary's Hill from the west, it stood in inky blackness between him and the silver eastern sky. The outline was as sharply defined as a silhouette, and on the very summit he saw the form of a cross and a kneeling figure. He watched the apparition for an hour, until the figure slowly arose and disappeared in the black woods of the hillside.

Not many mornings after he again saw the strange figure on the top of the hill engaged in his devotions. The advent of the anchorite soon became generally known in the neighborhood, and his home was discovered in a cave which he had dug in a gorge on the east side of the hill. No one disturbed him. His only occupation seemed to be his pilgrimages to the hilltop to pray. He gradually grew familiar with the inhabitants, sufficiently to answer their friendly salutations, and occasionally engaged in religious converse with them. One farmer became his confidant, and to him related the following history.

His name was Francois Soubrio. He was born some twenty miles from Strasbourg, and, being of high birth, was educated for the priesthood. He became enamored of a lady near the monastery where he was pursuing his course of study, and passion reciprocated, renounced his priestly vows and became openly betrothed. Disgraced in the eyes of his family and under the ban of the church, he postponed his marriage, and bidding farewell for a season to his affianced, he left, until the matter might blow over. At the end of a year, he returned to find his love fickle as well as fair, and in a frenzy of insane passion, slew her. He fled to America, landed at Quebec, and became a recluse in one of the monasteries of the old city.

Here Soubrio remained many years, tortured with remorse for his faithlessness to his religious vows and by the greater sin of murder that lay heavier on his heart. His only surcease from his troubles was in prayer; penance and in delving among some old French manuscripts that he had found in an obscure corner of his monastic retreat Among them was a manuscript purporting to be a diary kept by Father Marquette during the summer and fall of 1673, in which was a detailed account of his memorable voyage with Louis Joliet to the Mississippi River, via the Fox and Wisconsin Rivers, returning up the Illinois River and the western coast of Lake Michigan to Green Bay, from whence they started.

Soubrio's attention was particularly drawn to an account of an expedition from a creek, where the explorer had landed on his return voyage, a hard day's march west, to a steep and lofty cone-shaped hill which he climbed to the summit and thereon erected a rude stone altar, raised a cross, dedicated the spot as holy ground forever, in the name of his tutelary saint, Mary, and returning, left it towering in its solitude.

Francois felt that his mission, whereby to work out his full atonement, was declared to him. He fell on his knees, and vowed to rediscover the holy hill and reerect the long-ago decayed cross upon its summit. From this description of the coast and a rough map made by Joliet, which was with the manuscript, he had little difficulty in locating the spot.

Francois went to Chicago, where he was halted in his journey by a serious illness, which left him a confirmed paralytic with only the partial use of his lower limbs. In this crippled condition he at last reached the end of his pilgrimage, and late one evening crawled through the thick wood on his knees to the summit of the hill, where he spent the remainder of the night in prayer to the holy Saint Mary. With the dawn he rose from his knees in all the vigor of his early manhood, his palsy gone and health fully restored.

On the spot where his miraculous cure was wrought, he built a rude chapel, and each day and night, and often twice and thrice, he went up to pay his devotions, so often that the path he trod became definitely marked. Along the path he erected crosses at regular intervals, before which he knelt as he ascended and descended, doing extreme penance often by making the pilgrimage on his bare knees. The people had heard so much of his story as related to his miraculous cure that they began to seek relief from their bodily ailments through prayer at the hermit's shrine.

As for Francois, the hermit, he remained in the vicinity, in a rude hut built out from the mouth of the cave he first inhabited, for seven years, when he disappeared as mysteriously as he came. Whether he lived or died was never known. Some say he joined Union forces in the Civil War and was killed in battle. There was a rumor that he was seen in Chicago after his disappearance and it is sometimes told that his apparition is seen in the dusk of evening, kneeling, at some of the various crosses along his old path, or gliding in and out of a rude chapel.

Holy Island
Washburn County

A large peninsula at the southern tip of Long Lake, having the appearance of an island, was once a retreat established by a group of ministers.

Holy Land
Fond du Lac County

A nickname for the northeastern part of the county where many communities are named for their churches—St. Joe, St. Peter, Marytown, Johnsburg.

The Homme Homes
Shawano County

They were built by E. J. Hommes, who ran a farm, published three newspapers, operated four schools, raised and sold garden seeds, and sold a patent medicine of his own making called "Wittenberg Drops." He did all this to support his service programs. In a decade he built a church, a home for the aged, and an orphanage.

Honey Creek   *Sauk County*

Early settlers found many wild bees and rich stores of honey when they first came across this stream. It is the largest stream in the county, and there is a town named after it.

Honey Creek   *Walworth County*

It is said that in 1836 a band of wanderers traveling through the Territory of Wisconsin came to a small stream in an area where there were many bee trees. The name may also have been translated from Ah-moo-sis-po-quet-se-pee, meaning "large number of bee trees."

Hoosier Hollow   *Richland County*

Located in Eagle Township. Settlers such as William Miller and George G. Sharp came from the Hoosier state. The word "Hoosier" is said to come from the call "Who's here?"

Hope   *Grant County*

"Because we live in hope; the way farmin' is these days, a fellow's got to," said one old-timer.

Hopewell Ridge   *Richland County*

Located in Forest Township. Hopewell, Pennsylvania, was the place of origination of some of the settlers.

Hopokoekau Beach   *Fond du Lac County*

This subdivision is located on the east shore of Lake Winnebago in Taycheedah. It was named for Ho-po-ko-e-kau, a Ho-Chunk woman. She was the mother of a celebrated line of chiefs, and at one time was married to a high-ranking French army officer. When he returned to Canada, she refused to accompany him rather than lose her tribal status. The officer's name was De Kaury, but her sons spelled it "Decorah." Hopokoekau means "glory of the morning," and was given as a name to the queen because of her great beauty.

Horicon   *Dodge County*

Maunk-shak-kah, meaning "White Breast," was a Ho-Chunk village of some two thousand people here. In 1832 it is listed as Elk Village, and subsequently Indian Ford. In 1839 Henry Hubbard obtained the land, and it was called Hubbard's Rapids. A group of settlers from Lake George (formerly called Lake Horicon) in New York State were attracted to the location. William Larrabee, at a gathering of pioneers in his home, suggested the name be changed to Horicon. There were Horicon Indians mentioned in the writings of James Fenimore Cooper. The word in the Mohican language means "clear water."

Horlicksville   *Racine County*

The Horlick family built the Horlick malted milk plant here.

Horns Corners   *Ozaukee County*

Frederick W. Horn owned land here and built his house at the corner of a road crossing. He became State Commissioner of Immigration and was also state senator, state assemblyman, and speaker of the assembly from 1851 to 1854.

Horse Bluff   *Sauk County*

One day several hunters were camped in this area, seated around a blazing fire smoking their pipes, when they were startled by the neighing of a horse. As they watched, a pony, saddled and bridled, came trotting into the camp, riderless. For two days a search was made for the owner, without avail. The only European settlers known in that vicinity at the time were James W. Babb and his son, John, on Babbs Prairie. This mystery never was solved, and since that day the elevation has been known as Horse Bluff. H. C. Palmer related this peculiar story of the elevation located just west of the village of La Valle.

Horse Creek   *Richland County*

Located in Richland and Marshall. Samuel Swinehart called the stream Horse Creek after his horse became mired in the creek and died. Some say that it was named after a dead horse was found in the water.

Hortonville   *Outagamie County*

Alonzo Erastus Horton obtained the land patent for this quarter section from President Zachary Taylor on September 1, 1849, and founded this village. He is also said to be the founder of San Diego, California.

Houlton   *St. Croix County*

The location of a large sawmill in the early 1900s, it was named by lumbermen who came from Houlton, Maine. Houlton is situated on a bluff overlooking the St. Croix River.

Howard   *Brown County*

Brigadier General Benjamin Howard was a military commander in the War or 1812. Fort Howard was also named after him.

Howard   *Chippewa County*

Curt Craft, the first settler on the land, named the site Craft to honor his father. The name was changed to Howard to honor an official of the Soo Line Railroad.

Howard's Grove   *Sheboygan County*

The community was first called Pitchville, a name derived from the German word pech, meaning "pitch" or "cobbler's wax." H. B. Howard, one of the earliest businessmen in the area, established a trading center here in 1850. He built Howard's Hotel and was the first postmaster.

Howinch   *Rock County*

Ho-Chunk name for the Indian village at the mouth of the Yahara River. It existed for at least a hundred years before the first settlers came to this region.

Hub City

Located in Henrietta Township. T. G. Mandt made wagon parts here, some say only hubs. In another version of its naming, a daughter of Mr. Mandt told of visiting the little "town" as a child of eight or nine and hearing her father tell of naming the settlement for a close friend by the name of "Hub" Atkins, who was a Chicago railroad magnate.

Hubbard

The first government land sale in this area was a five-hundred-acre tract to Governor Henry Hubbard of New Hampshire.

Hubbleton

Known as Hubbleville in the early days, it was probably named for Levi Hubble, who owned a nearby section of land in the northeast corner of Milford Township. A busy shipping center for the products of the area, it was the only station between Watertown and Waterloo on the Chicago, Milwaukee, and St. Paul Railroad. A post office was established in 1850 and a school district was formed in 1859.

Hudson

Originally this settlement at the mouth of the Willow River was called Willow River. In 1848, Joel Foster, having just returned from the Battle of Buena Vista, suggested Buena Vista as a new name because of the beautiful view from the settlement. In 1851 J. O. Henning petitioned the Legislature to establish the name Willow River because he had platted a subdivision under that name. This caused considerable dissatisfaction until 1852, when Alfred Day petitioned to have the name changed to Hudson, as a traveler noticed a resemblance of the St. Croix River to the Hudson River in New York State.

Hughey

A logging station in the town of Cleveland at the eastern end of the Omaha Railroad. When the timber was gone, the railroad was removed.

Huilsburg

J. Huils was an early settler in that area.

Hull

David B. Hull was a pioneer settler in the area.

Hulls Crossing

J. D. Hull owned the land on which the station was established.

Humboldt

Discontinued post office in the town of Ironton, probably named after the geographer, Baron Alexander von Humboldt.

Humbolt

May have been named after Von Humbolt, the famous naturalist.

Hundred Mile Grove *Dane County*

Located near Dane and Vienna. The surveyors' stake marking the first one hundred miles from Fort Crawford to Fort Winnebago on the old Military Road was driven in this grove. Another local explanation for the name is that farmers hauling wheat to Milwaukee took this grove as being the one-hundred-mile mark from that city.

Hungry Hollow *Wood County*

This was a section in the city of Marshfield where poor residents once lived.

Huntington *St Croix County*

A corruption of Huntingdon, the town of origin of the first settlers of the 1850s. It was the site of a gristmill until 1948. The old millpond and a spillway still remain.

Hurlbut Corner *Crawford County*

Located in Scott Township. The only location where natural millstones were located, it was named after an early family.

Hurley *Iron County*

The Milwaukee, Lake Shore, and Western Railroad platted the town in 1885 and named it after Judge M. A. Hurley, a lawyer from Wausau and prominent iron ore mining operator.

Hurleytown *Wood County*

Timothy W. Hurley and his partner, Mr. Burns, established a mill and boardinghouse about the year 1855. The mill was sold to John Rablin in 1870.

Huron *Chippewa County*

The Huron Indians were a branch of the Iroquois that had been forced to move westward. They traveled the Great Lakes, the Fox River, the lower Wisconsin, the upper Mississippi, and the Black River to this area in Wisconsin. French traders named them Hurons, meaning bristly, rough haired, or savage.

Hurricane *Grant County*

A bad storm destroyed many trees here.

Husher *Racine County*

Originally, Husher started out as a post office called "Hoosier," a name probably chosen because it was near what was then known as Hoosier Creek. When the name was registered, it was misspelled as "Hisher." It is believed that through the natural erosion of language it eventually became "Husher."

Husher Ridge *Crawford County*

Michael Husher lived on a farm here in 1886. Husher Park is named after this ridge.

Hustisford *Dodge County*

The site was first known as Rock River Rapids since there is nearly a half mile of rapids here. John Hustis was the first settler in 1837. The township was named after him in 1848, with "-ford" added because the Indians had used a fording place here for centuries. For a short while it was called Hustis Rapids.

Hustler
Juneau County

The village was platted from the farm owned by Harmon Ranney in 1894. One street was called Hustler Street, no doubt with the intention that the hustlers in the village were to locate there. The Omaha Railroad built a freight-loading platform and a short spur for setting out cars. J. A. Morrill, who handled the freight, thought there should be an extension to the spur for loading farm produce, but the railroad company refused. He built a warehouse and kept after Mr. McCabe, the superintendent, to extend the spur until Mr. McCabe remarked that "all he had for breakfast, dinner, and supper was Hustler." Mr. Morrill replied, "That's all you will get, until Hustler gets what it wants."

When the farmers, or hustlers, offered to do the grading if the railroad would furnish the steel and ties, the spur track was built. It was then necessary to name the station and establish a post office. A list of names was submitted, but all were duplicates of other names in the state except Hustler. One account says that a prankster inserted Hustler at the end of the list as a joke. At any rate, this was the name the post office department chose.

Hustlers Ridge
Richland County

Located in Richland Township. First known as Coon Ridge, presumably because of some incident involving coons, the change allegedly was made when Frank Scholls remarked that his neighbors on the ridge needed to be hustlers.

Huston Heights
Richland County

J. W. Huston owned a quarry on the hill west of Richland Center, and in 1895 he built his home from stone from his quarry.

Hyland Corners
Dodge County

Amasa Hyland is said to have plowed a furrow from Beaver Dam to Watertown, following an old Indian trail, about where Highway 26 is now located.

Hynek Hollow
Richland County

The Hynek family came from Bohemia and settled here at Bloom.

The Ironton Hotel, against the backdrop of Sauk County's rolling hills, ca. 1923

⇥ I ⇤

Ice Age Reserve   *Fond du Lac County*
On August 6, 1973, the federal government set aside this area of glaciated lands in an effort to preserve its natural beauty.

Iduna   *Trempealeau County*
This post office, established in French Creek Valley in 1899, flourished for a short time with John Hovre as postmaster but ceased to exist when rural free delivery was established. Legend says the Post Office Department sent Mr. Hovre a blank, asking him to suggest three names. But Hovre, being short on inventing names and likewise on grammar and spelling, decided to let the government do the selecting. So he wrote across the blank, "I dono." Whether officials misread the final vowels or changed them for the sake of euphony is not stated.

Legends properly embalmed by time and firmly established in the affections of mankind, unless harmful, ought not to be destroyed. But this legend is too modern to have any special sanctity. The true origin of the name is said to be this: When the government blank was received by Mr. Hovre, he sent it to A. H. Anderson, who had assisted him in getting the post office. Knowing that this is a big country with an almost unlimited use for new names, Mr. Anderson at once turned to his Norse mythology and selected three names, which he sent to the post office department. Among them was Iduna, the custodian of the apples of immortality, which the gods tasted from time to time to perpetuate their youth. Loki, the spirit of evil, once stole the golden apples, causing great grief in Valhalla. Iduna's husband was Bragi, the divine bard.

Inch   *Columbia County*
William McDonald, a Scotch Highlander, started this small community, but the exact reason for his giving it this name is not known. It may come from the obsolete Gaelic word inis or innis, meaning "island." Or the word inches, meaning "meadow" or "meadowland," may have been the origin. One account states that a small creek running through the area was so narrow in most places it was called Inch Creek.

Independence   *Trempealeau County*
The town was platted during the year of the centennial celebration of American Independence. Giles Cripps suggested the name.

Indian Creek   *Polk County*
"A small trading center and social center has sprung up on Indian Creek and absorbed that name." This hamlet is in Lorain Township.

Indian Creek   *Richland County*

Located in Orion Township. Thomas Matthews, co-owner of the ferry at Muscoda, named the creek for the Indians he saw hunting along its banks.

Indian Crossing   *Waupaca County*

Probably used by the Indians as a portage at one time, this channel or outlet connects Round and Columbia Lakes.

Indian Ford   *Rock County*

In 1836 Black Hawk and his men forded the Catfish River on the site of what is now this village.

Indian Hollow   *Richland County*

In pioneer days the frames of wigwams were found on the Squire Sheafor farm at Akan.

Interwald   *Taylor County*

A German word meaning "in the woods."

Iola   *Waupaca County*

The Potawatomi tribe migrated from the Eastern Great Lakes region to Green Bay and then to the territory known as Waupaca County. Iola was an Indian girl, said to have been the daughter of Old Red Bird, brother of Chief Waupaca. She married a son of Chief Schenectady and returned to New York State in later life. The village site was named after her in 1829.

Iowa County

The Iowas were one of the southern Sioux tribes. The Indian word was Ah-hee-oo-ba or aiaouez, meaning sleepy or drowsy ones. One account states that the Iowa tribe was once part of the Ho-Chunk nation and was nearly annihilated by the Sioux, who gave them this name.

Irish Hollow   *Green County*

A valley in the southwest corner of Exeter township so named because all the early settlers came from County Antrim, Ireland.

Irish Ridge   *Crawford County*

Located in Scott Township. A large number of Irish families settled here.

Irish Road   *Calumet County*

A road that crosses Calumet County and along which lived many sons of the Old Sod.

Irma   *Lincoln County*

The town was officially laid out as Courtland by the Milwaukee Land Company in 1887. Later the name was changed to Irma after the depot agent's daughter.

Iron Belt
Iron County

This valley town, scooped out of the Penokee Mountain Range, was born of those two giants of frontier industry, lumber and iron ore. A sawmill and thirteen iron mines drew the original settlers.

Iron County

The discovery of iron ore in the Mesabi Mountain Range prompted the name.

Iron Mountain
Dodge County

This is a translation of the Ojibwe name biwabiko-wadjiw, meaning "metallic mountain." The Indians said that Manitou obtained some of the metal for his thunderbolts here.

Iron Ridge
Dodge County

In the early 1800s a few hardy settlers started this community because of the iron ore mines that were started at Old Iron Ridge by the Wisconsin Iron Company. When the railroad was completed, Iron Ridge Station was established and changed to the Village of Iron Ridge, incorporated in 1913.

Iron River
Bayfield County

A small stream flowing north from Iron Lake into Lake Superior was called Biwabiko-sibi by the Ojibwe Indians, meaning "metallic river." When a survey was made for the railroad to cross this stream, it was planned to have a railroad construction camp there named Iron River. When the railroad was completed and the construction camp left, it became a flag stop. About 1890 John D. Pettingill obtained homestead land and started the town.

Ironton
Sauk County

Early surveyors reported the presence of iron in the area because of variation in their compass needle, and iron ore was discovered near here in 1849. Jonas Tower, an experienced miner, platted the village and gave it this name.

Irvine
Chippewa County

William Irvine was manager of the Chippewa Lumber and Boom Company about 1846.

Irvington
Dunn County

Although in the 1880s there was a large sawmill and a cooperative creamery here, there are very few buildings now. Named after George Irving, who came by steamboat up the Mississippi and Chippewa with other pioneers from Iowa, Irvington is located on the Red Cedar River at the mouth of Irving Creek, two miles south of Menomonie.

Island Park
In Lake Winnebago

A Ho-chunk village was formerly located here called Pe-she after the warrior Pesheu, or Wild Cat. At one time it was also called Garlic Island.

Itasca *Douglas County*

Henry Rowe Schoolcraft was head of a commission appointed by the president of the United States to explore the coast of Lake Superior after the War of 1812. He is said to have coined the name Itasca from the Ojibwe word totsha, meaning "woman's breast."

Ives Grove *Racine County*

About 1837 Joseph Call sold his claim to Marshall M. Strong and Stephen N. Ives, who in turn sold it to Roland Ives. Soon after a post office was established and given the name of Ives Grove.

Ixonia *Jefferson County*

When the Town of Union was divided, Township 7 was called Concord, but there was great divergence of opinion as to what to call Township 8. To satisfy all factions, it was agreed to put the letters of the alphabet on slips of paper and have young Mary Piper draw them until a word was formed. The result was Ixonia. It is the only town of that name in the United States.

⇥ J ⇤

Jackson   *Burnett County*

G. L. Millet, a Prairie du Chien attorney, invested heavily in property in the eastern part of Burnett County and personally petitioned the state legislature to establish this new town named in honor of Stonewall Jackson.

Jacksonport   *Door County*

The site of an old Potawatomi Indian village called Medemaya-Seebe, meaning "old woman's creek." It was supposed to have existed for four hundred years or more. It was renamed in honor of President Andrew Jackson.

Jamestown   *Grant County*

James Boyce discovered lead ore here in 1827, and when prospectors moved in, the post office of Centerville was established. The settlement was abandoned within a few years due to the cheap price of lead ore, and the post office was moved to another location. When the community began to grow again the new post office was named Jamestown after James Gillmore, the postmaster.

Janes' Settlement   *Rock County*

In 1842 the Janes family settled in this now defunct settlement.

Janesville   *Rock County*

E-nee-poro-poro was the name of the Ho-Chunk village that flourished here. The name means "round rock," from the large stone outcrop in the Rock River, later called Monteray Point. When settlers found the site during the Black Hawk War it was known as Black Hawk. In 1837 Henry F. Janes, who had started a ferry service across the river, petitioned for a post office and was told there already was a Black Hawk in the territory. A federal officer then selected the name Janesville and appointed Henry Janes the postmaster. The first post office is said to have been a cigar box nailed to a log.

Jebaiesa Supet   *Shawano and Oconto Counties*

Menominee name for a group of Indian mounds on the east bank of the Wolf River near a spot called Five Islands by settlers. The name means "where the little corpse lies."

Jefferson and Jefferson Junction   *Jefferson County*

One account says it was named by Perry H. Smith, an early railroad officer, in honor of President Thomas Jefferson. Another account says that the site was abandoned by Captain Robert Masters and two other men who had petitioned the government to have the county seat located on their property. The petition was granted in 1838 with a blank left for the name, which Captain Masters filled in with the name Jefferson, the others agreeing.

Jefferson County

The county is said to have been organized by the territorial legislature in February 1839 on the petition of Patrick, Peter, and James Rogan and Judge Hyer, who had come from Jefferson County, New York.

Jeffris   *Lincoln County*

David K. Jeffris built a sawmill here in 1891 and named the settlement for his brother, James K. Jeffris of Janesville. Its post office was called Bundy after McG. Bundy of Grand Rapids, Michigan, who had large timber interests here. The post office is closed.

Jennings   *Oneida County*

David Jennings of Milwaukee owned land in the vicinity. The station was named Lennox.

Jericho   *Calumet County*

It is believed to have been founded as a toll gate station on the Brothertown-Sheboygan Plank Road, and some travelers tried to crash it. This suggested the name from the biblical village whose walls were destroyed by an outside group of people.

Jericho   *Waukesha County*

A little inn was built by Jerry Parsons with a sign over its door which read Jerry, Co.

Jerusalem Corners   *Pierce County*

A black family entertained people of the area with spirituals. The man was a good singer, and someone gave it this name.

Jewett   *St. Croix County*

First called Jewett's Mills, it was started by a Mr. Jewett, who came from the East in the 1890s. The "founder" had ambitions to create a bustling metropolis from this site of a small sawmill and gristmill. After selling many "city lots" he disappeared.

Jim Falls   *Chippewa County*

James Ermatinger, a native of Canada, was the first to settle here. He operated a trading post, a portage, and a logging operation and married Miss Cadotte. He originally named the town Vermillion Falls because the ground or clay was so red. Later it was called Ermatinger Falls and then shortened to Jim Falls.

Jimtown   *Dane County*

Located in Montrose. Named for Jim Wilson, a blacksmith, who tried to get people to give up the name "Jimtown" when the Montrose Post Office was established. Despite his insistence, they clung to the name.

Jimtown   *Richland County*

Located in Akan Township. It was named for two Jims: Jim Bachtenkircher, who operated a little store, and Jim Burns, who lived near a big spring where some of the settlers came for water.

Joe Snow Road   *Lincoln County*

Joe Snow built Joe Snow Road and homesteaded on Joe Snow Hill. He was a member of the crew that built a dam and sawmill for Andrew Warren, who was the first permanent settler in Jenny (later Merrill).

Johannesburg   *St. Croix County*

Settled by Johannes Johnson in the early 1870s, this community along the Apple River sprang up on lands owned by Isaac Staples, a Stillwater, Minnesota, lumber magnate.

John Gray Cave   *Richland County*

Located on the John Gray farm in Rockbridge Township, it is now buried under a plowed field. Spelunkers from the University of Wisconsin called it Squirrel Cave because a squirrel ran out just as they were about to enter the 710 feet of caverns.

John Muir Country   *Marquette County*

Originally from Scotland, John Muir traveled over these roads to such early settlements as Kingston and Pardeeville. He attended the University of Wisconsin, but he left before completing his studies to travel out West on foot. He persuaded Congress to pass the National Park Act in 1890.

John Muir View   *Columbia County*

John Muir (1838–1914), "father of the national park system" and world-famous naturalist, would often stop here to admire the view as he walked from his home in Marquette County to the University of Wisconsin.

Johnny Cake Gulch   *Richland County*

Located in Rockbridge Township. Melvin Poole named this sandy ravine, selecting this name, perhaps, because the deep yellow color of the sand reminded him of johnnycake.

Johnsburg   *Fond du Lac County*

Named for the St. John the Baptist Church located here. The parish was founded by six families who arrived from Trier, Germany, in 1841.

Johnson Creek   *Crawford County*

Running from Wingers to the County Line, it was named after the Johnson family.

Johnson Creek   *Jefferson County*

Timothy Johnson and Charles Goodhue, two courageous and daring young men, made a joint claim to the land where Johnson Creek now stands in 1837. They erected a dam and a sawmill and called the settlement Belleville. By 1873 mail was being missent to Belleville in Dane County, and a meeting was called and it was voted to change the name to Johnson Creek after its founder.

Johnson Hill   *Crawford County*

Located in Freeman Township. People by the name of Johnson operated a gravel pit on this hill.

Johnsonville *Sheboygan County*

This community was called Schnapsville (Whiskeyville) from earliest times, but the name was thought to be inappropriate and was changed to honor Andrew Johnson, president of the United States.

Johnstown *Crawford County*

Located in Clayton Township. A family here had three boys with the name of John, and several other people in the town also had that name, so by mutual agreement they named the place Johnstown.

Johnstown *Polk County*

The town was named for John Pauling, an early settler. He was a Civil War veteran and was a prisoner at Andersonville during the war.

Johnstown *Rock County*

Horace McElroy's "The Forgotten Places" gives this account of an early Johnstown incident:

> *John A. Fletcher purchased of the United States government on February 21, 1839 the East half of the South-East quarter of Section twenty-three in what is now the town of Johnstown. Shortly after his purchase of this land he concluded that it would make a good town site. No map of the place is on record, and it does not appear even to have been named. The good Squire Fletcher had just driven his last stakes when a land hunter came by, who said he was from Milwaukee, and was looking up some desirable tract that had not yet been entered; then he added, "It must be very sickly around here." "No it ain't," said Mr. Fletcher. "It's the healthiest country in the United States. What makes you ask such a fool question as that?" "Well," the man replied, "I only ask because I see you are laying out a thundering big burying ground."*

Jonesville *Sauk County*

This discontinued post office in the town of Spring Green stood on an Indian burying ground and has since been eaten away by the Wisconsin River. Thomas Jones was the first postmaster.

Juda *Green County*

This community is largely on land claimed by one Jehu Chadwick in approximately 1835. The original name of the village when platted was Juda, but the reason for the name is not known. Since the early settlers were Baptists and deeply religious, it probably refers to ancient Judah—they felt they had come to the Promised Land. When the railroad was built there was an attempt to change the name to Springfield and for many years the village was known by both names.

Juddy Smith Hill *Crawford County*

Named for Juddy Smith, it is located between Highway 131 and county trunk W.

Jump River
Chippewa County

The first settler was Barney Broeder, and the settlement was called Broederville. Residents changed it to Jump River because it is located at the river rapids. Big and Little Jump Rivers are so named by the Indians, who used them for tests of athletic prowess near their sources.

Junction City
Portage County

The tracks of the Wisconsin Valley Railroad (later the Chicago, Milwaukee, and St. Paul) and the Wisconsin Central Railroad (later the Soo Line) crossed at this point. A post office established in 1847 was named, officially, Junction. The citizens liked Junction City better, and the village was incorporated under this name in 1911. The first records list the following personal property in the village: eight horses, twelve cows, some swine, and nine wagons, carriages, and sleighs.

June
Burnett County

Gilbert Slayton had a daughter named June. He lived for a short time near Viola Lake, twenty-five miles east of Grantsburg.

Juneau
Dodge County

The village was first settled in 1844 by one Martin Rich. Being victorious in the battle for the county seat over Fox Lake and Watertown, it was first called Victory. In 1848 it was re-platted and renamed Dodge Center because of its geographical location. There was already a Dodge Center in Wisconsin, so the name was changed in honor of Solomon Juneau, founder of Milwaukee.

Juneau County

Solomon Juneau was an early French trader at the site of Milwaukee. He was born in Canada and came to Milwaukee in 1818 as an employee of Jacques Vieau. He was the first postmaster and the first mayor of the city.

Kaukauna's Grignon House, built in 1836 by Charles Grignon, the son of one of Wisconsin's first permanent settlers. The house was originally called "The Mansion in the Woods."

⇢ K ⇠

Kah-Puk-Wi-E-Kah *Bayfield County*
An Ojibwe Indian campsite in Siskowitt Bay on Lake Superior that had a fine sand beach.

Kalkberg *Dane County*
Located near Berry. The German word for "lime-hill" identifies this well-known quarry, the site of kilns.

Kane Hollow *Crawford County*
Located in Marietta Township, it was named for the Kane families who lived here.

Kansasville *Racine County*
Captain John T. Trowbridge, the first settler, had been a sea captain for twenty-five years on whaling vessels and lake boats. He also fought in the War of 1812 and had been captured by the British and imprisoned in India. In 1836 he decided to settle down and built a three-sided cabin for his family that kept them for the first winter. Later he built a two-story log house that became a stopping place for settlers passing through. When Captain Trowbridge became the first postmaster he named the town Brighton. Later, when the town was organized, it was called Dover. Apparently the Brighton Post Office in Dover Township was renamed Kansasville during the days of the Kansas-Nebraska Bill agitation in Washington, D.C. It is said that a family moved from here to Kansas, but because of the drought they returned, and the village was named in their honor.

Karlsborg *Burnett County*
M. J. Kalmen, an early settler, chose this name after the place in Sweden from which he and other settlers had come. It means "Charles's fortress."

Katherine Evans School *Fond du Lac County*
This school on the west side of Fond du Lac was named for a teacher and principal with forty-three years of service in the city's school system.

Kaukauna *Outagamie County*
The Menominee Indian word was okakaning, often shortened to kakaning, meaning "place where they fish for pike or pickerel," or "long portage," or "crow nesting place." It was the Indian term for rapids in the Fox River and has evolved into Kaukauna.
From the Manitowoc Herald, March 18, 1919:

> Some years ago Kaukauna farmers became wildly excited over a reported find of gold. It is a mystery whether the discovery was not a press agented affair, since it helped a student of Lawrence College to earn a portion of his way through school.

Early in 1900 a pair of students were specializing in chemistry at Lawrence College. In that same year a countryman, young, but roughly dressed, feet muddy, strolled into a saloon in Kaukauna, and showed the bartender a hunk of brilliant glistening rock, sparkling like gold, declaring that young as he was, he had hunted gold in the wilds of Canada, and knew ore when he saw it He begged for a drink in return for a bit of inside information on where he had found the "gold."

And for a drink he disclosed—later some thought too carefully—the location of the gold mine, and how he planned to go to Appleton and get the college laboratory to make an assay to find out how rich it was. Exit the goldfinder. No one ever saw him again.

The brilliant rock had been found in large quantities on several farms near Kaukauna. One of the owners of a farm took specimens to Appleton. There was no assayer in the city, but a student at the college was willing—for a fee—to make a test.

The young student chemist was honest. Looking at the specimen he said: "I'm sorry, my friend, this is not gold. It is iron pyrites, known as "fool's gold."

However, the student was persuaded to make an assay—for a fee of five much needed dollars. And the test showed only iron and sulphur.

Other farmers wanted assays made. There was a rush to Appleton to have specimens tested.

The farmers who paid $5.00 each for an assay never admitted they had been lured by fool's gold. So the students received material aid in financing an education.

Iron pyrites were thus proved to exist in quantities in the Fox River Valley.

There is gold in small quantities all through the iron ranges of Northern Wisconsin and Michigan. It is mined profitably in some localities, and the gold is a valuable by-product in the copper mining region.

Wisconsin also has a streak of diamond-bearing gravel running from northwest to southeast through the region of Stevens Point and Waupaca, but not over a half dozen diamonds—and these small—have been found.

Kawaga
Oneida County

Ojibwe Indian term for "whittlings" or "shavings." The Indians found a man whittling shavings here.

Keesus
Waukesha County

Said to be a Potawatomi Indian word for "sun."

Kegonsa
Dane County

This name is taken from the lake called Gi-go-sen-sag by the Ojibwe Indians, meaning "lake of small fishes."

Kekoskee
Dodge County

A Ho-Chunk Indian village was located here, the term meaning "friendly village."

Kellnersville *Manitowoc County*

A sawmill was established in 1849 by John (or Michale) Kellner. Later he built a gristmill and a general merchandise store and saloon. It was called Kellner's Corners at first, but the post office became Kellnersville.

Kelly *Grant County*

A settlement named after Valentine Kelly.

Kelly *Marathon County*

Nathaniel Kelly was a prominent businessman in Wausau.

Kempster *Langlade County*

Dr. Walter Kempster was born in London, England, and came to Syracuse, New York, with his parents and brother, John, at the age of seven. He became famous for his medical work during the Civil War and for research in the field of mental illness and psychology. He was the first superintendent of Winnebago State Hospital and professor of mental diseases at the Wisconsin Medical College. He also served as a witness in the trial of Guiteau, slayer of President Garfield. It is not clear whether it was Dr. Walter, or Dr. John, or both doctors, who received title to large tracts of timber land in this area north of Antigo in 1881. Apparently Dr. John Kempster lived in the area for a few years.

Kendall *Lafayette County*

John Kindle, the earliest settler, built a mill and the schoolhouse. The county board voted to change the spelling of the name to Kendall because it would be more easily written and spoken.

Kendall *Monroe County*

L. G. Kendall was a railroad contractor who purchased the right-of-way in this area and other property, and then resold it to W. P. Medbury, who had it surveyed and platted into lots. Mr. Kendall never lived in the area.

Kendall's Corners *Walworth County*

Captain George Washington Kendall owned a tavern at this corner.

Kennan *Price County*

Originally this was a part of Chippewa County and later was known as the town of Ripley. The story the old-timers tell is that many years ago a Soo Line tax lawyer, K. K. Kennan, set up his headquarters here and built a log station house that he named Kennan Station. It was shortened to Kennan.

Kenosha *Kenosha County*

Potawatomi Indian villages here were called Kenosha, meaning "pike" or "pickerel," and the first European hunters and trappers used this name. The settlement was first called Pike, and later Southport because it was the southernmost port in Wisconsin. When the village was incorporated as a city in 1850, it took the original Indian name.

Kenosha County

An old paper filed in Detroit whereby Indians ceded land to the settlers mentions this section as Kenosha, for the pike that apparently were plentiful in the creeks. Longfellow in The Song of Hiawatha spells it Kenozia.

Kepler Hollow *Richland County*

William F. Kepler, a farmer and carpenter, came to Marshall with his father, Henry, in 1853 or 1854. His spinning wheels could be found in many of the pioneers' homes.

Kerby Hollow *Richland County*

Located in Marshall Township. Joseph Kerby and his family came here from Maryland before 1857.

Keshena *Shawano County*

The Menominee Indian village here was said to have been named for Chief Keshi-ne. The word means "swift flying" and supposedly was chosen because the chief's father had a dream in which he saw the air filled with eagles and hawks.

Keska Kwutino *Calumet County*

This is a rock ledge, supposed to be sacred to the Menominee Indians because the thunderbirds who became the ancestors of the tribe alighted here and turned into men.

Kettle Moraine State Forest *Southeastern Wisconsin*

This area is characterized by a succession of curiously rounded glacial hills and valleys, interspersed by numerous lakes, ponds, streams, swamps, and woods or kettles.

Kewaquesaga *Oneida County*

This Ho-Chunk word means "the third daughter."

Kewaskum *Washington County*

A Potawatomi Indian chief had his camp here and died about the time the township was organized in 1847. The word means "going back," "returning on the back track," "a man able to turn fate whichever way he pleases," or "his tracks are toward home." Jesse H. Myer, who built the first log house, a sawmill, and a gristmill, chose the name.

Kewaunee *Kewaunee County*

In 1796 Jacques Veaux established a trading post at the mouth of the Kewaunee River. A few years later a hunter named Wood took possession of the vicinity and allowed no one to trespass for miles around. Gossip had it that gold had been found. In 1836 the site was chosen by John Jacob Astor as a trading post, and a city larger than Chicago was platted. Kewaunee is the Indian name for the site and is said to mean either "prairie chicken" or "the way around or across a point of land."

Kewaunee County

The Potawatomi Indian name is supposedly a corruption of Kaki-we-onan, meaning, "I cross a point of land by boat," referring to the river in the peninsula between Green Bay and Lake Michigan. The area was known as Woods or Woods River until 1834, when Joshua Hathaway, an early surveyor, gave it the Indian name, which he translated as meaning "prairie hen."

Keyesville   Richland County

Located in Ithaca Township. In 1872, when a post office was to be established, Norman L. James, who was elected to the assembly in 1872, was to choose the name. Mr. James consulted Judge E. W. Keyes, a former mayor of Madison. Judge Keyes mentioned "Jamesville" while Mr. James suggested "Keyesville." These two men and three others took a vote. Two were cast for "Jamesville" and three were for "Keyesville."

Keystone   Chippewa County

Original settlers came from Pennsylvania, the Keystone State, to establish a trading post and later a small village.

Kickapoo   Vernon County

The Kickapoo Indians, whose name is believed to mean "he stands out" or "now here, now there," lived in the valley and along the river.

Kickapoo Indian Cemetery   Crawford County

Located in Marietta Township. In 1867, fifty to two hundred Indians who were encamped here were decimated by an epidemic of smallpox. Discovered in the spring of that year, no one was buried here before or since the disaster.

Kiel   Calumet County

Kiel had its beginning in Manitowoc County, but a part of it grew over into Calumet County. Charley Lindermann purchased the land where the village now stands in 1862. Mrs. Lindermann asked Tante Gretchen, a kindly lady, to name the town. She chose Kiel in memory of her home in Germany.

Kiel   Manitowoc County

Colonel Henry F. Belitz bought a large tract of land in 1854 in the town of Meeme. Through his efforts the southwest corner of the county was set off from Meeme as a new town, which Belitz wanted named Schleswig after the Danish province in North Germany. But an amendment to the original petition named the new town Abel, in honor of the first settler, D. Abel, who had come in 1847. By 1856 Colonel Belitz was successful in getting the name changed to Schleswig. Five years later the name was changed to Kiel, said to have been Colonel Belitz's home in Germany.

Kieler   Grant County

George Kieler came from Germany in 1857. He was a shoemaker by trade and continued to make shoes in the small general store he built here. The post office was given his name.

Kilbourn   Columbia County

Byron Kilbourne was a Wisconsin pioneer and capitalist, said to have been influential in having the railroad built through this site instead of through Newport. He became tired of correcting those who dropped the "e" from his name and finally dropped it himself. Kilbourn City was recorded on a plat in 1856, but it is now known as Wisconsin Dells.

Kimball
Iron County

Named for Congressman Kimball of Pine River in Waushara County.

Kimball Park
Grant County

Mr. Kimball, who lived here at one time, is said to have had four wives and twenty-one children.

Kimberly
Outagamie County

One of the earliest government maps of the region shows an Indian trail on the south bank of the Fox River to Smithfield, where a school and several cleared fields are plainly marked. Another source refers to the old mission site of Smithfield. This is on the south bluff of the river across from where the Treaty of Cedars was signed. Kimberly Clark and Company acquired the land and water rights at The Cedars and built a pulp and paper mill in 1889. The settlement grew, the trail became a road and then a street, and in 1910 The Cedars was incorporated as the Village of Kimberly.

Kim-Me-Con
Vilas County

A trading post on the east shore of Catfish Lake. Later three logging camps were built here, a bank was established, and an effort was made to start a large settlement. But the entire business closed in the Panic of 1857. Joshua Fox, foreman of the lumber camps, is said to have given the site this name because his Indian guide said, "Kim-me-con" to him, meaning, "have you found it?" Mr. Fox was searching for a beautiful site.

Kingsbridge
Manitowoc County

Mr. King built the bridge across the West Twin River here.

Kings Corners
Sauk County

A discontinued post office in the town of Sumpter named for Solomon King. The village plat was called New Haven.

Kingston
Green Lake County

A gristmill built in 1848 by Drummond and Jewett was sold about a year later to Mr. J. E. Millard. His very beautiful and charming wife came from Kingston, Canada.

King Veterans' Home
Waupaca County

Known as Grand Army Home from 1890 to 1896, the name was changed in 1896 to Wisconsin Veteran's Home. In 1941 it was renamed King, after General Charles King, who participated in the Civil War and the Spanish American War. He was also the adjutant general in Wisconsin and was active in Wisconsin military life.

Kinker's Corners
Fond du Lac County

Frank Kinker once maintained a feed mill and grocery store here, in Friendship.

Kinnickinnic   *St. Croix County*

This is a Potawatomi Indian word referring to ceremonial tobacco made of toasted willow or sumac bark.

Kirkwood   *Sauk County*

N. C. and Timothy Kirk owned the land and gave the town its name. They operated a vineyard and made wine.

Kishkekwanten   *Brown County*

A Menominee Indian word meaning "sloping to the cedars." A cedar swamp is located at the bottom of the cliff.

Klevenville   *Dane County*

Iver Kleven was an early settler.

Klondike Corners   *Wood County*

Located in Cameron. The Klondike Saloon, owned by Anton Bast from 1898 to around 1900, was located at the corners. The name is not as well-known as it once was.

Kloten   *Calumet County*

"The first stranger coming into our midst will name this settlement," said the pioneers. The first stranger came from Kloten in Switzerland.

Knaggs Ferry   *Winnebago County*

James Knaggs operated a ferry here for nineteen years.

Knapp   *Dunn County*

John H. Knapp and William Wilson started a lumbering firm here that later was known as Knapp Stout and Company. The railroad was completed in 1871 and the stop was called Knapp Station, but the post office was called Knapp.

Knapps Creek   *Richland County*

Located in Richwood Township. An early hunter named Knapp built his cabin at the mouth of the stream.

Knappville   *Polk County*

"Started when Capt. Oscar Knapp, a pioneer of Osceola, bought 680 acres of timberland on which was located a natural spring and stream, with an abundance of trout." He built a trout-rearing pond, then in 1900 sold all of Knappville to Charles E. Lewis, who built the hamlet of Lewis. He renamed it "Seven Pines" for a group of seven pine trees located at the spring. One of the original seven pines still remains.

Knellsville   *Ozaukee County*

Knell was a farmer who came about 1860 from Luxemburg.

Knowles *Dodge County*

Said to have been named for the many knolls in the vicinity.

Kodan *Kewaunee County*

Wenzel Ullsperger, who operated a cheese factory, was the first postmaster. He had come from Kodau near the border of Germany and Bohemia, and wrote to the US government requesting a stamp for this new post office with this same name. Evidently someone misread his u for an n because when the stamp came, it read Kodan instead of Kodau. Wenzel remarked, "Well, you can't do anything with the government anyhow. We may as well keep the stamp."

Koepenick *Langlade County*

E. S. Koepenick, who owned and operated a sawmill here, is said to have been the first settler.

Kohler *Sheboygan County*

A farmer named Balkins first platted this land and named it Riverside, because it overlooked the Sheboygan River. In 1912 the Kohler Manufacturing Company, producer of enameled plumbing ware, moved its plant from Sheboygan to Riverside, and the village was named Kohler.

Kohlman's Hill *Dane County*

In 1848 Charles Kohlmann, a farmer, was robbed and murdered here when he was setting out with an oxcart for Milwaukee, on his way to buy supplies for himself and some neighbors.

Koll *Chippewa County*

This railroad crossing and sidetrack is thought to have been named for a family living nearby.

Konin *Oconto County*

A plain just below Oconto Falls, where a Menominee village once stood. The name means "where the tornado passed."

Koshkonong *Jefferson County*

This is the Indian term for the lake and creek that has been adopted for the town. There are various interpretations of its meaning. Potawatomi: "place of the hog" or "what he kept for himself." Ojibwe: "shut in," "close in," or "where there is heavy fog." (Heavy fog is said to hang over the lake and creek.)

Kossuth *Manitowoc County*

The Potawatomi village of Old Katose, which was called Kah-kah-be-gah-sing, meaning "small falls," was located here. Some early settlers wanted to name it Bismark, because he was the reason for their leaving Germany, but it was decided to name it after General Kossuth of Hungary, a Revolutionary War hero.

Krakow
Shawano County

J. J. Hof, a real estate man, named the village in honor of the ancient capital of Poland, because he wanted to entice Polish emigrants to settle here.

Kreinersville
Burnett County

E. O. Kreiner was one of the first settlers of this region and helped to get the post office established.

Krok
Kewaunee County

Judge Vojta Stransky, who came from Krok, Czechoslovakia, gave the community this name.

Kronenwetter
Marathon County

Sebastian Kronenwetter was a prominent pioneer of Marathon County.

Kruger
Burnett County

Paul Kruger, president of the Transvaal Republic and leader during the Boer War, is the man for whom this post office was named. Charles Benz, in whose house the post office was first located, was an enthusiastic German and suggested the name. The post office has been discontinued.

Kuehn
Vilas County

Charles S. Kuehn was an old settler.

Kunz Island
Washburn County

Charles Kunz was the first owner of this large island at the western side of Long Lake.

Kushkanong
Rock County

Probably taken from Lake Koshkanong, this settlement no longer exists.

⇥ L ⇤

Lac Court Oreilles   *Sawyer County*
Name given to a band of Indians by the French traders who first visited them at Ottawa Lake. The name means "Lake Short Ears." The Frenchmen thought the Ottawa Indians had cut the rims off their ears.

La Crosse   *La Crosse County*
When the French explorers and traders ascended the Mississippi River they saw Indians playing a game on the prairie that stretched two miles eastward from the bluffs. It was a ball game played with a long-handled racquet that reminded the French of their tennis game that they called la crosse. The French word is said to have originated in the fact that the racquet resembled a bishop's crozier. The settlement was first known as Prairie La Crosse.

La Crosse County
Named after the village of La Crosse. French explorers saw Indians playing this ball game where the city now stands.

Lac du Flambeau   *Vilas County*
French traders saw Ojibwe Indians fishing from their canoes at night by the light of flaming torches. The French for "lake of the flaming torches" became the name of the reservation and the town.

Lac Vieux Desert   *Vilas County*
Some maps claim this area as a desert, which is said to be a mistranslation of old French maps as "the old deserted place." The term actually means an old clearing or planting ground. The Ojibwe name was Kat-a-kit-lekon and referred to the place where they grew and stored food before the settlers came.

Ladoga   *Fond du Lac County*
Said to be an Indian name meaning "rising sun."

Ladysmith   *Rusk County*
When Bob Corbett built a sawmill on the Flambeau River here it was known as Corbett, then as Flambeau Falls, and later as Warner. In 1900 the name was changed to Ladysmith in honor of the bride of a woodenware company's manager to entice him to bring his factory there. The factory came, but Lady Smith never visited the town.

La Farge
Vernon County

In 1856 Charles Seeley built a sawmill on the Kickapoo River, one and a half miles north of what was known as the Crossroads, or Corners. The site was in Stark Township, so the post office in the settlement known as Seeleyburg was called Stark.

Four miles south of the Corners, Sam Green opened a post office and needed a name for it. Lacking entertainment, the Greens had a custom at family gatherings of opening the Bible and having someone close his eyes and point to a verse at random. The verse would be read at the family meal and its meaning discussed. The verse would govern the conduct of those present until the next meeting. Someone suggested that they take a list of place names in the United States and select a name as they did the biblical verse. Clara Hull ran her finger down the column, stopping at La Farge.

In time La Farge was moved to the Corners and absorbed Seeleyburg, which completely disappeared.

Lafayette
Chippewa County

First settled in 1843 by Arthur McCann and J. C. Thomas, who erected the "Blue Mills." It was organized in 1857 as French Town, the name not being changed to Lafayette until some later date. Lafayette Mill (later sold to Lafayette Lumber Co.) was built in 1863 by Charles Coleman.

Lafayette County

Named in honor of the Marquis de LaFayette.

LaFollette
Burnett County

This township was set off in 1902 during the term of Governor Robert M. La Follette.

LaGrange
Walworth County

The township is said to have been named after the native town of General Lafayette in LaGrange, France.

Lake Barney
Dane County

Located in Fitchburg. Named for Barney McGinty, who owned the land around it from 1846 until about 1850.

Lake Bernice
Fond du Lac County

Originally known as Schrauth's Pond, the lake was renamed by John Schrauth for his niece Bernice Berg when he platted the area.

Lake Church
Ozaukee County

This settlement started as a Luxemburg community. It has several very old stone buildings, including the Catholic church of St. Mary's, which suggested the name.

Lake Deneveu
Fond du Lac County

Named when Gustav deNeveu came to Wisconsin in 1838.

Lake Emily   *Dodge County*

Lake Emily, neighboring Lake Maria, and the now arid Lake Sarah made the trio of small lakes that in 1843 Hamilton Stevens named for his three young daughters. The springs of this lake feed one of the small tributaries to a branch of the upper Fox River.

Lakefield   *Ozaukee County*

This very small community is near Lake Michigan, and also near beautiful fields.

Lake Geneva   *Walworth County*

The Potawatomi Indians named the lake after their chief, Muck-Suck, meaning Big Foot. The French called it Gros Pied. About 1836 John Brink surveyed this vicinity and thought the lake was too beautiful for such an uncouth name. The lake reminded him of Seneca Lake in New York, which has the town of Geneva on its shore. Since this lake is smaller than Seneca Lake, he thought one name would serve for both the lake and the village.

Lake Kegonsa   *Dane County*

The Ojibwe Indians called it the "lake of small fishes." The Ho-Chunk called it "hard maple grove lake."

Lake Koshkonong   *Rock County*

Thiebeau, a French trader and early settler at Beloit, claimed that the name Koshkonong was of Ho-Chunk derivation and means "the place where we shave." When he and another trader first came to this area, they established their headquarters at the lake. They would return to the lake to shave after returning from fur-trading activities with the Indians.

Lake Marinuka   *Trempealeau County*

Named for Marinuka, granddaughter of Chief Decorah.

Lake Marion   *Dane County*

So named by Frank Murrish of Mazomanie, because his aunt, Frank [sic] Marion, on a visit from Chicago, fell into the lake. The "lake" is actually a millpond.

Lake Mills   *Jefferson County*

Captain Joseph Keyes and his family came to the lake in 1837 and built a sawmill and a gristmill at the outlet. The settlement was known as Keyes Mills. Mr. Keyes was instrumental in having it officially named Lake Mills, but in 1870 the name was changed for one year to Tyranena, the name given by the Indians. In deference to popular sentiment the state legislature restored the name Lake Mills.

Lake Mohawskin   *Lincoln County*

A contest determined the name of this lake in 1926 when Mr. Herbert Atcherson chose the name Mohawskin—MO from Somo, HAWK from Tomahawk, SIN from Wisconsin—the names of the three rivers that met at that point. Originally called Lake Tomahawk, the name was changed to avoid confusion with the Lake Tomahawk in Oneida County.

Lake Nebagamon   *Douglas County*

The Ojibwe Indians called the lake me-bay-go-mow-win, which means "place to still hunt deer by water." They built fires in the evening and shot the deer when they came to the water's edge to drink.

Lakeport   *Pepin County*

John McCain, who piloted a raft on the Mississippi, came in the spring of 1846. The site was first called Johnstown, but Mr. McCain gave it the name of Lockport, later changed to Lakeport.

Lake Puckaway   *Marquette and Green Lake Counties*

An expansion of the Fox River, it is eight miles long and three-quarters of a mile wide. The Indian name may signify "wild rice field," from the abundance of wild rice that annually feeds hundreds of ducks and blackbirds upon the surrounding marshes. Puckaway has also been interpreted to be an Indian name for syphilis.

Lakeside   *Washburn County*

A telegrapher was given a little shack in which to operate near a lake. He told of watching the wolves run past at night. It was called Lakeside and the name was transferred to the lake.

Lake Tomahawk   *Oneida County*

The town was settled on the east shore of the lake after the Milwaukee, Lakeshore & Western Railroad from Rhinelander to Hurley was built through this site. According to tradition a peace council was held somewhere on the shores, and a tomahawk was buried as a symbol that the two warring tribes had settled their differences.

Laketown   *Polk County*

Numerous lakes dot nearly every section of this township.

Lake Waubesa   *Dane County*

The name is an adaptation of the Indian name for the lake. In the Potawatomi language it was Wapishka, meaning "white foam." In Ojibwe it was Wabisi, meaning "swan lake."

Lake Wingra   *Dane County*

Located in Madison. From the Ho-Chunk word meaning "duck," this lake was in early times a great resort for ducks.

Lakewood   *Oconto County*

The Western Town Lot Company laid out this site in 1897. There was a lake in the nearby woods.

Lallier Park   *Fond du Lac County*

This playground in the city of Fond du Lac is on land once owned by the Lallier family. When the Lalliers cultivated and sold vegetables here, they called it French Gardens in honor of their homeland.

Lamartine   *Fond du Lac County*

The town was first called Seven Mile Creek—it was located on the creek that crossed the Old Military Road about seven miles from Fond du Lac. It was renamed in honor of Alphonse de Lamartine, a French poet and historian who became popular during the French Revolution of 1848.

Lamberton   *Racine County*

Named after William E. Lamberton.

Lamont   *Lafayette County*

Daniel Lamont was a member of President Cleveland's cabinet.

Lampson   *Washburn County*

Frank Lampson bought a large tract of land, built a home, and established a store and post office on the shore of a beautiful lake.

Lancaster   *Grant County*

The town was first settled in 1828 and was platted in 1837 by Major G. M. Price, who proposed the name of Ridgeway. A relative who had emigrated from Lancaster, Pennsylvania, induced him to adopt this name.

Land O'Lakes   *Vilas County*

State Line was the first name given to this site because the railroad ended here on the Michigan border. A sawmill known as Otto Mill was built and later sold to the Mason-Donaldson Lumber Company, and the post office was changed to Donaldson. The mill burned in 1908, but it was two years before the lumber was shipped out. Because there was a two-room school building and a town hall it was still considered the township headquarters. Then two brothers named Maas started a little store and took over the post office, which was changed back to State Line. They were both called into service in World War I, and Washburn Bates became postmaster. It is said that Aunt Ella, his wife, read all the postcards.

The State Line depot had been built half in Michigan and half in Wisconsin, but due to the Wisconsin eight-hour law it was moved across the line into Michigan. In 1928 it burned to the ground, and the new building was erected on the old location, half in each state. George St. Clair went to an outdoor show in Chicago and attended a party at which a number of summer home owners from this area brought up the subject of a new name. The post office department had requested it because there were State Line post offices in Minnesota and Mississippi. Mr. St. Clair submitted the name Land O'Lakes, which became official in 1926.

Langlade   *Langlade County*

Charles de Langlade was thought to have been the first permanent European settler in Wisconsin. It is now known that he did not come until 1764 and was therefore preceded by several others.

Langlade County

From the Antigo Herald, December 5, 1919:

The pioneer settler and well known attorney George W. Latta tells this story of how Langlade County received its name.

In Mackinaw (now Michigan) in 1729, Charles Michael de Langlade was born; he was the son of the Frenchman Agustin de Langlade, and of Domitilde, widow of Daniel Villeneuve, and sister of Nis-cono-quet, the principal Chief of the Ottawas.

At the head of the Ottawas in 1755 he planned an ambuscade that resulted in the defeat of Gen. Braddock on Monongahela River. After that he retired to Green Bay. The following year he returned to Fort Duquesne, where as lieutenant of infantry he rendered valuable services to the command at that post in obtaining information of the movements of the English in the vicinity of Fort Cumberland. In 1757, at the head of a band of Ottawas, he joined Montcalm just as that general had completed the investigation of Fort George. For the aid he gave the French on that occasion he was, at the end of the campaign, appointed second in command of the post of Mackinaw by the Canadian Governor Vaudruil.

He was again with Montcalm during the siege of Quebec by General Wolfe in July, 1759; planned an attack on a detachment of Wolfe's army, 5,000 strong; and had he been properly supported he probably would have put an end to the English expedition. He took an active part in the battle of the Plains of Abraham in April, 1760, fought under the Chevalier de Legis when that officer was at the head of the Canadian militia.

At the time of the Pontiac conspiracy in 1763, he gave the western garrisons timely notice of that chieftain's treachery, and, had it been heeded, the massacres at the frontier posts would not have occurred. So much for his activities with the French armies.

At the beginning of the American Revolution, Langlade attached himself to the English cause, and at the head of a large body of Indians composed of Sioux, Sacs, Foxes, Menominees, Winnebagoes, Ottawas, Chippewas and other western tribes, joined Burgoyne's army at Skenesburough, New York, in July, 1777. Upon the murder of Jane McCrea, and the severe reprimand which that event called forth from Burgoyne, the Indians deserted the British general almost to a man, leaving Langlade no alternative but to return with them. He was subjected to a bitter attack by Burgoyne in the parliament, since, had his influence been exerted to detain his Indian allies, Burgoyne's subsequent disaster would not have occurred. Langlade does not seem to have been censured by the English government, since in 1780 he was made Indian Agent, and later Indian Superintendent and Commander-in-chief of the Canadian military, which last two posts he retained until his death. He was also granted by the English government a life annuity of $800 for his services during the Revolution.

After the war he settled in Green Bay, where he became one of the most enterprising pioneers of the West. He is still known there as the founder and father of Wisconsin. During his life he took part in ninety-nine battles and skirmishes. He was of a mild and patient disposition and was respected by all. His integrity was proverbial, and his dealings and accounts with the English government were always remarkable for their exactness. August 12, 1754 at Mackinaw, he married Charlotte Amdroisnie Bourassa, by whom he had two daughters. None of his descendants are believed to be living now. He died in Green Bay in 1800.

Lannon
Waukesha County

Bill Lannon built a farm in 1840, and later a post office here at what was known as Lannon Springs. Stone quarries were opened on nearby farms, and the area became known as Stone City. Lannon stone, a superior quality of dolomite limestone, was quarried and shipped to Milwaukee. After Bill Lannon's death the people honored him by changing the name of the town to Lannon.

Lansing Dike
Crawford County

Part of Freeman Township. The roadway of the bridge to Lansing, Iowa, was named for the town of Lansing.

Laona
Forest County

Leona was a daughter of Norman Johnson, a local businessman, but in the legal papers it was misspelled Laona.

La Pointe
Ashland County

Father Claude Allouez named the region La Pointe de Chequamegon from the Ojibwe Indian name, and the Jesuit mission established by him was known as La Pointe du Saint Esprit. It was a haven for the Ojibwe and for French and English fur traders from attacks of the Sioux and other tribes. In 1693, the French officer Pierre Le Sueur arrived with a small detail of soldiers and a band of fur traders. He judged that the only safe place from which trade might be conducted was Madeline Island. He built a small fort at one end and named it La Pointe. It became a distributing point for the American Fur Company.

La Prairie
Rock County

A French term meaning "meadow" or "pasture."

Laque Hollow
Richland County

This small valley not far from the hamlet of Mill Creek was owned for many years by the Laque family.

Larsen
Winnebago County

The original settlement was located about a half mile north of the present location and was called Lee's Crossing as the land was owned by Mr. Halvor Lee. The Chicago and North Western Railway crossed the highway here and established a flag stop. About 1888 Philip Larsen built a small grocery store, and the name was changed to Larsen. In a short time the railroad moved its flag stop south, and Mr. Larsen also moved his store to the present site.

La Rue
Sauk County

W. G. LaRue was instrumental in locating vast beds of ore in the region.

La Valle   *Sauk County*

The village is said to have been named after a fur trapper by the name of La Valley who settled here. It was incorporated in 1883.

Lawrence   *Brown County*

Amos Lawrence, the founder of Lawrence College, purchased a large tract of land here. The town was set off and named in 1848.

Lawrence Hill   *Crawford County*

Located between DeSoto and Lawrence Ridge, it was named for the Lawrence family.

Layton Park   *Milwaukee County*

Mr. Layton was a prominent citizen of Milwaukee.

Lebanon   *Dodge County*

This name was proposed by William Woltmann, one of the principal promoters of the settlement and one of the original members of the Pomeranian Pilgrims who settled in the fall of 1843. He thought the biblical name very appropriate for a Christian settlement in the New World. The native pines reminded him of the cedars of Lebanon.

Lebansky Creek   *Richland County*

Located in Henrietta Township. The land on which this creek flows has been in the Lebansky family for nearly one hundred years.

The Ledge   *Fond du Lac County*

This ridge extends the length of the state and in the north forms the "thumb" of Door County. Officially called the Niagara Escarpment, it is over this same geologic outcrop that the Niagara River forms the famous falls. Marked by glacial erosion, The Ledge is the elevated ridge of a thick layer of limestone. Its elevation varies from low areas to the more usual steep perpendicular cliffs that have many springs gushing forth from the fissures in their faces.

Leeds and Leeds Center   *Columbia County*

Settlers from Leeds, England, gave it the name. There were also districts known as North Leeds and South Leeds.

Leef   *Burnett County*

John A. Leef was an early Swedish settler and the first postmaster.

Lee Lake   *Richland County*

Everett A. Lee left his farm in 1900 to begin his long business career in Cazenovia, where he operated a store and was president of the bank.

Leitner Hollow   *Crawford County*

In the Township of Seneca, the Leitner family once settled here.

Leland
Sauk County

A discontinued post office in the town of Honey Creek named for Cyrus Leland, a member of the state legislature.

Lemonweir River
Juneau County

From the Wisconsin Historical Collections:

> *This valuable stream, which gives name to the valley, derives its name from an incident of traditional history among the north-western tribes of Indians, many years prior to any modern white settlement within the territory of Wisconsin.*
>
> *An Indian Chief, who then held unbounded sway over the tribes of the West, from the southern end of Lake Michigan to the Mississippi, fearing the rapid encroachments of the white men, then spreading over the territories of Indiana and Michigan, formed the plan of an extensive league with the still farther western tribes around, and west of the Falls of St. Anthony; and, for the purpose of perfecting it, dispatched a messenger with a war belt of wampum, and a request for delegations of the Dakotas and Chippewas to meet in grand council at the big bend of the Wisconsin—now Portage City. The runner, in the course of his journey, encamped on the proposed council grounds overnight, next morning crossing the river, following the well-known trail to the West, again encamped on the banks of this beautiful stream. During the night he dreamed that he had lost his belt of wampum with which he was entrusted, at his last sleeping place. On awaking in the morning he found his dream to be a reality, and hastened back to recover the lost treasure, in which he was successful. On returning to the scene of his dream he again encamped, and before leaving on his mission, gave a name to the river, significant of the event—Le-mo-wee—the river of memory.*

Lena
Oconto County

The town was known as Maple Valley, but because there was another settlement by that name, George R. Hall, the postmaster, was asked to give two suggestions from which the government could choose a new name. The government rejected both his names, and his sweetheart asked why he looked so gloomy. He explained the reason, and then the idea came to him. "I'll send in your name," he said. So the post office was renamed in honor of Lena, who became Mrs. Hall.

Lenox
Oneida County

The name was adapted from Lenox, Massachusetts. It was the family name of the Duke of Richmond, who was the English secretary of state when the town in New England was established.

Leon
Monroe County

This town is said to have been named after the town of Leon in Mexico.

Leonard's Pond
Fond du Lac County

It is fed by a spring that used to operate the Mountain Mill owned by Charles Doty and Henry Conklin. This was the first gristmill in the county. S. B. Leonard later owned it.

Lepsic *Dodge County*

Settled by a number of German families in 1800 from the town in Germany.

Leslie *Lafayette County*

The first name was Grand View because of the town's location. It was later known as Belmont, from three shapely mounds nearby that early French travelers called belles mantes. The name was changed to Leslie for the son of M. Y. Johnson, who purchased the town site.

Lewis *Polk County*

Charles E. Lewis, a Minneapolis grain broker, owned a large farm, a lodge, and a trout pond hatchery about a mile southeast of the present town. It was called Seven Pines. When the Soo Line Railroad was built through the area, Mr. Lewis laid out the village and built the beautiful Lewis Methodist Church, the parsonage, and a large two-story general store.

Lewis' Landing *Richland County*

James Lewis was licensed to run a ferry and collect specified fees for conveying men, wagons, buggies, oxen, horses, and other domestic animals across the Wisconsin River at this point.

Lewiston *Columbia County*

E. F. Lewis was the first settler and, as sheriff of Columbia County, was involved in the John Baptiste DuBay murder trial.

Leyden *Rock County*

This community was named after Leyden in the Netherlands, the refuge of the Pilgrim Fathers before their emigration to America.

Liberty *Manitowoc County*

The town was first called Buchanan after President Buchanan. During the Civil War more Republicans settled here and wanted the name changed to Liberty. President Buchanan's attitude toward the problems of the North and the South were not popular with the inhabitants.

Liberty Prairie *Dane County*

Part of Cottage Grove and Deerfield. In the early 1840s a company of Fourth of July celebrators climbed to the top of Liberty Hill with a little brown jug. Inspired by the view of the prairie below, and by the height of the elevation, they named both the hill and the prairie for the occasion.

Lick Skillet *Richland County*

Some very poor people lived at this location in Richland in the early days.

Lightcap's Mill *Grant County*

Mr. Lightcap's stone mill is one of the most extensive establishments of its kind in Grant County. It was started in 1847 and took a year to build.

Light Foot Hollow   *Crawford County*

Running from Mt. Zion to the county line, it was named after the Light Foot family.

Lighthouse Harbor   *Fond du Lac County*

Originally called the "Big Hole," as a harbor it was unsatisfactory. It was dredged to a uniform depth of twelve feet in 1935. The name Lighthouse Harbor was officially adopted in 1935 because there is a lighthouse located here.

Lily   *Langlade County*

A stream in the area was first given this name. It was referred to as The Lily.

Lima   *Grant County*

The township is said to have first been known as Head of Little Platt. It was named Lima because of the lime kilns located there.

Lima   *Sheboygan County*

When the township of Gibbsville was divided, Lima became one of the new townships and was named by Hiram Humphrey in honor of his old home in New York. The settlement was once known as Wakefield, and later as Wheat Valley.

Lime Ridge   *Sauk County*

Mr. and Mrs. Charles Cushman built the first log house here in the early 1850s. When a post office was to be established they decided on Lime Ridge because of the outcroppings of limestone in the area and because the settlement was on a ridge.

Limery Ridge   *Crawford County*

Named after the Limery family, it is located in Prairie du Chien.

Lincoln

Many towns in different counties were given this name. Also Lincoln County was established, all in honor of President Abraham Lincoln.

Lind   *Waupaca County*

Named in honor of Jenny Lind, the great Swedish singer.

Linden   *Iowa County*

The original settlement was on the banks of a small stream called Peddler's Creek and had the same name. Gradually the settlement grew up the hill. It is said that in 1855 the government refused the name Peddler's Creek, so John Wasley suggested Linden because a big linden tree grew in front of the general store.

Lindsey   *Wood County*

The village was named for a former Neillsville man who was one of the first to carry on logging operations in this part of the state. This is evidently F. D. Lindsey, whose lumbering camp southwest of Neillsville was destroyed by fire in the late nineteenth century.

Lindwerm   *Milwaukee County*

Said to have been named for an early settler and owner of the land on which the town was platted.

Linn   *Walworth County*

Dr. Lewis Field Linn of Missouri was Colonel Benton's colleague in the United States Senate from 1833 until his death.

Lion's Den   *Ozaukee County*

This area about three miles north of Grafton was named by Jacques Donges. It is a sort of ravine near the lake and is said to have had two stones at the entrance with lions carved on them. During Prohibition bootleggers used to hide their booze in the den.

Lip Creek   *Racine County*

Named by Henry F. Janes, the History of Rock County gives this account of the circumstances of the naming:

> *He was of a roving disposition, and liked the excitement incident to a new country, and not much inclined to work himself, but to plan for others. He never was wanting for a good excuse to change his location. Accordingly, during the winter, he fitted out a horse team, and, with a small party, started west for Rock River. On arriving at Muskego Lake, they found the outlet frozen over, and, in attempting to cross, the ice broke, letting in the team, and, in getting the horses out, he hurt one of them, so that its lip became paralyzed and hung down, and it refused to eat, or could not, and, of course, soon died. Janes gave the name of "Lip Creek" to the stream. This accident, and other discouraging circumstances, caused the party to return. This name of "Lip Creek" as applied to the outlet of Muskego Lake, was retained for a long time.*

Litchfield   *Sauk County*

A portion of the plat of the city of Baraboo named for Litchfield, Connecticut, by R. G. Camp.

Little Black   *Taylor County*

The township is named for the Little Black River.

Little Chute   *Outagamie County*

Falls in the Fox River were originally known as La Petite Chute by early French explorers. It is believed that Father Vanden Broek, who built the first church and settlement in 1836, translated the name.

Little Kohler   *Ozaukee County*

Martin Roller came from Bavaria and purchased a section of land in 1846. He donated land for the church, which was known as the Koller Kirche (Koller Church). Some years later, after a cheese factory, saloon, and other dwellings were built, the people applied for a post office. It was granted under the name of Kohler. Until rural free delivery was established there were post offices at both Kohler and Little Kohler.

Little Norway   *Dane County*
Part of Blue Mounds. A sort of museum, the buildings and equipment are of Norwegian style, original and in reproduction.

Little Suamico   *Oconto County*
This is supposed to have been an ancient Menominee Indian campground. The name is derived from the Indian word suamakosa, meaning "little sand bar," "yellow sand bar," or just "yellow sand."

Livesey's Spring   *Dane County*
Named for James Livesey and his descendants, it was important in the history of the Pheasant Branch region because Michel St. Cyr, the first local settler, had his fur-trading post nearby, and many travelers knew it. The spring is now filled in.

Livingston   *Grant County*
Irish people settling in this locality called it Dublin. The railroad built from Galena to Montfort Junction passed through the settlement in 1878. It is said that Mr. Hugh Livingston was so glad to have the railroad that he gladly gave his farmland for the roadbed. He said it would do the people more good to have a railroad than for him to have one thousand acres for a farm. He then sold lots to build the village. Mr. Thomas Watson is said to have suggested it be named after Mr. Livingston.

Lizard Mound State Park   *Ozaukee County*
Named for its most outstanding mound, the park contains thirty-one examples of effigy mounds. Except for a few examples in adjoining states, effigy mounds are found only in Wisconsin.

Loddes Mill   *Sauk County*
This discontinued post office in the town of Prairie du Sac was first named Rowells Mills for Henry Rowell, and later Loddes Mill for Martin Lodde.

Lodi   *Columbia County*
There is no authentic account of how the city was named. According to tradition, Judge Isaac Palmer, a very early pioneer, drove into the area about 1845 from the South, and when he saw the trees for building materials, flat lands for agriculture, and a fine creek for water he decided it was a good place to settle. But he also saw two hills over a narrow valley with a low flat fan-shaped area funneling the creek. What could be better for a dam and waterpower to run a gristmill, flour mill, and lumber mill? This rosy vision prompted the judge to exclaim, "This is the idol of my eye!" Later he reversed idol to Lodi.

According to another story Judge Palmer, who was a scholar and barrister, read a great deal of history. His imagination fancied a resemblance between this place and Lodi in Italy, the locale of one of Napoleon's battles.

There is also a possibility that the settlement was named after Lodi in New York State.

Loganville
Sauk County

Chauncey P. Logan was given a quarter section of land by his wife's uncle and built a one-room house in 1853. Mrs. Logan was the first teacher in the little red schoolhouse, which also served as a church, town hall, meeting house, lecture hall, and singing school. When a two-room school was built, the old one was moved downtown and used for a wagon shop. Main Street was laid out by Logan Kinsley, and Mr. Logan named the village Loganville. Steven Kinsley had the first post office and Chauncey Logan had it next, and then it was moved in with the village store.

Lohrville
Waushara County

The Lohr Granite Company of Milwaukee was a big customer and backer of Mr. Rothman, who owned the Rothman Quarry that started this settlement. Much of his stone was sent to the Milwaukee Lohr mill to be polished and made into monuments.

Lomira
Dodge County

The son of Chief Black Hawk is said to have camped in this vicinity while blazing a trail from Milwaukee to Green Bay. The first European settlers came in 1843 and called the settlement Springfield. In 1849 the name was changed to Lomira, probably after Lomira Schoonover, daughter of Sam Schoonover. It is also believed the name was chosen because of the loam soil in the area.

London
Dane County

Early settlers chose this name from London, England.

Lone Rock
Richland County

At one time a remarkable pile of sandstone stood on the prairie a short distance from the left bank of the Wisconsin River. It became a landmark for the early raftsmen who traveled the river and was called The Lone Rock. It was later destroyed, and only the site remains. When Lone Rock City was laid out in 1856 there was only one log house on the plot, occupied by Mr. Calder, the first blacksmith. A number of other buildings were erected later that year.

Long Hollow
Richland County

Near Akan Township. Andrew Anderson and his family, the first homesteaders in the valley, purchased the land at one dollar per acre from the Northwest Development Company. The land looked big and long in comparison with their smaller valley in Norway, so they called it Stordalen. After they learned some English and other English speaking families moved in, Stordalen became Long Hollow.

Long Lake
Florence County

The town is located on the shore of Long Lake, named by government surveyors because it was longer and narrower than others in the area.

Long Lake   *Washburn County*

The lake was called Little Bear by Ojibwe Indians who camped on its shore. Later the Rice Lake Lumber Company set up camps on one side and the Knapp Stout Company took over the opposite side. There were many fights between the crews of the two camps. It is believed the Rice Lake Company changed to Long Lake and the township also took that name.

Long Range   *Grant County*

There is a very large lode of lead that ran from Cuba City to Potosi, later known as Mud Range. It contained a great quantity of mud that handicapped the mining, but it was one of the most fought-over ranges in this area.

Loraine   *Polk County*

Loraine Ruggles was an early settler. The first hotel built in this township in 1873 was called the Gillespie Stopping Place, "a great rendezvous for loggers and lumbermen."

Loretta   *Sawyer County*

Edward Hines, who owned a lumber company here, had a daughter named Loretta.

Loretto   *Sauk County*

This is a discontinued post office in the town of Bear Creek, named by Reverend Father T. A. Byre for Loretto, Italy. It was sometimes spelled Loreto.

Lost Hollow   *Richland County*

Part of Willow Township. Most credence is given to the story of a child from the Gray family, who was lost in the wood in the Loyd area and found lying dead by a log. Another version tells a story of the rescue of two lost children.

Lost Lake   *Dodge County*

One of a party of government surveyors became mired in the marsh at the outlet of the lake, went down, and was never seen again. There is no visible inlet or outlet to the lake.

The Lost Village   *Dane County*

Named because it was rather isolated from Madison. Part of the Forest Lake plat, it did not develop as much as expected.

Lotus Lake   *Dane County*

Also called Turtle Lake, it was once thickly grown with yellow pond lilies, or "lotuses."

Louisburg   *Grant County*

In 1850 people began a settlement known as Puckerville. In 1881 the town was known as Lewisburg after the last minister who preached in the little Methodist Episcopal Church, a Reverend T. J. Lewis. Another account states it was named after Lewis Curtis, an early pioneer who came in 1827. By 1900 the early settlements of Jamestown, North Jamestown, and South Jamestown or Puckerville all joined together as Louisberg, but there is no explanation why the spelling of the name was changed.

Louis Corners   *Manitowoc County*

Louis Senglaub owned a tavern where the post office was first established. Later he became the county treasurer.

Lovass   *Vernon County*

Jacob Lovass was the first settler in this area.

Lowell   *Dodge County*

The early settlement, established in the 1830s, was known as Town Ten. A mill was built in 1844 by Clark Lawton and Henry Finney. Mr. Lawton asked that the new community be named after his hometown, Lowell, in Massachusetts.

Lowville   *Columbia County*

Jacob Low, son of Captain Gideon Low of Fort Winnebago, was the first settler. The town was created in 1846 but no longer appears on highway maps. There is nothing left but a tavern.

Loyal   *Clark County*

It is claimed that during the Civil War, every eligible male in the township enlisted in the armed forces. The name Loyal was adopted as a tribute to these men.

Lublin   *Taylor County*

Marvin Durski, a land agent from Chicago, sold the land in this area. He had come from Lublin in Poland.

Luck   *Polk County*

The settlement began as a stopover for settlers traveling from around Cumberland, Wisconsin, to Taylors Falls, Minnesota, to get supplies that came by boat up the St. Croix River. They felt that if they made it halfway by nightfall they were lucky, so this stopover on Butternut Lake was called Luck. The town was moved west about half a mile when the railroad was built through the area. Another account states that Daniel F. Smith organized the town and chose this name because, as he put it, "I propose to be in luck the rest of my life."

Luco   *Fond du Lac County*

Luke La Borde, an early settler, was nicknamed Luco. The creek on which he kept his boat was called "Luco's Creek," and eventually the name was applied to the surrounding community.

Ludington   *Eau Claire County*

This crossroads settlement was started in the 1860s as part of Bridge Creek Township. It became the center of a logging district and had a shingle mill, handle factory, sawmill, and blacksmith shop. It became a separate township in 1877, named for Governor Harrison Ludington.

Luxemburg   *Kewaunee County*

The people who settled here were from the city of Luxembourg, Belgium.

Luxerin *Fond du Lac County*

This name for the Sheridan Farms was created by combining the first syllable of Luxembourg, the homeland of Sheridan's mother, with "Erin," his father's homeland.

Lyndhurst *Shawano County*

According to the History of Place Names Connected with the Chicago and North Western Railroad, "This name was made up for this place. It has no specific meaning."

Lyndon *Sheboygan County*

This town was named after a place in Vermont.

Lynxville *Crawford County*

The steamboat Lynx brought the surveyors who laid out the original plat. It was built as a stop for Mississippi River steamers.

Lyons *Sauk County*

This suburb of Baraboo was named by Harvey Canfield for Lyons, New York, where he once resided. The New York town was named for Lyons, France.

Lyons *Walworth County*

This township was set off from the town of Geneva in 1844 and named Hudson. It is claimed the first settlers came from the Hudson River area in New York State. Among them were William, James C., and Thomas K. Hudson, although their names were not found in the earliest records. In a few years the city of Hudson in St. Croix County had become more prominent, so the name was changed to Lyons after Thomas Lyons and his sons, who had built a dam and a sawmill by 1840. The railroad station was first called Lyonsdale and then Lyons.

Milwaukee's commercial district, looking north over the Milwaukee River from the Michigan Street Bridge

→❯ M ❮←

Mackford
Hiram McDonald, popularly known as Mack, was one of the prominent settlers of the area. Mack's ford was the place where the trail crossed the river. The letter s was dropped.

Mackie Spring
In 1841 Thomas Mackie built the first log house on this site in the present city of Beaver Dam. The spring at which he located is the head of Springbrook.

Madeline Island
The largest of the Apostle Islands, called Monine-wun-kaning by the Ojibwe Indians, meaning "place of the lapwings or golden-breasted woodpecker." Michel Cadotte, son of old Jean Baptiste Cadotte, the French Canadian fur trader, visited the island in 1785 and married Equa-say-way, daughter of the village chief. At their marriage the priest rechristened the wife, giving her the name of Madeline. When Michel Cadotte revived the North West Company trading post at La Pointe, the chief decreed that the island should be called by his daughter's Christian name.

Madge
While James S. Devereaux was postmaster at Shell Lake he established a star route into the settlement north of Long Lake and named it Madge after his daughter. William H. Todd had the first post office in his home and was the first postmaster. Each time a new postmaster was chosen the post office was moved to his house.

Madison
Indians have lived here between the beautiful lakes formed in the glacial period for thousands of years. Ho-Chunk Indians had a village here called Dejop, meaning "four lakes." The site was chosen for the capital of Wisconsin Territory in 1836, when there were no European settlers living here at all. James Duane Doty promoted it. Mr. Peck of Blue Mounds immediately decided that a tavern or inn would be a sound business proposition here. He built a triple log house on the site of 128 South Butler Street. Moses M. Strong and John Catlin surveyed Capital Park and staked out lots around it in 1837. John Catlin was chosen as the first postmaster, and he hired a man to build a post office where Manchester's Store would later stand. One end of Mr. Peck's tavern was used for the post office in the meantime. Madison was incorporated as a village in 1846 and a city in 1856. It was named in honor of President James Madison.

Madsen
The Soo Line Railroad was built on land owned by a Mr. Madsen.

Magenta *Eau Claire County*

This settlement was a railroad siding in North Eau Claire on the Chippewa River at what was known as Dells Pond. It was named for the depot agent, a Mr. Magenta.

Magnolia *Rock County*

This township was named indirectly in honor of Dr. Pierre Magnol, the noted botanist, for whom the magnolia tree was also named.

Maiden Rock *Pierce County*

This is one of the most striking landmarks of the upper Mississippi River, a rocky bluff that towers four hundred feet above the river where it widens to form Lake Pepin. A legend of an Indian with a number of variations accounts for the name. The Dakota, a band of the Sioux, lived in a village called Keoxa on the Minnesota side of the river. Their chief, Red Wing, had a beautiful daughter named Winona, who was supposed to marry Kewanee, a young Dakota man. But she was secretly in love with an Ojibwe man named White Eagle. One account says that White Eagle was killed by Red Wing's warriors. Kewanee presented so many gifts to the chief for Winona's hand that her father decided the wedding must take place immediately. Winona wandered off and appeared on the top of the high bluff, where she sang her death song and then leaped to the water below.

Maine *Marathon County*

A Mr. U. E. Maine is said to have been the first settler here.

Maine *Sheboygan County*

An early settlement of people from the state of Maine once lived along County Highway I between Five Corners and Hingham.

Ma-Kah-Da-Wah-Gah-Cok *Manitowoc County*

The name of a Potawatomi village on the East Twin River, about eight miles north of Mishicott, said to mean "black earth."

Malcolm *Langlade County*

Malcolm Hutchinson was the first settler here.

Malone *Fond du Lac County*

The early name for the settlement was St. Johns. After the Chicago and North Western Railway was built, H. T. Malone, an official of the railroad company, became the station agent and first postmaster. He also built the grain elevator and the general store.

Malvern *Oneida County*

The battlefield in Virginia known as Malvern Hill was the inspiration for this name. There is only a railroad siding now.

Manawa
Waupaca County

The first settlement was called Brickley, but the first post office was named Elberton after Elbert Scott, the first postmaster. On December 21, 1874, the name was changed to Manawa in honor of the hero of an Indian legend:

The Ho-Chunk had a village at this site headed by Chief Wecopah, a man of influence and power among all the surrounding Indian nations. But he was haughty and vindictive in nature, and a group of his people decided to replace him with the more popular Manawa, son of a former chief. A feud developed, and Manawa offered to fight Wecopah with bow and arrow.

Wecopah feared Manawa's great skill but was afraid that if he refused the challenge he would be branded a coward. On the day of the contest, the tribe assembled on the bank of the Little Wolf River. The enemies, with bows drawn, stood facing each other. The signal to shoot was given, and Manawa fell dead with an arrow in his heart. His own bowstring had snapped in two, and his arrow fell harmless at his feet. His friends gave him a princely burial on the bank of the river.

The legend says that Manawa means "long bow," or "one skilled in the use of a bow." The word is also said to mean "he has no tobacco" in the Menominee language.

Manchester
Green Lake County

The town was first called Albany and then Hardin. It was changed to Manchester in 1858 because English people from Manchester settled there.

Manitou Island
Bayfield County

One of the Apostle Islands, named Manitou Miniss or "spirit island" by the Ojibwe. Former names are said to have been Devil's Island and Tate's Island. The Indian spirit Manitou could be either good or bad and therefore either a god or a devil.

Manitowish
Iron County

This is a corruption of the Ojibwe word that means "evil spirit." The Indians believed there were evil spirits in the waters here.

Manitowish Waters
Vilas County

Peter Vance, guide, cruiser, and typical North Woods man, was the first settler to establish a residence in this locality. He came with two helpers in 1884. They traveled in three canoes up the Chippewa River to the Flambeau River to the Manitowish River and through Sturgeon and Bension Lakes to Rest Lake. The township was originally part of Lac du Flambeau but was separated by an act of the legislature in 1927 and named Spider Lake Township. The name was changed to Manitowish Waters in 1939 because there was another Spider Lake post office in Wisconsin.

Manitowoc
Manitowoc County

The first settlers thought the Indians called the place where they speared white fish at the mouth of the river Munedowk, but the accepted phonetic spelling became Manitowoc. In the Indian language it meant "spirit land" or "river of bad spirits" and also "devil's den."

Manitowoc Rapids   *Manitowoc County*

The town was first called Conroe after its first settler, Jacob W. Conroe.

Mankato   *Sheboygan County*

Once a small settlement on the Mullett River in the town of Plymouth, Mankato enjoyed only a brief existence. In 1859 Caroline Preussler acquired the site, and she platted it as a town in 1866. The settlement came to an end in the late 1870s. The origin of the name is unknown.

Man Mound Park   *Sauk County*

A park in the town of Greenfield, it is named for a large Indian effigy mound shaped like a man, the only known man mound in the world.

Maple   *Douglas County*

Early settlers were French and Irish Canadians who crossed Lake Superior to cut the dense growth of white and Norway pines. They named the settlement Little Canada. When the timber was gone and fire had consumed the slashings, maple trees grew. Finnish immigrants coming into the area renamed it Maple.

Maple Bluff   *Dane County*

The village was incorporated as Lakewood Bluff in 1930, and then changed to Maple Bluff because of the maple trees growing on the bluff on the north shore of Lake Mendota.

Maple Grove   *Manitowoc County*

Ava Smith is said to have suggested the name.

Maple Ridge   *Crawford County*

Located in Marietta Township. Sugar maples were very plentiful here in the past and are still highly visible in the fall.

Mapleton   *Waukesha County*

Sam Breck, the first postmaster, chose the name because of the trees.

Maplewood   *Door County*

German and Irish settlers called the Catholic church the Maplewood Church. Maples trees were cut for firewood, as there was no sale for the logs. The trees were also burned in piles to clear the land for farming.

Marathon and Marathon County

W. D. McIndoe selected this name in 1850 after the battlefield of ancient Greece.

Marblehead   *Fond du Lac County*

It was named for the lime rock in the quarry—even though the rock is lime and not marble. The Nast brothers began working the limestone ledge in 1871, producing two hundred thousand barrels of lime annually.

Marcellon
Columbia County

The name suggested to the Post Office Department was Massilon, in honor of the great French pulpit orator, but there was a town of that name in Ohio. The settlers insisted on having their own way even if a post office was refused. Some poor speller wrote it as Marrsellon on the plat, later changed to Marcellon. Dr. Lyman Foote of the Fort Winnebago garrison took up the first land grant in the township and platted a dream town he called Wisconsinapolis, but it was never developed.

Marengo
Ashland County

Said to have been named after the Battle of Marengo, in which Napoleon Bonaparte defeated the Austrians.

Marian Park
Sauk County

A park at Prairie du Sac, it was named by W. H. Jacobs for his daughter.

Maribel
Manitowoc County

The railroad brought people who settled and started a village about 1900. The Charles Steinbrecher family purchased property that had a number of horizontal caves in solid limestone. There was also a mineral spring thought to have great medicinal value. A hotel was built that soon became a popular tourist attraction. Mrs. Steinbrecher managed the hotel and served wonderful meals. The building is a large three-story structure of solid stone resembling an old castle and is still standing.

The Rev. F. X. Steinbrecher, who took a great interest in developing the beautiful grounds, is credited with coining the name. "Mary is for the month of May when we started to build," he said. "And we should add something to it to ring the bell—like Marybell. How would that be?" The caves were called Maribel Caves and the railroad station became Maribel Station. The village was developed by hardworking German farmers who took great pride in building the only church, St. John's Evangelical Lutheran.

Marietta
Crawford County

In 1853 Mrs. McShoolar was a very pretty and modest woman. Her first name was Marietta.

Marigaard Ridge
Crawford County

Named about 1941 for a family that lived here. It can be found just off Lawrence Ridge in the township of Freeman.

Marinette and Marinette County

Both the city and the county are named in honor of a remarkable woman who established a fur trading post on the banks of the Menominee River. She was born at Post Lake in Langlade County in 1784 and christened Marguerite Chevallier, daughter of the Frenchman Bartland Chevallier, who had come from Canada. Her mother was a daughter of Menominee chief Wauba-Shish. Marguerite was nicknamed Marinette, a shortened form of Marie Antoinette, then queen of France.

Bartland Chevallier moved to Green Bay in 1800 and went into partnership with John Jacobs from Canada. Marinette married the English Canadian, and they had three children. When the fur trading business slumped during the War of 1812 Jacobs started a school. In 1823 he moved to the present site of Marinette City and went into partnership with William Farnsworth at a trading post established by the American Fur Company. Within a few years John Jacobs went to Canada and never returned, and Marinette married Farnsworth. They had two sons and a daughter.

By 1831 Farnsworth had left to settle in Sheboygan. Marinette remained and developed the trading post into a large trading center. She was called Queen Marinette and became well-known for her business ability. She died in 1865. Her son, John B. Jacobs, platted the town.

Marion
Waupaca County

The town was formerly called Perry's Mills, for J. W. Perry, a sawmill owner in 1856. There are three accounts of the change to Marion: B. F. Dorr, surveyor of this area, is said to have named it after his hometown of Marion, Ohio; patriotic citizens are claimed to have renamed it after the famous Revolutionary War general, Francis Marion; it is also said to have been named after Marion Ransdell, an early settler who was a Civil War veteran of some repute and is buried in the Greenleaf Cemetery here.

Markesan
Green Lake County

Formerly known as Granville. It is said to have been renamed after the Marquesas Islands in the Pacific Ocean, since the people were as hospitable as the islanders supposedly were.

Marquette and Marquette County

Father Jacques Marquette, the French Jesuit explorer, passed through this region in 1673. He and his companion Louis Joliet stopped for several days in the village of the Mascouten Indians where Marquette now stands. A Vermonter named Luther Gleason established a trading post here in 1829.

Marshall
Dane County

The first land within the limits of this town was obtained in 1836 by three men from New York, A. A. Bird, Zenas Bird, and a Mr. Petrie. They entered into a contract: Zenas Bird was to erect a frame building of suitable dimensions for a public house; A. A. Bird and Petrie were to improve the waterpower in Maunesha Creek and build a sawmill that was to be completed and running within a year. Zenas Bird got the public house erected, and the others had the lumber ready and piled for the mill. Then all hands went to Madison for supplies.

While they were gone the prairie caught fire, burning house, lumber, and all. The frame of the house did not burn entirely and remained standing for six years before it fell to the ground. The place was called Bird's Ruins.

A. M. Hanchett bought property and established a store at Bird's Ruins. A good school was built and the village obtained a post office. Mr. Hanchett was the first postmaster and named the village Hanchettville. He later erected a gristmill and a new dam. In 1859 the Madison, Watertown, and St. Paul Company built a railroad to Hanchettville and called the depot Howard City in honor of the railroad contractor. When Mr. Hanchett was obliged to sell his property to Porter and Marshall, the name was officially changed to Marshall.

Marshall
Richland County

Named for John Marshall, who settled here in 1851.

Marshfield
Fond du Lac County

The area was originally part of Calumet and Forest townships. In 1852 it was named Kossuth. Three years later it was renamed Marshfield because of the large tracts of marshland covering the township.

Marshfield
Wood County

There is a difference of opinion as to how the city was named. One account states that John J. Marsh of New York City owned the greater part of the town and gave it his name. Another states that J. J. Marsh came from Haverhill, Massachusetts, and named the town after his uncle, Samuel Marsh, who was one of the original owners of the land. When the Wisconsin Central Railroad Company built its line from Stevens Point to Abbottsford, the stopping places were known by numbers indicating the number of miles from Stevens Point. Marshfield became Number 32. It is claimed the railroad company then named it after Marshfield, Massachusetts.

Marshland
Buffalo County

A large stretch of marshy land that was converted into fertile fields.

Martell
Pierce County

Joseph Martell was one of four Frenchmen who first settled here.

Martinville
Grant County

A Martin family resided in the area.

Marxville
Dane County

Part of Berry Township. Named for Johannes Marx, the owner of considerable lands here. Marx was not one of the earliest settlers, so there was some resentment. Some felt that the village should have been named Myer's Corners, and that Marx's friendship with the town chairman had unduly influenced the decision. It is said that Marx reconciled the situation by setting up a barrel of beer for a village celebration.

Marytown
Fond du Lac County

Named for the Church of the Visitation of the Blessed Virgin Mary, which dominates the settlement.

Maryville
Richland County

Part of Bloom Township. J. J. Shoemaker platted this village in 1856. After having been in the county less than six months, he disappeared, leaving many debts behind him. Maryville was left with a few lots sold and a log house. The "village" was auctioned for $1,150. The wife of Mr. Shoemaker may have been named Mary.

Mash-Ke-Da-Sing   *Sheboygan County*

Just southeast of the village of Cascade was a large Indian village known as Mash-ke-da-sing, or "little prairie."

Mather   *Juneau County*

About 1875 the Milwaukee Railroad built what was known as the Old Valley Line connecting Tomah in Monroe County with Babcock in Wood County. About halfway it came to a junction with the Goodyear Lumber Company railroad. The Goodyear Company built a general store at this junction, and its first manager was John Mather.

Matteson   *Waupaca County*

Roswell Matteson was an early settler here.

Matthew's Stopping-Place   *Wood County*

This overnight resting place in Saratoga Township was used by travelers bound for Friendship or Arkdale or Grand Rapids. It was owned by Michael Matthews and was maintained by him from the 1870s until about 1898; toward the end of that time it was used as a dance hall.

Mauston   *Juneau County*

In 1838 Dennis LaRonde and Walsworth had a trading post at the Indian village of To-ko-nee at this site. Within a few years a dam and sawmill were built by McNeil and McAllister. General M. M. Maughs of Galena, Illinois, became the proprietor of the mill, and the village became known as Maughs Mills. When Mr. Maughs platted the village in 1854 it was named Maughstown, eventually shortened to the present name.

Mauthe Lake   *Fond du Lac County*

Previously known as Off-set Lake and then as Moon Lake, it was named in honor of William Mauthe of Fond du Lac, who in 1927 was made chairman of the Conservation Commission of the state.

May   *Burnett County*

This post office was established from 1898 to 1905 in the general store of Justin Schoonover on the east shore of Big Clam Lake and named after his wife.

Mayhew   *Walworth County*

Jesse Mayhew owned the land on which the railroad station and post office were built.

Mayfield   *Washington County*

Mr. Andreas Reiderer, a native of the German part of Switzerland, was the founder of this little village. He named it in English after his birthplace, Maienfelden.

Mayville   *Dodge County*

The name Mayville was given to the trading post established where Chester and Eli P. May first settled in 1845. They were proprietors of the town site.

Mazomanie *Dane County*

All sources agree that this is a derivation of an Indian word, but there is a difference of opinion as to its significance. May-Zhee-Mau-nee or Walking Mat is said to have been a Ho-Chunk chief. Mo-zo-mee-nan were mooseberries, and mo-so-min-um were moon berries. The son of Chief Whirling Thunder was Manzemoneka, meaning Walking Iron. Manzemoneka had trouble with the agent at Fort Winnebago, Pierre Paquette, who dared the Indian to fire upon him. The Indian fired and Paquette was killed. Manzemoneka was tried for murder, giving wide publicity to his name. The newly founded village adopted Manzemoneka and bore the name for nineteen years. Then Mr. Edward Brodhead, chief engineer for the Milwaukee and Mississippi Railroad, changed the spelling to the present form.

McAllister *Marinette County*

About 1894, when the Wisconsin Michigan Railroad had been built, a man logging here ordered a carload of hay. His name was Pete McAllister. It seemed as good a name as any for the stop.

McAvoy Hill *Richland County*

James McAvoy came to America in 1852 and to Willow in 1861. The hill is in Richland; the road goes on into Willow.

McDowell *Burnett County*

A. L. McDowell lived on the shores of Lilly Lake and became postmaster for the settlement. He was a "sucker," meaning a cleanup man who piled up the branches that were cut off felled trees.

McFarland *Dane County*

William H. McFarland came here with the Milwaukee and Mississippi Railroad in 1854. He bought a large tract of land and had it surveyed and a village laid out. For a short time the name was spelled MacFarland but was officially changed back to McFarland in 1924.

McFarland Hill *Crawford County*

It runs from Bear Creek to Orchard Heights in the township of Clayton and was named after the McFarland family.

McGlynn Creek *Richland County*

Thomas McGlynn settled in the southern part of the town of Westford in 1850s.

McGregor Hill *Crawford County*

Mr. McGregor carved his name in a tree here in the village of Gays Mills. He came from Iowa, bought the land, stayed a few years, and then left.

McKinley *Polk County*

This township was named for President McKinley. The first post office came in 1888, the first school in 1889.

McKinney Creek
Richland County

In 1842 John S. McKinney was a mere child of five when he arrived in Richland County. At the time there were no more than twenty settlers in the area. Not only a farmer, he also dealt in furniture and was a pioneer undertaker.

McMillan
Marathon County

B. F. McMillan was a local lumberman.

McNaughton
Oneida County

The Bradley and Kelly Lumber Company hauled logs over a narrow-gauge railroad to the Wisconsin River and floated them downriver in the spring log drives. The Milwaukee Lakeshore and Western Railroad was built from Rhinelander to Hurley in 1888, and Cyrus Yawkey built a short railroad line from his logging operations in Hazelhurst to connect with it. He called his railroad the Hazelhurst and Southeastern, and the station where the two lines met, Hazelhurst Junction. His plan was to have two railroad outlets for his lumber mill. The Bradley and Kelly Company then erected a sawmill and hired a foreman named McNaughton, and the Milwaukee Lakeshore and Western ran a spur line to the mill, calling the switch station McNaughton.

In 1893 the Chicago and North Western Railway bought the Milwaukee Lakeshore and Western, and Cyrus Yawkey pulled up the tracks of the Hazelhurst and Southeastern because he was moving his logging operation farther north. Several years later Bradley and Kelly closed their mill, and the Chicago and North Western Railway renamed the Hazelhurst Junction station McNaughton.

The settlement still has a post office and a combination grocery store, tavern, service station, and restaurant in one building, which serves a rural resort area. There is not even a flag station on the railroad.

Meadowbrook
Sawyer County

It took some thirty or forty years for the Chippewa Falls lumber interests to cut off all the white pine in this area. When the shingle and lath mill was discontinued, the settlers took up farming. Grubbing out the tough pine stumps with the aid of horses and oxen was hard work. At this particular location a stream passes through a meadow that had a luxuriant growth of marsh grass instead of pine trees, distinguishing it to the pioneer farmers. They named the settlement Meadowbrook, but it was officially part of Weirgor township until 1919.

Mecan
Marquette County

Mikana is the Ojibwe word for "trail"; Mecan may derive from it.

Medary
La Crosse County

A junction was formed here with a railroad that ran to Winona, Minnesota, and the settlement was originally called Winona Junction. It was renamed in honor of a local citizen who became governor of the state of Kansas, Samuel Medary.

Medford *Taylor County*

Two different versions of the story of the naming of Medford are told: In 1873 a young lad who was homesick for New England sat down beside the Wisconsin Central Railroad right-of-way to eat his lunch. He pulled a pencil from his pocket and wrote the name of his hometown, Medford, Massachusetts, on a flat white rock. When the track was laid a crude shack was built to serve as a temporary depot. Railroad officials saw the name on the rock and lettered it on the shack.

Frank Perkins was one of the contractors who cut out the Wisconsin Central right-of-way through Taylor County. He and another workman from the eastern states were sitting on a hemlock stump one day. The other man peeled the bark from the stump and whittled the word Medford into its surface.

Medina *Dane County*

The early settlers were principally from the town of Medina, Ohio.

Medina *Outagamie County*

Another town named after Medina, Ohio.

Medina Junction *Winnebago County*

Close to Medina in Outagamie County.

Meeme *Manitowoc County*

Ojibwe for "wild pigeon." Anton Walterbach was an early settler.

Meenon *Burnett County*

Meenon is the Ojibwe word for blueberries. It is said this was a "land of jack pines and blueberries," and blueberries were an important source of income to early settlers here.

Meggers *Manitowoc County*

Ferdinand Ree built and operated a store and tavern for a few years and then sold it to Andrew Meggers.

Mellen *Ashland County*

Samuel O'Grady Bennett received homestead land from President Grover Cleveland in 1886 and platted a village called Iron City. He gave a deed to the Penokee Railroad for a branch line to be built eastward into the Gogebic Iron Range from the mainline Wisconsin Central Railroad that ran from Chicago to Ashland. A farsighted stipulation was demanded from the Penokee Railroad by Mr. Bennett: "There shall be established and thereafter maintained a regular station in connection with said Penokee Railroad as well as said Wisconsin Central Railroad." The depot was built and named after Charles Sanger Mellen, an official of the Wisconsin Central Railroad and an associate with J. P. Morgan Sr. in many of his railroad ventures. The town grew, and at one time the train conductor would call out, "Mellen—change for Hurley, Ironwood, and Bessemer." Now there are no passenger trains, and only occasional freight trains pass through.

Melnik   *Manitowoc County*
Named after an early settler.

Melrose   *Jackson County*
On April 13, 1839, Robert Douglas landed alone at a point on the Black River he called Douglas Prairie. In 1845 more of the Douglas family arrived from Dumfries, Scotland, and the area was also referred to as Dumfries.

William H. Polley stayed with the Douglas family while he built his beautiful, spacious twenty-two-room Victorian home. The Polley home has been kept in excellent condition and is a splendid example of the fine workmanship and gracious living of this period in our history.

In 1856, Mark Douglas built a house on his farm, and then a barn that was called "Travelers Joy and Farmers Friend." A lovely dance was held on the main floor of the barn. Still farther north a village was named Bristol after the thriving city in England. In 1860 Bristol was changed to Melrose by Hugh Douglas after Melrose Abbey in Scotland. There was already a post office in Kenosha County and a township in Dane County named Bristol.

Menakaune   *Marinette County*
This is an Indian word meaning "where the lodges are," or quite literally, "the village."

Menasha   *Winnebago County*
It is believed that Jean Nicolet counseled with the Indians here as early as 1634. In 1848 Curtus Reed and Governor Doty started the settlement. Mrs. Doty named it Menasha, the Menominee word for "thorn" or "island." It was incorporated as a city in 1874.

Menchalville   *Manitowoc County*
Stephen Menchal had a store and saloon here.

Mendota   *Dane County*
The Ho-Chunk name for Lake Mendota or Fourth Lake is Wonk-shek-ho-mik-la, meaning "where the man lies." The name Mendota, given to this lake in 1849 by Frank Hudson, a Madison surveyor, is a Sioux Indian name meaning "the mouth of the river." The Prairie Potawatomi called the lake Manto-ka, "snake maker," referring perhaps to the abundance of rattlesnakes along its shores.

The Four Lakes region was known to the Ho-Chunk Indians as Tay-cho-pe-ra. The other three lakes are Monona, Waubesa, and Kegonsa. Lake Wingra, a smaller lake, is connected with Lake Monona by a creek. The Yahara or Catfish River (Myan-mek) flows into Lake Mendota on its north shore. This stream connects the four lakes with each other.

The earliest American travelers to visit the Four Lakes were Ebenezer Brigham, James D. Doty (afterwards territorial governor of Wisconsin), Morgan L. Martin of Green Bay, and Lieutenant Jefferson Davis (afterward president of the Southern Confederacy), then stationed at Fort Winnebago at Portage. John Catlin and Moses Strong staked out the center of the plat of Madison in February 1837. Mr. and Mrs. Eben D. Peck, the first settlers, came to the site of Madison from Blue Mounds, April 15, 1837.

They erected a log cabin near present King Street, overlooking Lake Monona. Here the men who came to erect the first Madison state capitol building were boarded. Oliver Armel, a Frenchman, then had an Indian trading cabin between the capitol and Lake Mendota. At West Point, on the northeast shore of the lake, Wallace Rowan, another Indian trader, had a cabin in 1832. In 1833 he sold this post to Michel St. Cyr, a French Canadian, who traded with the Ho-Chunk Indians until after the building of Madison. The Sauk chief Black Hawk with his warriors and women retreated over the site of Madison on his way to the Wisconsin River in July 1832. A monument on the upper university campus marks the line of his pursuit by US troops.

Ho-Chunk villages and camps were located at a number of places on the shores of Lake Mendota before and after settlers came to this region. Their dome-shaped wigwams consisted of a framework of bent saplings covered with strips of bark or rush matting. They grew corn at all of their villages. In 1837 one of their large villages was located on the shores of a large marshy area, now Tenney Park, on the east shore of the lake and the adjoining lakeshores. It had several hundred inhabitants. Its name is given as *Chee-nunk*, "village."

Another village was located on the banks of the Yahara River and the north shore of the lake. This was *Ne-o-sho*. One of its planting grounds was on the lakeshore lawn of the state hospital and another at the eastern boundary of Morris Park, where Indian corn hills can still be seen. The best-known village was at the mouth of Pheasant Branch on the northwest shore of Lake Mendota. This was known as the "Four Lake village" or *Tay-cho-pe-rah*. It had at times, it is reported, from several hundred to five hundred inhabitants. White Crow, *Kaw-ray-kaw-saw-kaw*, was one of its chiefs.

Other Ho-Chunk campgrounds were at Mendota Beach, Merrill Springs, Second Point, and Picnic Point Bay and below Observatory Hill on the University of Wisconsin grounds. From these villages and campsites, and from other lands about the shores of Lake Mendota, large numbers of implements, ornaments, and ceremonial objects of stone and native copper have been collected. Many of these are preserved in the exhibition halls of the Wisconsin Historical Museum. Some are attributed to an Indian people who occupied some of these sites in prehistoric time, before its occupation by the Ho-Chunk.

Yellow Thunder, *Wa-kun-zah-gah*, was the war chief of the Ho-Chunk of the Four Lakes villages. His oil portrait hangs in the museum. The Ho-Chunk call themselves *Ho-chun-ga-ra*, "fish eaters." They are a tribe of the great Siouan stock of North American Indians.

The Sauk Indians, an Algonquin tribe, whose village was located at the present site of Sauk City and Prairie du Sac on the Wisconsin River, in 1766, also camped and hunted in the Four Lakes region.

More than eleven thousand Indian mounds have been located in Wisconsin by the State Archeological Survey. These earthworks consist of conical or round, oval, platform or flat-topped, linear or embankment-shaped, and animal or effigy mounds, pits, and enclosures. Most remarkable of these are the effigy or emblematic mounds; two were constructed in human form, and one of these is preserved in Man Mound Park near Baraboo. The most famous of the enclosures is known as Aztalan and consisted of the earth heaped about the wooden stockade that protected the prehistoric Indian village. Some of the outworks (mounds) of this ancient village (Cahokia culture) are preserved in Aztalan Mound Park, near Lake Mills. Among the numerous effigy mounds in southern and central Wisconsin are representations of bear, panther, wildcat, fox or wolf, buffalo, beaver, mink, deer, elk, turtle, frog, fish, snake, eagle or thunderbird, wild goose, and other birds.

About one thousand Indian mounds were formerly located about the five Madison lakes. Many of these have been destroyed in the cultivation of land, in road building, and in the growth of Madison. There were about 350 mounds on the shores of Lake Mendota. Mounds or mound groups remain on the campus of the University of Wisconsin, in Burrows Park, at Maple Bluff, Bernards Park, the State Hospital and the State Memorial Hospital grounds, Morris Park, Fox Bluff, Kennedy Pond, West Point, Camp Sunrise, Mendota Beach, Merrill Springs, Black Hawk Country Club, Eagle Heights, and on Picnic Point. Some of these are permanently preserved and are marked with descriptive tablets; others are being protected.

The finest of these mounds are on the lawn of the State Hospital at Mendota, on the north shore of the lake. A bird effigy there has the immense wingspread of 624 feet, the largest bird effigy mound in the world. Near it are two other huge bird mounds. A panther or water spirit effigy has a large tail that curves over its back. At the YMCA camp at Morris Park there is a large panther effigy with a large, tapering, straight tail. On a fairway of the Black Hawk Country Club there is a large wild goose effigy. Near it are three bear mounds. On Observatory Hill on the university grounds a bird effigy and a turtle effigy are preserved. Linear and round mounds are also found among the Lake Mendota mound groups.

Many of the mounds located here have been evacuated. These contained human interments of several kinds—bone reburials, flexed or folded burials, and full-length burials. One mound showed evidence of human cremation. Rude stone altars and burned stones were found. A stone chamber built of large lake boulders was found in one mound. One was constructed of layers of several different kinds of earth. Stone and copper implements, earthenware vessels, stone and shell implements, and animal bones were also found.—CHARLES BROWN, Wisconsin Historical Museum

Menomonee Falls   *Waukesha County*
Menomonee is an Indian word meaning "wild rice." A tribe of the Algonquin Indians was known by this name, and it is presumed they lived or camped along the river. The town was once called Nehsville after Frederich Nehs, the most prominent settler, who built the first mills and lime kilns here. The town of Menomonee merged with the village of Menomonee Falls in 1958.

Menomonie   *Dunn County*
Menomonie County
This is a different spelling of the Indian word meaning "wild rice."

Mequon   *Ozaukee County*
It is claimed that Chief Waubaka had a daughter named Wau-Mequon, or White Feather. The Indians used colors to denote the order of children in the family; white was for the firstborn.

Mercer

Dan Shea was sent here by the Brooks and Ross Lumber Company of Merrill to build a dam and start logging operations. He built the Shea Dam near Fisher Lake so logs could be floated down the river. Two tote roads were also built, and slowly settlers came into the area as the logs were taken out. Old Ed Evenson, who later served as town chairman for eighteen years, and George Richardson were instrumental in establishing the new town named in honor of John Mercer, one of the prominent timbermen of northern Wisconsin.

Meridean

There are several versions of the name's origin, but the most likely appears to be that recounted in the Curtiss-Wedge History of Dunn County:

> *In the third story it is related that in the pioneer days of this region a certain Mrs. Dean came up the Chippewa River on a steamboat, being on her way to join her husband, who was employed in the lumber traffic. She was accompanied by her bright little daughter Mary, who from her sweet character soon became the pet of all on board, so that the rough manners and profane conversation of the boatmen and lumberjacks were for a time, at least, softened into a semblance of decency and higher manhood. But she was suddenly taken dangerously ill and had to be taken ashore, the craft being tied up to the bank at the time, while with tearful sympathy those present watched her life ebb away until death ended her suffering. A little coffin was improvised from an empty box, and with a few ceremonies but many tears she was buried under a tree, where later the company's blacksmith shop was built. In loving commemoration of her, those present gave her name to the place. The grave and tree was later (1884) washed away by a flood.*

Meridean is located on the south bank of the Chippewa River in the southeastern corner of the county. At an older location farther up the river the village supported a large lumber milling operation in the 1860s–1880s.

Merrill

This lumbering settlement on the Wisconsin River was first called Jenny Bull Falls. Rivermen said the fast rapids sounded like a bull roaring in the distance. Jenny was the name they gave to an Indian girl, the daughter of a Potawatomi chief. The rivermen courted her, and when she died in pregnancy, her father wanted her honored. The name was shortened to Jenny Falls and then to Jenny. In 1881 an act of the state legislature changed the name to Merrill in honor of S. S. Merrill, general manager of the Wisconsin Central Railroad.

Merrillan

Benjamin H. Merrill and his brother, Leander G. Merrill, were the founders of this village. L. G. Merrill erected a sawmill in 1870 and asked his brother to plat the town and build a hotel. A number of co-partnerships grew up around the sawmill in which the senior member was one of the Merrills: Merrill and Loomis, Merrill and Ice, and others. The repetition of "Merrill and" suggested Merrillan.

Merrimac

One of the earliest settlers on this part of the Wisconsin River was Chester Mattson, who started a ferry here in 1848. The settlement was known as Mart's Ferry. Within a year Mr. Mattson was granted a post office, named Colomar after the postmaster general at that time. But farmers and stagecoach drivers continued to call it Matt's Ferry. J. G. Train is credited with having the name changed to Merrimack, after a county and river in New Hampshire. Later the "k" was dropped. This is also claimed to be an Indian word meaning "sturgeon," or "swift water."

The Merrimac Ferry

Charles Mattson was Merrimac's first permanent settler and the operator of this ferry. Today, the Merrimac Ferry is the last of upward of five hundred ferries chartered by territorial and state legislatures before the turn of the century.

Merton

Until 1849 this town was called Warren, after Sylvanus Warren and his fourteen children, who subsequently scattered all over the town. Mrs. Henry Shears suggested the name Moreton after the English town of Cromwell's fame. The spelling was later changed to Merton.

Me-Shee-Gah-Ning

This was a very large, old Potawatomi Indian village. The name meant "cleared land."

Messerli Quarry

Most of the rock in the state capitol building came from this quarry. It was owned by Mr. Carl Messerli and is located in Bridgeport Township.

Metomen

The word means "a grain of corn" in the Menominee language. The first town meeting was held at the home of F. D. Bowman, who suggested the name.

Michigan Island

The Indian word mishigan was said to mean "a bone with hair," and a similar term meant "he had scarcely any hair on his head." This island in the Apostle group was called pagidabiminiss by the Ojibwe Indians, signifying an island where they set lines with several hooks to catch fish. Michigan is also thought to be a form of the Indian word michigami, meaning "a large body of water."

Middle Inlet

The name was taken from the stream that is the middle of three streams flowing into Lake Noquebay.

Middle River

This name is also taken from the adjacent river, the one between Amnicon and the Brule.

Middleton *Dane County*

The first settlers were Horace Hall and John Alcott, who came in 1839. The area was heavily timbered with burr oak, hickory, poplar, and elm. Harry Barnes, the first postmaster, chose the name after Middleton in Vermont.

Milan *Marathon County*

In 1870 three men gained control of a number of acres of timberland in the western part of Marathon County. Their names were Rietbrock, Johnson, and Halsey, and by 1889 they had built the Abbotsford and Northeastern Railroad as an outlet for their products. They named the stations on the railroad after European cities.

Military Road

This route was surveyed in 1831 and 1832 to connect Fort Crawford at Prairie du Chien and Fort Howard at Green Bay, the first overland route to replace the water route by the way of the Fox River and Lake Winnebago. The Black Hawk War was an important factor in its construction, thus the name Military Road. It was completed in 1838 but was passable chiefly when the ground was either frozen or very dry. Hunters, traders, pioneers, soldiers, Indians, trappers, and confidence men traveled it, as well as military personnel.

Milladore *Wood County*

The original name was Mill Creek, but since there was already a Mill Creek post office in the state, postal authorities asked that a new name be chosen bearing some resemblance to the old one. Orlow Everetts and the section foreman made up the name of Milladore, which was accepted. Since there was a sawmill, a stave mill, and a feed mill, people thought the name should retain the word mill.

Millard *Walworth County*

First known as Backer's Corners. Later named Millard in honor of President Millard Fillmore.

Mill Creek *Richland County*

Located in Eagle and Dayton Townships. It was named for the mills on its banks, the first one constructed as early as 1841–42.

Miller *Burnett County*

Located three miles east of Swiss, it is named after John Miller, on whose land the post office is located.

Miller Hill *Crawford County*

Jay Miller, an early pioneer, lived on this hill just northwest of Wauzeka village.

Miller's Grove *Richland County*

Sunday school picnics and other large gatherings were often held here the W. H. Miller farm south of Richland Center.

Millersville   *Sheboygan County*

Henry G. Mueller, in partnership with a Mr. Halbach, constructed a steam sawmill here in 1866. Apparently the town was spelled with the more usual English form.

Mill Home   *Manitowoc County*

This name was selected because there were so many mills located here.

Millston   *Jackson County*

The family of Hugh B. Mills, a lumber baron, built the town. Mr. Mills built a large home and later added a two-story addition with six large rooms to accommodate loggers. Scandinavian farmers in the area left their homes after the fall harvest was finished and came to cut timber during the winter months to supplement their income. The Mills home had a large kitchen with a big iron range used to prepare meals for loggers. The Indians called the settlement Big Gut Depot because Hugh Mills had a large tummy.

Milltown   *Polk County*

A sawmill was the only building of any kind for a number of years.

Millville   *Grant County*

Another settlement that originated from the lumbering industry.

Milton   *Rack County*

Grainfield was the first name; pioneers found the land covered with tall grass. When a post office was applied for, the name Prairie du Lac was submitted because of the lakes around, or possibly with reference to Lake Koshkonong. This name was rejected because Prairie du Sac was already recognized, and the two might be confused. Milton was the name given in 1839. Tradition says that the pioneers thought of the places in the East that they had left as Paradise Lost and this little village as Paradise Regained and selected the name of the author of these classics. It is also possible it was named after Milton in Pennsylvania.

Milton House   *Rock County*

Located in Milton, this frontier inn was erected in 1844 by Joseph Goodrich. A pre–Civil War station in the Underground Railroad, it is still connected by a secret escape tunnel to the old log cabin. It is currently operated as a museum.

Milton Junction   *Rock County*

The Chicago, Milwaukee, and St. Paul Railroad was built through the village of Milton in 1853. In 1858 the Chicago and North Western Railway crossed the St. Paul road about one mile to the west. The settlement that grew up here was first called West Milton, later Milton Junction.

Milwaukee   *Milwaukee County*

A Potawatomi Indian village was discovered near the mouth of the Milwaukee River as early as 1649. The real translation of the word is uncertain, as the Indians with whom early missionaries and traders came in contact differed in their statements.

In 1679 Father Hennepin thought the name was Millecki or Melchi, meaning "good land." Father Zenobe thought it was Millicki, meaning "there is a good point." John Buisson de Cosme in 1699 reported it as Milwarkik, or "great council place." Lieutenant James Gorrell in 1761 called it Milwauky, or "good earth." It was spelled Milwauki in 1779, Millewacki in 1817, Milwahkie, Milwalky, and Milwaukie.

The Ojibwe did not have "l" in their language and substituted "n"—thus *manewuk,* meaning "open place," referred to the sandy area near the mouth of the river, *manawa* meaning a "suck-hole" and *mendake* meaning "snakemaker," a name they gave to the river.

Mana-wau-kee is said to have been a root used by the Indians for medicinal purposes, and they thought this was the only place where it grew. The Ojibwe Indians would give a beaver skin for a piece as large as a man's finger.

By 1884 the spelling of Milwaukee was finally stabilized and was said to come from an Indian word meaning "rich, beautiful land," or, according to Joshua Hathaway, "a gathering place by the river." Long before its discovery by settlers and for many years afterward, it was a popular meeting place or council ground for different tribes of Indians.

Mimi Island

This is an Ojibwe Indian word meaning "pigeon."

Mina-Kakun
Brown County

This was the name of the Menominee village at Fort Howard in Green Bay; there were a number of villages on both sides of the Fox River here. Mina-kakun, "a fort," referred to the place where they camped under the fort wall and is the present site of the railroad station.

Mineral Point
Iowa County

Lead was discovered in 1824 on a high rocky point between two streams, and later it was found that lead and zinc abounded near the surface in the whole area. Chief Black Hawk is supposed to have mined lead here to carry on his war.

Pioneers from the East flocked to the area in open and covered wagons. This was the age when women wore shawls and men wore buffalo coats. At night they slept on straw ticks. Straw was piled on the floor, and a rag carpet stretched tightly over it, and tacked around the edge.

The famous Shake Rag Street is at Mineral Point. The miners' wives shook dishrags to call their men home to dinner.

Mineral Point Road
Dane County

So named because it joined Madison with Mineral Point. Part of it coincided with Military Road (from Pine Bluff to Blue Mounds), and part with Speedway Road (from Pine Bluff to Madison). This name has been in use since the earliest days of Madison's settlement.

Minnechara
Fond du La County

The site of an old Indian village located on a big bend of the Fond du Lac River and shown on a map of Fond du Lac, dated 1857.

Minnesota Junction *Dodge County*

Minnesota is derived from a Sioux Indian word meaning "cloudy water" or "sky-tinted water."

Minniwakan Spring *Dane County*

Located in Madison. This Dakota word means "water spirit," i.e., whiskey. Not a native name, it is not certain whether the namer was aware of the second meaning of the word.

Minocqua *Oneida County*

Early histories mention a Chief Minocquip of the Ojibwe Indian tribe who may have been the eponym. Minocqua has five townships, but the populated part is a small section of land jutting out to divide Lake Kawaguesago from Lake Minocqua, making it almost an island city.

Minocqua is in the heart of the headwaters region. One frequently used the water route connected to the Wisconsin River, the Tomahawk River, and the Chippewa River by way of short overland portages to the connecting waters of Tomahawk Lake, Shishebogama Lake, Fence Lake, and Lac du Flambeau. It took two days to make one such cross journey. Travelers drifted downstream on the Wisconsin River to the portage point and then walked overland or worked their paddles through chains of lakes until they reached Bear River, which took them downstream toward the Chippewa River.

The point of land known as Minocqua was about halfway along this route and was an excellent stopping place. It was dry and had plenty of firewood and good springwater. It was a campsite used by all travelers, including the first French missionaries, explorers, and traders. Pioneers have said that the word means "mid-journey," "noon-day rest," "stop and drink," or "a pleasant place to be."

Minong *Washburn County*

An Indian word said to mean "a good high place," "a pleasant valley," or "a place where blueberries grow."

Mirror Lake *Sauk County*

The erection of a dam near the village of Delton in 1860 formed this lake. As the people came to visit it for pleasure or fishing, the remarkably clear reflections attracted attention and exclamations, such as "What a mirror!" It is said that Mrs. C. A. Noyes of Kilbourn is credited with first applying the name.

Misha Mokwa *Buffalo County*

An Indian word meaning a "very large bear."

Mishicot *Manitowoc County*

This Indian word is credited with the following various meanings: "covered by clouds," "great branch," "a wide sheet or cloth," "turtle." More reliable sources say that Old Chief Mishicot, of the Ottawa, ruled over this territory. The town was settled by Daniel Smith in 1844. By 1853 a large number of Saxons had moved in and changed the name to Saxonburgh, but by 1855 it was restored to Mishicot.

Missabe Iron Range *Northern Wisconsin*
Missabe is the Ojibwe Indian word for "giant."

Mission of St. Francis Xavier *Oconto County*
On December 2, 1669, the Eve of St. Francis, Father Claude Allouez arrived at Oconto and founded this mission, the first mission in northeastern Wisconsin.

Mississippi Gardens *Crawford County*
Located in the township of Eastman on the banks of the Mississippi at the foot of Charme Hollow, it was named after a dance hall tavern and recreation area located here.

The Mississippi River Parkway *La Crosse County*
The parkway was the first to be planned and constructed as a portion of the parkway that eventually will extend from the source of the Mississippi River in Lake Itasca to its mouth in the Gulf of Mexico.

Mitchell *Sheboygan County*
When the town was organized in 1850 it was called Olio. In the following year a number of Irish settlers moved in and changed the name to honor John Mitchell, the Irish patriot.

Mohrsville *Sheboygan County*
This was a settlement located at the intersection of the Green Bay and Howard Roads, named for Paul Mohr, a tavern keeper.

Mole Lake *Forest County*
Apparently this is a translation of the Indian word maw-she-gwaw-caw-maw.

Molitor *Taylor County*
This township is said to have been named after one of the early settlers. In one section there was a popular store and tavern owned by Matt Ochs known as the Last Chance. In another part there was a large sawmill, and the land was known as Egle Place since it was owned by George Egle.

Monches *Waukesha County*
This settlement was first called Kuntz's Mills after Heinrich Kuntz, and at one time it was known as O'Connellsville by the majority of Irish settlers. One stormy night a group of townsmen assembled in the mill to choose a name for their new post office. None of the Irish neighbors showed up to defend the hamlet's name, and the spirit of the Indian buried on Blanket Hill must have been out wandering that night. When the Irish awoke the next morning their beloved hamlet had been renamed in honor of a deceased Indian. Monches was a Potawatomi chief of an Indian village that had once been located here.

Mondell Hill *Crawford County*
Named after a family, it is located in Prairie du Chien Township.

Mondovi   *Buffalo County*

Harvey Farrington was the first settler here in 1855. The area was named Pan Cake Valley and later it became Farringtons. Elihu B. Gifford was the only man in the village to subscribe to a newspaper. While reading the weekly New York Ledger he became interested in a story of Napoleon's Italian campaigns. A great victory had been won against the Sardinians in 1796 at a place called Mondovi. The name appealed to Mr. Gifford. Mr. Gifford left for Spokane, Washington Territory, in 1878, and later named a village Mondovi in that state also.

Monico   *Oneida County*

This was a logging town and is thought to have been named by B. F. Dorr, the early surveyor, but the reason for this name is not recorded.

Monona   *Dane County*

The name appears to be of Indian origin, but there is some conjecture as to what it means. In the Ho-Chunk language it is said to mean "lost" or "stolen," or "teepee lake." The Potawatomi word manoman meant "wild rice." The Sauk-Fox Indians had a similar word that meant "superwoman," a mythical person of supernatural powers who presided over the wigwam. However, most authorities claim it is a word meaning "beautiful," and that was first used to describe the lake.

Monroe   *Green County*

Monroe began as three separate towns that were merged into one community. The first house was built by two bachelors, Hiram Rust and Leonard Ross, who had come from New York State in 1834.

Green County was organized in 1838, and then the memorable battle over the selection of the county seat started. Judge Andrick laid out a town and called it New Mexico but failed to record it at the Mineral Point office. It was generally assumed that New Mexico would become the new county seat, and Joseph Payne tried to buy an interest in it. Judge Andrick refused. Mr. Payne then laid out his own town immediately to the north, and waited until the Burlington legislature designated New Mexico as the county seat. He rushed to the land office to record his town as New Mexico, with the irate Judge Andrick in hot pursuit. Mr. Payne won the race.

However, the next session of the legislature repealed the law and appointed three commissioners to select a Green County seat. They chose a town called Roscoe that was two and a half miles farther north. Citizens of the two New Mexicos protested loudly. The legislature then decided to put the matter to a vote.

Meanwhile, it was discovered that a well dug in Joseph Payne's town yielded no water even at forty feet. That put his plat out of the running, so Mr. Payne, a Mr. LyBrand and William S. Russell offered to give the county 120 acres near a spring that was northeast of the Payne plot. This was later called Spring Square. Judge Andrick gave up the fight for his New Mexico plat and joined a Mr. Sutherland and another promoter to back a location immediately south of the Roscoe site.

The election of May 1839 was worse than no election at all, since the vote ended in a tie. A second ballot in June ended the same way, although LyBrand had imported one

Elias Luttrell to add an extra vote—but Luttrell double-crossed him and cast his ballot for Judge Andrick's location.

For the August election Judge Andrick submitted a point in his new development that was supposed to be the exact center of the county, and was quite confident of getting the majority vote. But by this time pioneer bachelor Hiram Rust had found a wife, and Mrs. Rust came to the rescue of LyBrand's Spring Square. Her braided hats were popular with miners who were settling the area, and a bonnet was offered as a prize to a young man to round up the miners' vote. So in August of 1839 a hat turned the tide of victory for LyBrand, Payne, and Russell.

Dr. Harcourt as county commissioner named the new county seat Monroe, presumably after President James Monroe.

For several years the three different names persisted. Judge Andrick's house was the center of things in South New Mexico, which also had a post office and store building. In Payne's North New Mexico was LyBrand's store. In Payne's Spring Square there was John Hart's store, and the blacksmith shop of Buckskin Brown. Apparently the town of Roscoe was also absorbed into the new community. Evidence of these early communities can still be seen in the street jogs of the present city.

Monroe County
In honor of President James Monroe.

Montello   *Marquette County*
James Daniel settled here in 1849 and named the site Serairo after a place in Mexico where he had fought during the Mexican War. Later it was called Hill River because of the granite hills and the Fox River. There are two accounts of how the name of Montello came to be chosen:

1. In the fall of 1849 a meeting was held in the home of J. N. Dart. There were a number of suggestions, but Joseph R. Dart, who had read of Montello in a novel, carried the majority.
2. French voyageurs and fur traders named the location Mont l'eau, or "hill by the water."

Monterey   *Waukesha County*
A Mr. Hackley was the first postmaster and chose the name in honor of the battle in Monterey, Mexico, during the Mexican War.

Montfort   *Grant County*
In 1827 Richard H. Palmer followed an Indian trail into this area and stopped in a ravine to look for water. He found a spring and a stream, and also pieces of lead that had been brought to the surface by badgers digging in the hillside. The location was called Wingville after Marlin Burton caught a pheasant with his hands. It was also called Podunk for a time.

During the Black Hawk War the miners built a small post fort to protect themselves, but they were never attacked. The settlement was named Montfort, but the post office kept the name of Wingville for a number of years.

Montgomeryville
Crawford County

Named for several of the Montgomery families, it is located in the township of Clayton.

Monticello
Green County

Robert Witter built a sawmill on Little Sugar River here in 1843. Foster Steadman, who became postmaster on the mail route between Monroe and Madison, named it in 1845. The most striking peculiarity in this part of the county are the mounds bordering Long Hollow, the long valley that extends from Mt. Pleasant far into Washington. Mr. Steadman named the post office Monticello, meaning "little mountain," in reference to these mounds or bluffs.

Montpelier
Kewaunee County

Thomas Paddleford was the first settler. He came in 1855 and named the site after his former home, Montpelier, Vermont.

Montrose
Dane County

In the late 1820s, prospectors and traders journeyed back and forth over the ridge trail from the lead mining country at Exeter to Blue Mounds. The first settler was George McFadden, who built a tavern and a large barn in the Sugar River Valley in 1841. It became known as McFadden Springs and also as the Grand Springs Farm. The first school was held in Elam Elder's granary in 1853, and later in the old granary at the Cheney Bowker farm. The seats were nail kegs with a plank placed across them. A barrel with a board across the top was the teacher's desk. D. S. Smith said that as a student there he once climbed into the upper rafters where a keg of beans was stored, and in spite of threats and pleadings, shot beans at the teacher and the other students. Joseph Kendrick is credited with starting the settlement and chose the name Montrose after a town in Pennsylvania.

Montrose Siding
Manitowoc County

This place took its name from The Legend of Montrose by Sir Walter Scott.

Moonsgrove
Calumet County

This settlement near Stockbridge has practically disappeared, and few people know that it even existed. It was one of the towns voted on in the 1852 election to select a county seat. It was named in honor of the early Moon family.

Moquah
Bayfield County

A logging company forwarded supplies to this site in advance of a camp construction party. A caretaker and an Indian assistant were sent along to protect the provisions and equipment, which were stored under canvas throws. One Sunday morning the two guardians went to fish in a nearby lake. Several hours later they returned to find the supplies scattered all around the campsite. The Indian exclaimed Mu-qwu, said to be the Ojibwe word for "bear." The word was spelled Moquah and became the name of the logging camp. Later the Northern Pacific Railroad station also adopted it.

Moro *Burnett County*
Named after Moro Castle at Havana, Cuba, at the time of the Spanish-American War.

Morris *Brown County*
The name of one of the early settlers.

Morris *Chippewa County*
A station on the Wisconsin Central Railroad, sometimes referred to as Morris-Craft Post-office, that has since disappeared.

Morris *Shawano County*
Maurice Deleglise, a Frenchman, was the first settler. His first name was chosen, with a new spelling.

Morris Valley *Richland County*
Charles L. Morris, a farmer and beekeeper, bought his home in Richland in 1947.

Morrisonville *Dane County*
In 1841 James Morrison left his native home in Dundee of Scotland to emigrate to America, land of promise, with his wife and three sons. They arrived in Dane County in midwinter. Their first home was a tent of blankets on a knoll above the Yahara River. Morrison purchased a quarter section of land in the township of Windsor for $1.25 an acre. Other pioneers also came to convert the fertile land into farms. The big problem was transportation, as produce had to be hauled by oxen to Milwaukee. In 1871 when the Madison-Portage Railroad was built, Mr. Morrison gave land for the railroad right-of-way, and also for a village, providing the railroad company established a station at this site.

Morse *Ashland County*
Mr. Morse was the foreman in a mill in this settlement when it was separated from the town of Mellen. He suggested naming the new town after a Mr. Edwards, but instead Mr. Edwards named it after Mr. Morse.

Moscow *Iowa County*
There is no record of how this once-thriving community got its name. At one time it had a school, a hotel, a blacksmith shop, a post office, and several stores and small factories. It was platted in 1850 by Chauncy Smith, an Englishman, who had built a dam across the Bluemound branch of the Pecatonica River and also built a gristmill. Apparently the village failed to prosper because the Illinois Central Railroad bypassed it in 1888. Today only scattered ruins, a few remodeled homes, and a cemetery remain. There is no record of any Russian immigrants ever settling in the community. It was populated by English, Irish, German, and Norwegian immigrants.

Mosel   *Sheboygan County*

The first settlers came in 1847, and the town was organized in 1853 with William Wippermann as town chairman. Julius Wolff suggested the name after the Moselle River in Germany and France, since many of the early settlers had come from that region. The Mosel post office was established in 1869 and abandoned in 1903. There was a Mosel Station on the Chicago and North Western Railway that is also long since abandoned.

Mosinee   *Marathon County*

This Indian word in Ho-Chunk is said to mean "cold land," and in Ojibwe, "moose." As early as 1836 traders and explorers had called the site Little Bull Falls because the swift rapids in the Wisconsin River sounded like the roar of a bull. Ojibwe Indians were living here when the first settlers came in 1857. The first post office was established on the east side of the river. When a bridge was built to cross the gorge, it was decided to move the post office to the west side. Truman Keeler, the postmaster, objected to the name Little Bull Falls because he thought it was vulgar for ladies to write such a title on their letters. Joseph Dessert led the discussion of a new name. He wanted an Indian name and said he would see Mr. Connor, the trapper, about it. Mr. Connor suggested that Old Chief Mosinee be honored, and the citizens approved.

Mosling   *Oconto County*

Originally called Linwood from the linn or basswood trees that grew nearby. Mosling was chosen for a merchant who established a business here.

Moss Creek   *Richland County*

Located in Buena Vista Township. This little creek was named as early as the 1850s for the moss, tufts of plants, sods, and mats that covered the moist ground along its course.

Mother's Run   *Richland County*

Located in Buena Vista Township. Some adults can remember playing along the banks of this little stream that flowed through Sextonville when they were young, but the story connected with the name has slipped away from them.

Moundville   *Marquette County*

So named for the numerous mounds remaining from prehistoric times.

Mount Adin   *Eau Claire County*

This is a high hill in the city of Eau Claire named for a Randall brother who was among the first settlers. Mount Simon and Mount Tim were named for other brothers.

Mountain   *Oconto County*

This location on the bank of the north branch of the Oconto River was a stopping-off place where teams of oxen and horses hauling supplies to logging camps were fed. In 1877 Thomas McAllan built the first permanent home. The town grew up around the first store built by Harry Baldwin. A. C. Frost was another early pioneer, and he built the first hotel out of logs and became the first postmaster. He is credited with naming the town

Mountain for the numerous hills around it. This is part of the Laurentian Plateau, with granite outcroppings, some quite high.

Mountain of the Stars   *Taylor County*
A translation of the Indian name, this is a natural mound some thirty miles in circumference and several hundred feet high. From it the Black River flows to the south, the Eau Claire and Yellow Rivers to the west, and two branches of the Wisconsin River to the east. It was said to be covered with pine timber, and its rocks and sands showed indications of copper or some richer ore.

Mount Calvary   *Fond du Lac County*
The first settlers arrived in the township of Marshfield, Fond du Lac County, in 1841. Almost all of them were Catholics, and in 1846 they built their first little church, under the direction of the Reverend Caspar Rehrl, the noted pioneer priest who also built other log churches in the area. On one of his mission journeys from Sheboygan he saw the big hill in the distance where Holy Cross Church and St. Lawrence Seminary now stand. He climbed to the top, planted a cross made of branches of trees, and decided to build a church on the hill. Most of the men who worked on the building were named Nicholas, so the people voted to call it St. Nicholas Church. The parish and the little settlement at the foot of the hill were called the St. Nicholas Congregation.

In 1853 the bishop of Milwaukee, Martin Henni, came to administer the sacrament of confirmation. Because of the location of the church he wished it to be called Holy Cross or Calvary Church, and the place itself Mount Calvary. Both Father Caspar Rehrl and his brother who succeeded him, Father George Rehrl, thought Mount Calvary was the more fitting name.

Mt. Hope   *Grant County*
The story is that prior to 1875, when the legislature passed a law permitting the establishment of high schools by cities and villages, it was the desire of every community to attract an academy as an institution of higher learning. This village was no exception, and the residents "hoped" so hard and to such good purpose that the Mt. Hope Academy did materialize. It was located on a small hill or rise.

Mount Horeb   *Dane County*
In 1861 a post office was established in the eastern part of Blue Mounds Township in the farm home of George Wright. Mr. Wright, a Methodist minister, was the first postmaster and chose the name from the bible. He was highly regarded in the community and served as a town treasurer, served a term in the state legislature, and was assistant provost marshall during the Civil War.

Mount Morris   *Waushara County*
According to folklore, this hamlet and township was named when Solomon Morris beat Gunnar Gunderson in a footrace to the top of this mount. Morris received with his victory the right to name the mount after his family.

Mount Nebo   *Richland County*
Located in Forest Township. The biblical name meaning "lofty height" was applied because of the height of this mount in relation to the surrounding area.

Mount Sterling   *Crawford County*
William Sterling came here before the Civil War. The high hill north of the village is said to be the highest elevation in Crawford County.

Mount Tabor   *Vernon County*
John C. Tabor settled here in 1855 and became the first postmaster in 1856. Settled mostly by Bohemian people, Mount Tabor is situated 1,361 feet above sea level.

Mount Trempealeau   *La Crosse County*
This large bluff was formerly called Minne-chon-kaha by the Ojibwe Indians, meaning "bluff in the water."

Mount Vernon   *Dane County*
Joel Britts and George, his nephew, were instrumental in starting the village. They named it for George Washington's home in Virginia, their native state.

Mount Zion   *Crawford County*
In Scott Township, the name was first given to a church built here in 1866.

Muir Knoll   *Dane County*
In Madison on the University of Wisconsin campus, this high point on University Hill was named in 1918 by Professor Julius Olson. John Muir, "naturalist and father of the national park system," lived across the drive in North Hall when he was a student at the university.

Muwka   *Waupaca County*
This township was named after a Menominee Indian chief.

Mukwa-Muko-Min   *Walworth County*
The land above the Chapin place on the north shore of Lake Geneva was given this name by the Potawatomi Indians, meaning "where the black bear digs for a root."

Muk-Wan-Wish-Ta-Guon River
Accent the first and third syllables and half-accent the last syllable to pronounce this Indian name. It means "bear's head." There has been some effort on the part of recent settlers in the region to have the name changed to Wolf River. Bad success to them, say the old settlers, who prefer a bear's head to a whole wolf.

Mukwonago   *Waukesha County*
Before 1836 a large and populous Indian village, the chief village of the Potawatomi, was located here. There are a number of interpretations of the word: 1. "Mother gone away" or "crying for mother." 2. "Feather" or "ladle," because the band in the stream was thought

224

to resemble that very crooked utensil. 3. The most accepted translation is "bear," "place of the bear," "place of the bear constellation," "bear stars," "bear hole," "home of the bear," "bear lair," or "people of the bearskins." The village was said to have been where the Indian bear clan held meetings. It was spelled Mequanigo by Ira Blood when he surveyed the original plat. It is not recorded when or why the spelling was changed.

Mule Hollow   Crawford County
Located in Freeman Township. This was originally called Heald Hollow, after the Heald family, but Mathias Hanson, the owner of a span of mules, later changed it to Mule Hollow.

Mullet Creek and Mullet Lake   Fond du Lac County
Named for John Mullet, an early surveyor. He often lived in the wilderness for three months at a time, carrying his provisions.

Mullet River   Sheboygan County
The river was named after John Mullet, one of the government surveyors who surveyed the exterior lines in the county in 1833–34, and was probably named by Mullett himself.

Murphy Hollow   Crawford County
In Clayton Township, it was named for the Murphy family.

Muscoda   Grant County
The journal of Lieutenant James Gorrell, the first English commandant at Green Bay after the French and Indian War, records under June 14, 1763: "The traders came down from the Sack (Sauk) country, and confirmed the news of Lansing and his son being killed by the French."

When all the Sauks and Foxes had arrived at Green Bay a few days later, they told Gorrell their people were all in tears "for the loss of two English traders who were killed by the French in their lands, and begged leave to cut them (the French) in pieces."

In 1817 the journal of Willard Keyes, a young New Englander traveling with a party down the Wisconsin River, records: "Passed a place called English Meadow from an English trader and his son, said to have been murdered there by the savages, twenty leagues to Prairie du Chien."

Thus the site came to be called English Prairie, or English Meadow, from a gruesome crime committed in the early days of exploration and settlement. The post office was named Muscoda in 1843. The word is said to be a corruption of *Mash-ko-deng*, the Indian word for "meadow" or "prairie." A tribe of Indians called the Mascouten or Prairie Indians lived in the Upper Fox River Valley.

The spelling and pronunciation is said to come from Longfellow's *Hiawatha*:

And Nokomis fell affrighted
Downward through the evening twilight
On the muskoday, the meadow
On the prairie full of blooms.

Muskeg *Bayfield County*

The Indian word for swamp.

Muskego *Waukesha County*

The Potawatomi Indians had a large settlement here, and the name is a derivation of their title for the location. It meant "swamp," "cranberry bog," "fishing place," "sunfish"—interpretations of Indian names vary. There were lots of sunfish in the lake. The Muskegoe Indians were also said to be the people of the swamp, or marsh dwellers. More than eight hundred Indians lived around the shores of Muskego Lake under Chief Kaw-wis-sot, son of King O'Nau-te-sah, who was chief of the Milwaukee-area tribes. Lavanlette Ellarson was one of the first settlers in 1836. Land was purchased for $1.25 an acre under the administration of President Martin Van Buren.

Muskego Center *Waukesha County*

The Indian name was Puk-woth-ic, meaning "high piece of ground" or "hill." At one time it was called Prattsburgh. No explanation is available for either name.

Mygatt's Corners *Racine County*

Wallace Mygatt settled here early in 1836.

N

Nabob   *Washington County*

This is the Menominee Indian word for "soup."

Nagawicka   *Waukesha County*

In the Ojibwe Indian language the word means "sandy" or "there is sand." It is also said to mean "songstress."

Nakoma   *Dane County*

A subdivision of Madison, the name was taken from Baraga's dictionary of Ojibwe, in which its meaning is given as "I promise him to do something." For promotional purposes this was changed to "I do as I promise," and this was made the "official" meaning.

Namekagon   *Bayfield County*

An Ojibwe Indian word meaning "sturgeon," "where the sturgeons are plentiful," "home of the sturgeon."

Nasewaupee   *Door County*

The name of a Menominee Indian chief who had a village a few miles west of here. The town was organized in 1859.

Nashotah   *Waukesha County*

The word means "twins" or "one of a pair." It was first applied to Upper and Lower Nashotah Lakes. The settlement was a terminal on the Watertown Plank Road. Later, when the railroad was built, it was known as Nashotah Station.

Nash Ridge   *Crawford County*

Named after the Nash family, it is located in the township of Freeman.

Nashville   *Forest County*

G. V. Nash was an early settler who came from Forest City, Arkansas.

Nasonville   *Wood County*

Two brothers, Solomon L. and William G. Nason, came here in the spring of 1855.

Natanano   *Shawano County*

This is the Menominee Indian word for smoky falls.

Nebagamon   *Douglas County*

This is a corruption of an Ojibwe Indian word meaning "watching for game at night from a boat," "hunting of deer by canoes at night," "a lake where they float in the night waiting for game."

Nebraska Hollow   *Richland County*

Located in Ithaca Township. Named for its resemblance to a hollow in Nebraska. Nebraska is an Indian word meaning "water valley."

Necedah   *Juneau County*

This word is said to be a corruption of the Ojibwe word nissida, meaning "let there be three of us," and was applied to the river. It is also said to be a Ho-Chunk word meaning "land of the yellow waters."

The river was named Yellow River by settlers who adopted Necedah as the name for their town. The first settlers were Thomas Weston and J. T. Kingston, who laid up a few rounds of a log shanty in 1848. They blazed a tree on both sides of the Yellow River with their names and the date of their claim, and took formal claim to the land according to the laws of that time.

Necedah immediately became a large logging center, with a drive of seven hundred thousand feet of logs from Cranberry Creek to the site of the proposed mill. The mill was completed in 1851, and within a few years five other mills were also operating. Others were added over the years. Two railroads were built. During the first nine months of 1881 more than nine hundred cars of lumber were shipped out. Eighteen miles of cars were loaded, and the railroads were unable to secure cars to fill the still pressing orders.

In October 1898, the mill whistles were tied down to signal the final closing of the mills, and the lumbering business in Necedah was ended. Farming has been the major industry since that time.

Neda   *Dodge County*

This small community grew up at the site of main iron mine shafts and was noted for the production of Iron Ridge Red Paint.

Nederloe Ridge   *Crawford County*

Located in the Township of Utica, it was named for families that lived here.

Neenah   *Winnebago County*

In 1835 the US government established a settlement to teach the Indians the refinements of white civilization. It became the first permanent town in this section of the Fox River Valley and was called Winnebago Rapids. The first permanent settler was Harrison Reed. Judge James Doty, who later became governor of the state, also settled here. One day he asked an old Indian the name of the river. The Indian thought he wanted to know the Ho-Chunk word for water so he answered neenah, the word that means "running water." Judge Doty gave the name of the town in 1843. In 1873 Neenah was incorporated as a city.

Nee-Rut-Cha-Ja *Jefferson County*

The Indian name for a ford in the Rock River about six miles north of Janesville. The white settlement here was known as Indian Ford. It was an old and important river crossing, and the Ho-Chunk word Nee-rut-cha-ja means "river crossing."

Neillsville *Clark County*

James O'Neill was the proprietor of lumber mills known as O'Neill's Mills. In 1854 the small community was chosen over Western Rapids as the county seat. It was connected to La Crosse by a four-horse daily stagecoach that carried the mail. The name was later changed to Neillsville.

Nekimi *Winnebago County*

A corruption of the Indian word nikimi or nee-kee-min, meaning "wild goose berry." The wild berries grew along the shores of rivers and lakes in this region, and wild geese often fed on them. Nigimi or Nekimi is also said to mean "he grumbles like a dog," "he acts as if he wanted to bite."

Nekoosa *Wood County*

A Ho-Chunk word meaning "running water." It was given to the locality because of the rapids in the Wisconsin River. Daniel Whitney, one of the first settlers, built a sawmill here in 1834 and called the site Whitney's Rapids. In 1847 it was called Point Boss or Point Basse after a lumberman named Basse and often called just Boss. Thomas Nash, owner of the Nekoosa Paper Mill that became the prominent industry, named the town Nekoosa in 1893.

Nelson *Buffalo County*

James Nelson, an Englishman, settled here on the Mississippi River at the mouth of the Chippewa River in 1843. The site was called Nelson's Landing and became a popular stopping place for river travelers. For a time a ferry ran between Nelson's Landing and Reed's Landing in Minnesota. Mr. Nelson seems to have disappeared, but the settlement kept his name.

Madison Wright was the first permanent settler in 1848. He lived in the bottoms near the ferry and traded in Wabasha, Minnesota. As time went on he spent most of his time in Wabasha and seldom visited Nelson. When he died Wabasha sent the Nelson town board a bill for his funeral, but the board replied that if Wright died penniless, it was because he had spent all his money in Wabasha; therefore, they should bury him.

A business center grew up in the neighboring settlement of Fairview, but the combined village took the name of Nelson. A post office was established in 1858 with E. A. Warner as postmaster.

Nelsonville *Eau Claire County*

Jerome Nelson purchased land from the government in 1854 and built a gristmill that he operated for many years. A store and a blacksmith shop were added. The small community was settled mainly by Norwegians during the 1870s.

Nemahbin Lake   *Waukesha County*

This is the Indian word for a kind of fish—the common sucker, a kind of trout, or possibly the cisco.

Nemet-Sakou-At   *Douglas County*

This is the Sioux name for the portage between the northern end of the Brule River and the St. Croix River.

Neopit   *Shawano County*

This was the name of the second son of Tshe-Katch-ake-mau, or Oshkosh-the-Brave, who was chief of the Menominee Indians after his brother, Aqui-ni-mi, defected. Chief Neopit died in 1908. The word means "fourth one in a den" and is sometimes spelled Neopet. It can be pronounced with the accent on either the second or third syllable. The name was legally given to the post office created at the Menominee Indian Mills after the La Follette Act of 1908 provided for this industry.

Neosho   *Dodge County*

This word is said to be a corruption of the Indian word meaning "a point of land projecting into a lake" or other body of water. It is also said to mean "small water hole." The Menominee Indians are also said to have given the name to this location, and in their language it means "clear water" and refers to the very clear water of the river. Daniel E. Cotton and an old gentleman named Rathburn were the first white settlers. After purchasing some land from the government in 1845, Mr. Cotton erected a sawmill, and the site was called Cotton's Mill. L. S. Van Orden, who came soon after Mr. Cotton, started the first general store and became the first postmaster.

Neptune   *Richland County*

Located in Ithaca Township. When Dr. Joseph Sippy had the little village platted in 1855, he accepted the name that the government had given to the post office here.

Nero   *Manitowoc County*

Guido Pfister, a Milwaukee industrialist, established a tannery near what was called Nero, located on the Sandy Bay Road between Two Rivers and Kewaunee. No explanation of the name is available.

Neshkoro   *Marquette County*

This is probably a Ho-Chunk word meaning "salt" or "sweet water." But the name of the town is said to have been coined from Nash and Kora, names of two early settlers near here. The first settlers were Mr. Dakin and his sister, Mrs. White, who came from New York State, and many people wanted the town named Dakinsville. One of the early postmasters, whose writing was poor, is said to have sent in the name Nashborough, and when the returns came back from Madison it was spelled Neshkoro.

Neshonoc   *La Crosse County*

The Indian name for a village on the La Crosse River. In 1858 the Chicago, Milwaukee, and St. Paul Railroad was built through the town, but the station was located at Salem, which later became West Salem. The merchants of Neshonoc moved their buildings and merchandise to Salem, and Neshonoc became a ghost town.

Neshoto · Manitowoc County
An Ojibwe word meaning "twins," "two families," "two rivers," or "one of a pair." In the Dakota language it means "kicks up smoke."

Neuren · Kewaunee County
This name is said to have been brought by a Mr. Kreilkamp from Austria.

Neva · Langlade County
Neva was chief of a tribe of Ojibwe who visited here on their way north to Post Lake. Neva Corners was named first, and the neighboring settlement also took the name.

Nevels Corners · Richland County
Located in Dayton Township. George W. Nevel operated a large grain and dairy farm at the corner of the road from Boaz to McGrew and the other road from Richland Center to Mill Creek. He was located here as early as 1895.

Nevers Dam · Polk County
Nevers Dam was built on land originally owned by Chas. Nevers. It is said to have been the largest pile-driven dam in the world. "Its purpose was to control the flood of logs that came down the river from northern pineries to the sawmills at Stillwater." Before its construction gigantic logjams occurred, and this vexed the lumber companies because breaking logjams was a very expensive process. In 1883 at Angle Rock in the St. Croix a jam took fifty-seven days to break. These jams always made headlines, and trainloads of spectators came for miles to watch the work and witness the breaking of the jams.

New Albertville · Chippewa County
Old maps show an Albertville post office that became New Albertville and is now part of the town of Howard.

Newald · Forest County
This small community was platted in 1905 by the Western Town Lot Company as Ross, for Charles Ross, an early settler. The name was changed the next year to Newald, to honor a local property owner.

New Amsterdam · La Crosse County
Immigrants from Holland chose this name. The town was laid out by a Mr. Bonnema and originally called Friesland, as he had come from Friesland, Holland

New Auburn · Chippewa County
In 1858 the site was known as Cartwright's Mills, and later as Cartwright. The township of Auburn had its voting place in Auburn Center. The village of New Auburn was incorporated in 1902. No explanation for the names is given.

New Berlin   *Waukesha County*

In 1838 this township was separated from the town of Muskego and given the name of Mentor. Sidney Evans, a Yankee settler whose home had been New Berlin in New York State, is said to have changed the name in 1840. Later a great many Germans came to settle in the community.

Newbold   *Oneida County*

Fred Newbold was a nephew of F. W. Rhinelander, president of the Milwaukee, Lakeshore, and Western Railroad when it was built through the area. Mr. Newbold owned and operated a sawmill at Tigerton, Wisconsin.

New Buffalo   *Sauk County*

This town is no longer on the map. Many of its residents came from Buffalo, New York.

New California   *Grant County*

The post office was established in 1850, discontinued in 1855, and restored in 1856. There is no explanation for the name.

New Cassel   *Fond du Lac County*

In 1846 the village was called Crouchville. Emil Brayman changed the name to New Cassel in 1846 to honor Hesse-Cassel, his birthplace.

New Centerville   *St. Croix County*

This is a town that died. It was once noted for its large dance hall, which continued into the 1940s.

New Denmark   *Brown County*

So named by Danish settlers.

New Diggings   *Lafayette County*

Miners moving in around 1824 gave the settlement this name.

New Franken   *Brown County*

A group of German immigrants arrived in Green Bay in 1845, and after looking over the surrounding territory chose this site for their new home. During the next five years the settlement was known as the Bavarian Settlement or the Dutch Settlement. Most of the people had come from Franconia in Germany, so it was named New Franconia, and later shortened to New Franken.

New Glarus   *Green County*

The name was adopted from the canton in Switzerland from which the first settlers came in 1845. A famine and unemployment in much of Switzerland in the early 1840s required drastic measures for relief. So in canton Glarus the authorities decided to send some families to the United States. Families were selected by lots, and a total of about 190 people left Switzerland. The colonists were instructed to find a new home that looked like the old home, purchase land, and set up a settlement

From the Monroe Sentinel, August 19, 1885:

On the 17th day of August, 1845, arrived the greater part of the immigrants who were the founders of our colony of New Glarus. Seventeen families—about 100 people, old and young, were left from a band of nearly 200 who said goodbye forever in April, 1845, to their beloved mountain home of "Old Glarus," in Switzerland. It took them nearly five months to reach their new home in the Territory of Wisconsin, then almost a wilderness.

Forwarded to Baltimore by dishonest agents, instead of to New York, where friends were waiting for them, they were sent in flatboats down the Ohio to St. Louis, where the terrible news awaited them that their leaders, Messrs. Durst and Streiff, who had been sent ahead to secure a location in one of the Northwest Territories had "died somewhere up North"—or if not dead, had run away with the money. What a blow to these poor, homesick people! But through God's blessing it proved to be untrue. Rumors reached them that the two men were somewhere near Galena looking for land, and two men were picked out to find them—George Legler and Mathias Duerst. They found Durst and Streiff fixing up a shelter for the long expected wanderers, on the hill where the church and schoolhouse of New Glarus now stand.

One of the party started back at once to bring the rest and let them know that Durst and Streiff were alive and well, and waiting for them. On the 17th of August they arrived in New Glarus, foot-sore, homesick, and destitute, so that they were forced to catch fish, of which there were, happily, plenty in the creek. The first winter was a mild one—through God's blessing—and New Glarus was saved.

New Haven   *Sauk County*

Named for New Haven, Connecticut, it is now an abandoned village plat in Sumpter.

New Holstein   *Calumet County*

About 1840 Ferdinand Ostenfeld left Schleswig-Holstein, Germany, for America. He arrived in New York and with a few others sailed up the Hudson River to Albany, through the Erie Canal to Buffalo, and by way of the Great Lakes to Sheboygan, Wisconsin. Here they took an oxteam overland through Plymouth and Greenbush to Fond du Lac. From there they walked in a northerly direction along the east shore of Lake Winnebago to the settlement called Calumetville where George White operated a hotel.

George White was the land agent for Benjamin Fields, who had acquired large tracts of land from the US government. Mr. Ostenfeld told Mr. White that he had friends in Germany who were anxious to leave because of the political unrest and impending war. In 1847 the two men made the trip to Germany to tell these people about the land and conditions in Wisconsin. It was hard for them to decide to make such a long journey, but Mr. Ostenfeld gave such a glowing picture of the country, the life in America, and the beauty of Lake Winnebago that they were convinced.

It was then that Mr. Ostenfeld remarked, "As I look at you people gathered around, all coming from the same place or near it, I think it would be a good plan to name our new settlement in Calumet County New Holstein to remind us of the land from which we all came."

A group of these settlers built their homes a short distance west of New Holstein and called the community Altona. Later they discovered another community in the state with a similar name (Altoona), so they dropped Altona and became a part of New Holstein.

New Lisbon
Juneau County

According to Ho-Chunk folklore, the present site of New Lisbon was a winter stopping place from which the men went north on hunting and trapping expeditions. The Indians migrated from their summer homes on Lake Winnebago and pitched their winter camps here in the fall. The encampment was called Wa-du-shuda, meaning "we leave canoe here."

In the fall of 1836 Samuel B. Pilkington and John T. Kingston heard of the extensive forest of pine timber and the splendid waterpower on the Lemonweir River. The Indians had just sold their lands on the south side of the river to the government, so the two men decided to explore the possibility of a lumber business here.

In December of 1837 they packed their ponies and started out from Racine for the North. When they arrived at the Lemonweir they decided to follow the stream to its mouth and camped one night at Provonsal's trading post, which they found unoccupied. It took a week to travel the length of the river, and on the morning of the seventh day they had breakfast of two crackers each on the present site of New Lisbon.

The first post office was called Mill Haven, but by 1868 it was changed to New Lisbon. The origin of the name is a matter of conjecture. One account states that Moses Kenyon chose the name. Another says it was chosen by Larmon E. Saxton, who had come from Lisbon in the state of Ohio.

New London
Outagamie and Waupaca Counties

A trading post was established here in 1851. The next year, the developers, Reeder Smith, Ira Millard, and Lucius Taft, purchased land to establish the city. It was named after the birthplace of Reeder Smith's father, New London, Connecticut.

New Munster
Kenosha County

Settled largely by German immigrants during the troubled years of the 1840s. It was named after Munster in Germany.

New Paris
Sheboygan County

In 1856 William Schwartz built a flour mill here. It took a man with an oxteam all summer to scrape out the millrace. The mill changed hands several times, and in 1869 it became the property of Vollier Wattier, who platted a village. Since he was a Frenchman, he named it New Paris. Shortly after this Peter Brickbauer purchased the property and added a cider mill. The popular name then became Brickbauer Mill.

Newport
Columbia County

When lumbermen changed their landing place below the Wisconsin Dells gorge from one side of the river to the other, they called the new landing New Port. It became a promising village that was wiped out when the railroad was built through Wisconsin Dells. The township took the name.

New Prospect *Fond du Lac County*

First called Jersey, because a number of settlers had come from New Jersey, the name was changed in 1861 when the New Prospect Post Office was established here.

New Richmond *St. Croix County*

In 1855 Mr. and Mrs. B. C. Foster and their two children journeyed from the state of Maine to St. Croix County. Mr. Foster, with an eye to lumbering, found a place on the banks of the Willow River that seemed a good site for a sawmill. The little settlement that grew up was called Foster's Crossing—there was a crossing nearby used by logging teams. The man who surveyed the town was Richmond Day. His first name was used for the town, but "New" was added because people thought there was another town called Richmond in the state.

Newton *Manitowoc County*

It is said that while they strove to clear enough land to grub out a bare existence, the people of this new town were always singing. It was called the Land of Song but was named after Sergeant John Newton, a Revolutionary War hero from South Carolina.

Newton's Woods *Fond du Lac County*

Owned by J. J. Newton, it was converted into a county park in 1928.

Niagara *Marinette County*

The word is of Iroquois Indian origin, probably a derivation of Oh-nia-ga, meaning "bisected bottom land."

Nichols *Outagamie County*

Albeit L. Nichols of Chicago, Illinois, formed the Nichols Land Company and came here to build a village. The land was platted and a sewer and water system installed in 1917, an unusual modern development for that era. Mr. Nichols started the Nichols State Bank and promoted businesses and homes in the small community. Until his death in the 1950s he had high hopes that it would become a large metropolis.

Nicolet National Forest *Oneida County*

Named in honor of Jean Nicolet, who in 1634 was the first European man known to have traveled into what is now Wisconsin.

Niganis Omanigan *Langlade County*

A former Indian settlement on the Menominee Reservation near the mill site of Phlox.

Niland Ridge *Crawford County*

Part of Marietta Township. Running from Pohlmann Hill to Steuben, it was named after the Niland family that lived here.

Nin-Do-Nah-Hun *Bayfield County*

This is the region around the Kakagon sloughs and adjoining lands that was so named by the Ojibwe because it had such an abundance of wild game and plants. The word means "my dish." In addition to wild rice, blueberries, and cranberries, there were plenty of fish, muskrats, deer, and rabbits.

Nine-Mile Island and Nine-Mile Slough   *Pepin County*
These two sites are in the same area and are so named because they are nine miles long. At one time there were so many passenger pigeons that settlers told of not being able to see the sun when they were in flight. At night they roosted on Nine-Mile Island and broke the branches of trees with their weight. Men caught them in nets and shipped them to Chicago.

Nine Mound Prairie   *Dane County*
In the summer of 1840 a party of ten or twelve early settlers of Verona chanced on this location after they set out to explore the upper Sugar River Valley. They found nine circular Indian mounds on the prairie.

The Nine Springs   *Dane County*
Located at the head of Nine Springs Creek, there are many more than nine springs, though perhaps nine of them could be considered to be the main ones.

Nip and Tuck   *Grant County*
This is the name of an old landmark church. When it was being built the committee bought a load of lumber and said it would have to be enough to do the job. As the church progressed, workers began to worry whether or not they would run out of lumber. Someone remarked, "Well, it is sure going to be nip and tuck!" And the church was given this label.

Nissedahle   *Dane County*
Located in Blue Mounds. Named for Nissedal, Norway, with the ending altered to conform to the surname of Isak Dahle, the founder and namer, whose family was from Nissedal. Dahle bought the land in 1927 and set out to make a reproduction of a typical Norwegian farm. Today the farm is more commonly known as Little Norway.

Nix Corners   *Eau Claire County*
Andrew Nix was the first postmaster in this small community.

Noah's Bluff   *Trempealeau County*
This bluff in East Arcadia was named for Noah Comstock.

Nobleton   *Washburn County*
A discontinued post office named after N. B. Noble, who was superintendent of the Rice Lake Lumber Company, which had many logging camps near Long Lake. The mail was brought by stage from Rice Lake.

Nora Corners   *Dane County*
Located in Cottage Grove. Named for the local post office, the name is intended to suggest Norway. A. A. Prescott, the first postmaster, wanted to give a Norwegian name to

this Norwegian settlement. Many of the names suggested sounded too un-English, so they retained the first syllable of Norway and Norwegian and approved the name Nora.

Norman   Kewaunee County
Norman Carlton is doubly honored by having both Norman and the town of Carlton named after him.

Norman Valley   Richland County
George Norman settled in the town of Henrietta after coming from Canada in 1855.

Norrie   Marathon County
Gordon Norrie was treasurer of the Milwaukee Lakeshore and Western Railroad for many years.

Norseville   Eau Claire County
Norwegians settled here in the early 1870s. The post office was discontinued in 1905.

North Andover   Grant County
This settlement was established at the intersection of two streams. A flour mill was built in the early days to grind wheat, and later other grains that were used to feed livestock. The mill was known as the Oliver Mill. The machinery for it came from Andover in Massachusetts. The word "North" was added when the name was chosen because it was thought that this settlement was located farther to the north than the New England one.

North Bay   Racine County
This is a small village platted in 1926 and probably given the name because it is on a bay of Lake Michigan, north of Racine. It is thought that the surveyor, Louis F. Pope, selected the name.

North Bend   Jackson County
Robert Douglas, who first started a settlement at Melrose, also settled North Bend. He and his brother Thomas landed here on the Black River in April of 1839 with only a hatchet as a weapon. By January of 1840 their food supply was nearly exhausted, and Robert decided to walk 160 miles alone through the wilderness to Prairie du Chien. He made the trip and then decided to carry a sack of flour back on his shoulder.

Meanwhile, Thomas waited in the lonely cabin for many days. When Robert returned, injured and exhausted, and pulled the latch string on the cabin door, Thomas managed to get to his feet to lift the sack from Robert's shoulder as it was more precious than a sack of gold.

In April they sowed their first grain by hand. One lone kernel of corn was found in the seed and was carefully planted on May 15, 1840. It grew to maturity and produced two well-developed ears of corn, which were carefully stored for seed for the next year.

The two brothers built the first sawmill in Melrose, but it failed and the machinery was moved to North Bend for their second sawmill on Mill Creek. The first hotel was built on the riverbank a short distance below the sawmill. This location on the north bend of the Black River gave North Bend its name.

North Cape   *Racine County*

The first settler was Mons K. Adland, who named the area after his homeland in Norway. He was born in 1795 in Norway and came to the North Cape area in Racine County in 1840.

North Clayton   *Crawford County*

Takes its name from the Clayton Township.

Northern Highland   *Forest County*

Covering fifteen thousand square miles in northern Wisconsin, this area is underlain by the crystalline rock of an ancient mountain range comparable to the Rockies, the peaks of which were worn down by glacial and other geological processes over time. One of the greatest concentrations of lakes in the world lies within this forest region.

North Freedom   *Sauk County*

The first settlers came here in 1846, and the community was called Hackett's Corners after the Hackett family. When the railroad was built two plats were made—one called Bloom after George W. Bloom, and one called North Freedom. Bloom Station was incorporated into North Freedom. Later, when iron ore was discovered, the name was changed to Bessemer in honor of Sir Henry Bessemer, who invented the Bessemer process. North Freedom was the name finally decided upon in 1890, and the village was incorporated in 1893. The name was suggested by the location of the village in the north part of the town of Freedom.

North Grimms   *Manitowoc County*

This small settlement grew up around a tavern a half mile north of Grimms, the community named after Louis Grimm, who owned the property where the railroad depot was built.

North Hudson   *St. Croix County*

The village was laid out by D. A. and A. H. Baldwin, real estate promoters. D. A. was also a promoter of the West Wisconsin Railroad, which is presently part of the Chicago and North Western Railway system. In 1872 some railroad car shops were established here, and this operation employed several hundred persons until about 1950. Located on the Willow River across from Hudson to the south, it is now a sizable "suburban" community for many who work in St. Paul, Minneapolis, and neighboring areas.

North Lake   *Waukesha County*

The Potawatomi Indians lived here when the settlers first came in 1850. Ho-Chunk Indians also traveled through the area. It is said that the Indians named the lake Wa-zia-yata, meaning "north." The white people also called this lake North Lake, since it is the most northerly lake in a connecting chain of lakes. Ralph Allen was the first white man to own land here. He staked a claim in 1837, which was later purchased by Colonel Henry Shears, who built the first sawmill. An early Indian name applied to the lake was Shana-koonebin, meaning "south cloud water."

North Luck *Polk County*
In the incipient stages of its growth, a creamery was the focal point of this small business center just north of Luck.

North Prairie *Waukesha County*
This area was once a beautiful prairie with a heavy growth of grass. The early settlers made hay to winter their stock. Since there was also a prairie some two miles to the south, this one was identified as the north prairie. Joseph Smart and Thomas Sugden, who settled here in 1836, are given credit for the name. The village did not flourish until 1851, when the railroad, which was built from Milwaukee to Milton, passed through North Prairie.

A single grave, situated along the railroad track on the outskirts of the village, has a ten-foot stone marker with this inscription:

George E. Price
Died at Milton March 23, 1859
Late Conductor on M and M RR
This Monument is erected as a tribute of respect
By employees of the Milwaukee Railroad Company.

Mr. Price died as a result of a train wreck at Milton, but no one seems to know why he was buried at North Prairie.

North Range *Polk County*
A settlement grew up around a grocery store here several decades ago when Highway 8 was moved north of Old Range.

Norwalk *Monroe County*
S. McGary, one of the first settlers in the county, named this town after Norwalk in Ohio, the beautiful little city near which he had lived for many years. The Ohio village was named after Norwalk, Connecticut, which is said to have originally been an Indian word meaning a "point of land."

Norway *Monroe and Racine Counties*
These settlements were named for the nationality of the early settlers.

Norway Point *Burnett County*
This point of land, where the St. Croix River bends sharply, was the site of a ferry and log landing in 1880. It was so named by the loggers because of a stand of Norway pine.

Norwegian Road *Crawford County*
Following Johnson Creek in Clayton Township, it was named for the many Norwegian families that settled here.

The Octagon House, Wisconsin's largest single-family home at the time of its construction in 1854

O

Oak Center

Perry H. Smith, an officer of the original Chicago and North Western Railway, chose this name for a town in a grove of oak trees.

Oakdale

In 1857 the Monroe County Board set aside a portion of land, six miles square, to form Leroy Township. The small village was called Leroy Station. Five years later both names were changed because confusion had developed in the mail addressed to Leroy and Elroy. Oakdale was chosen as the new name because the north half of the township was heavily timbered with oak trees.

Oakfield

The first settlement in this township was started in 1840 and called Avoca; the local cemetery still carries this name. In 1846 the township was divided, creating the new township of Lime, so named because of extensive quarries of limestone. The next year the name was changed to Oakfield because there were large stands of oak trees with open vistas in between. Russell Wilkinson, the first settler, built a log cabin that was ransacked and burned by the Indians. He was forced to move but returned within a few years.

Oak Grove

Major Pratt built the first log cabin here in 1841. Later he built an inn called the Oak Grove House, which burned in 1935. Fairfield was the first name of the village, but there was already another Fairfield in the state. Oak Grove was chosen as a name because there were no oak trees at all in the neighborhood!

Oak Hall

Located in Fitchburg. Taken from the name of a hotel built about 1860 by a man named Wood.

Oak Island

One of the Apostle Islands, named Mitigominikang by the Ojibwe, meaning "acorn." It is the highest island in the group and had many oak trees. The remains of several old logging camps are here. For some years one of them was the home of a hermit fisherman named Martin Kane, dubbed by one of the local newspapers King Kane of Oak Island.

Oakland

There were small areas of oak trees in the midst of a countryside covered with jack pine.

Oakley

This was once known as Spring Grove. Isaac Kline erected a carding mill here in 1843.

Oak Ridge *Crawford County*

In Freeman Township, there is an abundance of oak trees in the area.

Oaks *Sauk County*

An abandoned post office in the town of Woodland that was once called Friendswood from the Friends in the neighborhood.

Oconomowoc *Waukesha County*

This name was chosen by the Indians before there was any white settlement. Coo-no-mo-wauk is said to mean "waterfall," "place where the river falls," "beautiful waters," "beaver dam," or "beaver dam woods." It is also said to mean "river of lakes," which would refer to the string of lakes that are joined by the Oconomowoc River.

Charles B. Sheldon, who built a claim shanty here in 1837, was the first European settler. His friend John Rockwell built a dam and a sawmill. According to the story, Mr. Sheldon became acquainted with John Dority, who was married to an Indian woman of the band of Whirling Thunder, a Ho-Chunk chief. It was John Dority who told Mr. Sheldon that the name of the area was River of Lakes or Oconomowoc. The name was officially adopted in 1844.

Oconto *Oconto County*

In 1695 a map published by Cornelli in Venice, Italy, referred to the Oconto River as the Katon River. Missionaries called it Lagaspardi River. Farnsworth, a French fur trader, called it the Cantone River in 1825, and Brevort called it the Counton. In 1831 Samuel Stambough, a US government agent, officially reported the river as named the Gillispie. However, the first official US map in 1840 referred to the river as the Oconto River.

Okato, o-kon-toe, or oak-a-toe is said to have been the Menominee Indian name and means "pike place," "boat paddle," "the place of the pickerel," "red ground," "river of plentiful fishes," or "black bass." Early maps of 1820 to 1850 showed the river as Black Bass River. The Ojibwe Indians are said to have called it okando, meaning "he watches," "lies in ambush," or "watching outpost."

When Green Bay was a famous trading center, all tribes came to the area, including those hostile to each other. The Ojibwe had a small settlement on the river to keep their people informed of enemy movements. The city took its name from the river and was also the site of an ancient Menominee village on the sand dunes where the old dam was located. It was called Wasa-kiu, meaning "high sandy bank." Oconto Red Banks was named from the Indian word meaning "big high banks."

Oconto Falls *Oconto County*

The first settlers came up the Oconto River from the waters of Green Bay to settle here in 1846. The beauty of the falls, with their potential power for sawmills and later pulp and paper mills, influenced them to make it their home. A Menominee Indian village called Nepeus-pa-pen-ino, meaning "where water falls," is said to have been located here.

Octagon House   *Jefferson County*

Exemplifying an unusual architectural design that was in vogue briefly before the Civil War, this five-story solid brick house is eight sided. Claimed to be Wisconsin's largest single-family residence at the time, it has fifty-seven rooms and a cantilever spiral staircase.

Odanah   *Ashland County*

The Ojibwe Indians gave the village this name. Because of the fertility of the soil and the abundance of berries and wild rice, the area was originally known as Old Indian Gardens and also as Kie-tig-ga-ning, or "agricultural paradise."

In 1831 when the historian Henry R. Schoolcraft led his expedition up the Bad River, he wrote of the splendid gardens he saw in the vicinity. In the spring the Indians collected maple sugar and planted their gardens, and then went hunting or fishing. They returned in the autumn to harvest their crops and to gather wild rice. Odanah is the Ojibwe word for "town" or "village."

Ogantz   *Fond du Lac County*

This was a village plat near Fond du Lac. The name means "little pickerel."

Ogdensburg   *Waupaca County*

Judge Ogden came here in 1848 and started a village because there was potential waterpower.

Ogema   *Price County*

First settled in 1876 by people of various nationalities, with the Irish predominating. Lumbering attracted the settlers. The town grew up at the division point at the end of the railroad. The first lumber mill was owned by a Mr. Holmes, whose name was suggested for the town, but he objected strenuously. The town was named Dedham after the eastern town from which Mr. Holmes had come, but most of the people thought that "dead ham" did not sound very pleasing.

An Indian tribe was passing through the town. The people heard the chief addressed as Ogimau and decided to adopt his name. The word actually means "chief." In time the spelling was changed from Ogimau to Ogema.

Oil City   *Crawford County*

Located in Seneca Township. In the early days prospectors set out to seek oil in this area.

Ojibwa   *Sawyer County*

Ben F. Faast of Eau Claire organized the Wisconsin Colonization Company and purchased large tracts of land here. He set up a real estate office in Radisson and then moved it to the new town that he organized in 1918. His land office was the first building, and he had visions of a prosperous city that would be supported by modern farms growing up where the loggers had left slashings.

The land was advertised as fertile and very cheap. A number of thrifty, honest, and industrious people bought the land, which they farmed in the summer and then left to work in logging camps in the winter. Mr. Faast named his town Ojibwa because of its nearness to the Ojibwe River and the Lac Court Oreilles Indian reservation, home of the Ojibwe Indians. "Ojibwa" is the original Indian name of this tribe. It was often pronounced jibwa, omitting the initial o, and this was corrupted as Ojibwe. The two names refer to the same tribe of Indians.

Okauchee

The first structure in this section of Oconomowoc Township was a sawmill built in 1840 by Orson Reed. It was known as Reed's Mill and furnished a large portion of the lumber used in the construction of the Milwaukee to Watertown Plank Road.

The Okauchee Stagecoach House, a famous wayside stopping place, was built by Israel McConnell in 1845. It is said that taverner McConnell had many of the characteristics of Bailey, the keeper of the Tabard Inn, plus a few traits of the lesser lights in Chaucer's Canterbury pilgrim. Okauchee House operated until 1913, when the automobile brought its business to an end. Most of the material in Okauchee House came from the sawmill of Harrison Reed—very thick solid planks. Mr. Reed also hammered out the square iron nails that held the planks together.

In 1844 Curtis Reed and his brother Orson held a caucus to take over the Oconomowoc Township election. They gathered recruits from all the neighboring towns and met in a hollow under a hill, which was known long afterward as Caucus Hollow. According to plan they went to the town meeting in a body and elected Curtis Reed as town chairman along with all the other officers.

Okauchee is of Indian origin and is claimed to mean "something small," "pipe stem," "very long," or "the chief is come."

Okee
Columbia County

The Indians who accompanied Father Marquette and Louis Joliet are said to have named this site in June 1763. In most Algonquian tongues it means "ground" or "earth," or "black earth." It may also mean "good fishing grounds" and "evil spirit."

Old Copper Culture Cemetery
Oconto County

Old Copper Culture Indians buried their dead here approximately 7,500 years ago. They are the earliest known people to inhabit Wisconsin. Ranking among the world's first metalsmiths, they hammered the native copper into tools and weapons.

Old Johnstown
Rock County

A village in the town of Johnstown, it was named in contradistinction to Johnstown Center.

Old Lake
Dane County

Located in Bristol. This lake is now less large and less lakelike than it once was.

Old Settlers Park
Racine County

The Union Grove home of the Racine County Fair. It was named in honor of the Old Settlers' Society, founded in 1870.

Old Stockade Site
Douglas County

This stockade was built during the summer of 1862, when the Sioux uprisings in Minnesota, which culminated in the New Dim Massacre, caused great alarm in Superior.

Ole Military Road

This was established by act of Congress on March 3, 1863. It was built from Green Bay to Lake Superior along a well-traveled Indian route known as the Lake Superior Trail.

Oliver
Sauk County

A village site, platted in the Town of Freedom in 1911, and named for Henry W. Oliver, who was engaged in the mining industry.

Oliver's Mill
Grant County

Douglas Oliver, an early settler, built a gristmill and later a woolen mill, and a thriving community grew up. The name was changed to North Andover.

Olivet
Pierce County

Early settlers were very religious and were said to have named the community after Mount Olivet from the Bible. Another less convincing faction claims that the frogs in a pond in the center of the village seemed to cry: "Oll wet, oll wet!"

Olson Hill
Crawford County

Located in the Township of Clayton, it was named after the Olson family.

Omro
Winnebago County

Trading posts had been operated at this site, known as Smalley's Landing, from about 1836 until English immigrants came to settle. David Humes arrived in 1847, and shortly afterward the steam sawmill of Elisha Dean and Nelson Beckwith was built, followed by gristmills, hotels, general stores, and other sawmills. It became known as Beckwith Town but was officially named Omro on June 23, 1849, when Joel V. Taylor, along with Mr. Dean and Mr. Beckwith, laid out the village plat. They chose this name in honor of Charles Omro, an Indian who was one of the first traders to come here. The street names of the town are also historic Indian names.

From the Milwaukee Sentinel, February 14, 1897:

> *Twenty years ago, although the population of Omro did not exceed 1,000 souls, this pleasant village was the most important Spiritualistic center in the state. Now the society has practically disappeared, but a substantial monument bears witness to their period of growth and activity—the large plain brick hall toward the upper end of the main street where they used to meet, and where some of the most famous lights came many miles to teach and demonstrate.*
>
> *A spirit of inquiry gave the society birth. Early in the '60s when the fame of the Rochester knockings reached Omro a circle was formed to investigate these and other manifestations. Seven persons—Mr. and Mrs. R. C. Richardson, Mrs. E. H. Cheney, Mrs. Charles Follett, and Mr. and Mrs. H. Gilbert—held meetings every Sunday for two years, with the result that, though they had begun with a spirit of scepticism, they ended by becoming fully convinced and converted.*
>
> *In the meantime other circles had been formed, and Spiritualism became the absorbing subject of village life. The groups united, and employed leading Spiritualists to deliver public lectures. These meetings were held frequently, and*

the project of owning a hall of their own was broached. Thereupon a general organization was formed called the First Spiritualist's Society of Omro, with a membership of nearly a hundred, and the hall was built at a cost of $2,500. A novel Sunday school was formed called the Children's Progressive Lyceum. Sixty children composed it, divided into twelve groups, each designated by a name and banner. The exercises, which opened and closed with a hymn, included the "silver chain" recitation, and the "banner march." The former consisted in the conductor and the children alternately reciting lines from a little book of instruction, and the latter in the execution of various evolutions about the hall to music, each child carrying the American flag. Calesthenics and talks by the conductor completed the programme.

The theme of the recitations and the hymns was always Spiritualistic, and the talks were meant to instruct the children how to become upright and independent men and women.

Among the celebrated speakers who addressed the society was Victoria Woodhull, then at the height of her fame. This was before The Woman Who Did had been written, or the sex problem, so-called, had become a subject for plain speech, and her views of marriage, popularly termed "free love" had gained her notoriety in two hemispheres. Although she was not, strictly speaking, a Spiritualist, and the society did not necessarily indorse her views, they were seeking after light, no matter from what source it came, and paid her $100 for the lecture. This was a considerable sum for so small a place, but the audience that gathered to hear her fully justified the outlay, and no address before the society ever gave such general satisfaction.

Famous Spiritualists and mediums who visited Omro in those days were the Davenport brothers, Mrs. Warner of Berlin, Leo Miller of Michigan, Moses Hull of Boston, Benjamin Todd of Michigan, C. W. Stewart of Missouri, Hannah Sterns of Menasha, now of Pennsylvania, Susan Johnson of California, J. O. Barnett of Minnesota and James Peebles of California, who was afterward American consul at one of the China ports.

A subject worthy of the best efforts of the local and visiting mediums was the mysterious murder of John Sullivan, a farmer living a few miles in the country. He had been in the village during the day trading, and started homeward between 9 and 10 o'clock at night over the bridge across the Fox river. He had proceeded but a short distance on his journey when a cry of alarm was heard, followed by the discharge of a gun. Sullivan was found dead by the roadside. The investigation which followed was attended with no great success. But at the seances thereafter one of the most frequent questions asked was: "Who killed John Sullivan?" The spirits did not answer, that is not directly; they chose a different method.

One night a Mr. Wilson was crossing the bridge. Suddenly he beheld a man walking on ahead carrying a gun over his shoulder, and a voice at his ear said: "That is the gun that killed John Sullivan!" There was a cry of terror, a loud report, and then the apparition vanished. Wilson ran back to the village and told his experience, affirming that he would recognize the weapon should he ever again behold it. Sometime afterward he claimed to have seen the very gun which the spirit carried. Who, then, was the owner? Wilson declined to state, and the spirit refused to make any further disclosures. The murder is still a mystery.

As the seances multiplied and the mediums evoked powerful spirits, materialized with such distinctness that a number of photographs are owned here showing a living person with a hazy spirit looking over its shoulders. The photographer was always a medium, since it was necessary to call up the spirit at the instant the picture was taken. These spirits represented all the Seven Ages of Man and both sexes, but generally they belonged to the Caucasian race. A startling exception occurred, however, in the case of Robert Richardson, one of the earliest and most prominent members of the society.

One day he suddenly realized the presence of an Indian about him. He could not shake the spirit off and finally became curious to know how it looked. He resolved to sit for a spirit photograph. Two negatives were taken which proved unsatisfactory, but as he was leaving the gallery he was stopped by the spirit. He turned back and sat again, and the result proved highly successful, for just behind him an Indian was plainly discernable with a cap upon his head and a blanket about his shoulders—a noble savage who might have been a mighty sachem in his day. Mr. Richardson was satisfied, but some doubted whether the Indian had been all spirit. At a seance shortly thereafter a medium said to him suddenly:

"I see behind you the spirit of an Indian."

"Now," thought Mr. Richardson, "I will set all doubts at rest." He asked: "Would you recognize his likeness?"

"I would," replied the medium.

The photograph was brought in and immediately identified by the medium as that of the spirit which he had just beheld. Mr. Richardson believes there should be no further doubt about the genuineness of his spirit; as for himself he has never had the slightest.

But the life of the society was not all sunshine. Enemies sprang up within and without. A certain Dr. Hurd, who claimed to be a medium, met with the society all one winter and participated in numerous dark circles. In the spring he appeared as a reformer and advertised a meeting at which he would undertake to expose the methods of spiritualism. Admission was charged, but only sixteen attended and the affair wound up in disorder. Then he offered to show how the people were being hum-bugged for nothing, and a great crowd gathered. The rope test was made the feature. After having been securely tied by an old sailor who happened to be present, he proceeded to liberate himself in full view of the audience. But the objection was raised that he had used his hands, and a member defied him to fill them with ashes and shuffle off the coil without spilling it.

It is alleged that he called the obstreperous person aside and offered to make the matter all right with him if he would keep quiet. But the disturbance increased and the meeting ended in a tumult. Then the religious denominations, especially the Methodists, became hostile. The Rev. George Haddock, who was afterwards assassinated in Iowa on account of his warfare against the liquor interests, was extremely bitter in his denunciation of the society. One summer a Methodist camp meeting was held here and several of his sermons were directed against the Omro spiritualists. He denounced their work as fraudulent and they offered to prove it *genuine; he declared that Spiritualists had no regard for the marriage relation and generally dissolved it by divorce, and a member who had looked up the record of Omro since its settlement claimed that of sixty divorced persons three were Spiritualists and fourteen church members. The controversy resulted in a public joint debate between Haddock and J. S. Loveland of California, which proved extremely rancorous and left both sides more bitterly hostile than before.*

In the early days the various societies in this part of the state were united into the North Wisconsin Spiritualist association and met quarterly. Later it was superseded by a state organization with headquarters at Milwaukee, which proved a death blow to the movement, since the societies were too much scattered and new men came in bent upon making themselves prominent. The organization here is still kept alive simply because of the worldly interest represented by the hall. Officers are elected annually, but no regular Spiritualistic meeting has been held for several years. All that is now left of the once flourishing movement is represented by a few ladies who meet occasionally under the inspiration of that modern offshoot of Spiritualism, Mental Science.

Onalaska
La Crosse County

It has been claimed that this word is Indian and means "bright water" or was the name of an Indian woman. A more plausible explanation is that it was named by William C. Rowe, an early settler who built a tavern here. He was fond of quoting poetry, particularly Campbell's "Pleasure of Hope" that has the line: "The wolf's long howl from Oonalaska's shore." The musical name of this distant fishing station in the far Aleutian Islands struck Mr. Rowe's fancy, and he adopted it for his new town, dropping the superfluous o. The name was also written Ounalaska and is probably of Russian origin.

Onamun Ustat

This is the name of a clay bank on the Wolf River near Wakitcon Omanikun, Chief Wakitcon's village. It contained red clay that was used by the Indians to make red paint.

Onegahning
Door County

This was a Potawatomi village at the east end of the Sturgeon Bay ship canal. The word means "to carry a canoe back and forth," indicating a portage.

Oneida
Brown County
Oneida County

The Oneida Indians were a branch of the Iroquois Confederation in New York State who came to Wisconsin early in the nineteenth century. The word means "people of stone" or "granite people." Tradition says that the Indian forefathers in New York State were out on a hunting and fishing trip when they were given a sacred red stone from a cleft in the granite rock. Some 654 Oneida Indians migrated to Green Bay as a result of the Iroquois Wars in the East.

Oneida
Outagamie County

An Episcopal church built here was known as the Oneida Indian Mission, and the Indians got their mail in care of this mission. They called it Ugwe-hu-we-neh, which meant

"Oneida settlement." The hymn book for the church was printed in phonetic sounds so the Indians could read it in their own language.

O'Neil Ridge
Crawford County

The O'Neil family settled on this ridge in the Township of Utica.

Onion Hollow
Richland County

Part of Buena Vista Township. Paul Siefert, the artist, planted a field of onions here.

Onion River
Sheboygan County

Dr. Joseph Mallory gave the name of Joppa to this place, but it was later changed to Onion River after the stream on which it is located. The river was so named by the government surveyors because of the abundance of wild onions they found growing along its course.

Ontario
Vernon County

Giles White laid out and platted this village in 1837. He named it Ontario at the request of O. H. Millard, who had come from Ontario County in New York State. The word in the Indian language means "beautiful lake," "beautiful rocks," "hills and water," or "village on the mountain."

Ontonagon River
Vilas County

This Indian word means either "fishing place" or "away goes my dish (in the stream)."

Oostburg
Sheboygan County

The community was settled by Dutch immigrants and was named after a village in Holland.

Orange
Burnett County

Orange Parslow was the first postmaster.

Oregon
Dane County

Rome Corners was the first name of this settlement in 1843. It was renamed Oregon when it was platted four years later, after the township that had been named for the state of Oregon.

Orfordville
Rock County

The village was surveyed in 1856. D. Mowe wanted to call it Moweville, and a Mr. Clark wanted to call it Clarkville. The surveyor, Joseph T. Dodge of Janesville, suggested the name Orford after a town in New Hampshire. It was changed to Orfordville because of confusion with Oxford.

Orion
Richland County

Originally called Richmond, when an application for a post office was made in 1851, another Richmond in the state was noted. Judge A. B. Slaughter suggested the name Orion.

Osceola *Polk County*

This area in the St. Croix River Valley was opened to settlers in 1837 by treaties entered into by the US government and the Ojibwe Indians. Opportunities for logging and lumbering led to land claims in 1844, when a mill company was organized by young men from the state of Maine. They selected the tract of land that included a creek and Cascade Falls on which to build a sawmill because of the great waterpower potential. The settlement was called Leroy in memory of a mill hand who was accidentally killed while cutting timber. James Livingston, of the St. Louis Lumber Company at St. Croix Falls, chose the name Osceola for the Seminole Indian chief of Florida. When the post office opened in 1854 it was named Osceola Mills, but Mills was dropped in 1897.

Oshaukuta *Columbia County*

An Indian word meaning "a great place for spearing" and probably refers to nearby Rocky Run Creek.

Oshkosh *Winnebago County*

Jean Nicolet passed through this valley in 1634. By 1839 there was a small settlement. The few scattered wooden houses were known as Athens. A meeting was held at the house of George Wright to select an official name, and a large number of people attended. The group headed by Robert Grignon from Butte des Morts included a number of his Indian friends and seemed to have an edge on the voting. They chose Oskosh, the name of the Indian chief. Originally the name was spelled Oskosh with the accent on the last syllable. In some manner the "h" was added, and the accent was changed to the first syllable. The Indian word meant "brave," "a claw," or "horny part of the foot" or "a hoof." Oshkosh was the site of the Indian village Pa-ma-cha-mit, signifying "the crossing."

Oslo *Manitowoc County*

Norwegian settlers chose this name.

Osseo *Trempealeau County*

The city was surveyed in 1847 by W. A. Woodard from New York, and two men from Richland Center, R. C. Field and W. H. Thomas. A. McCorkle and Caroline Sexton also owned land. The first house was built in 1860 by Thomas Love from jack pine lumber.

In 1865 the post office was moved from the Beef River station, where it was called Summer, to its present location, and named Osseo. William H. Thomas was postmaster. There are a number of explanations of the name: 1. Robert C. Field coined the name from the Spanish word oso, meaning bear. 2. Most accounts state that it is an Indian name and means "a stony place," "stone on stone," or "a place of river and stone." 3. Henry W. Longfellow, in his Song of Hiawatha, called Osseo the Son of the Evening Star.

Otsego *Columbia County*

Many of the early settlers emigrated from Otsego in New York State. It is an Indian word meaning "welcome water" or "place where meetings are held."

Ottawa   *Waukesha County*

The name of a tribe of Algonquin Indians, said to mean "bulrushes." It is also said to mean to "trade," or "he buys and sells." The Ottawa were intertribal traders.

Otter Creek   *Crawford County*

Located in Eastman Township. Wild otter were seen here at the time of settlement.

Otter Creek   *Eau Claire County*

The creek flowing through the settlement started in 1854 abounded in otter. The well-known McClellan House, a stage stop and inn, was built here on the Sparta Road.

Otter Creek   *Rock County*

Numerous otter slides were seen along its banks at the time of surveying.

Otter Island   *Bayfield County*

Henry Schoolcraft called the island Oregon, but the Indians named it for the number of otter found there.

Otterville   *Sauk County*

An abandoned post office near the headwaters of Otter Creek.

Ottman Corners   *Pierce County*

A small community southwest of Ellsworth was given this name after Mr. Ottman, a Dutch minister, who settled there with his family.

Outagamie County

The Ojibwe Indians gave this name to their ancient enemies, the Foxes, whom French explorers in the Wolf River Valley called Renards. Outagamie means "people living on the opposite shore," or "dwellers on either side of a river."

Outer Island   *Bayfield County*

One of the Apostle Islands, called Ohio by Henry Schoolcraft. The Indian name was Gachi-ish-qua-quin-dag, meaning "the furthermost island."

Owen   *Clark County*

The T. S. Owen Lumber Company built a lumber mill in 1892 and operated it until the 1930s. The city is now a dairy farming center.

Oxford   *Marquette County*

A fording place for oxen and wagons across Neenah Creek, important to early travelers.

Ozaukee County

This is said to be the true name of the main Sauk Indian tribe. It means "people living at the mouth of the river." It is also claimed to be derived from two Sauk words meaning "yellow" and "earth." According to tradition the first Sauk man sprang from the yellow earth.

Pierce County's Kinnickinnic Falls

⇥ P ⇤

Pacific
Columbia County

N. H. Wood, an early settler, thought the great expanse of waving grasses resembled the Pacific Ocean.

Packwaukee
Marquette County

The Fox River and Buffalo Lake were an important water route for Indians and the first settlers. There were many Indians living on both sides of the lake, and one large settlement was called Packwaukee. The word means "where the water is shallow," "forest spring," "forest opening on thin land," or "land with thin woods."

The Indians chose the name to honor Chief Packwaukee, a tall man who walked with a cane, who lived here for many years. The village was platted in 1850 and a post office established. A trading post building is still standing. Early settlers came here to buy things arriving by boats and sold their eggs to be shipped. Wild rice beds in Buffalo Lake were harvested by the Indians for many years.

Pail Factory School
Wood County

Located in Hurleytown. Later called Garrison School, after Frank Garrison, a sawmill operator, this earlier name evidently came from John Rablin's pail and tub factory at the site.

Pakanano
Oconto County

A Menominee village located on a long narrow point where the Little River joins the Oconto River. The word means "branch of a river."

Pakegama Lake
Sawyer County

Pakegama is an Ojibwe Indian word meaning "branch lake."

Palmyra
Jefferson County

This name was given the village by two students of the Bible, David J. Powers and his brother Samuel. When they arrived in 1842 they liked the looks of the area so much they named it after Palmyra, an oasis city in the Syrian desert. The word means "sandy soil," and there is sandy soil here.

Pancake Valley
Dane County

This is a well-known local humorous name for Vermont Valley. A homeless man is supposed to have concocted the name when, having asked for food at several of the settlers' houses, he was everywhere offered pancakes. This story is apocryphal, but there is no other explanation known for the name. The valley is not exceptionally flat.

Pansy
Burnett County

The first postmaster's wife, Mrs. John Vorpahl, liked pansies.

Panther Intaglio   *Jefferson County*

The only known intaglio effigy mound in the world. Increase A. Lapham found it in 1850, but it had been excavated for ceremonial purposes about 1000 AD by American Indians of the Effigy Mound Culture. Of ten other recorded intaglios, all now destroyed, eight were similar in representing the panther and two represented bears.

Paper City   *Grant County*

This was laid out as a large village in 1836 by an eastern syndicate but was never occupied. It was located on the south bank of the Wisconsin River, where it flows into the Mississippi River at the foot of Lookout Point, and is now Wyalusing State Park.

Pardeeville   *Columbia County*

In the fall of 1848 John S. Pardee, a merchant in Milwaukee, sent Reuben Stedman to build a store in this neighborhood. Mr. Pardee's brother-in-law, Yates Ashley, operated a gristmill and a sawmill. In 1854 Mr. Pardee was named US consul to San Juan del Sur, Nicaragua, and died there the same year. His father, also named John, came to Pardeeville to live in 1865 and is buried in the cemetery.

Parfreys Glen   *Sauk County*

Named for Robert Parfrey, there was once a mill and a distillery in this glen in Greenfield Township.

Parfreyville   *Waupaca County*

Robert Parfrey founded the settlement in 1851.

Paris   *Grant County*

Tou Le Jon came up the Platte River in 1828 and stopped where another stream entered it. He cast off a line and made it fast to a cottonwood tree. The crewmen went ashore, and while they prepared their first meal in the wilderness, Tou Le Jon surveyed the ground and mapped out a city with streets, public squares, and grand avenues to resemble its namesake in France.

Paris   *Kenosha County*

Seth B. Meyrick settled here in 1837 and named it after his former home in Oneida County, New York.

Park Falls   *Price County*

The town was settled in 1876 and called Muskallonge Falls until 1885. The lovely waterfall has been converted to a dam for the local paper mill. The parklike appearance of large stands of virgin pine suggested the new name.

Parkland   *Douglas County*

A name coined for the town and station by the county board when the insane asylum was established here.

Park Ridge   *Portage County*
The village is located on high ground adjoining the Plover River. Originally it was spelled as one word, Parkridge.

Parnell   *Sheboygan County*
This was a hamlet in Mitchell Township named after Charles Parnell, the Irish statesman.

Parrish   *Langlade County*
A small community established during the white pine logging period and named after Judge J. K. Parrish of the Tenth Judicial Circuit in 1889.

Patch Grove   *Grant County*
This site was originally called Finntown for Enos Finn, an early settler. Henry Patch arrived in 1836 and built a cabin near a grove of trees that was enlarged within a few years to accommodate travelers. The place became known as Patch's Grove.

Patzau   *Douglas County*
This town was settled by Bohemian farmers who chose this name after a village in their native Bohemia.

Paulson   *Chippewa County*
Andrew Paulson operated the post office and store.

Peck   *Langlade County*
Named in honor of George W. Peck, governor of Wisconsin from 1891 to 1895.

Peculiar   *Dane County*
Located in Vermont. This corner area was named for an early post office. When Thomas A. Denney was awarded the post office, he wanted to name it Denney Post Office, but vigorous local opposition arose, and for some time a decision could not be reached. All the alternative names submitted turned out to be the same as, or too much like, others in existence. The Post Office Department lost patience waiting for a name, and wrote that it was peculiar, or that they were peculiar people, if they could not decide on a name; whereupon Denney suggested that they adopt the name "Peculiar," and so it was done.

Peebles   *Fond du Lac County*
The Peebles family, the first to settle here in 1847, was the prominent family in Peeblesshire, Scotland, before 1296. Robert Peebles and his family came to New England in 1718. Ezra Peebles, the second son of ten children born to Sanford S. Peebles and grandson of John Peebles IV, came to Wisconsin in 1845. He and his wife settled in the big forest of Taycheeda Township among the Indians. One day while Mrs. Peebles was rocking her infant son, she saw an Indian man at the window. He motioned to her to open the door and made her understand that he wanted a butcher knife. She gave him one, and about an hour later he returned it along with a quarter of venison.

The town was settled about 1857, and in 1875 Ezra Peebles built a cheese factory. When the railroad was built, the officials asked him what he would pay to have the town named after him. He answered, "Not a damn cent, but if you want to name it after me, you can."

Some years later the railroad company started a stone quarry that was responsible for the Peebles gold rush. Some workmen found bright stones they thought were gold, but examination proved them to be feldspar.

Peeksville   Ashland County
Mr. Peek bought a large tract of land, built a hardware store, and laid out a town.

Peet   Burnett County
Ed Peet started the newspaper in Grantsburg in 1895 and published it until 1905. He was known throughout the state for his promotion of the cutover lands in northern Wisconsin and his advertising of Burnett County. Mrs. Ida M. Nichols, the first postmaster in this settlement, gave the post office his name.

Pe-Ji-Bo-Nau-Ga-Ning   Sheboygan County
Between Seeley Hill and Follett's Creek on one side of the Sheboygan River, and another prominent bank about one-half mile to the west, it is a large flat area. On the western side of this prairie, and on both sides of the Sheboygan River, was the largest Indian village in Sheboygan County. The name means "fish dam." The Indians had constructed a dam in the river for catching fish.

Pelican Lake   Oneida County
Rivermen who brought supplies north to the logging camps noticed white pelicans at certain times of the year at Pelican Rapids on the Wisconsin River and also on this large lake. The state of Minnesota has three Pelican Lakes, so these birds, or some similar species mistaken for pelicans, must have been sighted this far north. The hamlet that grew up here took the name also.

Pembine   Marinette County
The word is derived from an Indian term meaning "water berries" or "cranberries." Government surveyors in 1847 gave the name to a stream flowing into the Menominee River, and also to falls on the river.

When the Milwaukee and Northern Railroad and the Minneapolis and Atlantic Railroad formed a junction at this site, the station was called Pemene Junction, then Pembine Junction, and finally, Pembine. The small stream that flows through the village is now called Pemen-Bon-Won. A man from Green Bay who had heard the stream was good for trout fishing approached a French Canadian and asked him where there was good trout fishing. The Frenchman pointed in the direction of the stream and said, "La Pemene c'est bon won," meaning to say, "La Pemene, it is a good one."

Pendarvis   Iowa County
Located in Mineral Point. Named after a village in Cornwall by Robert Neal and Edgar Helium in 1935, it was originally the location of some Cornish miners' homes. These men had an expert knowledge of stoncutting and masonry, which they used to build limestone houses like those they had left in England. Most of these stone and log houses were

located on Shake-Rag-Under-the-Hill Street. According to legend, the women would signal the men that it was time to eat by shaking rags from their doorways.

Pe-Ney-We-Se-Da-Ink
Manitowoc County

This was a Potawatomi village north of Cato. The word means "partridge feet."

Penokee
Ashland County

This is a corruption of a Ojibwe Indian word meaning "land of wild potatoes." It may also have originated in a printer's mistake for a word meaning "clean or cleared land" or "iron."

Pensaukee
Oconto County

A corruption of the Ojibwe Indian word meaning "inside the mouth of a river." There was a village located at this site. A similar Indian word means "goose land."

Pepin
Pepin County

The lake, which is a widening of the Mississippi River, was given this name by early French explorers before 1700. It seems probable it was named for one of the companions of Duluth, who was in the vicinity in 1679. Another account names it in honor of a French king, Pepin le Bref. It was also called Lake of Tears, because the Sioux Indians had a habit of weeping over their friends when they came in contact with European settlers and wept more than usual at this site. The county and the town were named after the lake.

Perida
Burnett County

Perida Frank Parsons was postmaster here from 1899 to 1908. It is now deserted.

Perley
Barron County

A deserted village named for John Perley, a lumberman.

Perrot State Park
Trempealeau County

Nicolas Perrot established a trading post here in 1685 that was abandoned about 1732.

Perrot's Post
Trempealeau County

After building Fort St. Nicholas at Prairie du Chien in the summer of 1685, Perrot moved north and spent the winter here "at the foot of the mountain behind which was a great prairie abounding in wild beasts."

Perry
Dane County

Named in honor of Commodore Perry.

Peshtigo
Marinette County

An Indian word meaning either "snapping turtle" or "wild goose."

Peshtigo Fire Cemetery
Marinette County

The greatest forest fire disaster in American history wiped out the Peshtigo community on October 8, 1871. The fire claimed at least eight hundred lives and destroyed every building in the area. Three hundred fifty unidentified men, women, and children are remembered at this nearby mass grave.

Petenwell

According to legend, a settler named Peter Wells strayed into an Indian village and was so friendly he was invited to live there. One day he met the chief's daughter, Clinging Vine, who was promised to Gray Wolf, a sullen warrior.

Peter and Clinging Vine fell in love and decided to run away together. But Gray Wolf was jealous and watchful, and he told the chief of their elopement. The lovers were captured and brought back, Peter to be burned at the stake at sunrise, and Clinging Vine to be given to Gray Wolf, who took her to his tent. She was able to soothe Gray Wolf to sleep using her soft words and ways, and then slipped out and released Peter from his bonds.

Again they stole away. The Indians tracked them to the large rock next to the river. A thunderstorm arose and sheets of rain fell like a solid wall to separate the lovers from their enemies. A blinding flash of lightning revealed them standing hand in hand on the edge of a cliff before they leaped into the dark rushing waters of the river below. The name was distorted to Petenwell and given to the landing where early settlers took their oxcarts to meet flatboats loaded with equipment and supplies for the Necedah area.

Petersburg
Crawford County

Peter Haskins laid out a village here in 1855.

Petrifying Springs Park
Kenosha County

The name refers to a calcareous formation that is found on the South Ravine of this 350-acre county park. The stony clusters, formed by rainwater and chemical action, resemble petrified flora material.

Pewaukee
Waukesha County

Asa Clark and Charles Bell built a dam at the outlet of the lake in 1835. It was called Pewaukeewinick, or "snail lake," by the Potawatomi Indians. The first school was held in Asa Clark's parlor. The village developed rapidly, spurred by the increasing use of the Watertown Plank Road from Milwaukee. During the Civil War the Octagon House on High Street became a stop on the Underground Railroad. It was incorporated as a village in 1876.

Although the name was taken from the lake, there are other versions of exactly what Indian word was used. Pee-wau-naw-kee, "a flinty place," is one. "Little lake," "swampy lake," "a timber opening," "scattered wood," "soggy ground," "clean land," and "a dusty place" are other translations of various words claimed to be the lake's name.

Pewitt's Nest
Sauk County

A waterfall and gorge on Skillet Creek, it received its name in 1843 because of a workshop built by an ingenious, eccentric mechanic in a recess of solid sand-rock. The workshop was located ten feet above a deep pool of water that was confined within the walls of a canyon that had been dug out by the plunge of water over a fall eight or ten feet in height. The approach to the workshop was either through a trapdoor in the roof or through a trapdoor in the floor. If through the roof it was by climbing down the rock wall to it; if through the floor it was by a floating bridge upon the pool with a ladder at its end leading to the trapdoor in the floor. The shop could not be seen from the mouth of the canyon or from the top from any direction save one. Hence, the early settlers dubbed it "Pewitt's Nest."

Phantom Lake   Waukesha County
The settlement was named after the lake that is said to be a lake of mystery, with an Indian legend of love and death. The Potawatomi Indian name was Nish-ke-tash.

Phelps   Vilas County
This village was first named Hackley after the Hackley, Phelps, Bonnell Company, who were its founders in 1902. William Phelps became superintendent of the store and general manager of most other things, so his name was adopted about 1915.

Phillips   Price County
Elijah B. Phillips was general manager of the Wisconsin Central Railroad Company in 1876 when tracks were laid to Elk Lake and this village was platted.

Phlox   Langlade County
John Jansen, one of the first settlers, chose the name. One resident said, "I recall hearing my parents tell that when they settled on a homestead about three miles out of town, they walked to a little store and post office through a path in the woods, and the ground was a blanket of blue phlox flowers."

Picatee Hollow   Crawford County
Part of Eastman Township. Taken from a French song, "La Toria the Picatee," the name also came from the word "Picardy," meaning gentle meadows and soft landscape.

Pickerel   Forest County
In 1900 Mrs. George Jackson, the postmistress, named the office after the large lake nearby. "Flo" Jackson had come to the community as a young schoolteacher.

Pickett   Winnebago County
Armine Pickett and his family moved here from Lake Mills, in 1846. The post office was then called Weelaunee and was established in their home. Mrs. Annie Pickett was postmistress. When the railroad was built in 1871, the station was named Pickett. Soon the post office name was also changed to Pickett. Annie Pickett was the first cooperative butter and cheese maker in Wisconsin in 1840.

Picture Rocks   Grant County
When the large cave in Wyalusing State Park was first discovered, it was under a large waterfall. Ice was often found there as late as the Fourth of July. The walls were of multi-colored sand.

Pierce County
In 1853 the state legislature split St. Croix County to form two other counties named after US presidents. This one was named for President Franklin Pierce.

Pierce
Kewaunee County

James Pierce was a Canadian who rose in arms against the queen's government. He was captured with his fellow conspirators and banished from the country. After a series of adventures he brought his family to the woods of Kewaunee and became a romantic pioneer personality.

Pier County Park
Richland County

This ten-acre piece of land near the natural bridge at Rockbridge was donated for use as a park in 1947 by the heirs of William Pier, founder of the Richland County Bank.

Pier's Spring
Richland County

This was a favorite picnic ground, on land owned by W. H. Pier at Dayton.

Pigeon
Trempealeau County

The township was named after Pigeon Creek. William B. Bunnell and William Smothers saw great flocks of wild passenger pigeons roosting along the creek while on a hunting trip.

Pigeon Falls
Trempealeau County

Peter Ekern, a Norwegian immigrant, discovered the small natural falls, which he harnessed for a feed-grinding mill in 1881. He also built a store where farmers could purchase supplies. In those days there were many wild passenger pigeons.

Pigeon Island
Bayfield County

In the Ojibwe language it was called Eshkwegondens, meaning "a small island at the end of a larger island," or "a point of land." It was also called omini-miniss, meaning Pigeon Island. It is one of the Apostle Islands.

Pigeon River
Sheboygan County

The river was called Memee or Memee sibi by the Indians. Memee is the Ojibwe word for "pigeon" or "dove," and si-bi or se-be means "river." This name was probably applied because somewhere in the vicinity of the river, or in the vicinity of Pigeon Lake, its source, there was an extensive wild pigeon roost.

Pilsen
Kewaunee County

Bohemian immigrants named it after Pilsen.

Pinch Gut Hollow
Richland County

In the early days a family lived in this tiny valley near Steamboat Rock. They were so poor that one winter they ate elm bark.

Pine Creek *Crawford County*

In Seneca and Eastman. Many white pine trees grow along the banks of the creek.

Pine Creek *Trempealeau County*

Towering pines grew here, in some places in abundance. One was used by a farmer as a tower for his windmill.

Pine Grove *Brown County*

A beautiful grove of tall pine trees located on the farm of Mrs. Katie Hendricksen, between the public school and the Catholic church, prompted this name.

Pinehurst *Eau Claire County*

So named because of the extensive pinelands.

Pine Knob *Crawford County*

Part of Utica Township. This huge, rocky mound has white pines growing along its sides and on top. Years ago it had a clump of tall pine trees on top, which could be seen for miles around.

Pine River *Richland County*

A company from Mineral Point penetrated the wilderness about 1840 or 1841 and discovered stands of pines along this stream.

Pine River *Waushara County*

The Lange family, who were early settlers here, wanted the new town site named Leon, after a community in upper New York State. Others liked the name Pine River, because pine trees bowered over the beautiful river here. As a compromise the township was named Leon and the village Pine River. The Indian name meaning Pine River was Poy Sippi.

Pine Valley *Richland County*

This valley in the Mill Creek area was named for the pines that no longer grow in Rock Canyon.

Pipe *Fond du Lac County*

The name is an English translation of the French word "calumet" meaning "pipe of peace." It was an important stopping place on the trip from Green Bay to Fond du Lac, a three-day trek.

Pittsfield *Brown County*

A number of settlers from New England chose this name from a town in Massachusetts.

Pittsville *Wood County*

Oliver Wright Pitts came here with his bride in 1856 from Pennsylvania. Later his father and three brothers joined him. They built a sawmill on the Yellow River, and lumbermen in the surrounding area called the community Pitts' Mill. As the settlement grew, the name was altered to Pittsville.

Pius
Sheboygan County

Thomas F. Heraty named this post office after Pope Pius IX, according to his own diary.

Plain
Sauk County

Cramers Corners was the first name of this settlement because Solomon, John, and Adam Cramer owned the land. In 1852, when the logging began, there were only a few log houses, so it was generally referred to as Logtown. Then a stage route was established between Spring Green and Reedsburg, and a post office was applied for. The residents did not think Logtown was appropriate. A Catholic priest who stopped there suggested Plain because the land reminded him of Maria Von Plain in Austria. It has also been said that Plain was chosen because the residents were "just plain people."

Plainfield
Waushara County

The first settler in 1848 was William N. Kelly from New York State, and the site was called Norwich. Elijah C. Waterman came the following year and laid out a village. He offered free lots to settlers if they would build and live on them. A gristmill, a sawmill, and a general store were soon added. When the post office was established, Mr. Waterman was appointed the first postmaster and officially changed the name to honor his earlier home in Plainfield, Vermont.

Plain View
Crawford County

Located in Marietta Township. It offers a plain view.

Platteville
Grant County

It was called Platte River Diggings in 1827 when early settlers arrived. John H. Roundtree and his neighbors petitioned for a post office and asked that it be named Platte River. For a few months during 1828 the name was Lebanon, and then changed to Platteville. Alonzo Platt, a prominent citizen, came in 1828, but the Platte River had been named before that time. It is said the Indians smelted their lead and put it into what was known as plats, or bowl-shaped masses, which usually weighed about seventy pounds.

Pleasant Prairie
Kenosha County

The flat prairie attracted settlers who found it a pleasant place to live.

Pleasant Ridge
Crawford County

Also called Taylor Ridge, it is said to be very pleasant. It runs from Seneca east.

Pleasant Ridge
Richland County

Enoch Gray built a home on this ridge in the town of Willow after the Civil War. Those who lived here later said that "it is as near heaven as they could ever get" and named it Pleasant Ridge.

Pleasant Springs   *Dane County*

A large spring and numerous smaller ones are found in different parts of the town.

Pleasant Valley   *Eau Claire County*

The community was settled in 1858 and called Machias. The name was changed when it was established as a township in 1870.

Pleasant View   *Crawford County*

Located in Marietta Township. This ridge is said to have a pleasant view, anywhere along its path from Niland Ridge to Maple Ridge.

Pleasantville   *Trempealeau County*

This settlement is in the valley of Elk Creek, which is known as Pleasant Valley.

Plover   *Portage County*

The meaning of the Ojibwe name is "prairie." It was the terminal point of an old Indian portage between the Wisconsin and Wolf Rivers. The city is named after the Plover River, which was called the River of Flags. No explanation of the word Plover is given.

Plug Town   *Crawford County*

Located in Scott Township. Also known as Childstown, it was given its name by an early horse trader, who traded in common work stock, or "plugs."

Plum City   *Pierce County*

The first settlers called the creek Plum Creek. Frank Moser named the town site Plum City, saying, "So long as the stream is called Plum Creek on account of the many wild plum trees which grow along its bank and in the valley, it is no more than right to name the town site Plum City."

Plum Creek   *Crawford County*

Located in Eastman Township. Wild plum trees grew in the valley through which this creek runs.

Plum Run   *Crawford County*

Located in Clayton Township, it was named for the abundance of plum trees in the area.

Plymouth   *Sheboygan County*

In 1845 Henry Davidson and his son Thomas, of Hartford, Connecticut, were attracted by the natural beauty around The Springs. The Fond du Lac–Sheboygan Trail also passed this site, so they erected a building to serve as a home and an inn. Henry Davidson wanted to call the settlement Springfield. Other settlers suggested Brookfield. At one time a fight raged over the name, with one group favoring Plymouth and another Quit-Qui-Oc. The state legislature changed the name from Plymouth to Quit-Qui-Oc. The next year another act of the legislature changed it back to Plymouth. Thomas Davidson chose the name in honor of his sweetheart, who had lived and died in Plymouth, Massachusetts.

Podunk   *Sauk County*

An abandoned hamlet about halfway between La Valle and Wonewoc. Farmers hauled potatoes and cordwood here to load on trains of the Chicago and North Western Railway. The potato warehouse still stands as a landmark.

The Point of Beginning   *Grant County*

In 1831, when Wisconsin was still in Michigan Territory, Lucius Lyon, US Commissioner on the survey of the Wisconsin-Illinois border, built up a mound six feet square at the base and six feet high to mark the intersection of the border and the fourth principal meridian. All Wisconsin public land surveys began from this point. The mound built on the border disappeared long ago, but every surveyor's monument in the state, the borders of all townships and counties, the locations of villages and cities, the position of roads, lakes, and streams, all were determined and mapped from lines and distances measured from this Point of Beginning.

Point Jude   *Richland County*

One romantic tale tells of a young maiden, Judith McCloud, who, pursued by Indians, jumped off this cliff on the old Madison road. This story may have come from an equally legendary incident in which Robert McCloud, who was being pursued by Indians, scrambled down the face of the cliff and hid in a cave that was unknown to the Indians. The McClouds were a family of early settlers who had several skirmishes with the Indians.

Pokegama   *Douglas County*

The Ojibwe word means "water at the side of a river," "the river divides," "water that turns off to one side."

Polander Hollow   *Crawford County*

This is the first ravine about Lynxville, and the place where a man from Poland once settled.

Polar   *Langlade County*

Originally the settlement was called Mueller's Lake. When the Webster Manufacturing Company erected their mills here in 1888 it was renamed Sylvan Lake by Mrs. Weeks, the postmistress. The millpond was a fairly large body of water. When the Webster Manufacturing Company sold their interests the name became Mueller's Lake again until the citizens voted to name it Polar in honor of Hiram B. Polar, an Indian trader and prospector. Mr. Polar had come to northern Wisconsin in 1861 and traveled down the old Lake Superior Trail from Lac Vieux Desert to Langlade County. He lived among the Ojibwe. Later he became the proprietor of a so-called stopping place.

Polivka Corners   *Manitowoc County*

John Polivka owned a tavern here.

Polk County

Named in honor of President James K. Polk.

Pollander Hollow   *Crawford County*

Located in Seneca Township, it was named for two Polish families that settled here. The other people referred to them as "Pollanders."

Pollander Ridge   *Crawford County*

Reverend Pollander was a pioneer clergyman who settled here. This spur ridge is south of Dutch Ridge.

Poplar   *Douglas County*

The first settlement was a part of the town of Brule. The land was covered with white and Norway pine that was logged off, leaving the country completely barren. Poplars were predominant among the softwoods that grew up to cover the naked land.

Porcupine   *Pepin County*

There are two stories about the naming of this hamlet:

1. A surveyor and his companion saw a porcupine when they were driving around the county. In talking about this particular section afterward they referred to it by saying, "Where we saw the porcupine."
2. Eli Place, a pioneer hunter, claimed to have shot a very large porcupine here and nailed it to a tree. He then named the creek and the settlement.

Portage   *Columbia County*

The Fox–Wisconsin River portage here was a landmark in early Wisconsin history. The name was given to it by French explorers who called it le portage. No other place in Wisconsin has a more colorful history, for Portage saw Indians, explorers, fur traders, voyagers, soldiers, and settlers. It was the site of Fort Winnebago. Marquette and Joliet portaged here en route to the Upper Mississippi.

Portage County

The original county was much larger and included the site of the city of Portage, where the Fox and Wisconsin Rivers come within one mile of one another. When the county was divided, representatives from the northern part wanted to keep the record books and thereby save a few dollars, so they kept the name for the new northern section.

Port Andrew   *Richland County*

Located in Richwood Township. The little Indian town of Tippisaukee was the site of this little village laid out by Captain Thomas Andrew, a pilot on the Wisconsin River in the 1840s.

Port Edwards   *Wood County*

John Edwards Sr., in partnership with Henry Clinton, built a sawmill here on the Wisconsin River in 1840. The settlement was known as Frenchtown due to the large population of French people. In 1869 the settlers renamed it in honor of its benefactor. The river divides at this point to flow on both sides of a large island, which provided a place to store logs, sort logs, tie up lumber rafts, and load supplies. Since there were two channels, logs could be diverted to holding ponds or sent downstream.

Porter
Rock County

The township was named after Dr. John Porter.

Porterfield
Marinette County

John Porterfield was the owner of a large farm here and also a business block in Marinette.

Portersville
Eau Claire County

Edward Porter had the largest lumber mill on the Chippewa River. This community was started in 1863.

Port Hope
Columbia County

Jonathan Whitney platted this town during the days of great hope of a canal being built from the Wisconsin to the Fox River. He named it in hopes it would be chosen as a town site by the company doing the job.

Port Washington
Ozaukee County

This site was settled in 1835 by a group led by Wooster Harrison, and his plat was the first to be recorded in the federal land office at Green Bay. Solomon Juneau also owned land here. The site was called Wisconsin City. In 1843, because of confusion with other similarly named cities, the name was changed to Washington after George Washington, sometimes with the prefix Sauk added. When a large new pier was constructed, bringing commerce and new settlers, the name was changed to Port Washington. It was also known as The Little City of Seven Hills.

Port Wing
Bayfield County

Axel L. Johannson came by boat from Duluth, Minnesota, to take homestead land here in 1891. Within a few years there were sawmills, stores, dwellings and a post office. No explanation for the name is given.

There had been some thought of naming it Flag River because of the blue flag lilies that grew in the marsh at the mouth of the river.

Posey Hollow
Crawford County

It runs from Highway 131 to Maple Ridge, and it was named after the Posey family.

Poskin
Barron County

Originally the settlement was named Cosgrove after the founder. In 1895 it was renamed Poskin Lake, in memory of a well-known Indian who drowned in the lake, or, according to another source, in honor of Mary Poskin, the wife of Captain Andrew Taintor of Knapp Stout and Company, who had a lumber camp at the lake. When the railroad came in 1917, Lake was dropped from the name.

Post Lake
Langlade County

On the east shore of the lake there are ruins of an old trading post.

Potawatomi State Park   *Door County*
There is a tradition that the Potawatomi, Ottawa, and Ojibwe Indians were a united
nation of tribes living around the straits of Michilimackinac. When they separated, the
Potawatomi perpetuated the sacred fire that had been shared during the federation.

Potosi   *Grant County*
Until 1845 this town was called Snake Hollow. Two reasons are given: the area was
infested with snakes, and the valley winds between bluffs to the river in a snakelike manner. Potosi may be an adaptation of the Indian name Potosa, the wife of Julien Dubuque,
but most accounts agree that it is derived from the Spanish word meaning "lead." Willis
St. John was the patriarch of the Potosi mines. He discovered a cave in a bluff that was
rich with lead that is still known as St. John's Cave.

Potter   *Calumet County*
At one time this community was called Muskratville, a name that farmers along the Manitowoc River resented. It was also known as Rantoul Center in honor of Robert Rantoul, a
railroad man. Since there already was another Rantoul in the state, the name was changed
to honor the Potter family. The Potters had large land holdings here and became well-
known during the Civil War era. It was one of the Potter clan who organized a band of irate
Calumet County farmers to ride into Cato Falls one dark night and blow up the dam. They
thought the dam on the Manitowoc River was the cause of poor drainage of their lands.

Pound   *Marinette County*
Before 1882 there were a number of settlers and logging camps here in the area called
Beaver Creek country. When the Milwaukee and Northern Railroad was built, a station
was named after Thaddeus C. Pound, who was the representative in Congress from the
Eighth Congressional District, which included the northern part of the state at that time.
He had also been lieutenant governor from 1870 to 1872.

Powers   *Pepin County*
This community started as a railroad station on the Powers' farm, where farmers brought
their milk to ship by train to Eau Claire several times a week. There was a little house
where the section boss lived.

Powers Lake   *Kenosha County*
The name is believed to honor an early settler.

Poygan   *Winnebago County*
This is a corruption of a Ojibwe word meaning "a place for threshing wild rice" or another
word meaning "a pipe."

Poygan Paygrounds   *Winnebago County*
The Menominee Indians ceded to the US government all their lands between the Wolf
and Fox Rivers in 1836. Every October, for twenty years, payments of the twenty annual
installments were made on these grounds.

Poynette

James Duane Doty, who was to become governor of the Territory of Wisconsin, laid out this village and named it Pauquette, in honor of Pierre Pauquette, the intelligent, faithful Indian trader and interpreter who had lived here. Pauquette, a man of gigantic strength, was murdered by Iron Walker, grandson of Chief Black Hawk. The name of the town was garbled by the post office into the meaningless Poynette, and attempts to correct the error have been unsuccessful. So the town stands with the wrong name, and Pierre Pauquette is forgotten.

Poysippi

The Pine River was called Poygan Sippi by Potawatomi Indians, because it flowed into Poygan Lake. The name was contracted to Poy Sippi. It is also said to be a corruption of an Indian word meaning "Sioux river."

Prairie Du Chien

The prairie here where the Wisconsin River enters the Mississippi was neutral ground where Indians met to barter. In 1673 it was part of the vast territory claimed by Marquette and Joliet in the name of King Louis XIV and came under the French flag. Nicolas Perrot established a depot for furs here in 1685 and named it Fort St. Nicolas. The first settlers known to have lived on the prairie were Jean Mario Cardinal Sr. and his wife, who came around 1755.

The area came under the British flag in 1763 and continued as a fur trading center. More pelts were shipped out of here than from any other place in the Upper Mississippi Valley. George Rogers Clark's conquest of the old Northwest gave Virginia claim to the region, and after the Revolutionary War it was ceded to the United States. It was then incorporated into the Northwest Territory, the Indiana Territory, the Illinois Territory, the Michigan Territory, and the Wisconsin Territory.

Prairie du Chien is the second-oldest settlement in the state of Wisconsin. Fort Shelby was established here in 1814, and the British captured it the same year. The first Fort Crawford was built in 1816. The largest number of Indians ever known to have assembled in the United States for the purpose of holding council convened on the prairie in 1825. The Red Bird Massacre took place near the southern end of the prairie, and Chief Red Bird was imprisoned and died in Fort Crawford. The second Fort Crawford, where Chief Black Hawk surrendered and was made prisoner, was built in 1830.

The name comes from the Fox Indian chief who was known as Dog. Early French voyagers called the place Dog's Prairie, or Prairie du Chien.

Prairie Du Sac

Traces of a Sauk Indian village have been found here, and the place was called Prairie du Sac by the French, or Sauk Prairie. It has also been claimed that the name means the prairie or meadow of the bag or sack, suggested by the shape of the land and not the Indian name.

D. B. Crocker established a village when, in 1840, he built a log store. Joshua Abbott with Archie Hill built a frame hotel and tavern, and soon a blacksmith shop and a wagon shop were added.

Prairie Farm   *Barron County*

Named by a group of men who came up the Hay River from Menominee to look for farmlands for the Knapp Stout Lumber Company. They climbed the two-hundred-foot bluff rising from Hay River and saw the prairie area beyond the trees. The Knapp Stout Company established farms here to raise grain and hay for their horses and cattle and farm produce for their lumber camps. A school was organized for children of company employees, and the village began to grow.

Prairie, River and Lake   *Barron County*

Derived from the Ojibwe words mockode iawsibi, meaning "prairie river."

Preble   *Brown County*

Peter Faenger and other German settlers came here as early as 1836. It is believed to have been named after Commodore Edward Preble, early nineteenth-century senior officer in the US Navy.

Prentice   *Price County*

Alexander Prentice and four companions came here in search of a site for a lumber mill in 1882. They found it on the banks of Jump River. Mr. Prentice became the first postmaster but left when the mill was completed. It has also been recorded that the name was chosen for Jackson L. Prentice, an early surveyor.

Prescott   *Pierce County*

The site was first known as Mouth of the St. Croix and also Lake Mouth. Later it was known as Elizabeth, in honor of the first girl here born to European settlers, the daughter of Mr. and Mrs. George Schasser.

In 1827 a company of officers at Fort Snelling, Minnesota, organized themselves to obtain land to divide and sell as lots. They raised $2,000 and elected Philander Prescott, an Indian interpreter, to obtain lands at the junction of the St. Croix and Mississippi Rivers. He got twelve hundred acres and established a trading post. In 1837 a treaty was made with the Sioux Indians giving the US government clear title to all lands east of the Mississippi. In 1841 Congress passed an act forbidding ownership of public land by a private syndicate, and the size of Prescott's claim was reduced to about two hundred acres. In 1851 Mr. Prescott laid out a few lots, and the village was started.

Presque Isle   *Vilas County*

This small settlement was created by the lumber industry, and the name changed every time there was a new owner-manager of the lumber mill. J. J. Foster built the sawmill and planing mill and began logging operations in 1905. He was president of the Vilas County Lumber Company and named the settlement Fosterville. William Winegar was hired to superintend the business and became so successful the town was renamed Winegar in 1912. At a later date a Mr. Bonifas is supposed to have been in charge, and the town was called Bonifas. The present name is French and means "nearly an island."

Preston   *Trempealeau County*
Susan H. Reynolds, the wife of Edmond M. Reynolds, one of the earliest settlers, chose this name. She came from the old New England family of Prestons.

Prestonville   *Vernon County*
Obadiah S. Preston laid out this small settlement.

Price   *Jackson County*
Price   *Langlade County*
Price County
William T. Price was president of the state senate when the county was formed. He was born in Pennsylvania and moved to western Wisconsin at an early age. In 1851 he was register of deeds for La Crosse County and then served in the state legislature. From 1854 to 1859 he was county judge for Jackson County. After many terms as assemblyman and state senator he was elected representative to Congress. He died during his second term in 1886.

Primrose   *Dane County*
Mrs. R. Speers suggested this name at a meeting held at the schoolhouse in 1848. She had heard her father sing an old song that began, "On Primrose hill there lived a lass . . ."

Princeton   *Green Lake County*
Royal C. Treat arrived here in 1848, staked out a claim, and erected the first building, the boards for which were hauled from Stevens Point. He was joined by Nelson M. Parsons, and the site was known as Treat's Landing. Later Royal Treat and his brother, H. B. Treat, secured the title to 132 acres of land and laid out the village that they called Princeton, but there is no record of why this name was chosen.

Progressive Ridge   *Crawford County*
This ridge in Seneca Township was so named because the fanners in the area were considered to be progressive.

Prospect   *Waukesha County*
Dr. John Ingersoll, the brother of the great agnostic Robert Ingersoll, chose this name because of the 360-degree view into four counties from the top of the hill.

Pukwana Beach   *Fond du Lac County*
Located on Lake Winnebago, the name is an Indian word for "smoke" or "that which comes from a pipe." Calumet, Pipe, and Pukwana are place names found in the area that all refer to the pipe of peace. Tribal councils were held in the vicinity at which the pipe of peace was passed.

Pulaski   *Brown County*
Mr. J. J. Hoff, a Norwegian, obtained large tracts of land in this area and advertised them extensively in newspapers of large cities to get buyers. He was a good businessman. He

chose this name to honor a Polish hero so Polish people would settle here. Count Casimir Pulaski was a Revolutionary War hero.

Pulcifer
Shawano County

Daniel H. Pulcifer was post office inspector during the Harrison and Cleveland administrations. The people of this community asked for a post office, and he was influential in helping them get it. Later he served in the Wisconsin state senate and became a newspaperman, the sheriff of Shawano County, and the first mayor of Shawano. He was editor of the Wisconsin Blue Book in 1879.

Pumpkin Center
Dodge County

As far as anyone knows, there are no pumpkins. Until 1971, Pumpkin Center was only the village's nickname, but steps were taken to legalize the name that year.

Pumpkin Hollow
Richland County

Located in Ithaca Township. A stock buyer remarked to Alfred Misslick one day that he had never seen so many pumpkins as he saw in this valley. "Well, it is Pumpkin Hollow," he replied, and the name stuck and replaced the original name of Misslich Hollow.

⇥ Q ⇤

Quaker Bluff   *Crawford County*

Early settlers were reminded of Quaker churches in the east by this bluff in the village of Gays Mills.

Quarry   *Manitowoc County*

The settlement was first called Slab City. A marble quarry was started here, but the stone was found to be too soft to market successfully.

Quarrytown   *Dane County*

Now included in Madison, a small early settlement here was built around the three quarries.

Quinney   *Calumet County*

This is the name of a prominent Indian family. John W. Quinney led a group of Stockbridge Indians from New York and figured as their sachem. Electa Quinney is acclaimed to be the first woman teacher in Wisconsin. Phoebe Quinney, an Indian woman, lies buried in the Indian Cemetery at Stockbridge.

Quisisana   *Sauk County*

This is the name given to a resort on the Wisconsin River near Wisconsin Dells. It means "here you find health" and was selected by Mrs. Lydia Ely of the town of Kilbourn.

View from the Racine courthouse, with Lake Michigan visible in the distance, ca. 1888

⇢ R ⇠

Racine
Racine County

The Potawatomi called the river ot-chee-beek, or "root," because tangled roots grew out of its banks that impeded the passage of canoes. St. Cosme, a Jesuit priest, gave it the French name for root, Racine, in 1699. The Jesuits said no man could find a better place to send out strong roots for a prosperous and satisfactory life.

The city is built on a beautiful site where French traders and explorers often stopped. Jacques Vieau built a trading post here in 1794. In 1834 Captain Gilbert Knapp started a settlement he named Port Gilbert. Later he decided to keep the old French name and incorporated it as Racine in 1841. The city has also been called the Belle City of the Great Lakes because of the beauty of its surroundings.

Racine County

Named for its principal town, which was first called Port Gilbert and was located on the Root River. "Racine" is the French translation of Root River.

Radisson
Sawyer County

This small logging town was started in 1902 by Orrick Whited, a real estate dealer, and Henry LeBeau, editor of a paper. Mr. Whited platted lots and built a home, a large bank and store building, and a land office. He named the town in honor of Pierre Esprit Radisson who, with his brother-in-law Sieur des Grosseilliers, passed through the area in 1659. The Omaha Railroad was built in 1903.

Randall
Burnett County

James J. Randall was an early New Englander who settled west of this site.

Randall
Kenosha County

The township was named for Alexander Randall.

Randolph
Columbia and Dodge Counties

The first settlement was called LeRoy, after the Frenchman who preceded Pauquette in transporting boats across the Wauona Trail between the Fox and the Wisconsin Rivers at Portage. LeRoy built the surgeons' quarters at Fort Winnebago for his own home but sold it to the government. The name was changed to Conversville by Jon Converse, an early settler. It was changed again to Westford in 1864 and incorporated as Randolph in 1870, after Randolph, Vermont, from which some of the first settlers, including Mr. Converse, had come.

Random Lake
Sheboygan County

The lake was named by government surveyors in 1835. The village was first settled in 1848 as a trading post. When the railroad reached it, the station was called Greenleaf, after E. D. Greenleaf, financial agent of the railroad company. It was changed to Random Lake in 1907, as the railroad tracks ran along the edge of the lake.

Rangeline
Manitowoc County

The community grew up on the Rangeline Road from Manitowoc to Larrabee.

Rankin
Kewaunee County

Congressman Joseph Rankin gave the post office to the community, so loyal Democrats gave it his name. The post office has been discontinued.

Rantoul
Calumet County

Robert Rantoul was a popular member on the board of directors of the Illinois Central Railroad. The town was organized in 1855.

Raspberry Island
Bayfield County

The Ojibwe name was Mis-ko-mini-kan, meaning "raspberry place" or "where raspberries grow."

Rathbun
Sheboygan County

James E. Rathbun was the first postmaster.

Rattlesnake Knob
Sauk County

Rattlesnakes inhabited this elevation in the town of Dellona.

Rattlesnake Point
Crawford County

This rock outcropping is located in Marietta Township. Rattlesnakes used to abound in the area.

Rattlesnake Rock
Richland County

Circus performers and other showmen came here to get snakes for use in their work. The rock is in the Fiddlers Green area.

Raymond
Racine County

Governor Henry Dodge approved an act of the territorial legislature establishing this town, and decreed the first town meeting should be held in the house of Elisha Raymond.

Readstown
Vernon County

Daniel Read built the first home here in 1848 and platted the village in 1855. Two years later the post office was established, one of the first in the Kickapoo Valley.

Red Cliff
Bayfield County

The Indian village at this site was called Passa-bikang, meaning "steep cliff." There is no explanation of why it was changed.

Red Cloud Park   *La Crosse County*

Commemorates a descendant of the Ho-Chunk, Corporal Mitchell Red Cloud Jr., who died in Korea in 1950. Holding off an enemy attack with his machine gun fire, he saved the lives of many of his comrades. He was posthumously awarded the Congressional Medal of Honor.

Red Granite   *Waushara County*

William Bannerman, a Scottish immigrant, first found a red granite formation near Berlin and operated two quarries there for a time. He found, however, that the hard stone would not split properly in cold weather. He looked around for other deposits and found the very fine rock underlying five or six farms in an area known as Sand Prairie. Crops could not be raised in the thin soil on top of the granite, and the land was considered valueless. He purchased the 126-acre Cronk farm at a very reasonable price in 1889 and found the stone under it was unusually hard and saleable. Although the quarry he operated had a comparatively short history, the town that grew up on the edge of it boomed. The quarry became a water filled pit in back of the post office. It serves as a swimming hole and tourist attraction. Older residents like to remember that the streets of some of the largest cities in the United States are paved with the hard red granite from their area.

Red Hill   *Richland County*

Part of Akan Township. William Helm, a farmer, said that the clay on the hill was the reddest he had ever seen.

Red River   *Kewaunee County*

A small stream, which found its way over red clay into the water of Green Bay, was called Red River on the earliest maps of the county.

Redville   *Taylor County*

Many red buildings in the settlement prompted this name.

Reeder's Grove   *Walworth County*

John Reeder settled in this section of the town of Sharon in 1837.

Reedsburg   *Sauk County*

David C. Reed, an early settler, is credited with founding the town in 1850.

Reed's Landing   *Grant County*

This site was named after an early settler in 1840.

Reedsville   *Manitowoc County*

The settlement was first named Mud Creek. An early settler named Reed operated a sawmill here in the 1850s. When the Chicago and North Western Railway was built, the station was named Reedsville in honor of Judge George Reed of Manitowoc, who lost his life when the Newhall House burned in Milwaukee in 1871.

Reeseville   *Dodge County*

Samuel Reese came to Wisconsin in 1844. A son, Adam Reese, surveyed and platted a town and named it in honor of his father. Adam Reese farmed his land, taught school in the winters, and later was elected supervisor, assessor, justice of the peace, and county superintendent of schools. When the railroad was built in 1858, the depot carried the name Lowell Station, but it was changed to Reeseville in 1865. Adam Reese then became postmaster, express agent, and grain buyer.

Reichmann Slough   *Crawford County*

Located in Wauzeka Township. The Reichmann family owned land in this area.

Rewey   *Iowa County*

J. W. Rewey platted this village in 1880.

Rhine   *Sheboygan County*

German settlers chose this name after the Rhine River in Europe.

Rhinelander   *Oneida County*

The site was originally called Pelican Rapids, probably because rivermen claimed to have seen white pelicans here. The advantages of the site for a sawmill town were noticed by Anderson Brown of Stevens Point, who came here in 1871 to look for timber stands below Eagle River that could be logged easily.

The Brown Brothers Lumber Company purchased this site and platted a town in 1882. The Milwaukee Lakeshore and Western Railroad was built to the town in November of that year, and the name was chosen to honor F. W. Rhinelander of New York, president of the railroad company. The town grew and became a supply center for dozens of logging camps. The Soo Line Railroad was built through in 1886, and during the 1890s it was known as the busiest and most prosperous lumbering center in Wisconsin.

By World War I the heavy stand of pine to the north and east, estimated to contain about 700 million board feet, and the hemlock and hardwoods, thought to contain about 300 million feet, had been just about harvested. The last log drive was made down the Pelican River in 1923. Rhinelander is also known as the City of the Hodag, a mythical creature invented by the famous cruiser, surveyor, and prankster, Eugene Shepard.

Rhodes Station   *Trempealeau County*

Joshua Rhodes settled in this section of Caledonia Township in 1853.

Rib Falls   *Marathon County*

The Rib River begins in and winds around a very high elevation that was named Rib by the Indians and is now known as Rib Mountain.

Rib Lake   *Taylor County*

J. J. Kennedy and his brother came here to start a sawmill. They brought a crew to Wellington Lake, and in cruising around looking for timber they came to a larger lake that was much better situated for a mill. It was surrounded by beautiful tracts of hardwoods, hemlock, and enormous pine, in a growth so dense as almost to shut out the sky. They immediately moved their equipment to the new site and began building the sawmill and a town. Someone mentioned the lake was shaped like a rib, and Mr. Kennedy decided to name the town Rib Lake. In the 1920s the mill was one of the largest in the state, running day and night.

Rib Mountain and Rib Mountain State Park *Marathon County*

The Ojibwe word for this hill, which is said to be the highest elevation in the state, was O-pic-wan-a or O-pi-gegan-ama, meaning "rib," "back," "his back."

Rice Lake *Barron County*

In 1868 the Knapp Stout and Company lumber firm established a logging camp south of the Red Cedar River. Along the river's edge were wild rice pools and rush swamps. There were Indians living in a village here, and other Indians also came to gather wild rice and to capture the wild fowl that fed on it. There were many battles between the Ojibwe and the Sioux over possession of these rice beds. After building their logging camps, Knapp Stout and Company built a dam that transformed the rice pools and swamps into Rice Lake. In the 1870s the Knapp Stout and Company was said to be the largest lumber company in the world.

Richardson Hollow *Richland County*

William Richardson came from Ohio in 1855 and settled in Henrietta in 1858.

Riches *Sauk County*

This is a discontinued post office in the northeast portion of the town of Troy that was named after Robert Riches.

Richfield *Washington County*

The first settler was Philip Laubenheimer, who came in 1842. No explanation for the name is given.

Richland County

The name was chosen because of the rich soil in the area. It has also been suggested that some of the settlers came from Richland County, Iowa.

Richland Center *Richland County*

The town was named in 1851 by its founder, Ira S. Haseltine. He purchased a quarter section of land from the government and had a part of it platted into village lots. It was located in almost the exact center of Richland County.

Richmond *Walworth County*

The township was set off in 1841. Thomas James, Perry James, and Robert Sherman came here from Richmond, Washington County, Rhode Island.

Richwood *Richland County*

This township was rich in soil and timber.

Ridgeland   *Dunn County*

The first community was known as Annesburg on the southern edge of Barron County. It was moved a mile farther south into Dunn County in 1900 when the Dallas and Menomonie Railway, which later became a branch of the Soo Line, was built through the area. Apparently a location for the railroad station at the "Y" that was extended to Rice Lake was one consideration in moving the village. The land was obtained by George Huss and called Ridgeland because it has wooded ridges on either side. Most of the first homes were built for railroad employees. The village plan is unique in that it has a square that used to be enclosed by a board fence that made a good hitching rail for horses. Over the years this square has been used summer and winter for all manner of community activities.

Riefs Mills   *Manitowoc County*

The first settlers were the Rief Brothers, who built a sawmill, a planing mill, and a casket factory.

Rienzi Cemetery   *Fond du Lac County*

This cemetery was set off from land owned by Abby Tallmadge, wife of N. P. Tallmadge, territorial governor of Wisconsin. The family's arrival in 1844 was soon followed by the death of their son, William Davis Tallmadge. He had just graduated from Union College and was about to return to New York to enter a law firm. While looking over the new home of his parents, he remarked that he would like to be buried on a certain hill.

Two weeks later he died and was buried here. "The first to lie beneath these sacred oaks" was inscribed on his stone. Governor and Mrs. Tallmadge set aside this part of their farm for the community to use as a burying ground. "I will name this cemetery Rienzi. Rienzi was the last of the Romans, and my son was the last of the Tallmadges," the governor remarked. Cola de Rienzi engineered a revolt in Rome and ruled for three years before he was dethroned.

Rietbrock   *Marathon County*

The township was settled through the efforts of Frederick Rietbrock of Milwaukee. He owned timberlands and was influential in getting the railroad built.

Ringle   *Marathon County*

The Ringle Brick Company was an important industry here.

Rio   *Columbia County*

Most of the land in Columbia County was settled between 1844 and 1864. Along the Military Road, from Fort Winnebago at Portage to Fort Dearborn at Chicago, were the small villages of Wyocena, Otsego, Fall River, and Columbus. Between Wyocena and Otsego was a region known as the Ohio Settlement, because most of the settlers came from that state.

About 1852 Delos Bundy built a roadhouse, known as The Ohio House, a blacksmith shop, and a country store half a mile northwest of the present village of Rio. Bundy also secured an appointment as postmaster and requested the post office be named Ohio. When he received his commission the name appeared as Rio. The change may have come about from illegibility or careless reading of the word, or perhaps the officials objected to a name that was so well established elsewhere.

In 1864 the Chicago, Milwaukee, and St. Paul Railroad was built into the area, and Abram Van Aernam offered a free right-of-way through his land and a free site for a depot, but the most favorable site for a village seemed to be the property of N. D. Dunlap. Dunlap hired A. Topliff, the county surveyor, to plat part of his land, and the railroad depot was finally built on this. The first lot was sold to Jacob Ulrich who began building a hotel. N. D. Dunlap began to erect a store building about the same time, and there was quite a contest over who would finish and occupy his building first. A Mr. Welch built a small warehouse for the storage of grain, and it was used by the railroad company as a depot until another one was built in 1865.

Rio Creek   *Kewaunee County*
The settlement was known as Krichmann's Place, probably because August Krichmann gave it the first store, a log building erected in 1889. There is no explanation of why the name was changed.

Riplinger   *Clark County*
In 1910 the Soo Line Railroad built a track from Spencer to Owen, Wisconsin, and established a station between the two towns named Osborn, until they found there already was another Osborn in the state. Frank Riplinger and his sons, Ben and Fred, built a store, so the railroad company adopted their name.

Ripon   *Fond du Lac County*
This settlement was started in 1848 by the Wisconsin Phalanx, an association that settled in the valley below. The next year David P. Mapes built a sawmill and a hotel nearby. The two settlements grew together and were known as Morena. When the city was chartered, however, Mapes asked Governor Horner to name it, and the governor chose Ripon after Ripon, England, the home of his ancestors.

Rising Sun   *Crawford County*
When T. H. Wilder first came here to settle it had been raining steadily for two weeks. The next day the sun came out.

Rising Sun Grange   *Fond du Lac County*
Chester Hazen erected the first commercial cheese factory in the state. The rising sun was the trademark of the factory and is etched on Hazen's tombstone. "Rising sun" is the English translation of the Indian word Waubun, the intended name for the township that was misspelled Waupun.

River Falls   *Pierce and St. Croix Counties*
In 1850, two years after Joel Foster first came here, the community was known as Kinnickinnic after the Indian name for the river. Four years later a meeting was held at the home of Osborne Strahl and the name of Greenwood was chosen and entered on the books of Pierce County. When the community petitioned the government for a post

office, it was discovered that there was already a Greenwood in the state. The community then chose River Falls, after the falls in the Kinnickinnic River.

River Hills

Edwin B. Bartlett of Milwaukee writes this account of how he named the village:

> One of our members had a home called for many years Riverdale, I believe. I thought that name was corny. I met Ludington Patron, a prominent member of this village, and begged him not to consider Riverdale or any name like it. On the spur of the moment I suggested River Hills. Mr. Patton presented it to the Committee; it caught on; and they adopted it. It is a nice name, river and hills, a pleasant country. I believe this happened in 1920 to 1928.

Riverview
Richland County

First it was called Briggstown, after J. W. Briggs, who came to Buena Vista in 1848. In the 1850s it was changed to Gage's Ferry, and then to Law's Ferry. When the day of the ferries was over, the view of the river suggested the name of Riverview. The ridge above the river was given this name.

Roberts
St. Croix County

In 1885 a group moved into the township of Warren, settling a mile north of the present village limits, in the center of the township. When the railroad was built, the town was moved south to its present location and a post office established. It was renamed Roberts after one of the men working on the railroad.

Roche a Cri Creek
Adams County

Roche a Cri means the shouting (or whooping) rock. The circumstances of the naming are unknown. Two affluents of the Wisconsin River bear this name, Big and Little Roche a Cri Creeks.

Rochester
Racine County

Rochester was one of three townships established within Racine County by an act of legislature. According to tradition the name was selected by some of the first settlers, who had come from Rochester in New York. Joshua Hathaway tells how he tried to give the community another name. He inscribed Waukeeshah on an oak tree, with the consent of settlers Cox and Myers. Waukeesha was an Indian name probably meaning "fox." He also says that when the town began to grow, the name was changed to Rochester because it had waterpower, as did the town in New York.

Rockbridge
Richland County

Located in Richland Township. The Indians worshipped this natural rock bridge as a gift from the Great Spirit. Samuel Swinehart passed through it in a dugout canoe in 1843.

Rock County Rock

The county has a rocky prairie within its limits, and there was an exceptionally large rock there. The Rock River is said to have been named first from the rocky character of the soil through which it flows. There is also a story that early French explores called the river Rivière des Kickapoo because there was a village of the Kickapoo Indians living on it. In the 1700s it was called Rivière de la Roche, a translation of the Indian word for the river, meaning "river of the rock." Rocks at the mouth of the river cause rapids.

Rockdale   Dane County
The original name, Clinton, was changed to Rockdale when it was found there was another Clinton in the state. Apparently Rockdale was chosen because the village is located in a valley between two rock ridges.

Rock Falls   Dunn County
William Plaisted was the first settler. He called the section of the river from Rock Falls to the Chippewa "Rock Run" because of the rocky gorge it flows through. It is now known as Rock Creek, and a natural waterfall of some eighteen feet gives the town its name. A township called Rock Creek was established in 1857.

Rockfield   Washington County
Peter Klumb and his family lived in the area when the Chicago and North Western Railway was built, and they boarded some of the railroad employees. It took about four years of work before depots were erected, and names had to be chosen. Mr. Klumb chose Rockfield for this stop because bedrock lies very close to the surface and protrudes through the top soil in many places, making rocky fields.

Rock Island   Door County
This island is about a mile square and lies off the extreme northeastern corner of Wisconsin at the very end of where Green Bay meets Lake Michigan. It was the first place visited by white explorers, since the customary Indian route south from the Straits of Mackinac followed the shore of Upper Michigan to Point Detour and then along the islands across the mouth of Green Bay to the west shore of the Door County peninsula.

On the north and east shores of this island were limestone ramparts that rose in perpendicular grandeur from the lake to a height of a hundred feet and more. The first settlers on the island were John A. Boone, James McNeil, George Lovejoy, David E. Corgin, Jack Arnold, and Louis Lebue. Fishermen and trappers came here from the Island of St. Helena in the Straits of Mackinac in 1835. A village known as Illinois Colony was established but was abandoned when settlers left for better, more profitable areas.

Rockland   Brown County
The name was inspired by the prominent rock ledge.

Rockland   La Crosse County
At the south edge of the village is a large rock, about fifty feet high and thirty to forty feet in diameter at the base, surrounded by level land for some distance.

Rockland   Manitowoc County
There are numerous outcroppings of coral limestone in the Kettle Range near here. The area was once the site of a great Ojibwe Indian settlement.

Rockmont   *Douglas County*

A rocky peak overlooking the station on the Omaha and South Shore Railroads prompted this name.

Rock of Lincoln   *Richland County*

A rock that bears a resemblance to a profile of Abraham Lincoln tops a hill south of Richland Center.

Rock Springs   *Sauk County*

The founder called the village Excelsior, the motto of his native New York State. Later it was called Rock Springs from the natural springs running out of rocks. Still later it was called Ableman's Mills, and then Ableman after Colonel Stephen Van Rennselaer Ableman, the first permanent settler, who built sawmills and gristmills there. In 1947 the name was officially changed from Ableman to Rock Springs.

Rockville   *Manitowoc County*

The Sheboygan River runs shallow over rocks here.

Rockwell   *Manitowoc County*

The settlement has also been known as Rockwood and is named after the Rockwell Lime Company.

Rocky Branch   *Richland County*

Located in Richland Township. This was the only stream Samuel Swinehart found in the 1840s that had a gravel bottom.

Rocky Island   *Bayfield County*

One of the Apostle Islands, called Maple Sugar Island by the Indians. Henry M. Rice, who at one time owned all of the stumpage on the island, named it.

Rocky Roost   *Dane County*

This small, rocky island in Lake Mendota was formed when the lake level was raised in 1850 but has been joined to Governor's Island since about 1940 by a strip of sand and vegetation. The "roost" is probably in reference to a cottage built on the island.

Rocky Run   *Columbia County*

A creek here was called Rocky Run because of its many rocks. "Run" comes from an old New England name for a small stream.

Rodell   *Eau Claire County*

The community was first called Rosedale because of the abundance of wild roses. When the railroad was built, the name was changed in 1856 to Rodell because there already was a station named Rosedale in Lincoln Township.

Rogersville   *Fond du Lac County*

Named for the Rogers family, who arrived in 1848.

Rohn Hollow   *Richland County*

It was about 1850 when the first Rohn family came to Buena Vista.

Roi-Porlier-Tank Cottage   *Brown County*

The oldest standing house in Wisconsin, it is named for three of its owners: Joseph Roi, Jacques Porlier, and Niels Otto Tank.

Rolling Grounds   *Crawford County*

Located in Clayton Township. The hills and grounds in this area are rolling.

Romance   *Vernon County*

This community is located in a valley between hills of beautiful forests, conducive to a romantic mood. It once had its own post office.

Rooney   *Burnett County*

This abandoned town was named after James Rooney, who owned lands in the area. Nearby Rooney Lake was named first.

Roosevelt   *Burnett County*

This township was set off in 1903, when Theodore Roosevelt was president.

Roosevelt Wayside   *Fond du Lac County*

There is a bathing beach here on the east shore of Lake Winnebago. The land was set aside for public use during the first presidential term of Franklin D. Roosevelt.

Root Bridge River Crossing   *Crawford County*

Named for the Root family, it leads from Barnum into Haney Valley.

Rosalietown   *Sauk County*

A deserted hamlet on the Wisconsin River, between Merrimac and Prairie du Sac, that was named for Rosalie Naffz, wife of Charles Naffz.

Rosecrane   *Manitowoc County*

Rose Crane owned a store and tavern and stopping-off place here.

Rosemere   *Manitowoc County*

First called Rosement, later changed to Rosemere, after a lady who lived in the vicinity named Rose Mary.

Rosemeyer Ridge   *Crawford County*

Located in Clayton Township. Also known as Halverson Ridge, it was named after a family by the name of Rosemeyer.

Rosendale   *Fond du Lac County*

One of a pioneer group coming by overland caravan in 1845 is said to have selected this name. Upon reaching the big hill east of the village he looked down on a perfect dale of roses and exclaimed, "We'll call our new home Rosendale!" Another account gives Mrs. George D. Curtis the credit for choosing the name.

Rosenow School   *Fond du Lac County*
In the city of Fond du Lac, it was named for Henry Rosenow, who served on the school board from 1918 until his death twenty-five years later.

Rosholt   *Portage County*
J. G. Rosholt platted and developed this village.

Rosiere   *Kewaunee County*
Rosière is the French word for "queen of roses" and was chosen by Belgian settlers.

Rostok   *Kewaunee County*
A discontinued post office and trading center settled by Czechoslovakian immigrants and named after a city in Bohemia.

Rothschild   *Marathon County*
The village was started in 1909 when a group of Wausau businessmen built a pulp and paper mill here on the Wisconsin River. A man who lived in an old shack here was referred to in local conversations as the Baron de Rothschild. There were some stories that this man was actually a member of the Rothschild family who had run away to be alone in the wilderness. Other stories say he was humorously given this title because he was a recluse who kept exclusively to himself.

Round Lake   *Forest County*
An English translation of the Potawatomi name Wahwiyagamy.

Round Top   *Fond du Lac County*
This conical-shaped hill near Dundee is one of the many glacial formations in the area.

Rowe's Spring   *Dane County*
Located within the University Arboretum in Madison, it was named for R. W. Rowe, a former owner of the farm on which it flowed.

Rowley's Bay   *Door County*
Peter Rowley left the little frontier post at Fort Howard and settled here in 1835.

Roxbury   *Dane County*
James Steele, an early settler, suggested the name Roxbury because his birthplace was Roxbury, New York. Mrs. Burke Fairchild suggested the name Nelson, after the English admiral. A vote was taken, and it was tied after everyone but the secretary had voted. He cast the deciding ballot, but misspelled the name as "Rocksbury," and it appeared as such on maps and elsewhere for a few years.

Royalton   *Winnebago County*
Ellis N. Royalton built the first store here in 1853.

Rubicon   *Dodge County*
When a post office was established outside the present village it was called Upton. Later it was moved to the village and the name changed. A schoolteacher from New York who had come from the Isle of Man is said to have chosen the name from the Rubicon River Caesar crossed in 49 BC.

Ruby   *Chippewa County*
E. L. Hawn, founder of the firm of Sill and Hawn, came here in 1902 and organized the Ruby Lumber Company, named after his only daughter. Later Ruby Hawn became Mrs. Dan Anderson and a graduate of the university in veterinary medicine and agriculture when that field was unheard of for women. She was the first woman to do cow testing in the United States.

Rudolph   *Wood County*
The first persons to file claims here were John Draper, Paul Kingston, and Harrison Kellogg Fay, who came in 1840. Later Francis Harkness arrived and built the first house. Anna Harkness was the first girl born to European settlers here. The town was named in 1856 after Frederick Rudolph Hecox, the first boy born to European settlers in the area. According to the story, Horace Hecox, the boy's father, and several other pioneers were sitting around a table trying to select a name for the town they were planning to build. The child creeping around under the table pulling at their trouser legs received little attention until someone remarked that it might be a good idea to name the town after him. None of them wanted to call it Frederick or Hecox, but all agreed on Rudolph.

Rudolph's Grotto   *Wood County*
This is a shrine devoted to the Virgin Mary, on Grotto Avenue in Rudolph. Father Philip Wagner established it in 1928 in fulfillment of a vow to Mary and in gratitude for his answered prayers that she restore his impaired health and enable him to enter the priesthood.

Rumsey's Landing   *Dunn County*
Only the foundation stones remain of the grain depot buildings once used to store wheat brought down from Sherbourne Prairie in central Dunn County. During the Civil War the grain was shipped by steamboats on the Chippewa and Mississippi for the Union armies. Located on the Chippewa River in southeastern Dunn County, it was named after John and H. T. Rumsey, early pioneers.

Rural   *Waupaca County*
Originally known as Nepewan, an Indian name meaning "the little waterfall," Rural was named by J. H. Jones in 1851.

Rush Creek   *Crawford County*

Part of Freeman Township. It originally received its name from a man called Rust, but the name was changed by community agreement.

Rush Lake   *Winnebago County*

The wild rice and rushes around its border prompted the naming of the lake, and the post office took the same name.

Rusk   *Burnett County*

This township was set off in 1899, the last year of the term of Jeremiah M. Rusk, governor of Wisconsin.

Rusk   *Dunn County*

Until the invasion of the chintz bug the village was the center of a large wheat-growing area known as Sherbourne or Rusk Prairie. Named in honor of Governor Jeremiah Rusk, it is located four miles east of Menomonie.

Rusk and Rusk County

The community was originally named Gates, in honor of John L. Gates, a prominent Milwaukee lumberman and capitalist. It was changed to Rusk in 1905 in honor of Governor Jeremiah M. Rusk. Governor Rusk had moved to Viroqua, Wisconsin, in 1853. He became a member of the legislature, and then served in the Union Army during the Civil War. Later he became bank-comptroller, member of Congress, and from 1882 to 1889 governor of the state. He was the first secretary of agriculture under President Benjamin Harrison.

Russell   *Sheboygan County*

John Russell, a pioneer settler, was prominent in local government. The town was named after him in 1852.

Russell   *Trempealeau County*

William Russell came here to settle in 1864.

Rutland   *Dane County*

The township of Rutland was organized in 1846 and named after the city in Vermont.

Rutter Hill   *Crawford County*

Located in Freeman Township, it was named after the Rutter family.

Ryan   *Kewaunee County*

The community was named after a popular Irish family, the Ryans.

Ryan Hollow   *Richland County*

Part of Akan Township. Named for Matthew Ryan and for his son born in 1862, who lived many years on the homestead.

S

Sabin *Richland County*

Oliver Corwin Sabin, a land agent, had a store in the eastern part of the town of Sylvan. He was disappointed with the development of the area, so he tried again with Corwin. Next he went on to Ladysmith, where he was more successful.

Sacramento *Green Lake County*

This small village was platted in 1849 and named by a Mr. Hatch, who had come from the California gold rush with memories of Sacramento. It was temporarily the county seat when Waushara County was organized. It was absorbed by the town of Berlin.

Sage Batomen *Dane County*

Norwegian for "Saw Mill Bottoms," the name is still widely used in this strongly Norwegian settlement.

Sagole *Outagamie County*

This is the word used by Oneida Indian men in greeting each other. For women the word is sagu.

St. Anna *Calumet and Sheboygan Counties*

Immigrants from Luxembourg, Germany, and Belgium settled here and built a Catholic church that they dedicated to Saint Anna.

St. Catherine *Calumet County*

This is a forgotten village that appears on very old maps. It was laid out in 1852 on the east shore of Lake Winnebago. There were several business places and a church that served lake travelers. It is thought to have been named after St. Catherine of Siena.

St. Cloud *Fond du Lac County*

Benert Moesch, the original owner of the town site, named it after St. Cloud in France.

St. Croix County

This is one of the oldest names in the Northwest. It is French and means Holy Cross. There are several explanations of its origin. One is that French missionaries named the lake and river St. Croix because the river enters the Mississippi nearly at right angles, thus forming a cross, and because the waters are a dark red color, being stained by roots of tamarack trees at high water time. Another story states that French explorers, traveling by boat, saw a cross in relief on the rocks of the Wisconsin side. The most accepted story states that an early French explorer named St. Croix was shipwrecked and drowned at the mouth of the river. This report was made by Le Sueur when he went up the Mississippi River in 1700 to explore some mines that were said to exist in Minnesota.

St. Croix Falls *Polk County*

At one time there was a waterfall on the St. Croix River where the Northern State Power Company's dam now stands. It had a drop of twelve to twenty feet over a stretch of about one hundred feet. Much logging was done in the upper St. Croix area, and this site had several sawmills.

St. Croix Junction *Chippewa County*

This was a junction formed where the Wisconsin Central Railroad connected with the Soo Line. An old sugar factory was built there.

St. Francis *Milwaukee County*

The Indian name for this settlement was No-gosh-ing, meaning "snake" or "enemies." No explanation for the present name is given.

St. George *Sheboygan County*

A post office was established at the intersection of six highways and called Six Corners. But it was officially named after the Catholic church, St. George.

St. Germain *Vilas County*

The history of this community has been traced back to the late seventeenth century, when traders were regulated by the French government. Those who refused to buy licenses and follow government regulations went farther into the wilderness to trade with Indians and sold their furs to the Hudson Bay Company. The French governor revoked all licenses and in 1696 ordered all traders and soldiers to return to Ottawa, New France.

Soldier Jean Francois St. Germaine had married an Indian, and rather than return to New France, he deserted and settled with his wife's tribe. In 1747 Antoine St. Germaine, a fur trader, was living in this area, and by the 1800s several St. Germaines were recorded by the Northwest Fur Company. Leon St. Germaine served as a Ojibwe interpreter in the War of 1812 and was employed by the American Fur Company in Lac du Flambeau. Big St. Germain Lake was so named for this French-Indian family. The community took the same name, dropping the final e. The statue of Chief St. Germaine that stands in the village honors the many Indians who had this name. There was no Chief St. Germaine.

St. Joe *Fond du Lac County*

It consists mainly of a store and a few houses located at the foot of a hill surmounted by St. Joseph's Church.

St. John *Calumet County*

The hamlet was known as Woodville until a post office was to be established, when it was found there already was a Woodville. The Catholic church of St. John the Baptist was the first building in 1862, and the community grew up with the organization of the parish.

St. Marie *Green Lake County*

Father Marquette, in his journal of his voyage to the Mississippi River, called the old Indian village at this site Lacote St. Marie, or St. Mary's hill or bluff. When Colonel Shaw moved here he named it St. Marie.

St. Nazianz *Manitowoc County*

A pamphlet published in 1867 gives a history of this community, beginning in the Black Forest of Baden in Germany. People left their homes there to come to America, where they could worship God according to their conscience without being molested and persecuted. Father Ambrose Oschwald organized his parishioners for the purpose of leaving Germany to form a Catholic village. To prepare for the journey he studied practical medicine for two years at the University of Munich.

The group embarked in two ships from Le Havre, France, in 1854 and sailed for fifty-five days. After landing in America they came to Milwaukee by train. Here Father Oschwald bought 3,840 acres of land in Manitowoc County at $3.50 an acre. The settlers traveled by boat to Manitowoc and by oxteams through the forest. Part of the way had to be cut through with axes. When they reached their land they built two log block houses and then a church, which they named in honor of St. Gregory Nazianz.

St. Philips *Crawford County*

Part of Clayton Township. The community is named for the church located here.

St. Rose *Grant County*

Father Samuel Mazzuchelli, an Italian missionary priest, purchased land and built a Catholic church in 1851 that he named St. Rose. The first settlers were J. V. Donahoo, John O'Neill, and Joseph Banfield. The town was first called St. Rose of the Prairie by Father Mazzuchelli.

Sakemao Watena *Waupaca County*

The site of an old Menominee village on the Wolf River. The name means "mosquito hill."

Salem *Kenosha County*

This section of Wisconsin was settled chiefly by people from New York and New England who were a generation or more removed from the British Isles, and they brought with them the place names of their former homes. Salem was one of these townships. When the settlement was started in 1840 it was called Brooklyn, and there were also places known as Liberty and Brass Ball. When the railroad was built, Salem was established as the name of the main village as well as the township.

Salmons Hollow *Crawford County*

Part of Utica Township, and named for the Salmon family.

Sanborn *Ashland County*

Supposedly this township was named after Senator A. W. Sanborn, who held a large area of land here.

Sand Creek *Crawford County*

The sand in the bottom of the creek gave it its name. It runs from Bell Center to the east.

Sand Creek   *Dunn County*

Norwegian settlers, the Toycen and Myron families, came here in covered wagons along Indian trails that followed the Red Cedar River. They built cabins and cleared the land for farming. There was a firm sand and gravel bottom in the river at this point that made it easy to ford, so the settlement began to grow. Knapp Stout and Company of Menomonie started a logging industry here.

Sanders Park   *Racine County*

Formerly Forest Park, it was renamed Sanders Park in memory of Edwin F. "Pop" Sanders, a well-known naturalist in the area. As a high school teacher in Racine, he frequently took his students on field trips to his favorite spot, Forest Park. Sanders Park is recognized as an official State Scientific Area. It is an eighty-acre natural hardwood forest where it is possible to see a portion of southeastern Wisconsin that is virtually unchanged since the time of the first settlers in Wisconsin.

Sand Island   *Bayfield County*

The Ojibwe name was Waba-biko miniss, meaning "white rock island." Henry Schoolcraft called it Massachusetts. There is a sandy shoal connecting it with the mainland two miles away; geologists believe it will eventually make a peninsula of the island.

Sand Lake   *Burnett County*

Big Sand Lake was named for its beautiful sandy beaches. The community took the same name as it became a famous tourist attraction.

Sand Prairie   *Richland County*

This sandy flatland is located along the Wisconsin River in Richwood Township.

Sand Prairie   *Rock County*

A level, but sandy, prairie.

Sandusky   *Sauk County*

William Dano and Joshua Holmes, early settlers, named it for Sandusky, Ohio, their former home. The Huron Indians are said to have called the site Ot-san-dosti, meaning "cool water."

Sandy Bay   *Kewaunee County*

A small bay in the shores of Lake Michigan was known by this name when it became an anchorage for lake navigators.

Sandys Hill   *Crawford County*

Located by Sugar Creek in the Township of Freeman, it was named after the Sandy family.

Saratoga   *Rock County*

Platted in 1837, the beautiful flow of pure water from deep in the earth reminded settlers of the famous springs. The spring is now called Caledonia Springs.

Saratoga *Wood County*

This is a word derived from the Iroquois Indians. It was originally proposed as a name for the state before Wisconsin was chosen.

Sarona *Washburn County*

In 1898 Fran Sauer and his family settled on 120 acres of cutover land purchased from the Shell Lake Lumber Company. The following year a group of German people came to the area to settle as a Mennonite colony. The train station where they stopped was called Bashaw, but they didn't think it was an appropriate name. They met with Mr. Sauer in his cabin and asked him if they could name their town Sauerville, but he modestly refused. It was suggested that Sharon be selected from the biblical reference to a place of abundance and pasture. The Mennonites were impressed with the luxuriant grasses that made the region favorable for stock raising. They supposedly combined Sharon and Sauer to coin the name Sarona.

Satterlee *Oconto County*

The name of a Menominee Indian village that was once called Pik-wu-ku-noa Omani-kun, meaning "outdoor in shooting town"—the shooting referring to an act performed with otter-skin medicine bags inside the medicine lodge. Satterlee is said to have been the name of a Menominee chief.

Sauk City *Sauk County*

The village site was originally named Harszthy for Count Augustine Harszthy, who platted it in 1840. As this name was difficult to remember, it was changed to Westfield. The area had historically been known as Sauk Prairie from the Sauk Indians, and as the word "city" was popular at that time it was decided to rename it Sauk City.

Sauk County

According to a French Jesuit missionary, the Indians living in this prairie area called themselves the Saukies. In Indian sign language the word was translated to mean something sprouting up. The more popular translation is "yellow earth," as opposed to red earth, the symbol of the Fox Indians. Some references claim the Sauk Indians painted in yellow ochre, thus giving rise to their name. Saukies was shortened to Sauk, and in some names the French spelling Sac was used.

Saukville *Ozaukee County*

The founder of the village was William Payne, who erected a gristmill and a sawmill in 1846. The name is apparently taken from a Sauk Indian village that was located here. They cultivated maize in clearings along the river and furnished the European settlers with fish and game. The village site was important as the meeting place of two much-used Indian trails, the Green Bay Road going north and south, and the Dekorra Road going east and west. The early settlements of Voelker's Mills, Schmit's Mill, Mechanicsville, and St. Finbars have all been incorporated into the present village of Saukville.

Saw-Mill Bottoms *Dane County*

Located in Vermont. Sawmills were built along a stream here in 1847 and 1851. They continued their operations into the 1860s.

Sawyer County

Philetus Sawyer of Oshkosh was a congressman in the House of Representatives and later a US senator for two terms. He came from Vermont to Wisconsin in 1847 and started a sawmill at Oshkosh.

Sayner *Vilas County*

Orrin Wesley Sayner, with his family, got off the train at Eagle River in 1890 to take a job as caretaker for the summer home of Civil War Confederate Colonel Tatum. The country was completely wild except for scattered logging camps and Indians. In a borrowed lumber wagon Sayner hauled his wife and three small children the sixteen miles to Lake Content. The Indians took care of the family the first winter, showing them how to make moccasins and mittens out of deer hides. Three years later they lived an entire summer in a tent, eating the muskellunge fish caught by the two boys. The first order of the day was to catch a muskie, then they could play. Mr. Sayner built a summer resort and became the first postmaster of the settlement.

Saxeville *Waushara County*

In 1849 Justice Noble staked out a claim at this site. He then returned to Milwaukee and interested Edward J. Saxe, captain of the schooner North Star that journeyed from Buffalo to Milwaukee, in his investment. Saxe advanced $1,500 toward building a sawmill, then moved his family to the site and acquired full title to Noble's claim. Soon his brother Jacob Saxe from Vermont secured a government land grant on surrounding territory and joined him. The village was surveyed and platted in 1854.

Saxon *Iron County*

As early as 1865, military land was acquired from the government and later divided into homesteads for the earliest settlers. Supplies had to be carried on foot following a path through the dense forest from Hurley, a distance of thirteen miles. When the Chicago and North Western Railway was built, a flag stop known as Siding Four was established. In 1885 the Duluth South Shore Railroad was built through the area also, and for some unknown reason the name was changed to Dogwood. In 1899 the first depot was built between the two railroad tracks. A Mr. Grey, a Frenchman, worked in the station, and after he put the mail on the train, he would call out, "Sacks on." He continued this practice for many years until the nickname of Sacks-on became popular, and in 1892 Dogwood was changed to Saxon.

Scandinavia *Waupaca County*

One of the first settlers was a Mr. Magnus, and since all of them were Norwegian or Scandinavian, the name Scandinavia seemed appropriate.

Scarboro *Kewaunee County*

It has been assumed that Scarboro Creek received its name from a lumberman from the state of Maine as there is a Scarboro Creek at Casco, Maine. When a sawmill was built on the creek and a settlement started, it took the same name.

Schleisingerville *Ozaukee County*

B. Schleisinger Weil founded the village in 1845–46.

Schleswig *Manitowoc County*

The settlement was first called Abel, but predominantly German settlers brought the name Schleswig from Germany.

Schoens Crossing *Crawford County*

An early crossing into the Wisconsin bottoms near the Bush Creek and Wisconsin River confluence, it was named for a family in the Wauzeka Township area.

Schofield *Marathon County*

Dr. William Scholfield came to this locality in the 1840s and erected a sawmill known as the Scholfield Mill. The village name dropped the first l.

School Hill *Manitowoc County*

A prominent school on a hill brought about this name.

School Section Bluff *Dane County*

Located in Mazomanie. An old log schoolhouse known as Howarth's School was built on this bluff in the settlement of the British Temperance Emigration Society in 1849. The land later changed hands, and the new owner would not give up the school building, so one night the building disappeared and reappeared the next day in a different location, off the bluff, and it has been there since.

School Section Hollow *Richland County*

Located in Ithaca Township. The Land Ordinance of 1785 set aside a section of each township for school funds.

Science Hill *Richland County*

Located in Richland Township. John Ross, who taught the children in a little log school here for three years, named it Science Hill.

Scotch Lane *Dane County*

Adam Davidson, a prominent settler in this Scottish settlement, built high rail fences to keep other people's cattle off his land, thus giving the road the effect of a lane. This is a local nickname for the present Highway G.

Scott *Brown County*

The township was first named Liberty when it was set off from Green Bay in 1859, but this name did not suit John P. Arndt. He proposed Pochequette, the French title for the site of many former Indian villages. It was Robert Gibson who urged Scott, probably in honor of Sir Walter Scott

Scott   *Burnett County*
G. L. Miller chose this name in honor of General Winfield Scott, commanding general of the US Army during the Mexican War. Mr. Miller, a Prairie du Chien attorney, became a booster for this area and personally petitioned the legislature for new townships that he named after famous generals.

Scott   *Columbia County*
Scott   *Sheboygan County*
Both said to have been named for General Winfield Scott of Mexican War fame.

Selfridge Park   *Fond du Lac County*
H. Gordon Selfridge was born in Ripon. He entered the mercantile business in Chicago and after his retirement moved to London, where he built one of the largest department stores in that metropolis.

Seminary Springs   *Dane County*
Located in Burke. The lands around this corner were originally among those set aside for use by the university under an act of congress (June 12, 1838), "An act concerning a seminary of learning in the Territory of Wiskonsan."

Seneca   *Crawford County*
Samuel P. Langdon named the village at the suggestion of Nicholas Morgan, who had come from Seneca in New York State. Mr. Langdon, a native of Massachusetts, laid out the village plat. The Senecas of New York State were a tribe in the Iroquois nation. The name means "a place of stone."

Seneca Hollow   *Crawford County*
Part of Seneca Township. Running from the east end of Taylor Ridge to Haney Valley, it was named after the town of Seneca.

Sessions Prairie   *Waupaca County*
Named for an early settler in the area.

Sevastopol   *Door County*
The town was organized in 1859 under the name of Laurieville, but this did not suit the farmers of the area. Sebastopol was suggested by J. P. Simon as a fitting suggestion of the town's future greatness, for the Crimean seaport on the Black Sea.

The '76 Farm   *Dane County*
Located in Burke. Alexander Botkin put up a sign on his farm about 1840 with this name on it. It refers to the year of the signing of the Declaration of Independence.

Sextonville *Richland County*

Ebenezer Morris Sexton had this village in the Township of Buena Vista platted in 1851.

Seymour *Eau Claire County*

A dam and sawmill were built in 1857 on the Eau Claire River, named after an early settler.

Seymour *Lafayette County*

The town was laid out in 1869 and named in honor of Governor Seymour of New York, who was the Democratic candidate for president that year.

Seymour *Outagamie County*

Tradition says that an early name for the site was Squeedunk, possibly of Indian origin. The first settlement was made at Lime Rock, about a mile west of the present city. When the railroad was built in 1870, the people of Lime Rock moved to the railroad and a post office was established. It was named after Horatio Seymour, governor of New York State, who had received land grants here in 1845.

Shake-Rag Street *Iowa County*

This is a street in Mineral Point that was named from a custom of the early settlers. At mealtimes, Cornish women shook rags that could be seen by their men working at the windlasses on the eastern ridge.

Shanghai Ridge *Crawford County*

Henry Bailey was one of the first settlers on Shanghai Ridge. He was tall and thin, over six feet tall. At this time, there was a common breed of chickens called Shanghai chickens, which were quite large and scraggly. A neighbor of Bailey's gave him the nickname of shanghai because of his supposed resemblance to the chickens. Soon the ridge became known as Shanghai Ridge.

Sharon *Walworth County*

Supposedly some of the first settlers came from the town of Sharon in New York State. The first people to settle here were William Van Ostrand and a Mr. Southard, who came in 1842. By an act of the territorial legislature, approved March 21, 1843, this township was set off from Delavan Township and called Sharon.

Sharpe *Chippewa County*

R. A. Sharpe was supervisor of Ruby Township and acquired 240 acres of land in 1899. He operated a store, and the settlement took his name. Manley Sharpe was an early county agent, and Jesse Sharpe was the first director of the Chippewa County Fair.

Shaw *Eau Claire County*

George Shaw was the first postmaster here in the 1860s.

Shaw Hill   *Crawford County*

Thomas S. Shaw operated a rural post office here called the Shaw Hill Post Office, located in the Township of Seneca.

Shaw Hollow   *Crawford County*

Running east from Barnum, it was named for the Shaw Family. Located in Haney Township.

Shawano and Shawano County

Shawano is an Indian term meaning "to the south." According to a Menominee tradition, a band of these Indians traveling south along the Wolf River in search of food came to a large lake, where they found an abundance of wild rice. They called the lake Sha-wah-no-hah-pay-sa, or "lake to the south." The county and the city were later named from the lake. There is also an account of a Chief Shawneon, or "Silver," son of Chief Glade, living in the area.

Sheboygan and Sheboygan County

The word Sheboygan has an Indian origin. There are a number of words of two principal meanings from which it may have been derived. One series is said to mean any hollow object such as a pipe stem, reed, cane stalk, or hollow bone; or that with which one perforates or pierces through, hence a needle or awl. The other meaning refers to a passage away by water, or a river disappearing underground, or a noise underground.

One authority claims the Indian word meant "send through" and "drum," and referred to festive tribal occasions when the Indians carried their drums between Sheboygan Falls and Sheboygan and beat the cadence most properly suited to the event. There is also a tradition that a great noise coming underground from the region of Lake Superior was heard at this river.

Other explanations offered are that on quiet days sound carried an unusual distance if originated at the mouth of the river, and one Indian chief said the name referred to the sound heard if one placed an ear to the ground near the mouth of the river. The Sheboygan River was named first, and the county and city were named after it.

Sheboygan Falls   *Sheboygan County*

The first name of this site was Rochester, from the city in New York State, and is recorded on the plat of 1847. Later it was discovered that there already was a Rochester in the state. The first settler was Silas Stedman, and Stedman was suggested but not used. The Indian name of Coppacon was also suggested and discarded. The name was changed to Sheboygan Falls in 1850, after the falls in the Sheboygan River.

Sheboygan Indian Mound Park   *Sheboygan County*

Located in Sheboygan, the park has fifteen acres of ancient woodland and winding stream that hold eighteen rare Indian burial mounds, dated about 500–750 AD. The intaglio, conical, and linear mounds constructed by the Effigy Mound People were used for the burial of their dead.

Shelby
La Crosse County

Fort Shelby was named in honor of the famous governor of Kentucky, Isaac Shelby. When this fort was taken from the English, the first American flag was unfurled in Wisconsin.

Sheldon
Rusk County

Named for an official of the Wisconsin Central Railroad when it was built in 1906.

Shell Lake
Washburn County

It is claimed that the Ojibwe called the lake Mokokesese sahkiagin, which has been interpreted to mean "frog's navel." Another Indian name means "the lake is muddy, miry, shallow." The US government survey of 1855 labeled it Frog Lake, and it was known as such for some years. Later it was called Summit, probably by the railroad company when the town was laid out in 1881. By 1883 the lake and the town were both renamed Shell Lake, apparently because the contour of the lake resembled a shell, since it has no clams or shells worthy of mention.

Sheridan
Waupaca County

The original name was Sessions Prairie. Immediately after the Civil War the first group of settlers selected Sheridan after General Philip H. Sheridan, famous cavalry leader and Indian fighter of the area.

Sherman
Sheboygan County

It was first called Abbott after a prominent family in the community. Because of the family's Southern sympathies during the Civil War, the townspeople forced them to leave, and the name was changed to honor General William Tecumseh Sherman, the famous Union general.

Sherman Rock
Wood County

This large rock in the Wisconsin River just south of the Wisconsin Rapids Dam was named in honor of Simon A. Sherman, a famous pilot on the river. At one time it was a great hazard to pilots of lumber rafts as they came over the Grand Rapids.

Sherry
Wood County

Henry Sherry with a partner started logging here in 1880 under the name of Briggs and Sherry.

Sherwood
Calumet County

When the post office was established in 1858 it was called Lima, but there was another town by this name. Steven Nicolai arrived in 1859 from Prussia and built a log cabin, a store, and then a brick house. The community took the name Nicolai's Corners. Shortly after the Civil War, a one-armed veteran named Sherwood built a saloon and lent his name to the community.

Shesko Wabshkoke
Waukesha County

This was the Indian name of the former marsh at the southern end of Pine Lake, meaning "muskrat marsh."

Shields   *Dodge County*

General Shields, an Irish statesman, is said to have represented Illinois, Minnesota, and Missouri in the US Senate.

Shiocton   *Outagamie County*

Dominicus Jordan and Randall Johnson came here in 1856 and built the first house on land purchased from the government. A lumber town grew up, known as Jordan's Landing or Jordanville. A rival village a short distance to the north called Shioc was abandoned in a few years when the dam washed out. Mr. Jordan asked that the town be called Shiocton. Chief Shioc was a great war chief of the Menominee tribe that had a village near here. The name is said to mean "by force of wind."

Shivering Sands   *Door County*

The whole sandy shore at this location seems to shiver at times.

Shockley Hill   *Crawford County*

Located in Marietta Township and named by a man with the name of Shockley.

Shoe Lake   *Forest County*

The name is the English translation of the original Potawatomi name Wakissannibis.

Shopiere   *Rock County*

The settlement was first called Waterloo because of a battle between the Meeken family and the other settlers in the village. The post office was given the name Shopiere, the phonetic spelling of the French word for limestone, pierre à chaux or chaux-pierre. L. P. Harvey chose the name.

Shorewood   *Milwaukee County*

At this location, on the shores of Lake Michigan, is a deposit of Devonian rock, alternating soft shale and limestone 140 feet thick, known as the Milwaukee formation. Daniel Bigelow platted the village in 1836 and named it Mechanicsville. At that time it was considered an ideal site, and there were some who thought that Bigelow's village at the dam might even outstrip Juneau's and Kilbourn's on the swamp (Milwaukee).

But the depression of 1837 was a blow to the mills and other businesses. The village revived again when the railroad was built through the area. In 1875 J. R. Berthelet discovered that the limestone could be made into a cement, and the Milwaukee Cement Company built its first plant on the east bank of the river. In 1888 a second one was built. A post office at the second plant was named Berthelet, but the area was known as Cementville. In 1900 a petition was filed for the incorporation of the village under the name of East Milwaukee, changed to Shorewood in 1917.

Shorewood Hills   *Dane County*

This village took its name from its situation on the shoreline on Lake Mendota near wooded hills. The Mendota Heights Association acquired the land from David Stephens and his wife in 1892. In 1922 the Eagle Heights Land Company was chartered and filed the village plat. It was incorporated as a village in 1927.

Shoto   *Manitowoc County*

The name is a shortened form of the Indian word neshoto, meaning "two rivers."

Shullsburg   *Lafayette County*

Jesse W. Shull came from Philadelphia to Dubuque, Iowa, in 1816 to buy furs from the Indians as an agent for John Jacob Astor. In 1818 he arrived in the lead mining district of Wisconsin and established a settlement known as Old Shullsburg. The Reverend Samuel Mazzuchelli, a young missionary priest of noble Italian birth, platted a part of the present city and named the streets Judgment, Truth, Peace, Charity, Goodness, Friendship, Wisdom, Pious, Virtue, Justice, and Happy. The present city is usually considered as dating from 1827.

Sidemont   *Manitowoc County*

The site was so named because it was a railroad crossing, or siding.

Sigel   *Chippewa County*

General Franz Siegel was a Civil War general who had come to the United States from Germany in 1849. Some Wisconsin residents had apparently served under him and admired him enough to choose his name for the town, dropping one e.

Signa   *Ozaukee County*

This settlement was established as a railroad junction and siding of the Chicago North Western Railway near Port Washington. It is claimed the name is short for "signal point on the siding."

Signal Oak   *Fond du Lac County*

Once a landmark on the Butte des Morts Trail from Green Bay, the tree now stands at the corner of Ransom and Thorne in Ripon.

Signal Point   *Grant County*

At this site in Wyalusing State Park Indians built signal fires to communicate with other Indians on the prairies and in the valleys.

Silver Creek   *Sheboygan County*

The Potawatomi Indian name for the creek meant "red sand creek." John Silver was an early trapper. Another account says it was named after a place in New York State.

Silver Lake   *Kenosha County*

Supposedly named for the silvery sheen of the waters. Fred H. Schenning had a survey made of the village site in 1886.

Silver Mine Drive   *Eau Claire County*

A road lined with cottages following the north bank of the Chippewa River in the town of Union west of Eau Claire. It was named for a mythical silver mine that was promoted in the 1880s.

Sinipee   *Grant County*

In 1837 this was a boomtown, but it is now completely gone except for some cellar pits and an old spring located in Jamestown Township on the Mississippi River. The name is an Indian word meaning "lead ore." Payton Vaughn came here in 1827 and later built a large stone mansion with a dance hall on the second story. Zachary Taylor and Jefferson Davis came from Fort Crawford to attend the dances. The village had several stores, with merchandise brought in by the riverboats that took out loads of lead ore. John Plum Jr. called a meeting of the citizens here to promote the idea of building a transcontinental railroad from the Great Lakes to the Pacific Ocean.

Sinsinawa   *Grant County*

General George Wallace Jones bought land here for a lead smelter in 1827. In 1844 he sold it to the Reverend Mazzuchelli, who built a college here and started the Dominican Sisters. Edgewood College in Madison is a branch of this institution. Sinsinawa is an Indian word. In the Algonquian language it means "rattlesnake" and may have been adopted because the hills and bluffs of this region were once infested with many rattlesnakes. There is also said to be a rattlesnake effigy mound at this site. In the Sioux language the word means "home of the young eagle" and the college called its school publication The Young Eagle until it was moved to become Rosary College, River Forest, Illinois.

Sioux Coulee   *Crawford County*

Originally it was called De Sioux Creek when a warlike Sioux inhabited the area. An early French Canadian later changed the name.

Sioux Creek   *Barron County*

Sioux Indians who lived in western Wisconsin before being displaced by settlers were at war with the Ojibwe, who also tried to occupy this land.

Siren   *Burnett County*

Settlers moved into this area after 1870, and by 1895 a post office was established. The first postmaster was Charles F. Segerstrom, who had the office in his home. His home was surrounded with lilacs, so he suggested the Swedish word for lilac, Syren. The postal department changed the y to i in granting the application. Several years later the post office was moved a mile and a half west of the present village, where a store and creamery had been established on Little Doctor's Lake. When the Soo Line Railroad was extended from Frederic to Duluth it was moved to the present site.

Siresville   *Crawford County*

A village here was planned out but never developed. Alexander Sire and his brother William settled on land in Section 32 and laid out the village in 1853.

Siskiwit   *Bayfield County*

This Indian word means "kind of fish resembling trout," probably cisco.

Sister Bay   *Door County*

This bay on the south shore of Green Bay was named after the two Sister Islands. Increase Claflin gave them this name because they were close together and so near alike. There are actually two bays, and at one time they were called Little Sister Bay and Big Sister Bay. But since they are adjacent to each other, the habit of referring to them as one was gradually established, and the settlement that grew up on the shore of Big Sister Bay was named Sister Bay also. Schooners used to stop at Little Sister Bay to load cordwood. It was also known as Pebble Beach because of the many smooth, round pebbles deposited there by the action of the waves.

Skanawan   *Lincoln County*

An Indian name meaning "creek that runs through bluffs."

Skillet Creek   *Sauk County*

Captain Levi Moore built a cabin near Skillet Falls and named the stream and falls for the waterworm holes in the soft sand-rock because they looked much like iron "skillets."

Skunk's Misery   *Walworth County*

An old settler named Lennon attempted to domesticate skunks and raise them for their hides. His establishment in the town of LaFayette was given this nickname.

Sleepy Corners   *Crawford County*

Found in Clayton Township and named for the solitude of the area.

Sleepy Hollow   *Crawford County*

Also part of Clayton Township. Running from St. Philips Church to West Fork of the Knapps Creek, it was named because of the quietness of the area.

Sligo   *Sauk County*

A deserted Irish settlement in Winfield Township named after Sligo in Ireland.

Slinger   *Washington County*

This place was an important trading center for the Indians. The much-used Winnebago Trail, the easiest route through the heavily forested Kettle Moraine Valley, crossed the area. In 1830 the land around Cedar Lake was surveyed by two men named Brink and Burk, and by 1840 settlers began to move in. One of these was a man from France, B. Schleisinger Weil. He purchased a strip of land three miles long and one mile wide from the US government and built a log cabin.

In 1845 Mr. Weil received a deed from the government that is the original plat of Slinger, and apparently it was decided to name the town Schleisingerville about this time. Mr. Weil started a distillery, and other enterprises such as shoemaker, blacksmith, wagon maker, hotel, two taverns, steam flouring mill, tannery, store, grain elevator, and a stone stable. It is said that if the town could have obtained more land it would have grown larger and faster than any other in the area. In 1855 Mr. Weil used his influence to get the old La Crosse Railroad built through the town, and gave a big celebration to honor the occasion. The Village of Schleisingerville was incorporated in 1869. In 1921 the name was shortened to Slinger.

Slovak

The settlement was established by immigrants from Czechoslovakia, who named it after a place in their former country.

Smelser
Grant County

The township was named after an early family.

Smith Hollow
Richland County

Benjamin Smith was the first settler in the town of Willow.

Snake Creek
Richland County

This stream in Orion Township is very winding.

Snow Hollow
Richland County

Daniel and James Snow, sons of Horatio Snow, came by oxteam to Rockbridge in 1857.

Snyders Corner
Crawford County

Named for a shoe cobbler named Snyder. He operated a shoe repair business here on the corner of Highway 27 and Wall Ridge in Eastman Township.

Sobieski
Oconto County

Polish immigrants named the settlement in honor of King John Sobieski of Poland. A few of their log cabins are said to be still standing.

Soldiers Grove
Crawford County

A dam and a sawmill were built here in a large pine grove in 1857 by Joseph Brightman. By 1866 a store and hotel were also built, and the little community was known as Pine Grove. In 1873 the Post Office Department asked for a different name; there was already a Pine Grove in the state. Anxious to retain part of the original name, since people who spoke of coming to "the Grove" to trade, it was remembered that part of the army pursuing Black Hawk's band had camped in this large pine grove overnight.

Solon Springs
Douglas County

This site was named White Birch in 1888 when the railroad was built, and it became popular as a summer resort. Tom Solon was one of the early summer residents. He and his family homesteaded some land on which they found a flowing spring. Solon thought the water was good enough to sell. He built a bottling works, and the railroad built a sidetrack to his plant. The water was bottled in five-gallon glass jugs and dispensed from vending machines for a nickel a glass. Railroad stations in Wisconsin, Minnesota, and Illinois had Solon Springs water in their lobbies. Mr. Solon also bottled soft drinks and soda water until 1913. Apparently the industry did not make any money, but it did serve to put Solon Springs on the map.

Somers   *Kenosha County*

The town was officially named Pike by an act of legislature in 1843 and changed to Somers in 1851. There is no record of why the change was made. The settlers of Pike were developing a railroad line with the hopes of extending it all the way to Chicago. A wealthy Englishman named Somers came to Pike, and the citizens were either trying to interest him in providing money for this railroad, or were appreciating an investment he made in the line when they renamed their town in his honor.

Somerset   *St. Croix County*

General Samuel Harriman of Civil War fame founded this village. His father came from Somerset County in England, and it was thought that the Wisconsin location resembled the terrain of the English county. There is a Somerset County in Maine and also a Somerset in Massachusetts.

Sopher Hill   *Crawford County*

Before the highway across this hill was paved, it caused great consternation to travelers. The Sopher family had a farm close to the top of this hill in Clayton Township.

Soules Creek   *Richland County*

Mr. Soules took up a claim in Henrietta in partnership with W. H. Joslin. Indians drove him out, but he later returned to become a manufacturer of shingles.

South Buck Ridge   *Crawford County*

Located in Freeman Township. Known for the deer in the area. The north end of this ridge is connected to the south end of North Buck Ridge.

South Byron   *Fond du Lac County*

The first settlers came to the township of Byron in 1839. In the summer of 1844 John Polts with his wife and four children came from New York to the small community called Mound Prairie. Mr. Polts made a house of crotches on which he laid lone poles and thatched the roof with prairie grass. Blankets were hung on the sides. No record is given of when the name was changed to South Byron.

South Mequon   *Ozaukee County*

This small community at the crossroads of Donges Bay Road and Wauwatosa Road was affectionately known as Klatschbach, a German word meaning "gossip creek."

South Milwaukee   *Milwaukee County*

Originally this village was just the northeast corner of the town of Oak Creek where the post office was located. About 1890 a few ambitious men organized themselves into a real estate company and decided to boom the town. Some of the men had financial backing, and others had plenty of courage and the proper amount of persuasive power. They platted a village, sold the lots, and made efforts to interest factories and businesses to move there. The post office of Oak Creek was changed to South Milwaukee in 1891, and the following year the village was incorporated with a population of 517 people.

Southport   *Kenosha County*

This location is the southernmost point in Wisconsin at which a harbor might be constructed.

South Range   *Douglas County*

It is presumed that some mapmaker chose this name because of the range of hills that extends through the area from east to west. The post office was listed under that name in 1886.

South Twin Island   *Bayfield County*

The Indian name meant "Rabbit Island." Henry Schoolcraft called it Georgia when he was identifying the islands in the Apostle Island group. Later it was called Willey's and also Shoal.

South Wayne   *Lafayette County*

Omery Spafford and Francis Spencer cleared the first land for planting near the junction of Spafford Creek and Pecatonica River in 1832. While working in a cornfield, Spafford was killed by an Indian raiding party led by Little Priest.

About 1840 a stone-tub corn-cracker was built by John Hover, and Miles McKnight erected a sawmill. Later Albert Heindel built a store. The area had been called the Lost Township because of an error in early survey records. It was resurveyed in 1835, but one section was still left out until 1841.

The first town meeting was held in Amos Eastman's house. It opened with a discussion of what to name the new township, which developed into some heat. Finally old Amos Eastman took the floor and demanded silence and order. With dimmed eyes he faced the wrangling citizens and chided them for their foolish quibbling. He said, "We are descendants of men who served with Anthony Wayne. It is most proper that the town about to be born should be called Wayne."

The first post office was also called Wayne and was located in the home of G. M. Hobbs, the first postmaster. In reality his high hat was the post office, as he carried the few letters received until by chance he found the addressees. Later the post office passed from one house to another and finally settled in Heindel's store. He called it Spafford's Post Office, and then dropped the last two words so it was just Spafford.

About 1856 plans were made for a railroad to be built through the area, and a village plot was surveyed. The Civil War stopped the construction of the railroad, and the village died. Only two buildings were erected, and the site was dubbed Two Town. By 1880 the railroad was built about a mile from Spafford, and a depot was erected named Collins Station, after one of the railroad officials. A settlement began to grow around the depot, and the Heindel store moved into it. The post office was also transferred and took the name of Collins. This did not meet the approval of the citizens, who demanded it be called Wayne.

By this time there already was a Wayne post office in the state. Mrs. Roy Eastman, whose maiden name was Gretta Perrigo, told William N. Deetz that Dr. O. T. Woohiser, Postmaster Perrigo, J. H. Deetz, and L. Heindel went into a huddle and added South to the name of the village. A large white oak in the village was known as the Treaty Tree because when the Indians and settlers met for a parley, a sudden summer shower forced them to seek protection under its spreading branches, and this close proximity seems to have fused the treaty.

Sparta
Monroe County

A Mrs. Petia (or Mrs. M. Pettitt), wife of one of the pioneer founders, was given the honor of naming the city. She chose the name Sparta from the Greek.

Speedway Road
Dane County

Part of Mineral Point Road between Madison and Pine Bluff, when it was newly surfaced it was used by early autoists as a speedway.

Spencer
Marathon County

During the construction of the roadbed for the Wisconsin Central Railroad in 1871 the southern part of this site was known as Section 40 and later named Waltham. The northwestern part of the settlement was called Irene, in honor of the wife of James L. Robinson, who built the first lumber mill in 1874. Both of these hamlets were a part of Hull Township, and then Brighton Township when it was set off. In 1877 the name of the railroad station and the post office became Spencer, after a town of the same name in Massachusetts from which some of the early settlers had come.

Spirit Rock
Menomonee County

This story is taken from a marker at the site:

> *One night long ago a Menominee Indian dreamed that Manabush, a grandson of Ko-Ko-Mas-Say-Now (the Earth) and part founder of the Mitawin or Medicine Society, invited him to visit the god. With seven of his friends the Indian called on Manabush who granted their request to make them successful hunters. One of the band, however, angered the god by asking for eternal life. Manabush, seizing the warrior by the shoulders, thrust him into the ground and said, "You shall be a stone, thus you will be everlasting." The Menominee say that at night kindly spirits come to lay white veils among the trees. The legend is that when the rock finally crumbles the race will be extinct.*

Spooner
Washburn County

This city was first located in two different places. About two miles east of the present site there was a saloon and several residences. The people moved to Chandler, a settlement about two miles north that had a store, post office, saloon, and about thirty houses. The Chicago and North Western Railway had a turntable here. About 1882 the Chandler settlement was also deserted and moved to the present location of Spooner because it had a more suitable water supply near the Yellow River. A large forest fire had partially destroyed Chandler because there was insufficient water to fight the fire. The trains also needed water for their steam boilers.

Some buildings were moved from Chandler on railroad flatcars, and a new railroad terminal was established. A railroad corporation known as the Chicago, St. Paul, Minneapolis, and Omaha was formed as the railroads developed here. John C. Spooner, a lawyer, was associated with the development of this corporation. He was small but possessed tremendous vitality and energy. He had been an officer in the Civil War, and he later became a US senator.

Spring Brook
Crawford County

A spring feeds this brook in Wauzeka Township.

Springbrook
Washburn County

Both the post office and the township were called Namekagon until 1901, when the post office was changed to Springbrook. The name was apparently inspired by the small creek, which is spring-fed.

Spring Farm Phalanx
Sheboygan County

A colony of Fourierities settled in the town of Mitchell in 1846, attracted to the locality by some excellent virgin springs. They called themselves the Spring Farm Association after the adjacent springs, and adopted the motto "Union, Equal Rights, and Social Guarantees." In 1847 they petitioned for a special charter incorporating it under the name of Spring Farm Phalanx, but the territorial legislature denied the request. The organization lasted only three years and then was dissolved.

Spring Green
Sauk County

Mrs. Turner Williams was the first female settler to live in this township in 1843. When land surveyors came to this vicinity they boarded at her house. Mrs. Williams asked them to name the site Spring Green because to the north of her house were some hollows that faced south, and the green came here so much earlier in the spring than in surrounding territory.

Spring Hill
Richland County

There was a large spring at the foot of this hill in Marshall Township.

Spring Lake
Pierce County

A large spring near the center of the township formed a small lake here.

Spring Prairie
Walworth County

The original name was Franklin. A large log tavern was built by Dr. Hemminway in 1837 and used for religious services, public meetings, store, post office, and polling place. The name then adopted was Hemenway's, the spelling apparently altered a little for convenience. Abigail A. Whitemore Hemminway (or Hemenway) suggested the name Spring Prairie because of the natural springs that discharged into Spring Brook, a branch of Sugar Creek.

The Spring Slough
Dane County

Located in Roxbury. Because there is a spring here, it does not freeze over in the winter.

Spring Street, Milwaukee
Milwaukee County

The present West Wisconsin Avenue was formerly called Spring Street because so many springs welled up in the roadway. Later it was called Grand Avenue to match Milwaukee's ambitions but was changed to West Wisconsin Avenue because it connected with old Wisconsin Street of the east side.

Springvale
Fond du Lac County

The township was created in 1848. The name was suggested by either Dave Lamb or Warren Whiting because of the numerous vales and springs.

Spring Valley
Pierce County

The Eau Galle River arises largely from big springs in this valley. It remained a small, tight valley of farmland with scattered settlers until 1878 when iron ore was found in the hills. Soon a pig iron blast furnace was built, and a land rush was on. The census increased from 100 in 1890 to 1,200 in 1900. The furnace never operated full-time, for by the time it was ready to produce, the ore in northern Minnesota had been found. Millions of tons of low-grade ore still remain in the area. Two main springs remain: Eagle Springs on the north and Berghardt Springs to the southwest.

Spring Water
Waushara County

The township has a number of lakes and springs.

Staangji
Dane County

Norwegian, meaning "the pole," it referred to the presence of a flagpole, which the English-speaking settlers called the Liberty Pole. The village of Mount Horeb grew up around these crossroads.

Stangelville
Kewaunee County

Numerous Stangel families came to this vicinity as early settlers.

Stanley
Barron County

A Mr. Stanley surveyed the township.

Stanley
Chippewa County

L. C. Stanley and W. P. Bartlett of the Northwest Lumber Company platted the town in 1881. Mr. Stanley had come from New York State and was a schoolmaster, farmer, merchant, banker, judge, lumberman, railroad builder, and mayor of Chippewa Falls. He gave his name to the community but never lived in it.

Stanton
St. Croix County

When the town was started in 1880 it was named Ormes. In 1900 the name was changed in honor of E. M. Stanton, Lincoln's secretary of war.

Staples
Burnett County

Winn Staples was a prominent logger in the pineries on the St. Croix River and its tributaries.

Starkweather Creek
Dane County

John C. Starkweather, the sergeant at arms for the convention of 1846, was bringing a payroll from Milwaukee to Madison, and, unable to cross this creek, he felled some trees and made a bridge. The bridge remained in use for some time and gave the creek his name. The creek flows into Lake Monona.

Star Lake *Vilas County*

Star Lake was a development of the Williams and Salisch Lumber Company in 1894. Harry Star was killed by a pile driver as the track was being laid across a small bay of the lake to connect with a roundhouse and sawmill. Both the lake and town were named in memory of him.

Star Prairie *St. Croix County*

The first settlement was started in 1854 when Trueworthy and Thomas Jewell, with their families, came west from Lowell, Massachusetts. Both Trueworthy and Thomas had spent a winter in the lumber camps along the St. Croix River. They traveled down Apple River and made camp beside a beautiful brook. This became their home.

The first cabin was built of hand-hewn tamarack logs and had four rooms. It was the beginning of Jewelltown. The Jewell brothers obtained seven hundred acres and offered free lots to anyone who would build. They laid out a town and erected a sawmill and a gristmill. Major Edmund Otis, who married Emma Jewell, daughter of Trueworthy, is said to have given the town its more poetic name.

Star Valley *Crawford County*

Located in Utica Township, and organized and built in 1893, it was named for its first and only factory, the Star Valley Creamery.

State Center *Green Lake County*

This was a small town built in St. Marie Township in what was thought to be the geographical center of the state. When it became apparent it could not hang together, the town was carted away piecemeal.

State Line *Vilas County*

The town is on the northern boundary between Wisconsin and Upper Michigan.

Steamboat Rock *Dane County*

This large outcrop of rock at the top of a bluff resembles a steamboat.

Steamboat Rock *Richland County*

The wearing down of the hills left this rock formation south of Buck Creek that resembles a steamboat.

Steinthal *Manitowoc County*

The community was named after a tavern and store built of stone.

Sterling *Polk County*

The citizens were said to be of "sterling" character. This township was first called Moscow.

Stetsonville   *Taylor County*
Settlers came to this site as soon as the railroad was built in 1872. In 1875 Isaiah F. Stetson built the first sawmill.

Steuben   *Crawford County*
The settlement was first known as Farris' Landing. A name for the post office was needed in 1882. Henry Kast, the first postmaster, asked the government to select a name. Steuben was chosen in honor of the famous German general of the Revolutionary War, Baron Von Steuben.

Stevens Point   *Portage County*
When the Indians traveled the Wisconsin River, this site, just above a sixty-mile stretch of falls and rapids on the Wisconsin River, was known to them by a very long name that meant Hemlock Island. The hemlock trees that grew on it abundantly were otherwise rare in this region. Later it was known as First Island. There was a Menominee village across the river.

George Stevens was the first settler to come here in 1839. He traveled with two oxteams loaded with supplies. There was no trail to the Upper Wisconsin timber area except by the river. George Stevens established a settlement here as a gateway to the pineries and a supply point for the immense lumbering industry that began within a few years. There is also a story that a Reverend J. D. Stevens, missionary to the Indians, may have influenced this name.

Stevenstown   *La Crosse County*
C. A. Stevens was a shrewd lawyer and land speculator in this area along the Black River.

Stiles   *Oconto County*
This is the site of an old Menominee Indian village named Pak-wu-kiu, meaning "pointed hill."

Stinky Point   *Fond du Lac County*
Located in Lakeside Park in the city of Fond du Lac, this projection into the lake has earned its sobriquet from its proximity to the city's sewerage plant. Governor Doty sold this land in 1838 to his good friend Dr. William Beaumont, the army surgeon who became famous for his studies of the digestive processes in the wounded Alexis St. Martin.

Stinnett   *Washburn County*
This village grew from a section house built by the railroad crew. It was probably named for an early settler or lumberman who lived there.

Stitzer   *Grant County*
One account states the village was built on land formerly owned by Bernard Stitzer, an old settler, after the railroad came through in 1878. Another account claims that George and Ann Stitzer (spelled Stoetzer) came here from Germany in 1847. They gave the land for the first church school and post office. The town was given their name when it was set off from the township of Liberty.

Stockbridge   *Calumet County*

The Stockbridge Indians were given this name in the eastern United States where they once lived, by English settlers. The name traces back to England. Both the Stockbridge and Brothertown Indians migrated to Wisconsin during the 1830s by way of the Great Lakes, the Fox River, and Lake Winnebago. They were led by the Reverend Eleazar Williams.

In 1833 Reverend Marsh is said to have moved 230 of them from Kaukauna to this location overlooking beautiful Lake Winnebago to get them away from the evil habits of the European settlers. Marsh built a parsonage and the Presbyterian church and established a post office. He named it Stockbridge and was the first postmaster. In 1837 the American Presbyterian Board discontinued its mission among the Stockbridge Indians, and the very displeased Reverend Marsh left the community. Later the Indians were given US citizenship and moved to Shawano.

Stockholm   *Pepin County*

Swedish emigrants came here headed by Eric Peterson in 1855. They decided on the name Stockholm on Lake Pepin after the capital of Sweden, Stockholm on Lake Malaren.

Stoddard   *Vernon County*

Henry Hewitt White traveled from Vermont to Wisconsin with his family in 1868. He climbed Tiger Bluff and saw a beautiful field of corn below. He quickly decided that this was the land to own. The family occupied a vacant log cabin while a frame house was being built. Later he accumulated more land and laid out a village. He named it after Colonel S. Stoddard, who had been mayor of La Crosse and was much admired by Mr. White.

Stoddards Corners   *Richland County*

In Willow Township, five sons of Valentine Stoddard had adjoining farms here.

Stonefield   *Grant County*

Nelson Dewey gave this name to the rock-studded, two-thousand-acre farm he established along the bluffs of the Mississippi.

Stone Lake   *Sawyer County*

The original settlement was located in Washburn County prior to 1887. The first residents relocated their village on high land, choosing this hill in Sawyer County. Millions of board feet of pine and hemlock lumber were sawed and shipped from here. The settlement took the name of the lake, but there is no explanation of how Stone Lake received its name.

Stoney Point   *Crawford County*

A large number of iron-bearing rocks dot the surface of the land here, located in Seneca Township.

Story Creek *Dane County*

Located in Oregon. Named for L. M. Story, T. Story, and their families, who settled at the head of the creek in 1846–47.

Stoughton *Dane County*

Luke Stoughton bought the land from Daniel Webster in 1847 and platted it for a village.

Strader *Eau Claire County*

Joseph Strader was an early settler who came here in 1855 to build a store and blacksmith shop.

Stratford *Marathon County*

Land in this area had been granted to veterans of the War of 1812 by the US government. The Connor family of Auburndale bought many acres of timberland from the heirs of these veterans. When the Connors built a mill and established a village here they named it after the original home of the family, which had been Stratford, Ontario, in Canada.

Strawberry Islands *Door County*

Increase Claflin gave the islands this name because of the many wild strawberries.

Strawberry Ridge *Richland County*

Located in Richwood Township. John Coumbe found many wild strawberries here on his journey from Galena in 1838 to the site of what was to be the first settler's home in the county.

Stretching Waters *Waupaca County*

This chain of little lakes commences about three miles southwest of Waupaca. It was known to the Menominee as She-she-pe-ko-naw, which means "stretching waters."

Strum *Trempealeau County*

The hamlet was first called Tilden after Samuel J. Tilden, the statesman who was prominent in the first Cleveland administration. In 1890 Congressman William T. Price renamed it for his friend Louis (or Peter) Strum of Eau Claire, who became state senator from this district. There was already another village named Tilden in the state.

Stuckey Hollow *Crawford County*

Fred Stuckey and his father bought a farm here from the government in early times. The place is named for the Stuckey family and is located in Wauzeka Township.

Stuckeyville *Crawford County*

Named after an early Stuckey family, it is located in the west portion of Wauzeka village in the area of the old stagecoach stop.

Sturgeon Bay *Door County*

The city was first recorded as Graham in 1855. The History of Door County states that in 1857 Mr. Stephens, the state assemblyman, got a bill passed organizing the town as

Ottumba. Later it was changed back to Graham. In 1860 a petition headed by C. Daniels was presented to the county board to change the name to Sturgeon Bay. The bay had been given this name because the sturgeon fish were plentiful here and because it was thought to be shaped like a sturgeon.

Sturtevant
Racine County

The settlement was first established as Johnson in 1875. William M. Johnson was the first postmaster. The next year it was changed to Western Union Junction when a large railroad center was established here. In 1901 the name was again changed to Corliss as the Corliss Engine Works located in the town. And in 1923 it became Sturtevant when the B. F. Sturtevant Company was established here.

Suamico
Brown County

This name is taken from the Indian name of the siteous-suami-gong, which had several disputed meanings. Father Chrystom Verwyst explains it as "place of the yellow beaver." Father Jones said it meant "at the beaver's tail." Rev. E. P. Wheeler of Ashland said it meant "yellow beaver residence place." It has also been said to mean "yellow sand," "home of the beavers," or "point or tail of land." The Indians called one point "long tail" and the other "little tail," referring to projections of land along the shore of Green Bay.

The first lighthouses erected along this shoreline were known as the Tail Light Stations. This area was once a Menominee Indian village of some size.

Sugar Bush
Brown County

The name given to any sizable grove of sugar maple trees. Patches of hardwood trees were scattered through the virgin pine forests, and in autumn from a high place these looked like pools and streaks of gold against the dark green.

Sugar Creek
Crawford County

Families that lived and settled in this area named it for the sweet spring water they found here.

Sugar Creek
Walworth County

Sugar maple trees along the creek were tapped by the Indians for maple syrup. The Potawatomi Indian name was Sis-po-quiet-spee, meaning "sugar maples along the valley."

Sugar Grove Ridge
Crawford County

A grove of sugar maples in the area gave it this name, located in Clayton Township.

Sugar Loaf
Crawford County

It looks like a lump of sugar. This elevation is located in the village of Gays Mills to the west.

The Sugarloaf
Dane County

This striking, solitary hill stands out from the east bluff of the Wisconsin River, in Roxbury. The name was commonly applied to this type of hill, one that has a more or less conical shape. This probably goes back to early settlement days, when sugar came in conical loaves.

Sullivan *Jefferson County*

In 1879 the post office in this small settlement was called Winfield because of a space in the wooded area that was open to winds. There had been a post office named Erfurst at Heath's Mill, two miles to the south, in 1846. Casper Braun was the first postmaster at Winfield. In 1883 the name was changed to Sullivan. One story says that a transient workman named John Sullivan was killed near the railroad depot by a load of ties.

Sumac Lagoon *Dane County*

The inmost channel of Belle Isle, sumac plants grew here.

Summit *Douglas County*

Refers to the top of the divide between Lake Superior and the Mississippi River.

Summit
Summit Center
Summit Corners *Waukesha County*

The prairie area in this township was believed to be the highest elevation between the Fox and Rock Rivers. Summit Corners was a mail stop on Territorial Road that became a stagecoach station and center of business. A tornado destroyed it, and it was bypassed by the railroad. It declined.

Summit Lake *Langlade County*

The lake and the small settlement is thought to be the highest point in Wisconsin, some 1,726 feet above sea level.

Sumner *Trempealeau County*

The name honors Charles Sumner, an American statesman who was a member of the Abolition Party and an advisor to President Lincoln.

Sumpter *Sauk County*

This town was called Kingstown but was not the first of that name in the state. Sumpter was chosen in honor of Fort Sumter, where the Civil War began. The fort's name was wrongly spelled on an early map when the letter p was inserted. The misspelling was never corrected. Fort Sumter was named for Thomas Sumter of the Revolutionary War, and the word means "a packhorse" or "the driver of a packhorse."

Sun Prairie *Dane County*

In 1837 a group of forty-six workmen with six yoke of oxen carrying supplies left Milwaukee for Madison to erect the new capitol building. Nearly all of Wisconsin west of Milwaukee was unbroken wilderness, and they had to make roads as they went along. Commissioner August A. Bird was in charge.

They traveled for nine days in constant rain and mud until they reached the prairie east of Madison. Suddenly the sun shone. Two years later Charles H. Bird, who had been a member of this party, returned and built a home. His son, James Bird, was the first child born to European settlers in Sun Prairie. The nearest neighbors were a band of Ho-Chunk Indians camped along a hillside. Sun Prairie was the first town in Wisconsin, and the second in the nation, to have rural free delivery. It is called the Groundhog Capital of America.

Sunset Point   *Dane County*
In Madison, for many years this has been known as an excellent point from which to observe the sunset.

Superior   *Douglas County*
The village was incorporated in 1887, named after the lake. Samuel de Champlain labeled it Grand Lac on a map that he made in 1632. Father Marquette named it Lac Superieur de Tracy, and French traders and voyageurs continued to call it Superieur because it was the largest of the Great Lakes, and because it is the farthest north of all the Great Lakes.

Henry W. Longfellow in his Song of Hiawatha says the Ojibwe called it Gitche Gumee, meaning "big sea water." Ge-wa-de-nong is also said to have been the Ojibwe name, meaning "big north waters." The first Europeans to visit the city's location were Radisson and Groseilliers, who came in 1661. The site is also said to have been a battleground between the Ojibwe and Sioux.

Supple Marsh   *Fond du Lac County*
This large marshy area in Fond du Lac on the west shore of Lake Winnebago was a source of ice for Fond du Lac from 1888 until the 1930s. The Supple family owned this marsh and some warehouses on North Water Street. Blocks of ice were cut from the lake in January and February, some sixty thousand tons during peak seasons. The marsh was sold to the city in 1967, and in 1975 boat ramps were installed.

Suring   *Oconto County*
Joseph Suring and his wife were pioneer settlers at Hayes, where he established a lively trading business with the Indians. He gave up the Hayes store in 1882 and built a sawmill here. When the Chicago and North Western Railway was built through in 1896, Mr. Suring suggested the name Three Rivers because the North Branch, the South Branch, and Peshtigo Brook combine to form the Oconto River near here. But the state officials advised him that the name Suring had been selected, which surprised and pleased him very much.

Sussex   *Waukesha County*
The three Weaver brothers came here in 1834. They had come from Sussex in England and laid out this village to resemble the city in England. In 1842 they built St. Albans Episcopal Church as a copy of the church in England's Sussex. Dick Weaver made a fortune by raising hops, hanging them out to dry on long tamarack poles.

Swallow Rock *Wood County*

A former campsite for the Ojibwe Indians, this sandstone cliff is located on the east bank of the Wisconsin River in Nekoosa. Bank swallows make nests in holes in this stony elevation.

Swatek Ridge *Crawford County*

John Swatek, a Bohemian immigrant, was the first settler on this ridge, located in Eastman Township.

Swiggum Ridge *Crawford County*

Named after the Swiggum family that settled here, located in Utica Township.

Swiss *Burnett County*

When C. H. Chipman, the first postmaster, sent in the application for a post office, he suggested Big Island, for the island in the St. Croix River not far away. This name was refused, supposedly because it consisted of two words. Mr. Chipman was the owner of a particularly fine herd of pedigreed Brown Swiss cattle, so he submitted the name Swiss, which was accepted.

Syene Prairie *Dane County*

The biblical Syene was the southern frontier post of Egypt. The name may have been given to the settlement here in Fitchburg to suggest its remoteness.

Sylvan *Richland County*

The township was named for its rustic beauty. "Sylvan" means abounding in woods, groves, and trees.

Sylvester *Green County*

Amos R. Sylvester was one of the earliest settlers.

Bluffs and farmland in Trempealeau County, ca. 1945

T

Tabor *Racine County*

Tabor was an area north of Racine that was settled by Bohemians around 1852. Tabor reportedly is a word meaning "gathering place."

Tabor *Vernon County*

J. Clark Tabor was the first postmaster.

Taft Ridge *Crawford County*

Located in Haney Township, it was named after the Taft family.

Tainter Creek *Crawford County*

Running from the county line to the Johnstown Bridge, it can be found in Utica Township and was named after the Tainter family.

Tallman Homestead *Rock County*

Abraham Lincoln was a guest in this house when he came to Janesville to deliver a political address in 1859. Built by William M. Tallman in 1855–57, it was an Underground Railroad station that aided fugitive slaves in pre–Civil War days.

Tamarack *Trempealeau County*

Named after Tamarack Creek, the stream flowing through it. Tamarack is a larch tree.

Tanktown *Brown County*

This settlement was founded by Reverend Nils Otto Tank, a former Norwegian missionary who arrived here in 1850 to establish a "perfect" society. His plan failed tragically and his colony dispersed, part going to establish Ephraim in what is now Door County.

Tar Hollow *Richland County*

Some who came from Ohio may have thought that the pines in this valley in Bloom Township were reminiscent of those in Tar Hollow in Ohio. Pioneers are said to have used the pine tar as a healing salve.

Tarrant *Pepin County*

The Tarrant family lived in Durand and built a creamery there.

Taus *Manitowoc County*

The town was named after Taus in Bohemia.

Tavera   *Richland County*

This little settlement in Richwood Township was known as Ellsworth Mills at the time when Harry Ellsworth had a sawmill here, where he made sleigh runners and clothes racks. In 1878 a post office was to be established here, and the government, rejecting double-word ownership names, chose Tavera. The word is similar to the Latin word for "hotel," chosen because a hospitable little inn was located here for years.

Taycheedah   *Fond du Lac County*

An Indian village at this site was called Teecharrah, meaning "our camping place by the lake," or "our lodge by the lake." Francis McCarthy and Reuben Simmons, who came in 1838, were the first settlers. They built the home of Governor James Duane Doty where the Wisconsin Industrial Home now stands. Governor Doty chose the name.

Taylor   *Jackson County*

In 1873 the Green Bay and Western Railroad was built through this area. This village was named for one of the railroad officials. The vicinity had been settled in 1854.

Taylor County

William R. Taylor was governor of the state when this town was established in 1875. Governor Taylor had been born in Connecticut and emigrated to Dane County. He was known as the "farmer governor."

Taylor Hollow   *Richland County*

Thomas Orton Taylor, a brick maker and farmer, and his wife, Mary Hill Taylor, were the first settlers in the valley, located in Richwood Township.

Taylor Ridge   *Crawford County*

The name derives from the Taylor family. Located in Seneca Township.

Templeton   *Waukesha County*

A post office founded by James Templeton when the railroad was built. It was merged with the village of Sussex in 1932.

Tenney's Run   *Richland County*

William Tenney made a run for his life here when he was chased by a bear. This little valley is about a mile in length and is located at the mouth of Elk Creek.

Tennyson   *Grant County*

For many years this village was known as Dutch Hollow because of the nationality of the early settlers. No explanation is given for the change in name.

Terry Andrae State Park   *Sheboygan County*

Mrs. Andrae named the park in memory of her husband when she donated the land.

Tess Corners *Waukesha County*

The site of the crossing of Indian trails for Big and Little Muskego Lakes, the corner was named for Jacob Tess, a native of Mecklenburg, Germany, who became a prominent farmer in the vicinity. It was a pony express stop, with a post office established in 1867. Tess Corners is in the northeast corner of Muskego and is one of the oldest communities in the town.

Theresa *Dodge County*

This community was founded by Solomon Juneau, who also started Milwaukee. He often traveled the Military Road from Milwaukee to Green Bay as a trader for the American Fur Company. On these trips he became intrigued with the beauty of this location, especially a site on the hill overlooking Rock River. He built his home here, the first in the community, and a trading post that drew other settlers. He bought the land from the government, dammed the river, and erected a sawmill and a gristmill.

The village was platted in 1848 and named after Solomon Juneau's mother, Theresa. The community developed as a center for gamblers, "skin game" artists, and drunks. There were three breweries, a distillery, twelve saloons, bowling alleys, pool halls, and various other diversions. The Solomon Juneau home has been restored as a historic site.

Thiensville *Ozaukee County*

John Weston bought 148 acres from the US government here in 1839. He lived in a log house on the Old Green Bay Road, near the mouth of Pigeon Creek. He also established a store and a post office here that was called Mequon River after the Indian name for the river. In 1842 Weston sold his holdings for $800 to Joachim Heinrich Thien (popularly known as John Henry Thien), who had come from Germany. Thien laid out the village, built the first mill, and named the community Thiensville. The post office kept the name of Mequon River until 1883, and the village was considered part of Mequon until it was incorporated in 1912.

Thiry Daems *Kewaunee County*

A Belgian surveyor named Constant Thiry and a Belgian Catholic priest, Father Daems, were instrumental in encouraging the first Belgian settlers to come to this area.

Thompsonville *Racine County*

A Mr. Thompson was one of the early settlers.

Thorp *Clark County*

Named North Fork in 1870, the name was changed to Thorpe in 1880. The railroad company was in the habit of spelling Thorpe without the final e, so sometime after 1880 the post office designated Thorpe as Thorp.

Three Lakes *Oneida County*

The Lake Shore Traffic Company purchased the land around these lakes from the US government in 1881. When surveyors for the company surveyed a right-of-way for the railroad, they found a lake surrounded by large maple trees, which they called Maple Lake. From it they followed the range line between Sections 11 and 10 and came to another lake they called Range Line Lake. A mile to the north a town line crossed the range line and also another lake, which they named Town Line Lake. When the Milwaukee Lakeshore and Western Railroad was built here to bring supplies to the lumber camps, the station was named Three Lakes.

Frank McNinch came here with a logging crew in 1883. They had dinner in the lumber camp kitchen made of rough boards covered with tar paper. The only other buildings were a boxcar for a depot, a log building for lumbering supplies, and a bunkhouse. The town later became a famous lumbering center.

Thunder Mountain   *Oconto County*
The Indian name for this high hill in the northeast part of Oconto County near the settlement of Mountain was Chequah-Bikwaki. They believed the thunderbirds built their nests on its crest and attached a number of myths and legends to it.

Tibbets   *Walworth County*
The home of Samuel H. Tibbets served as a post office after 1842. Previously it had been located at Kendall's Corner.

Tichigan   *Racine County*
This is a Potawatomi word meaning "home of the dead" and refers to the Indian graveyard in the area.

Tierney Hill   *Crawford County*
In Scott Township, it was named for the Tierney family.

Tiffany   *Rock County*
This settlement was started in 1840 when the Chamberlain family homesteaded in the area, and a tavern site became a stagecoach stop. George Tiffany, a Milwaukee pioneer, operated the stage lines out of Milwaukee and also became a deputy postmaster under Solomon Juneau. Mr. Tiffany arrived in Milwaukee in 1830 and acquired land, money, and influence but apparently never lived in the community that took his name.

The Chicago, St. Paul, and Fond du Lac Railroad, which later became part of the Chicago and North Western Railway, built tracks connecting Gary, Illinois, and Janesville, Wisconsin, through this section of Rock County in 1855. A very remarkable railroad bridge crossing the Turtle River Valley was designed by a Mr. Van Mienen, who modeled it after ones he had known in France. Stone for the foundation was especially selected from the quarry at Waupun, and each stone was cut and placed by hand. It is a beautiful monument to fine design and workmanship. A station was established on the railroad at the tavern stagecoach stop. The post office was established in 1857.

Tigerton   *Shawano County*
The story is that the village was named about 1865 after Tiger Creek, which flows into the Embarrass River. The creek was said to have a section of fast whitewater that "roars like a tiger."

Tilden
Chippewa County

This township was separated from Eagle Point in 1883 and named for Samuel J. Tilden.

Tillinghast
Chippewa County

This hamlet was named after the first banker in Bloomer, who was also connected with the Northwestern Lumber Company.

Timberland
Burnett County

Located some forty miles southeast of Grantsburg, it took its name from the vast forests in this section at the time the post office was established.

Tioga
Clark County

Tioga, New York, the previous residence of N. C. Foster, lent its name to Tioga, Wisconsin. Mr. Foster owned much of the timberland around the settlement and built a railroad to aid his timber operation.

Tippisaukee
Richland County

Now part of Richwood Township. John Coumbe, the first European settler in Richland County, found this little Indian town when he crossed the Wisconsin River in 1838. The Indians told him that the word meant "beautiful view."

Tisch Mills
Kewaunee and Manitowoc Counties

Charles Tisch built a sawmill and gristmill on the Mishicot River in 1865. The gristmill was operated on a share basis to accommodate the farmers in the surrounding area. Rye flour was sold under the trade name Zitna Vedraska, a Bohemian name.

Token Creek
Dane County

Legend has it that the Indians dropped a token of tobacco or other gift into the creek when they crossed it, to appease the spirits.

Tomah
Monroe County

Chief Thomas Carron was the son of a Menominee Indian chief. Thomas was pronounced Tomah by the French traders, and so he became popularly known. He was born in 1752 in the Old King's village opposite Green Bay. Chief Tomah was said to have been a man of magnificent appearance, six feet tall with dark eyes and handsome features. He was peaceful, firm, prudent, progressive, and sincerely loved by both Indians and settlers.

The city was started as a result of land speculation. Robert A. Gillette, surveyor for the railroad, found that gamblers had purchased the land along the proposed railroad right-of-way and pushed the prices sky-high. So he quietly rerouted the road through this farmland area, which necessitated a lot of extra grading and the tunnel at Tunnel City. When the village site was selected in 1855, one of its founders is said to have read an old history stating that Chief Tomah once gathered his tribe here for a conference.

Tomahawk
Lincoln County

The city was started by William Henry Bradley at the junction of the Tomahawk River and the Wisconsin River. It was named after the Tomahawk River, which begins in the chain of lakes headed by Tomahawk Lake. Indians say this very old waterway was named as a result of a battle between the Sioux and the Ojibwe when a tomahawk or hatchet was buried on the shores to commemorate peace between the tribes.

Tomkins Green *Crawford County*

Located on Irish Ridge and part of Scott Township, it was named for the Tomkins family.

Tonet *Kewaunee County*

Originally the settlement was called Jonet, after a prominent local family. Some mapmaker who did not understand the Belgian word changed the J to a T, or perhaps he misread the first letter.

Tony *Rusk County*

Originally this settlement was called Deer Tail after the creek that flows through it. It was changed to Tony in honor of Anthony Hein, popularly known as Tony, of the Hein Lumber Company.

Tonyawatha Springs *Dane County*

Apparently this is a pseudo-Indian name, made on the pattern of "Hiawatha" and such. The name seems to have started after the construction of the Tonyawatha Spring Hotel, which was near the spring that "gushes forth to gladden the sight and heal the infirm." Said to mean "healing waters," it seems to be a pun on "tonic water" invented for commercial purposes. Located in Blooming Grove.

Torgerson Creek *Crawford County*

Named after the Torgerson family, it runs off upper Sugar Creek. Located in Freeman Township.

Torgerson Hollow *Richland County*

Part of Eagle Township. When he was five years old Gabriel T. Torgerson came from Norway with his parents.

Totagatic River *Washburn County*

It may mean "place of floating logs" or "boggy river," from the Ojibwe totogan.

Towerville *Crawford County*

Named for the Tower family, it was the site of a sawmill, woolen mill, and creamery. Now part of Utica Township.

Townsend *Oconto County*

While Mr. Smith was surveying this village here for the Chicago and North Western Railway, a land agent for the railroad named Charles Townsend stopped to talk to him. He mentioned that a new name would be needed for this location, which was known at the time as Johnson Siding. The surveying crew started suggesting names, and someone suggested Townsend.

Trade Lake   *Burnett County*
Trade River
The township, settlement, and river were named after the lake. A popular Indian trading
post was located on its shores.

Trego   *Washburn County*
This site, where two railroads cross, was first called Superior Junction, but it was confused
with the city of Superior. For a short period it was called Mills. In 1902 it was officially
named Trego.

Trempealeau and Trempealeau County
The first settlement was the trading post of Nicholas Perrot, established in 1685. It was
located at the foot of a high elevation completely surrounded by water, or a mountain
island. The Indians called it "mountain soaked in water." French traders put it into their
own language, La Montagne qui trempe à l'eau, and thus Trempealeau Mountain. The
Indian legend said this mountain had given offense to Wakanda and was slowly sinking
into the Mississippi River.

In the 1840s several log cabins were built by French fur traders and trappers about
a mile down the Mississippi River from Trempealeau Mountain, and this became the
nucleus of the present village. James Reed, a trapper, built a two-story log house with
spacious rooms that served as his home and also as an inn for river travelers. The settlement became known as Reed's Landing or Reed's Town. In 1852 William Hood surveyed
a plat of Reed's Landing, calling it Montoville or Mountainville. Soon another survey was
completed under the direction of Timothy Burns, who added Trempealeau to form the
name—Montoville-Trempealeau, which lasted for only a few weeks before it was shortened to Trempealeau.

Trevor   *Kenosha County*
This settlement was started when the Wisconsin Central Railway was built through the
area in 1885 and named for one of the officials of the railroad company.

Tripoli   *Oneida County*
This name is from the Greek meaning "three towns" or "triple city." The town borders
three counties: Oneida, Lincoln, and Price. An official of the Minneapolis, St. Paul, and
Sault St. Marie Railroad chose the name about 1888, because the railroad sidetrack also
crossed the three counties. The site is an old logging and sawmill center. In 1866 Israel
Stone, an Indian, built a logging camp there and a sawmill nearby on the Somo River. It
had been abandoned when the railroad was built. The sidetrack was put in so that work
trains could pass each other.

Trippsville   *Vernon County*
A post office was established in 1867 and named after the postmaster, Dier Tripp.

Trout Creek   *Crawford County*
It was given this name because of the plentiful and tasty trout in the waters.

Troy   *Sauk County*

Jonathan W. Harris chose the name after his former home in Troy, Miami County, Ohio. Troy was a famous city in ancient Asia Minor.

Troy   *Walworth County*

An early name for this settlement was Meacham after a tavern keeper known as Major Meacham. Another local tavern owned by Austin McCracken gave the name McCracken's for a short time. The first settlers came from Troy in New York.

Troy Center   *Walworth County*

This community was created by the railroad company because a station was needed here at a meeting of highways. In 1871 the railroad company bought land from Gardiner Briggs and laid out a village plat. A post office was established, as well as a hotel, stores, a warehouse, a blacksmith shop, and about thirty comfortable homes. It was named Troy Center because it was located in the center of the township.

Truax   *Eau Claire County*

Peter Truax was an early settler and large landowner here. The railroad station was established in 1875.

Truax Field   *Dane County*

It was named for Thomas LeRoy Truax of Madison, a lieutenant in the Army Air Force, who was killed in an airplane crash in 1941.

True Hollow   *Crawford County*

Part of Seneca Township. It was named for the families that lived here.

Trumbull Island   *Richland County*

Part of this island is in Richland County. The island was once owned by James Trumbull.

Tunnel City   *Monroe County*

The first settlement in 1850 was a station on the stagecoach trail known as the Blue Ridge Road. It consisted of several houses and the station, which furnished fresh horses for the long journey over the western ridge of hills. Several years later the La Crosse and Milwaukee Railroad, which later became the Chicago, Milwaukee, St. Paul, and Pacific, sent surveyors through Monroe County to choose a route for a new railroad line.

Since the ridge of hills was considered impassable, other routes were investigated. But a Mr. Jackson and a Mr. Moll, both landowners, were each trying to get the right-of-way over their own townships, even though it meant crossing the ridge. Mr. Moll won the decision for Greenfield township by offering more land. The new tracks were laid up to the ridge on both sides. The trains then crawled up the hill to the old stagecoach station that became Tunnel City. Here the passengers got off and walked over the hill to a train on the other side and continued their journey to La Crosse. Freight was hauled over the ridge by a team of horses.

This was a cumbersome business until the Weber Transfer Company thought of a better plan. Tracks were laid over the ridge, and a capstan post was erected on the brow of the hill, with teams of oxen driven around it to make it turn. Cables were fastened to the railroad cars, and they were pulled up the hill, then across the top, and then lowered to the other side. Freight was hauled in this way until the first tunnel through the hill was built in 1861. The tunnel was an enormous job, as it was done with pick and shovel, the sand and rock hauled out with wheelbarrows. It was cribbed up with timbers, and there were a number of earth slides before it was completed.

Turtle Lake   *Barron County*
Joel Richardson, one of the first settlers, named the town Skowhagen after his hometown in Maine. However, the lake had been named Turtle Lake in 1862 by government surveyors who noticed many turtles laying eggs on the bank. Later the Knapp Stout Lumber Company operated several logging camps on both sides of both Upper and Lower Turtle Lakes. Logs were hauled onto the ice in winter and driven downstream to the mills at Menomonie. After the Chicago and North Western Railway was built past the lakes, the lumber company began to use it for shipping their supplies, designating that they be unloaded at Turtle Lake instead of at the town. When the post office was established, it was also designated Turtle Lake, so the other name for the town was dropped.

Tuscobia   *Barron County*
This name was adapted from the Indian word tuscola, which meant "a level place."

Tustin   *Waushara County*
From the 1870s through to 1920 it was a thriving village and trading center. Not only the most important steamboat and sawmill center in the Lake Poygan area before the automobile-railroad era, it was also a popular mecca for duck hunters in the early years. It is now a favorably located residential lakeside area on the north shore of Lake Poygan in Waushara and Winnebago Counties. Thomas H. Tustin, an early settler and landowner, had this community named for himself.

Twin Bluffs   *Richland County*
At first this little "town" with no school, no church, and no cemetery was known as "Bug Town." In 1876 when there was to be a railroad depot here, the name seemed inappropriate. George Reed suggested "Twin Bluffs" for the two bluffs that seemed to stand guard over the little village. Part of Buena Vista Township.

Twin Lakes   *Kenosha County*
The community was settled about 1842, although General John Bullen is said to have built a tavern in 1837 on the main road at the Fox River to accommodate travelers. The Immesan family was the first to have twins, named Mary and Elizabeth. One day at a picnic it was decided to name the lakes Twin Lakes, and the town later adopted the same name.

Two Creeks   *Manitowoc County*
This town was originally called Rowley after Peter Rowley, who was one of the first men to establish businesses and homes here. For some reason the citizens petitioned to change the name to Two Creeks. Two creeks empty into the lake here.

Two Rivers *Manitowoc County*

The earliest mention of this site is a notation in the logbook of His Majesty's Sloop Felic-ity, which is recorded in the Wisconsin Historical Collection, volume 11, page 211. On November 4, 1779, pilot Samuel Roberts speaks of a certain trader named Monsieur Fay being at a place called Deux Riviers eighteen leagues from Millwakey to the north. The settlement must have started from travel on the Great Lakes at a very early date. It was named Two Rivers because of its location between the two rivers known as the North and South Twin Rivers.

⇉ U ⇇

Ula
Ulao
Port Ulao   *Ozaukee County*

This is an abandoned place with many roots in the historical past. James T. Gifford came here in 1847 to build a lake port on the site of what had been an Indian village. He hired surveyors Luther Guiteau and J. Wilson Guiteau to plat about fifty acres into streets and lots. He built a one-thousand-foot pier into the lake for loading cordwood onto ships.

The first macadam road in the country (a mixture of charcoal and clay) was built to the site. As wood was cut in clearing the farmlands of the surrounding countryside it was hauled to Port Ulao and sold to the lake ships for fuel. A Mr. Burhop had taken his load of cordwood onto the pier when his horses shied, and the wagon, wood, driver, and horses were tipped into the lake, where all were drowned and lost. A fishing station was added to the pier where fishing boats docked to clean and smoke their fish. By 1853 Daniel Wells and John Howe took over the project, but it soon declined as ships stopped using wood for fuel. The lake eroded the cliffs and shoreline, and only a few pilings of the pier are left.

West of the village there was a feed mill and the Ghost Town Tavern, near what was known as Ulao Station on the Chicago and North Western Railway.

The name is thought to have been adopted from an American general named Ulao who landed at the port sometime in the 1850s. He was a descendant of French Huguenots, and his name may have been spelled Ulaeua or in some other way, as efforts to trace him have been unsuccessful. There is also a story that the abandoned Ulao station was given this name because the train's whistle sounded like "You Lay-Oh." Charles Guiteau, the assassin of President Garfield, lived here until hanged for his crime in 1881. He was the grandson of General John R. Howe and the son of Luther Guiteau, the surveyor.

Underbill   *Oconto County*

This was a Menominee village called Kak-wani-kone, meaning "crossing the portage," since this was one end of the portage between the Oconto River and Lake Shawano. Settlers moved in during the late 1870s. William F. Underbill, from Vermont, built a store, sawmill, and creamery. He had a small herd of Ayrshire cattle that he tended himself, and he churned the cream for butter that was sold in his store. He married late and had one son, also named William. The Chicago and North Western Railway built through here in 1880, abandoned in 1936. There was also a saw and planing mill that flourished from 1900 to 1920.

Union   *Burnett County*

Captain D. W. Fox, a pioneer settler on Yellow Lake, chose this name in honor of the Union forces in which he served during the Civil War. He was attached to the staff of General Sexton and became prominent in local, county, and GAR affairs.

Union   *Eau Claire County*

The township was originally Oak Grove, later West Eau Claire. No explanation is given for the change.

Union   *Grant County*

According to one old-timer, the name was chosen because of the united meetings held here when folks had good times.

Union Church   *Racine County*

Several church denominations joined together to build a church.

Union Grove   *Racine County*

John E. Dunham built the first home on eighty acres of land that he had purchased in 1838. The first school was built in 1846 and called Union School. The village is presumed to have been named by Governor Dodge, who combined the school's name with "Grove" for the beautiful grove of burr oak trees on the west side of the highway.

Unity   *Clark and Marathon Counties*

Edmund Creed was the first settler in the area and was also the first postmaster. This is his account of how it was named: "When a post office was asked for at this place, Brighton was sent to the Post Office Department as the name selected, but as there was already a Brighton in the state, we tried again and sent in the name Maple Grove, only to be informed that there also was an office of that name in the state. Some now wanted this name and some another, and before we could come to an agreement the department took the matter into its own hands and gave the new office the name of Unity. The officials at Washington evidently were a 'unit' on that name, if the citizens of this place were not, and I was named as the first postmaster. There was some kicking because I was a Democrat, and in order to bring about peace in our little family of pioneers, I refused to accept the office, and John Sterling was appointed."

In 1931 Mrs. Edmund Creed, then a widow, gave this account: "When Uncle Sam asked that a name be selected for the new community, I suggested Maple Grove. Uncle Sam already had a post office in Wisconsin by that name, so I suggested the name be Unity, as the people of the community were so united."

Unity   *Trempealeau County*

When the town was organized, Dennis Lawler felt he was entitled to the honor of having it named after him. But P. B. Williams, another early settler, wanted to name it Unity after the town in Maine from which he came. Noah Comstock suggested the two draw lots. Williams drew the longest cut and won.

Usakewik   *Marinette County*

The name of a Menominee Indian village at the mouth of the Peshtigo River, meaning "at the mouth."

Upham   *Langlade County*

The township was named in honor of William H. H. Upham, governor of Wisconsin from 1895 to 1897.

Upson   *Iron County*

Three surveyors, one of them named Upson, laid out this town when lumbering and iron mining drew settlers to the area.

Utah   *Pierce County*

A local mill owner's leaning toward Mormonism was responsible for the name of this community. The settlement no longer exists.

Utica   *Winnebago County*

Edward B. Ransom came from New York in 1841, traveling with his oxteam, dog, and gun. He was charmed with the lovely and fertile country here and built a double log house, twelve by sixteen feet, with a hall through the center. One section was often filled with visitors and newcomers. Fish, venison, and prairie chickens were plentiful and made many good meals for weary and hungry travelers.

Indians often camped nearby, hunting and trapping. An Indian once called at Mr. Ransom's house and asked for bread and meat, saying he had no money but would come back in three days and pay. Mrs. Ransom gave him a loaf of bread and told him to go and that he was welcome to it. He took the bread, set his gun in the corner of the room, and left. In three days he returned with some venison, took his gun, and seemed very pleased with the trade.

The Reverend Hiram McKee, John Thrall, E. B. Fisk, and George Ransom were also early settlers here. Mr. McKee was the first minister in the town and was noted for his energetic style of preaching. After the last round of logs had been placed in position in one of the homes, Reverend McKee stepped on the porch of the building and proposed then and there that the town be given a name. The names of several of the settlers were proposed, but each declined the honor. The name Utica was proposed and adopted, probably after the city of this name in New York State. For a time it was also known as Utica Center. In 1865 it was changed to Weelaunee, probably an Indian name, but in 1867 it was changed back to Utica.

Utley   *Green Lake County*

It was named after Charles Utley, assistant superintendent of a division of the Chicago, Milwaukee, and St. Paul Railroad. The village of Utley was settled when a granite quarry was opened on the site after a railroad spur line was built from Brandon to Markesan in 1883. A depot, hotels, taverns, stores, and houses were constructed. When the quarry shut down, the community was abandoned. The depot was removed in 1904, and nothing remains today but the open quarry.

The Valders train station, ca. 1912

⇥ V ⇤

Valders *Manitowoc County*

Norwegian immigrants settled here from 1840 to 1860. A church was built, called Valders Norwegian Southern Church, as most of the settlers were from Valders in Norway. The Wisconsin Central Railroad built its track through the settlement from Neenah to Manitowoc. On July 4, 1895, the people all came out to witness the first train—a locomotive, a baggage car, and one coach. Officials of the railroad company inspecting the road were the only passengers. When they arrived and saw so many people gathered, the train stopped and they inquired about a name for the station. There was no reply. One officer looked off to the southwest and saw the church spire. He asked if that was a church and if it had a name. The citizens told him, and he then said that Valders would be a good name for the railroad station. The citizens agreed.

Valley *Vernon County*

Originally called "The Corners," it gradually came to be known as Valley, probably because of the terrain. It was settled in the 1840s, and the first business was started in 1877.

Valton *Sauk County*

This name was probably a contraction of Vale Town or Valley Town.

Van Buren *Rock County*

Laid out and platted in 1836, but since deserted. It was probably named for Martin Van Buren.

Vanceberg *Dunn County*

The site of what is purported to be the last Indian battle in Wisconsin, where a band of Ojibwe was attacked at "sugaring time" and massacred by a band of Sioux. Sources are not agreed on the date of this occurrence, but it was sometime near 1860. It is also the site of a vanished village once occupied by a fur trading post, sawmill, flour mill, dam and mill pond, post office, stagecoach stop, and school. Named after the pioneer Vance family, it is located six miles west of Ridgeland in the northern part of the county.

Vance Hollow *Crawford County*

Located at the middle of Bear Creek in the Township of Clayton, it is named for a family called Vance.

Van Dyne *Fond du Lac County*

In 1850 the State of Wisconsin granted 165 acres to Jonathan Goff. Later this parcel of land came into the possession of Daniel R. Van Dyne and in 1866 it was laid out into lots. The village consisted of a grocery store, feed or gristmill, blacksmith shop, cheese factory, and hotel and some old farm buildings.

Veazie   *Washburn County*

This town was originally built as a headquarters for the logging camps in the vicinity by George Veazie, a logger from Stillwater. A large dam built here on the Namekagon River in 1878 backed up the water and raised it some eight feet. Here logs were stored and then flooded downriver to the junction with the St. Croix River. Mr. Veazie built a town hall only about twelve by fourteen feet in size and placed a sign on it that read "Town of Veazie."

Vermont   *Dane County*

Old settlers named the community in honor of the Green Mountain State, from which they had come.

Vernon   *Waukesha County*

Settlers from Vermont are said to have selected this name because it sounded much like Vermont. It was once called The Burg because a German called Fritz kept a small hotel there. The first post office was established in Asa Flint's log house. The settlement was called Vernon Center for a number of years.

Vernon County

The county was first named Bad Ax after the Bad Ax River flowing through it. The Indian name for the river was Minnesheik, meaning "bad ax." It is said the Indians found the stones at the mouth of the river too soft to make good axes.

Bad Ax as a name sounded too warlike. County Judge Silvester Fish, a boyhood friend of George Vernon Weeks, who lived in the county, is said to have chosen the new name. Another account says that Judge William F. Terhune selected the name after George Washington's home, Mount Vernon, and because the word means green, and there were many green fields in the county.

Vernon Station   *Waukesha County*

When the Soo Line Railroad was built, a depot was established here known as Savannah Station on the edge of the Big Vernon Township marsh. A village was platted but never built.

Verona   *Dane County*

For many years this settlement was known as The Corners because it was at a crossing of main traveled roads. The north-south road was built by the army from Galena, Illinois, to Green Bay in Wisconsin. Lead and zinc ores taken from Mineral Point to Milwaukee brought about the east-west road. Some of the early settlers came from Verona in New York State, and one of them, William Vroman, suggested this name. It was first called Verona Corners, and then just Verona in 1848.

Vesper   *Wood County*

This community was started as a sawmill town in 1872 and was almost entirely destroyed by fire on August 28, 1894. The first settlers were a bachelor, Sam Boyington, and Mr. and Mrs. Joseph White. In trying to select a suitable name the citizens came up with

Hardscrabble, which was said to describe accurately the life in those early days. A Mr. Cameron of the Sherry-Cameron Lumber Company set up a post office and asked the Post Office Department to select a more suitable name. Vesper was chosen, and Mr. Cameron became the first postmaster in 1882.

Veteran   *Burnett County*
Captain D. W. Fox of the Pennsylvania Voluntary Infantry selected this name for the settlement on the west side of Big Yellow Lake to commemorate veterans of the Civil War.

Viall's Spring   *Dane County*
Andrew Viall acquired this property in 1859. The spring was obliterated when the Nakoma Country Club fairways were graded, but the water still flows across the golf course, eventually running into Lake Wingra.

Victory   *Vernon County*
The Battle of Bad Ax, which ended the Black Hawk War, was won near here in 1832.

Vienna   *Walworth County*
The community was first called Martinsburg, after the John Martin family who lived here. Winslow Page Storms built Vienna House here in 1848, a store, tavern, and post office. It is said that Mr. Storms came from a town named Vienna in New York State.

Vilas   *Dane County*
Vilas County
William Freeman Vilas of Madison moved to Wisconsin from Vermont and graduated from the University of Wisconsin in 1858. He was US postmaster general from 1885 to 1888, secretary of the interior for the next three years, and later a US senator.

Vinegar Ridge   *Crawford County*
Located in Haney Township. Also known as Burton Ridge. The vineyard quality was poor, hence the name.

Vineyard Coulee   *Crawford County*
Located in Bridgeport and Prairie du Chien. George Jacob Schoeffer brought to this area some grape culture from Alsace-Lorraine, France.

Vinney O'Malley's Hill   *Dane County*
Vincent O'Malley owned this land in the 1890s. The hill is the highest in Westport.

Viola   *Richland and Vernon Counties*
The first settlers arrived in 1854, and the village was laid out and platted the next year. In 1857 Viola Mach was born and given a lot because she was the first child born in the village to European settlers. Cyrus Turner bought out Mr. Mach's holdings and established the first post office, naming it Viola.

Viroqua *Vernon County*

Moses Decker settled here in 1846, and four years later the city was surveyed, platted, and named Farwell after Governor Farwell. In 1854 an official act of the county board changed the name to Viroqua, but there is no record of why.

There is a story that Viroqua was an Indian maiden, daughter of Chief Black Hawk, who drove her pony off a high cliff to escape capture by settlers, but facts indicate that Black Hawk did not have a daughter. One account says Viroqua was the name of an Indian girl in a novel. Another says she was a Mohawk Indian girl who performed in an eastern theater, where a Connecticut man who saw her liked the name and bestowed it on the Farwell settlement. Still another states: "Viroqua, sister of Dr. Oronhyetetha, the distinguished Mohawk Indian, was head of a troup of Indians giving entertainments at the Opera House in Brantford, Canada."

Voelker's Mills *Ozaukee County*

This is another one of Wisconsin's lost towns. Ernest Schmidt built a dam and erected a sawmill on the Milwaukee River here, four miles north of Saukville, in 1860. In 1875 V. Voelker became a partner and added a gristmill. The sawmill and dam were swept away in the flood of 1881 but were immediately rebuilt, and the place was called Voelker's Mills. George Kendall kept a store and saloon here for a number of years. The hamlet was later incorporated into Saukville.

Voree *Walworth County*

This settlement, in the town of Spring Prairie, was founded by Jesse James Strang, a Mormon, in 1844. He intended to build a city and temple here, but in 1847 he fled with his disciples to Mackinaw Straits. It is not known whether he found the name for his holy city in the Book of Mormon, or whether it was revealed to him in another way. Voree means "garden of peace." From the Beloit Herald, 1906:

> In Walworth county lives the sole survivor of the Wisconsin Mormon church, founded at Voree Sept. 13, 1845. Wingfield Watson, now nearing the end of his run of life, is still vigorous, and enthusiastic in his defense of the Mormon faith and its Wisconsin leader, James Jesse Strang.
>
> The founding of the settlement at Voree is one of the interesting stories of early Wisconsin. It was in Spring Prairie township, Walworth county, that followers of Joseph Smith took up with the new leader and founded the village of Voree.
>
> Strang bought 200 acres of fine land. The place was platted and named Voree, a name that hangs to it yet.
>
> Strang proceeded to appoint patriarchs, high priests, twelve apostles and "likewise a following of seventy."
>
> On September 13, 1845, everything being ready, Strang directed Aaron Smith, high priest Jirah B. Walker, J. M. Van Ostrand and Edward Whitcomb to an oak tree on the east line of Spring Prairie township. Digging beneath the roots of this tree there was unearthed three golden plates in a case of baked clay. The priest reported the find and Strang translated the inscription to mean that Joseph Smith had appointed him as his successor.

A number of houses were erected at Voree and a small city was soon built. In one of the buildings that is still standing was published a paper known as the Voree Herald. Later it became the Reveille, and finally the Gospel Herald.

Strang, although the possessor of one legal and faithful wife, at once "sealed" to himself a second wife, then a third, and soon afterwards a fourth. Mrs. Strang, the first wife, then returned with her children to her former home in Indiana.

It is alleged that Strang became so insolent and overbearing, practiced so many gross deceptions that an unbeliever named Scott set up a rival newspaper and attempted to unmask the prophet. Affairs at Voree began to go from bad to worse, until in 1847 Strang claimed to have received a revelation to move to Beaver Island, in Lake Michigan, and most of the outfit pulled up stakes and followed their leader.

Strang announced a revelation which declared that he was to be "King in Zion." He was crowned on July 8, 1850, with a metal crown having a cluster of stars, and burnt offerings were included in the program.

The downfall of Strang and his little kingdom came suddenly and in an unexpected manner. He decreed that the female members should wear a certain hideous costume of calico pantalettes, a garment that came to the ankles and resembled trousers. Over this was to be worn a flimsy skirt that reached the knee, with waists that were absolutely straight without a tuck, ruffle or puff. Beads, jewelry and all personal adornments were forbidden and the hair was to be "combed back and braided tight."

One brave woman, the wife of Thomas Bedford, flatly refused to don the toggery and although labored with persistently and at last threatened, she maintained her insubordination. Finally her husband was charged with encouraging his wife in her obstinacy, for which he was tied to the whipping post and unmercifully whipped.

The scene attending the diabolical scourging of Bedford aroused intense feeling all over the island, for he was deservedly one of the most highly esteemed men in the church. The female members joined in upholding Mrs. Bedford and encouraging her all they dared. The indignation grew to such intensity that finally one Alexander Wentworth, with his friend Bedford, conspired to commit regicide. Secretly they planned to shoot the king on the first opportunity. They had not long to wait. On July 9, 1856, the day after celebrating the royal anniversary, Wentworth shot Strang through the body with his rifle. Strang fell, mortally wounded, while Wentworth and Bedford immediately confessed their crime and gave themselves up, but they were never tried for the offense.

With the death of Strang the kingdom of the Latter Day Saints on Beaver Island fell.

Voree in Walworth county of today is a deserted place with a number of tumble-down stone buildings.

Wingfield Watson still believes in the divine calling of Strang as a prophet, seer, and apostle of Jesus Christ. He lives on one of the choicest farms in Spring Prairie township. Thomas Watson, his son, is the manager of the property, which is well stocked with sleek cattle, including a dairy herd. The home is surrounded with orchards, while the garden, the proprietor's pet, is a nursery of grapes, berries and small fruit. Mr. Watson was born in Ireland about seventy years ago, and by application and perseverance has acquired a good education. He joined with Strang on Beaver Island, and his loyalty, zeal, and superior qualifications soon distinguished him with his chief. All the records, books, papers and church property, including its most sacred emblems, are still in his keeping. His home is a museum of Mormon literature.

⇢ W ⇠

Wabeno   *Forest County*

This is the title of the fourth degree of the Medicine Lodge among the Ojibwe and Potawatomi Indians and denotes that they are conjurers and magicians in practicing medicine. It means "wise men," "crafty magicians," or "mysterious men." Another account tells of a tornado that passed through this area from Antigo northeast to Upper Michigan, leveling the forest. When the Indians came to this open area they called it wabeno, meaning "coming of light" or "rising sun."

Waboo   *Price County*

From the Ojibwe, wabus, meaning "rabbit."

Wachuta Ridge   *Crawford County*

Named for the Wachuta family, who have been longtime residents. It is located in Prairie du Chien Township at the junction of Limery Ridge on 27 east to Gran Grae.

Wade House   *Sheboygan County*

Built by Sylvanus Wade between 1847 and 1851 at a total cost of $300. Meetings for the discussion of Civil War issues were held here. It became the most important stagecoach stop on the plank road between Sheboygan and Fond du Lac.

Wagon Landing   *Polk County*

Pioneer settlers hauling lumber from the mills at St. Croix Falls found they could ford the Apple River here.

Wah-Bau-Ga O-Ning-Ah-Minh   *Portage County*

The Indian name for the portage trail between the Wolf and Wisconsin Rivers used by both Ojibwe and Menominee Indians. They carried their canoes on their heads the distance of eight miles between the two streams.

Wakefield   *Vilas County*

Named after an early settler, John Wakefield.

Walbridge   *Douglas County*

This was a railroad station named after Horace S. Walbridge of Toledo, who once tried to build a railroad here. A money panic interfered, and the project failed.

Waldo   *Sheboygan County*

In 1870 O. H. Waldo, a prominent lawyer of Milwaukee, E. D. Holten, and a Mr. Hilbert were the promoters of a railroad from Milwaukee to Green Bay. The township of Lyndon voted a $1,500 bond issue to aid the project, and by the fall of 1871 trains were running.

The railroad was called the Milwaukee and Northern Railroad, now the Chicago, Milwaukee, and St. Paul. The same year eighty acres were platted for a new village called Lora. Later the railroad company renamed it Lyndon Station, but as there already was a Lyndon Station in Juneau County, the name was changed to Waldo, after Mr. Waldo, who became president of the company.

Wales   Waukesha County
In the spring of 1840 John Hughes and his family set sail for America from Cardiganshire, Wales, finally settling in South Prairieville about four miles southwest of Waukesha. They found the hills, the fish and game, as well as the soil of this glacial drift area very attractive. Other Welsh settlers followed, and by 1853 there were some eighteen hundred people in the area. Old Government Hill and the village of Wales were near the center of the community.

Walhain   Kewaunee County
Florian Strickman, who settled here in the 1850s, came from Walhain in Belgium.

Wall Ridge   Crawford County
A large number of Wall families settled in the area, located in Eastman Township.

Walworth   Walworth County
Christopher Douglass broke ground on the prairie in 1837, plowing furrows two and one-half miles long. Later he built the first tavern, which became known as Douglass Corners. Just to the north was Bell's Corners, a trading center where a post office had been established since 1839. By 1851 the post office was transferred to Douglass Corners and renamed after the county.

Walworth County
Colonel Samuel F. Phoenix, founder of Delavan, suggested that the county be named in honor of Reuben Hyde Walworth, the last chancellor of New York State; the chancery court was abolished at the close of his term. He was known as a great equity jurist and a man of outstanding character in temperance work and other movements. Walworth was one of the very first counties in Wisconsin.

Waneka   Dunn County
An Ojibwe word meaning "he digs a hole" or "he excavates."

Wanless Hollow   Richland County
Archibald Wanless arrived in the spring of 1852. Located in Marshall Township.

Ward Ridge   Crawford County
An old pioneer by the name of Henry Ward lent his name to this ridge. It is located in Clayton Township.

Warrens   *Monroe County*

When the West Wisconsin Railroad Company built their line to this site in 1868, George Warren and James Gamble unloaded a small sawmill and started sawing pine logs into lumber. The settlement was called Warrens' Mills. Three years later the post office was established, and in 1892 the name was shortened to Warrens.

Warren Springs   *Dodge County*

In 1845 James H. Warren settled near Mayville at this onetime Indian settlement that had a spring.

Warsaw   *Rock County*

From Horace McElroy's The Forgotten Places:

> *The late Silas Hurd, who was one of the pioneer settlers of Rock County, used to tell the following story. One evening a stranger came to his home on the East side of Rock River and asked for a night's lodging, which of course was given to him. The stranger stated that he was from New York City, and complained bitterly of the hardships he had experienced on his journey West.*
>
> *In the course of conversation he asked Mr. Hurd how he could reach a place called Warsaw. Mr. Hurd told him that unfortunately his only boat was smashed up, and that there was no other within some miles of his place. "But," he said, "you go right down back of my house and swim Rock River easy enough. Then you will go about half a mile North and about a mile East, and there you will find a lot of stakes stuck in the ground. That's Warsaw."*
>
> *"But are there no houses there?" asked the man from New York City. "Not a house," Mr. Hurd replied, "there's nothing but stakes."*
>
> *"Well," the stranger said, "that settles it. I have bought a lot of property in Warsaw, and have been assured that it is a growing, thriving place with great possibilities in the near future, and I've had a good, tough time getting this far. If there's nothing but stakes in Warsaw, I don't care to look at it; and anyway, I wouldn't swim Rock River for all the land in this township. I'll go back to New York and get after the man who sold me corner lots in Warsaw."*

Wasa-Waugan   *Vilas County*

At the end of Lake Flambeau, on both sides of Bear River, is the Indian village now known as The Old Village. It has been in existence since very early times. The Ojibwe name is Wasa-Waugan, meaning "torch river."

Wascott   *Douglas County*

When the Chicago, St. Paul, Minneapolis, and Omaha Railroad was built north of Superior Junction, now the town of Trego, a section house was erected at this site for the men maintaining the tracks. It was named Twentieth Mile House, because it was twenty miles from Superior Junction. When a telegraph office was installed, a shorter name was needed. The president of the railroad at that time was W. A. Scott.

Washburn County

After the lumber mill was started on the shore of Shell Lake, the settlement grew rapidly, and by 1883 the people decided to separate from Burnett County to form Washburn County, named in honor of Cadwallader C. Washburn, governor of Wisconsin from 1872 to 1874. Washburn had come from the state of Maine to Mineral Point and served as congressman from this district for five terms. For many years he was president of the State Historical Society, and he gave the university its observatory.

Washington *Eau Claire County*

The first settlers were farmers who came to the area in 1852. The township was established in 1866 and named for President George Washington.

Washington *La Crosse County*

This township was named Buchanan when it became independent in 1857. But President Buchanan was unpopular in the vicinity, so the name was changed in honor of President George Washington.

Washington County

Named in honor of the first president of the United States.

Washington Island *Door County*

The Indian name was Me-she-ne-mah-ke-ming, or "leader island," probably because of its position in the island group at the head of the Door County Peninsula. After the War of 1812 this became US territory. Colonel Miller was sent to Green Bay in 1816 to take command. He brought five hundred men and considerable supplies on four large sailing vessels. They named the largest island in the bay Washington Island after the flagship of their fleet, which had been named in honor of our first president.

Waterford *Racine County*

Samuel Chapman and Levi Barnes were the first to settle here in 1839. Indians living in the area crossed the Fox River at this site by fording it. Oldsters believe the name was derived from the ford across the Fox River.

Waterford Woods *Racine County*

This wooded area in the Township of Waterford on the west bank of the Fox River was developed in 1927 by Willis J. Mehan and S. H. Harris Jr. It became a popular summer colony during the 1930s and 1940s, and during the 1950s the area was rezoned for permanent homes.

Waterloo *Jefferson County*

The Indian name of this site was Maunesha when Bradford Hill, the first settler, came. Waterloo is said to have been suggested by the battle of Waterloo.

Watertown *Dodge and Jefferson Counties*

The Indians called this area Ka-Ka-ree, meaning "oxbow," which describes the double bend in the Rock River here. The first settler was Timothy Johnson from Connecticut by way of Ohio. When he heard of the fertile land and abundance of game in the Territory of Wisconsin he sold his farm in Ohio and began to explore the Rock River Valley in 1836. At one place he recognized the potential value of the rapids in the river where there was a spring of good water nearby, and entered a claim for one thousand acres of land. He named the site Johnson's Rapids, built a cabin for his family, and encouraged others to come to share his claim. Mr. Johnson himself may have changed the name to Watertown, after the town in New York State.

Watertown Plank Road   Milwaukee County
This $100,000 road of white oak planks extended fifty-eight miles west from Milwaukee on a course roughly paralleling State Street, running past the Frederick Miller Plank Road Brewery through Wauwatosa, Pewaukee, and Oconomowoc to Watertown.

Waubeek   Pepin County
A big hill in this township was called Waubeek after an Indian woman. All evidence of the Indian village is gone, but apparently settlers mentioned the hill often by its Indian name, and it was adopted for the township also.

Waubeka   Ozaukee County
The Indian village of Chief Waubeka was located here on the north shore of the Milwaukee River.

Waubesa   Dane County
This is the Indian word for "swan," and there was a story that a large swan had been killed on the lake. The settlement took the name of the lake.

Waubesee Lake   Racine County
The name is an Indian word that has several possible meanings: "Mark in the center of the hair for clan mark, yellow or red," or "swan lake," or "a white bird flies along," or "swan." Waubesee Lake is the original name, but it was changed to Minister Lake during the time the parsonage of the Norway Lutheran Church was located on the lake, and then it was later renamed Waubesee Lake. It is found in Norway Township.

Waucousta   Fond du Lac County
The name is an adaption of Waukeag, an Indian word for a glacial kame, several of which mark the landscape.

Waukau   Winnebago County
An Indian chief by this name lived here for a time. The word is also thought to be the name of the Indian priest of the Grand Medicine Lodge who directed the initiation rites of candidates aspiring to become members.

Waukechon   Shawano County
Waukechon was a chief of the Menominee Indians. His name meant "crooked nose."

Waukesha   *Waukesha County*

Morris D. Cutler was the first settler to come here in 1834. Five years later W. A. Barstow built a gristmill on the shores of the Fox River. An Indian village called Tchee-ga-scou-tak had been located here. The name meant "burned land" or "fire land" and referred to the frequent prairie fires that ravaged the countryside. Settlers called the community Prairieville. When the county of Waukesha was formed, Prairieville was the leading settlement, so it was named the county seat. The name was then changed to Waukesha.

Waukesha County

When this county was separated from Milwaukee County, an Indian name was wanted. Waukesha was suggested because it was the Potawatomi word for "fox," and the Fox River, named for the Fox Indians, drains into Illinois from this area.

Waumadee   *Buffalo County*

It was named after a creek by the Ho-Chunk Indians. Waumadee means "clear creek."

Waunakee   *Dane County*

There are two accounts of how this settlement was established:

1. In 1870 the Chicago and North Western Railway was extending its line through this area to St. Paul. The route selected was two miles away from the present site of Waunakee, and it was planned to erect the depot at Peckham's Mill. Mr. Lewis Baker persuaded George Fish to join him in influencing the railroad company to change its proposed route. Railroad company officials demanded $1,500 and a two-mile right-of-way through the new area. Mr. Baker and Mr. Fish were able to raise the money by bonds and notes. When the new village site was chosen, citizens asked that it be named Lester, as this was the name of the nearest post office located near the Ferdinand Wilke farm. But these citizens who wanted to choose the name had refused to contribute toward the funds raised, so Mr. Baker and Mr. Fish refused them that honor. The two men then consulted Simon Miller and a Mr. Hill, Madison bankers, who submitted a list of names. Waunakee was among them and was chosen. It is an Indian word said to mean "you win," "sharp-shooter," "he lies," "he lives in peace," "he forgets something," or "he digs a hole."
2. The other account says that a flour mill and small settlement were established in the western part of Westport Township in 1850. In 1872 the Chicago and North Western Railway started building west from Madison, and plans were made for a new town site and depot. A squabble arose over the depot site and the price of land. Landowners put an exorbitant price on the property, hoping to make a killing. Two farmers named Baker and Bryant offered the necessary land free a mile to the west. The railroad was located on their land, and the new depot was named Waunakee after a friendly Indian who camped near the mill. Local citizens boast that there is no other place in the world with the name Waunakee.

Waunoma   *Richland County*

Robert G. Hurst and William McCollum platted this little hamlet in Buena Vista Township on June 13, 1853, naming it with the Indian word that means "pretty Indian maid." The settlement lasted only a few years.

Waupaca and Waupaca County

A number of interpretations are given for the meaning of this Indian name: "where one waits to shoot deer," "stalling place," "looking on," "white sand bottom," "pale water," and "the place of clear water." One interpretation claims it meant all of these things and also "tomorrow."

Waupee Lake   *Forest County*

It means "looking at it," from the name of a Potawatomi chief.

Waupun   *Fond du Lac County*

In 1839 the first settler, Seymour Wilcox, came here from a town called Madrid in the state of Vermont. He called his new home Madrid also. The next year a post office was established, with Mr. Wilcox as the first postmaster. But James Duane Doty, then a congressman from Wisconsin, had given Mr. Wilcox his commission and wanted an Indian name for the town. Mr. Doty's choice was Waubun, meaning "early light of day" or "dawn." Due to a mistake in spelling or writing, or poor eyesight, the name appeared as Waupun, and the township accepted it when it was formally organized in 1842.

Wausau   *Marathon County*

Voyageurs of the American Fur Company traveling north from the Indian station at Dubay heard a roaring sound that investigation proved to be falls or rapids in the Wisconsin River. To them it resembled the lowing of a bull, so they named the site Big Bull Falls. George Stevens of Stevens Point acquired property rights from the Indians here so he could use the waterpower. He built a sawmill in 1839.

Within a few years a settlement clustered about the falls. The honorable W. D. McIndoe selected the pretty Indian word wausau as a more fitting name for the town. The word means "far away." Perhaps the Ojibwe used this word in speaking of the place because it was far away from their ancestral hunting grounds in eastern Canada.

Wausaukee   *Marinette County*

John S. Monroe, an enterprising Yankee from New York State, came to Kenosha (then Southport), Wisconsin, in 1847. He had learned the shipbuilding trade at the New York shipyards and built his first important craft, the Lewis C. Irwin, on Lake Michigan.

Later he came to the Wausaukee site to establish a mill for preparing and marketing cedar posts. The nearest neighbor for the pioneer family was at the old Kitson Trading Post of the Northwest Fur Company, almost four miles away. He was influential in getting a railroad built to his site, and other pioneers moved in.

In time Mr. Monroe became the owner of a blacksmith shop, three teams of horses, several buildings, and most of the town plot of 160 acres. He built the first scow for transporting supplies and lumber between ships and shore at Oconto. He also built scows for the Norton Company, operators and shippers on the Oconto River. No record is given of why the Indian name of Wausaukee was given to the town. The word means "river among the hills," "beyond the hill," or "faraway land." For many years the settlement was called Big Wausaukee, but subsequently "Big" was dropped.

Waushara County

A Ho-Chunk chief known as Big Fox had an Indian name that became corrupted to Waushara, which means "foxes." An ancient Ho-Chunk village near the outlet of Fox Lake in Dodge County was called Waushara, and Fox Lake was called Waushara Lake by the Indians. Since the Indians had given the name to prominent locations in the county, it seemed a fitting name.

Wautoma   *Waushara County*

From the Wautoma Journal, May 15, 1858:

> *The Town of Wautoma was first organized in April 1851, and then embraced the county. The name was formed from the two words wau (or waugh) and tomah. The first (wau) is a very common word in the Indian dialect, but does not always have the same meaning. It forms a syllable in the names of hundreds of towns, counties, and cities. The writer has many times endeavored to ascertain its exact definition, but never succeeded. It is sometimes used for "good," sometimes for "life," and occasionally for "ground" or "earth" and in fact seems to drop in naturally anywhere and express whatever the occasion requires.*
>
> *Tomah was the name of an Indian chief. Whether Wau-toma was chosen as an appropriate name for this "neck of the woods," as meaning the "land of Tomah," or in order to follow the prevailing fashion of Wisconsin, to "wau" everything we what not, tradition is silent on the subject.*

Jabez Nelson Rogers and Charles and John Sumway purchased a sawmill and started manufacturing lumber here in 1849. The three men as partners owned and laid out the town. It was necessary to have a post office, so Mr. Rogers made the application through General King of the Milwaukee Sentinel, choosing the name Wautoma.

Wauwatosa   *Milwaukee County*

Before the settlers came, Wauwautosa was a forest primeval of gigantic trees on a cluster of hills rising abruptly from the meandering Menomonee River. Wild game abounded, and hovering over the misty rice swamps in the early evenings were swarms of fireflies. "Wau-wau-tae-sie," said the Indians, when they beheld these mysterious blinking insects.

In 1835, New England settlers started to move in. Hart's Mills was the first name, because of the sawmill and gristmill owned by Charles Hart. In 1841 the town was organized. Among the names proposed was Rushville, after Rushville in New York State, from which many settlers had come, and also Bridgeport.

Daniel Proudfoot proposed Wauwautosa, the name of an Indian chief found in a book on treaties with the Indians that was owned by Byron Kilbourn of Milwaukee. The chief was said to be a "great walker" or a "jaunty walker." This name was accepted, and a Mr. Longstreet, a very short man, presented it to the legislature. Through some error the u in the second syllable was omitted, and it became legalized as we now spell it. Other interpretations of the Indian word are "what he works for," "what he earns," "dim memory," "I grabbed something," and "he shines as he walks."

Wauzeka   *Crawford County*

Around the year 1800, give or take twenty years, an Indian said to bear the name Wauzega established a permanent camp at the mouth of the Kickapoo River, half a day's trip down the Wisconsin River to Prairie du Chien, or a day's trip back up the river. It is not known to what tribe he belonged. The Kickapoo originally were native to the area but were chased out toward the east by the Sioux. However, a small segment of the original tribe returned to the Kickapoo Valley, where they perished of smallpox in 1876–77. It has been guessed, however, that Wauzega was an exile from the Ho-Chunk tribe.

The first post office was established two miles west in 1848 but was moved to the present location in 1856 where a settlement named Wauzeka had started. It is not known how Wauzeka was chosen instead of Wauzega, except that the former word could have been easier to pronounce for the settlers not acquainted with the Indian's language. The name is also claimed to have been the name of an Indian chief. It means "pine," "white pine," or "wrinkled."

Wauzeka Ridge   *Crawford County*

Named after the village, it is located in the Wauzeka area.

Wayne   *Lafayette County*

It was named in honor of Mad Anthony Wayne, a Revolutionary War general.

Wayne's Corners   *Polk County*

This previously unnamed business center grew up in recent years around a popular eating place started by Wayne Greenlee. When giving the location of any other establishments in the area, an informant will say, "It's over by Wayne's place."

Webb Lake   *Burnett County*

There is no village, only a township named for the largest lake in its boundaries, Webb Lake. The lake was first called Webb's Lake. Mr. Webb is claimed to have been an old trader with a poor reputation who had a trading post near its outlet. Another account says he was a logger from Stillwater.

In 1909 G. L. Miller went to Madison and had a special act passed by the legislature dividing Jackson Township into three smaller townships. At a meeting in Mr. Miller's home, the Webb Lake Township was called Harrison for the purpose of allotting the proportionate share of assets and liabilities of Jackson Township. Later it was suggested it be named Miller, but the people objected and voted to change it to Webb Lake. However, the earliest post office was at the home of a Mr. McDowell and was named for him. At a later date the office was moved near its present site and named Weblake because the department wanted one-word names. The township name was subsequently corrected to Webb Lake, and the post office was discontinued.

Weblake　　　　　　　　　　　　　　　　　　　*Burnett County*

Weblake, some forty-five miles northeast of Grantsburg, derived its name from Webb Lake.

Webster　　　　　　　　　　　　　　　　　　　*Burnett County*

In 1896 a new post office was established in the settlement called Clam River. J. D. Rice, the leading pioneer of the community, applied to Congressman John Jenkins to have it changed to Webster after Noah Webster, the great lexicographer.

Webster　　　　　　　　　　　　　　　　　　　*Vernon County*

On the 7th of April in 1856, a band of hardy pioneers and early settlers gathered together at the house of Sol Richardson to complete the organization of a new town. It was named Webster after Daniel Webster.

Wedge's Prairie　　　　　　　　　　　　　　　*Fond du Lac County*

In 1844 Salmon Wedge brought his family to this expansive prairie.

Weedens　　　　　　　　　　　　　　　　　　　*Sheboygan County*

This was a station named after George W. Weeden, a farmer and cheese factory owner.

Weinberg　　　　　　　　　　　　　　　　　　　*Dane County*

German, meaning "Vineyard-hill"; an early experiment in wine growing was made here. The name is remembered in the large local German settlement but is no longer much used.

Welker Hollow　　　　　　　　　　　　　　　　*Richland County*

John Welker (1815–1884) came to Forest Township in 1854.

Wells　　　　　　　　　　　　　　　　　　　　*Calumet County*

When a post office was established to serve the people in the northeast area of Calumet County, two names were sent to the community by the post office department. Wells was the one chosen.

Wells　　　　　　　　　　　　　　　　　　　　*Manitowoc County*

This township was named for Congressman Owen A. Wells.

Wentworth　　　　　　　　　　　　　　　　　　*Douglas County*

This was a station established on the Northern Pacific Railroad that was named after the Wentworth Lumber Company, a large concern that was operating in the county at this time.

Wequayong　　　　　　　　　　　　　　　　　　*Brown County*

A large Potawatomi village was once located on the present site of Green Bay and known by this Indian name. It means "small harbor."

Wequiock *Brown County*

This is an Ojibwe Indian word meaning "it forms a bay," "there is a bay," or "bladder."

Werley *Grant County*

The name was chosen in honor of a prominent citizen, Gottlieb Wehrle, with an anglicized spelling.

Werner *Juneau County*

In 1851 John Werner built the first sawmill in Necedah. He later sold the mill to B. S. Miner and moved to the settlement of Germantown, where he set up another mill. He platted a village here and changed the name to Werner.

West Allis *Milwaukee County*

The name is derived from the principal manufacturing plant, Allis-Chalmers, which had begun operations a few years prior to incorporation of the village. The company's main plant was still on Milwaukee's south side near the lakefront, and the second plant was generally spoken of as the West Allis plant.

There was strong factional feeling about the naming of the village at the time it was incorporated in 1902. One area was known as North Greenfield, and many people wanted to retain that name. Those who preferred West Allis sent out a notice that the meeting to decide the issue would be held at eight o'clock. Then they told all the people on their side to come to the meeting at seven o'clock, after which the doors were locked so the others could not get in. The village of Honey Creek, which lost its name and became a part of West Allis, is the oldest section of the present city.

West Bend *Washington County*

This is a combination of two early settlements that grew up around a sawmill and a gristmill founded by Byron Kilbourn and Barton Salisbury in 1845. One was called Salisbury's Mills, and later Barton. The other was called West Bend, because of the sharp horseshoe curve in the Milwaukee River at that point. It was incorporated in 1885. In 1961 the two merged as West Bend, the county seat of Washington County.

Westboro *Taylor County*

Old-timers came here to work in the tanning and logging industries in 1875 from Westboro in Massachusetts. In the early days the logs were piled on rolleyways on the bank of Silver Creek during the winter. They were marked with a steel mall to identify them later. When the ice thawed in the spring, men called river rats rolled them into the river, where they floated into Jump River and into the Chippewa River to Chippewa Falls. Here they were sawed into lumber and shipped to market. In later years a large sawmill and planing mill were built at Westboro.

Early Westboro was known as a hard town where there were many fights, some gunplay, and a few knifings. There were five saloons. There were two Italian settlements. The Italians baked their bread in a community oven built of rocks and fired with wood. They would bake about a hundred loaves of bread at a time. One account says that officials of the Wisconsin Central Railroad, who had come from Westboro in Massachusetts, chose the name.

Westby *Vernon County*

In 1879 the Chicago, Milwaukee, and St. Paul Railroad completed its branch line from Sparta to Viroqua and chose this site for a station. They named it in honor of Ole T. Westby, who had built a store here in 1867. The town was incorporated as a village in 1896 and became a city in 1920.

West Denmark *Polk County*

This is a tiny Danish community where the people have continued the customs and traditions of their native land.

Westfield *Marquette County*

Robert Cochrane, the founder of this community, came from Westfield in New York State.

Westford *Richland County*

Asa and Levi Lincoln came from Westford, New York. Their store served as the meeting place at the time of the organization of the township.

West Fork *Crawford County*

Forks off Knapps Creek to the west, in Clayton Township.

West Kewaunee *Kewaunee County*

The original name of this settlement was Coryville, in honor of Abner Corey, the first county judge of Kewaunee County. In April 1857, a meeting was called at the home of Peter Laury to organize the town as a political unit, and the name was changed to Krok, by Judge Wojta Stansky, after his native town in Bohemia. Later the city of Kewaunee was incorporated, so the area remaining was renamed West Kewaunee.

West Lima *Richland County*

The first settler was Job M. Hurless. Others who joined him came from Indiana, so the place was called Hoosier. In 1855 Joseph L. DeHart came from Lima, Ohio, and started a store. Four years later he built a second store and was influential in getting the name established as West Lima.

West Marshland *Burnett County*

Marshland was the name given to a hamlet started by cranberry growers in the 1870s. It was thought that it would grow into a great cranberry capital. As the crops dwindled, so did the hamlet, and the name was applied to this large town of extensive marshes. Later, other townships were set off from it, leaving only the western part to be called West Marshland.

West Milwaukee *Milwaukee County*

Huge estates, elaborate summer homes, productive farms, and gravel pits were the beginnings of this community. The village was incorporated in 1906 by uniting portions of two existing governmental units. It is west of Milwaukee.

Westmorland *Dane County*

J. C. McKenna Sr., one of the owners, and his family decided together on the name of this subdivision of Madison. Because several other plats had recently been made to the west of Madison, Mrs. McKenna suggested that this would be "more land" platted in the "west." J. C. McKenna Jr. says that the treeless and rolling land suggested "moorland," and this idea was incorporated also. The name was also picked because it was euphonious and reminiscent of Westmoreland, England.

Weston *Dane County*

This once thriving village of 320 was named for Daniel Weston, a Dunn County pioneer of Rock Falls, who was a member of the first elected county board. At one time a large lumber mill operated here at the terminus of a railroad spur.

West Point *Columbia County*

When the petition for organization of the town was first presented, the name chosen was Portland. However, the committee of the county board changed it to Bloomfield. In some manner the formal order to create the township appeared with West Point, probably because of its location in the extreme west corner of the county. On the map it resembles a point.

Westport *Dane County*

This township was named for Westport in Ireland, because many of its early settlers came from there.

West Salem *La Crosse County*

The village was platted in 1856 by Thomas Leonard, M. L. Tourtellotte, and Oscar Elwell. The first name suggested was Rupert, as the Elwells had come from Rupert in Vermont. But Elder Card, the Baptist minister, insisted it be named Salem, because it means "peace" and would be a good omen. Mr. Elwell then remembered that their market town in the East had been Salem, New York, which was a thrifty town, so he too agreed to name it Salem. Soon mail became confused with the town of Salem in Kenosha County, which had already been in existence for some time. West was then added to the name.

West Sweden *Polk County*

The Swedes who settled here named it West Sweden because it was "west of Sweden." The only settler who could write English at the time was F. O. Johnson, the town clerk for thirty-five years. "He was surveyor, Justice of the Peace, Sec. of the creamery, storekeeper and postmaster all at the same time."

West Two Creeks *Manitowoc County*

This community was located one mile west of the village of Two Creeks, which has since disappeared.

Weyauwega   *Waupaca County*

An Indian village of this name was located here; the word means "here we rest." The site was a popular camping place for Indians traveling up and down the Waupaca River. There was said to be a Chief Weyauwega buried here.

Weyerhaeuser   *Rusk County*

Frederick Weyerhaeuser, founder of the Weyerhaeuser Lumber Company, developed his fortunes by harvesting the virgin forests of white pine timber in Wisconsin. One of his headquarters was located here in the 1870s, and the village that grew up was given his name. Mr. Weyerhaeuser built the first logging railroad in the state.

Wheat Hollow   *Richland County*

Part of Willow Township, it was named for Preserved Wheat, an early pioneer who lived in this valley.

Wheatland   *Kenosha County*

Named for its terrain.

Wheaton   *Chippewa County*

Early settlers raised wheat and no other crops at all for the first few years. They had phenomenal yields until the cinch bugs came and put an end to wheat raising.

Wheeler   *Dunn County*

Chester A. Arthur was president of the United States in 1881 when Maria L. Welton was granted homestead rights to 160 acres of land here. In 1864 Mrs. Welton sold a strip of her land to the St. Croix and Chippewa Falls Railway Company, which established a station named Lochiel. Part of the strip was platted into a new town named Welton.

About the same time a store was built by the firm of Sherburne and Wheeler. H. D. Wheeler of this firm became the first postmaster of the town and insisted it be named Wheeler. About 1892 the people persuaded the railroad company to change the name of its station to Wheeler. Gradually the settlement lost its triple personality and became Wheeler to the railroad, the post office, and the community. One of the early industries was a sawmill that manufactured railroad ties and wagon spokes. The harvesting of blueberries was also important, and at one time it was a potato center.

For a few years there were two brickyards operating near a deposit of especially good brick-making clay. Because it started with three names and had so many thriving industries, it was nicknamed Jumbo but never quite grew up to that size.

Whiskey Creek   *Dane County*

This stream is actually the upper Yahara River, above the entry of Token Creek. It was probably named because there was a much frequented tavern in the area, but this local story may also explain the name:

Hank Lawrence, an early settler, having been drinking at the nearby crossroad tavern, was returning home with a jug of whiskey. Instead of using the ford to cross the creek, he tried to make his horse cross on the footbridge. The animal became frightened and shied, and the jug plunged into the stream. The cork popped out, and as the whiskey gurgled away it seemed to say, "Good-good-good-good." "Yes," cried Lawrence, "I know you're good, but I can't get you!"

Whitefish Bay   *Door County*

The Indian name for this site was Ah-qua-she-ma-ga-ning, meaning "save our lives." There is a legend that six canoes of Indians went cranberry picking to Manitou Island. A heavy fog came up, and they became lost and drifted about. As they neared the shore they heard the waves dash against the rocks at Whitefish Bay Point. Fortunately they were able to land in safety.

Whitefish Bay   *Milwaukee County*

The name was originally given to the beautiful bay on Lake Michigan just north of Milwaukee because of the numerous schools of whitefish to be found there. The village was incorporated in 1892.

Whitehall   *Trempealeau County*

Benjamin F. Wing, the original owner of the town site, chose this name after Whitehall in Illinois, which in turn was named for Whitehall in New York State. The name may also have been chosen in honor of Whitehall in England, as most of the first settlers were of English descent.

White Lake   *Langlade County*

Before the lumber mill was built here in 1917 the lake bottom was covered with very white sand. There were a number of white sandy beaches. On the eastern and southern banks were stands of white birch trees. The lake was called White Lake, but its bottom was covered with debris from the mill, which may have also raised the water level. The village was a portion of the Town of Wolf River until 1925, when it was incorporated and took the name of the lake.

Whitelaw   *Manitowoc County*

One account says that the village was named after Whitelaw Reed, an officer of the Chicago and North Western Railway. Another claims it was named for a Mr. White, a lawyer who was supposed to have assisted in establishing the post office in 1892. Prior to this time it was known as Pine Grove Siding. However, there was another post office named Pine Grove near Green Bay, so this name was discarded. The population is predominantly of German ancestry.

White Mound   *Sauk County*

A hill called White Mound gave this settlement its name.

White Oak Springs   *Lafayette County*

Beautiful and unfailing springs, shaded by the foliage of miniature white oak trees, supply the town with water.

White Potato Lake   *Oconto Lake*

Translation of the Menominee name of the lake, *wapasipamiuk*.

White's Prairie   *Fond du Lac County*

Solomon White was one of the early settlers who started farming on this prairie in 1845.

Whitestown   *Vernon County*

Giles White was the first settler in the town.

Whitewater   *Walworth County*

Indians called the river Wau-be-gan-naw-po-cat, which means "white water" and referred to the white soft clay and sand in the bottom. When the town was organized in 1842 it took the same name. The first settler arrived July 1, 1837.

Whittlesey   *Taylor County*

Some believe the settlement was named after the first legislator to represent the district. Others say it was named by the railroad company, the word being derived from an Indian word meaning "sand-bar."

Wiehe   *Douglas County*

Chris Wiehe was secretary of the Hines Lumber County.

Wild Cat Mound   *Sauk County*

The redoubtable Indian warrior Pe-Sheu or Wild Cat was honored by the Ho-Chunk who named this site after him.

Wild Rose   *Waushara County*

The first settlers came from Rose, Wayne County, New York, in 1850. The township was named Rose, and the village that was organized in 1874 was named Wild Rose to distinguish it from the township, and also because there were many wild roses growing in the vicinity.

Wild Rose Ridge   *Richland County*

Originally it was called Maple Ridge, but due to confusion with cheese factories in Sauk and Vernon counties called Maple Ridge plants, the name was changed to Wild Rose Ridge. Located in Richwood Township.

Wildwood   *St. Croix County*

Only a lone section of a brick wall, part of a onetime mill, now marks the location of this once busy sawmilling town a few miles north of Woodsville. Situated in an area called the Big Woods, large quantities of hardwood products were manufactured here.

Willard   *Clark County*

N. C. Foster, who owned much of the timberlands in the area, named this location for his son, Willard Foster. He also built a railroad from Fairchild to Willard to transport his timber.

Williams Bay
Walworth County

Israel Williams was a New Englander who had fought in the War of 1812 as a captain. He came to the Lake Geneva region in 1836 with his wife, her aged mother, and his seven sons. He settled on the north shore of the lake on this bay.

Williamstown
Dodge County

The first settlers were Alvin and William Foster and Chester May, who arrived here in 1845 to select a site for their mills and begin work on the sawmill and dam. It is believed the township was named for William Foster.

Willington School
Dane County

Located in the town of Dane. A combination of the names Wilson (for Woodrow Wilson) and Washington (for George Washington), with an orthographic l added.

Wilmot
Kenosha County

The first settlers here were the Asabel W. Benham family in 1844. Mr. Benham claimed nearly all the land in the vicinity and built the first frame house, and also a small mill with power furnished by water from ditches through the marshes. Later he constructed a dam across the Fox River and enlarged the mill.

Mr. Benham named his village Gilead, in honor of the place in Connecticut from which his parents came. Four years later a meeting was called by all the citizens for the purpose of selecting a new name for the village. Much discussion ensued. Finally Mr. Wilbur said jokingly, "Well, since we are hearing much about the Wilmot Proviso these days, why not call our new town Wilmot." His suggestion was taken seriously, and a motion to that effect was made and carried.

Wilson
Eau Claire County

Originally this township was part of Ludington Township, and it was sparsely settled during the early 1870s. It became a separate township in 1916 and was named in honor of President Woodrow Wilson.

Wilson
Sheboygan County

David Wilson from Ohio was a commercial fisherman who settled here in 1840.

Wilson
St. Croix County

Trained donkeys at the sawmill here would pull logs from the millpond and stop at just the right point by the saws. Captain Wm. Wilson of Menomonie built the first sawmill in this once busy village in 1870.

Wilson Creek
Sauk County

A discontinued post office in the southwest corner of Troy that was named for Thomas Wilson.

Wilson's Creek
Sauk County

John Wilson, a Scotsman, located his claim in the western part of what is now the Town of Troy.

Wilson's Woods   *Fond du Lac County*

Once owned by S. Wilson. Picnics were often held here. It is located in Fond du Lac Township.

Wilton   *Monroe County*

Esau Johnson of Prairie du Chien unloaded his goods on a raft in 1842 and came up the Wisconsin and Kickapoo Rivers to the town of Sheldon. He was the first settler near Wilton and was soon followed by others who came with oxteams to establish new homes. It was a wild country, and it is related that one settler described it this way: "Surely God made this country for the Indians, and we ought to let them have it!" No explanation is given for the name.

Winchester   *Vilas County*

This village was an active lumbering center started about 1902 on the southern shore of North Turtle Lake. A man named Winchester was head of the Turtle Lake Lumber Company.

Winchester   *Winnebago County*

It was settled by Yankees in 1846 and by Norwegians in 1847. At the time it was referred to as "the Neenah Settlement." In 1852 the Yankees chose to rename the settlement Winchester, after the cathedral town in England. Both Clayton Township and Winchester Township were known as Winchester.

Wind Lake   *Racine County*

A lake in the area was given this name, probably because winds have a strong sweep across it. The settlement took the same name.

Wind Point   *Racine County*

The village is the site of the Wind Point Lighthouse, which was built in 1880. The 112-foot tower is said to be the oldest and tallest lighthouse still standing on the Great Lakes. It has been said that the lighthouse replaced a tall wind-blown tree that for many years was used as a navigation point to avoid the reefs off Racine. The area supposedly derived its name from this tree.

Windsor   *Dane County*

The Wheeler family came here in 1851 from Old Johnstown, east of Janesville. They traveled by oxcart, and the only thing they found was a nice grove of oak trees. Early settlers named the town after Windsor, Vermont, from which they had migrated.

Winfield   *Sauk County*

In 1852 it was decided to name this settlement in honor of General Winfield Scott of Mexican War fame. He had been nominated by the Whig Party to run for president of the United States against Franklin Pierce.

Winnebago *Winnebago County*

The name was given to the State Hospital community when its post office was established in 1876. William M. Walker, the first postmaster, owned many acres in the vicinity, and it is thought that he and Dr. Walter Kempster, superintendent of the hospital, selected the name.

Winnebago County

The Ho-Chunk Indians lived around this large lake in central Wisconsin. They were called "Winnebago" by a neighboring tribe. The name "Winnebago" means "people of the strong-smelling water." The Indian languages did not distinguish among things that had a strong smell. Europeans translated the Indian word for "strong smelling" as "stinking" and so they thought "Winnebago" meant "people of the stinking water" or "dirty water people."

Winnebago Rapids *Winnebago County*

The site of what is now Neenah and what was the location of a US government settlement established for the education and civilization of the Menominee Indians. When the government admitted the project a failure, the entire property was put up for sale and was purchased by Harrison Reed in 1844.

It was platted and recorded as a village in 1848 by Harvey Jones, the co-owner of the settlement. It was incorporated as a village in 1850 and became consolidated with Neenah in 1856, at which time the name was changed to Neenah. Ho-Chunk Indians at one time had a village on Doty Island near the rapids. They often exacted tribute for the privilege of being allowed to pass through their territory across the treacherous rapids. The name arose as a result of the people and the place.

Winneboujou *Douglas County*

Winneboujou is the first man created by Manitou in Ojibwe mythology. He was the traditional hero and demigod of their legends, and his story parallels that of Longfellow's Hiawatha. Once he went to sleep on the banks of the Brule River at this site, and the South Wind, being in a playful mood, blew his canoe down the river and far out into the lake. When he awoke he blew his whistle, and the North Wind brought it back. Ever since that time the North Wind was his favorite. The town was started as a station on the South Shore Railroad where it crosses the Brule River.

Winneconne *Winnebago County*

The word means "place of skulls" and was so named by the Indians because of a battle between the Sauk and Fox on one side and the French, Menominee, and Ojibwe on the other. A large number of human skulls and bones were scattered about the area afterward. The Sauk and Fox Indians were driven by the French from Butte des Morts to the shores of the Wolf River to die of wounds and disease. It is also said to mean "a dirty place" and "marrow of bones." The marrow of deer bones was a great delicacy with the Indians, and the place may have been one where feasts of this kind were held. An Indian mission was established here in 1620. The village was incorporated in 1847.

Winnequaw Point

The largest of the Ho-Chunk villages located about the Madison lakes was situated on the southeast shore of Lake Monona at a place then known as Squaw Point or Strawberry Point. Captain Barnes of steamboat fame called it Winnequaw, a name he made up from Indian syllables.

Winneshiek Bluff
Crawford County

Part of Freeman Township. A cross marks the burial site of an Indian woman atop this bluff. Winneshiek is an Indian name.

Winneshiek Wild Life Refuge
Grant, Vernon, and Crawford Counties

Winneshiek in the Indian language means "dirty, brackish, muddy" and was applied to water, and also to the yellow birch tree because the bark has a smoky color. Chief Winneshiek, who presided over the Pecatonica village in this area, was given this name by his people because he had a bearded face, which was unusual among Indians.

Winona Junction
La Crosse County

This name was given by Sioux Indians to the first daughter in a family.

Winooski
Sheboygan County

James Stone and the other early settlers in this locality came from Vermont State, where there was a town by this name. The word is of Indian origin and means "onion." There is an Onion River in Vermont, and also one here in Wisconsin.

Winter
Sawyer County

Before the axes of woodsmen began to fell the giant white pine trees, a stopping-off place was established near here for lumberjacks and occasional travelers. It was called LeBoef. Settlers began to move in after the Omaha Railroad was built from Rice Lake to Park Falls. The community was called Winter in honor of John Winter, an Omaha Railroad official who came from St. Paul to engage in the logging industry. The township was organized in 1905.

One of the most exciting and most publicized incidents in logging history took place in the town of Winter on the banks of the Thornapple River. The trouble resulted because of a clause in a deed that reserved flowage rights to the Chippewa Lumber and Boom Company.

An employee of this company, John Dietz, purchased a tract of land from the company through which flowed the Thornapple River, a stream used for log drives. Mr. Dietz had been employed as a watchman at Price Dam on the Brunet River. Shortly after moving to the Thornapple site he tried to collect wages that he claimed had not been paid to him while he was employed as a watchman.

Mr. Dietz refused to allow the company to drive the logs through his property unless it paid a fee of ten cents per thousand feet for the logs that had passed over this waterway since he had purchased the property. The company refused to pay. Mr. Dietz armed himself with a rifle and appeared at the dam to enforce his claim.

Arguments between Dietz and the company persisted for several years. The company paid the claim of $1,800 for wages, but still Dietz would not compromise. The company was forced to haul its logs to the Flambeau River, which resulted in additional expense. The company entered a legal complaint, and the sheriff and deputies were sent out from time to time to serve a summons on Mr. Dietz. No one succeeded in apprehending him. On Oct. 7, 1910, a pitched battle occurred in which Mr. Dietz was wounded. He surrendered to the sheriff and was tried by jury and found guilty.

Wisconsin

The derivation of the word is uncertain. Polish settlers have claimed the honor as partly theirs, since a certain Tadeucz Wiscont was an influential and prominent man in the southern part of the state.

The name was first given to the river by the Indians. Father Marquette, the first European to travel it in 1673, wrote the name as Meskousing, meaning "red stone," which was characteristic of the banks of the river.

Father Hennepin in 1683 called it Misconsin, with an initial *M* instead of *W,* and claimed it meant "strong current"or "wild rushing channel."

Early French maps spelled it *Oui-scon-sin* to convey phonetically the Indian pronunciation. The word has had other spellings and is also claimed to mean "holes in the bank of a stream in which birds nest," "muskrat lodge," and "a good place to live."

The territory took the name of the river, and when the state was formed in 1848, the legislature adopted the name with its present spelling. Most accounts say the word came from the Ojibwe as Wees-kon-san, meaning "gathering of the waters." Judge James Duane Doty claimed it was a Ho-Chunk word meaning "river of the flowering banks," Wis-koos-er-ah.

Wisconsin City   Rock County
Perhaps somewhat pretentiously named by John Inman, Josiah Breese, Edward Shepard, James S. Seymour; and John H. Hardenburgh on May 24, 1836.

Wisconsin Dells   Columbia County
The city was named Kilbourn for Byron Kilbourne. The name was changed to Wisconsin Dells in 1931, to clarify its location and make it easier for tourists to locate it.

Wisconsin Rapids   Wood County
This city is a consolidation of Grand Rapids on the east side of the river and Centralia on the west side. The first settler to build a permanent home in Grand Rapids was Nelson Strong, who came in 1838. The name was probably chosen because of the descent of forty-five feet that the Wisconsin River takes in passing this location. However, mail became confused with Grand Rapids in Michigan, so the name was changed to Wisconsin Rapids in 1920. Indians called it "rabbit's place."

Wissota Dam   Chippewa County
A dam above the falls on the Chippewa River was built by the Minnesota-Wisconsin Power Company in 1915. Louis G. Arnold of Eau Claire was the engineer and chose the name, combining Wisconsin and Minnesota.

Withee   *Clark County*

The first permanent settlers came here in the summer of 1870. James Boardman came first from Minnesota as a lumberman. George W. Richards and David R. Goodwin were the next to arrive. Soon a schoolteacher from Maine named Niran H. Withee settled here and became an influential figure in the logging camps. He acquired land and property, and the village was given his name. He did much to shape the policy and manage the affairs of Clark County and served as county treasurer from 1875 to 1882. When the post office was established in 1880 Niran Withee was the first postmaster.

Wittenberg   *Shawano County*

A sawmill located at this site was the reason for the Milwaukee Lakeshore and Western Railroad to build its line north from New London in 1880. It was then proposed that eight charcoal kilns be built, and the place be called Carbenero. Pastor E. J. Homme also came here, with the intention of building a Norwegian orphan home and home for the aged. A post office was established the same year, with Jonas Swenholt as postmaster.

Reverend Homme then wrote a request to the railroad company that the name be changed from Carbenero to Wittenberg. He said that when he came here it was the realization of a cherished dream to build homes for the fatherless and the aged. At a meeting with the officials he folded his hands and thanked God because he had found the right place and said, "We must find another name. Let us call it Wittenberg."

Witwen   *Sauk County*

A discontinued post office in the town of Troy was named for G. and J. P. Witwen, who built a mill here.

Wolf River   *Waupaca County*

Before the white settlers came, it was called Muk-wan-wish-ta-guon, which signifies "Bear's Head River." The early settlers substituted the name Wolf.

Wonewoc   *Juneau County*

This Ojibwe word means "they howl" and probably refers to wolves in the area. Before the settlers arrived, the country was an ideal haunt for many kinds of wildlife. It is thought that the hills and bluffs would echo and re-echo the calls and howls of wolves prowling in the night.

Wood   *Milwaukee County*

This is a large center operated for the hospitalization and care of veterans by the US government within the city of Milwaukee. It was opened May 1, 1867, to care for Civil War veterans and has provided that service ever since. A post office was named Wood in honor of General George H. Wood, who served as president of the board of managers of the National Home for Disabled Volunteer Soldiers for many years. General Wood served in both the Spanish-American War and World War I. He was an adjutant general of the State of Ohio.

Wood County

Joseph Wood was assemblyman from Grand Rapids, now Wisconsin Rapids, when the county was formed. He came to Grand Rapids in 1848 and after serving one term in the legislature, and one as county judge, was mayor of Grand Rapids.

Woodford   *Lafayette County*

The first settlers here were English, followed by Norwegians and Germans. John Magnus built a sawmill to provide lumber for the new homes. A farm about a mile to the south was a station on the Underground Railroad. The first post office was located in the home of John Kerns in 1885. Mr. Kerns chose the name for the large piles of cordwood that were hauled in from the surrounding area and piled up until they could be shipped out by rail. Ford was added for the fording place on the Pecatonica River at the edge of the community. Later travelers crossed the river by ferry. A cable across the stream was used to pull the ferry back and forth.

The Battle of the Pecatonica was fought about one mile north of Woodford on June 16, 1832. Colonel Henry Dodge had built a stockade at what is now Dodgeville to protect his cabins and lead mines. Colonel William S. Hamilton, son of Alexander Hamilton, had lead mines at what is now Wiota and built a stockade called Fort Hamilton about seven miles west of Woodford. Both Dodge and Hamilton were informed by a ranger that a band of Indians was in the area near Fort Hamilton.

The two men and a group of volunteers set out to find the Indians. They followed their trail to one mile north of Woodford, not far from the junction of two forks of the Pecatonica River. There, they cornered and killed up to seventeen Indians. Two of the white men were mortally wounded and another two severely wounded. This was considered the turning point of the Black Hawk War, one of the last battles between the Indians and the settlers on the east side of the Mississippi River.

Woodhull   *Fond du Lac County*

John Woodhull was the deputy postmaster when this community was established.

Wood Lake   *Burnett County*

Located five or six miles southeast of Grantsburg, on the shore of Wood Lake, it took its name from the lake on the wooded shores of which it is located.

Woodland   *Sauk County*

The name was probably chosen because of the abundance of timber at this location.

Woodlawn   *Sauk County*

This is a discontinued post office in the town of Washington that was named for Dr. William A. Wood.

Woodman   *Grant County*

In 1864 Cyrus Woodman and Ralph Smith laid out the lots for this village. A small sawmill that produced lumber, railroad ties, and laths provided work for the inhabitants.

Woodmohr   *Chippewa County*

This township's name was formed by combining the names of two men, Lawrence Mohr, an old settler, and assemblyman Woodard.

Wood River   *Burnett County*

This was the second post office established in Burnett County in 1862. The site was probably named by fur traders, explorers, timber cruisers, or loggers, who gave the name to the river and two lakes, Big and Little Wood. The post office was discontinued in 1867, but the name still applies to the township.

Woodruff   *Oneida County*

Early lumber camps at Three Lakes and Eagle River were operated by the Woodruff-Macguire Company. When the Chicago and North Western Railway built its line north, a terminal was established at Muskonegan Creek near here for unloading supplies. The railroad men became accustomed to using the phrase "for Woodruff," and the name was adopted. George Woodruff lived in Chicago.

Woodstock   *Richland County*

Some believe it was named for Woodstock, England; others think that the government assigned the name to the post office here. Located in Henrietta Township.

Woodville   *St. Croix County*

In 1872 a railroad siding was constructed by A. A. Kelly for shipping out logs to St. Croix. It was known as Kelly's Switch. The post office established in 1876 was also given this name, but it was subsequently changed to Woodville. Some think this was the name of an early settler. Others believe it was chosen because of the dense forest of pine, oak, butternut, maple, and birch that was often spoken of as the Great Woods. Kelly's sawmill was sold to the Woodville Lumber Company in 1879. The great forests soon disappeared.

Woodworth   *Kenosha County*

A station opened here when the railroad built in the 1850s was named for the Woodworth family, who lived on farms surrounding it.

Wooster Mills   *Crawford County*

Located in Clayton Township, it was named after the Wooster family.

Wright's Corners   *Trempealeau County*

Hollister M. Wright settled here in 1853.

Wrights Ferry   *Crawford County*

Captain Wright was the last ferry operator on the Bridgeport line. Located in Wauzeka Township.

Wrightstown   *Brown County*

Hoel S. Wright was the first settler here in about 1833. Some years later he built a hotel and then a ferry to cross the Fox River. The place was called Wright's Ferry. The first bridge across the river was also credited to him. The name was changed to Wrightstown in his honor.

Wyalusing State Park *Grant County*
This site was laid out as the village of Paper City in 1836 by an eastern syndicate but was never settled. Robert Glenn, who came from Wyalusing in Pennsylvania, gave it the new name because he thought the location resembled the Pennsylvania village. The word is derived from an Indian term that means "home of the old warrior" or "dwelling place of the hoary veteran," after an ancient warrior who lived near the Pennsylvania site.

Wyocena *Columbia County*
In the early days of the settlement a Major Dickason moved here. One night he had a dream about an Indian girl whose name was Wyocena. He liked the name so much that he chose it for the village. Another account of his dream states, "He dreamed he had been on a journey the night before to a country metropolis where all was business and bustle, and the name of the city was Wyocena." The word in the Potawatomi language is said to mean "somebody else."

The Yahara River in Dane County, ca. 1910

⇥ Y ⇤

Yahara River and Yahara Park   *Dane County*
The word is a phonetic spelling of a Ho-Chunk word that means "catfish." Mrs. Minnie White Wing, daughter of Chief Blue Wing, gave the name as Ho-wich-ha-hora. An old Indian trail crossed the river at the Black Bridge near Lake Monona. Oliver Lemere gave the name Ne-rucha-ja to the village located there at Frost's Woods in the early days of Madison settlement.

Yankeetown   *Crawford County*
It was named after New England settlers bearing colonial names. This is evidenced by a headstone in the cemetery. Located in Clayton Township.

Yellow Lake   *Burnett County*
The Ojibwe named the lakes and the river here for the yellow sand at their bottoms, or possibly because of a preponderance of yellow bloom or pollen that appeared in their waters. The Indian word Wess-awa-gamig meant "yellow water" and Oss-awa-gami meant "the water is yellow." Early French explorers who arrived before 1700 called the river Rivière Jaune. The settlement on Big Yellow Lake had a post office from 1890 to 1950, named for the lake.

Yellow River   *Washburn County*
Called the "River Jaune" by early French explorers because of the bright yellow sand on the bottom of Yellow Lake through which it flows.

The Yellowstone Trail   *Fond Du Lac County & Others*
Before our present system of national highways was established, this highway ran from Plymouth Rock to Puget Sound. Marked by yellow posts with an arrow encircled by stars, it crossed Wisconsin from Kenosha north to Oshkosh and then west.

Yolo   *Clark County*
This small hamlet was named after a county in California. The word was originally an Indian word meaning "abounding in rushes."

York   *Green County*
In the winter of 1841–42 a meeting of settlers was held to adopt a name for the settlement here. Green's Prairie was chosen. Some years later, when Wisconsin had become a state and the county of Green was organized, township subdivisions were laid out. It was then decided to name this town York, in honor of the state from which most of its settlers had come, New York.

Yorkville *Racine County*

The area was originally known as Waites Corners, deriving its name from Charles C. Wait, who came from Vermont to Yorkville in 1835, and his father, Reuben, who arrived in 1838 and settled close by (early records show Wait without an "e"). On February 7, 1842, the Wisconsin Territorial Legislature created the Town of Yorkville.

Yuba *Richland County*

The village was laid out in 1856 by the surveyor Joseph Irish, who was working for Edward Pinick, owner of the land. Mr. Pinick also erected a sawmill using power from the Pine River, the water being carried to the mill by means of a race half a mile in length, which secured a seven-foot head of water. An old-fashioned up-and-down saw was installed.

Pinick was suggested as a name, but Yuba was finally chosen, although just why is not certain. It may have been adopted from a city, river, or county in the gold mining area of California. The post office was established in 1857, with Edward Pinick as postmaster.

⇥ Z ⇤

Zachow *Shawano County*

Netley was the name given to this village by the Chicago and North Western Railway when they built their line from Green Bay to Eland Junction about 1903. It was later changed to Zachow in honor of the late W. C. Zachow of Shawano, a prominent business-man and pioneer from Cecil, Wisconsin. The community thrived as a cattle, sugar beet, and grain shipping center, and in 1907 Cargill Elevators, Inc. of Minneapolis established the Zachow Elevator and Lumber Company.

Zander *Manitowoc County*

Helmuth Zander was one of the early settlers here.

Zenda *Walworth County*

This was a name picked at random, said to have been suggested by the novel The Prisoner of Zenda.

IMAGE CREDITS